1 SAMUEL

ANTONY F. CAMPBELL, S.J.

The Forms of the Old Testament Literature

VOLUME VII

WILLIAM B. EERDMANS PUBLISHING COMPANY
GRAND RAPIDS, MICHIGAN / CAMBRIDGE, U.K.

© 2003 Wm. B. Eerdmans Publishing Co.

Wm. B. Eerdmans Publishing Co.
255 Jefferson Ave. S.E., Grand Rapids, Michigan 49503 /
P.O. Box 163, Cambridge CB3 9PU U.K.

Printed in the United States of America

08 07 06 05 04 03   7 6 5 4 3 2 1

Library of Congress Cataloging-in-Publication Data

Campbell, Antony F.
1 Samuel / Antony F. Campbell.
p.   cm.   — (The forms of the Old Testament; v. 7)
Includes bibliographical references.
ISBN 0-8028-6079-6 (pbk.: alk. paper)
1. Bible. O.T. Samuel, 1st — Commentaries.
2. Bible. O.T. Samuel, 1st — Criticism, Form.
I. Title: First Samuel.   II. Title.   III. Series.

BS1325.53.C36   2003
222′.4307 — dc21

2003040776

www.eerdmans.com

THE FORMS OF THE OLD TESTAMENT LITERATURE

Editors

ROLF P. KNIERIM • GENE M. TUCKER • MARVIN A. SWEENEY

*Published

To
Rolf and Hildegard
without whom
these volumes
would not have happened

CONTENTS

CONTENTS

ABBREVIATIONS AND SYMBOLS

I. Miscellaneous Abbreviations and Symbols

DH	Deuteronomistic History
dtr	deuteronomistic; when needed, "deuteronomic" will be written in full
Dtr.	M. Noth's abbreviation for his Deuteronomist
DtrN	the "nomistic" (= legally oriented) dtr editor/editing (used when discussing the hypothesis of an exilic DH with two revisions later in the exile, postulated by Smend, Dietrich, Veijola, and others)
DtrP	the later dtr editor/editing identifiable by interest in matters prophetic (used when discussing the hypothesis of an exilic DH with two revisions later in the exile, postulated by Smend, Dietrich, Veijola, and others)
LXX	Septuagint (= Greek)
LXX^A	Septuagint: Codex Alexandrinus
LXX^B	Septuagint: Codex Vaticanus
LXX^L	Septuagint: Lucianic recension (often equivalent to the mss. group boc^{2}e^2)
MT	Masoretic Text (= Hebrew)
PR	Prophetic Record
4QSam	Samuel material from Cave 4 at Qumran

N.B.: The asterisk (*) is used throughout this volume to indicate that only the relevant parts of the verse or verses so marked are referred to. In other words, the asterisk (*) is a signal that a part or parts of the text involved are excluded from the reference.

→   indicates terms in the Glossary.

II. Publications

AASF	Annales Academiae Scientiarum Fennicae
AB	Anchor Bible
ABD	*Anchor Bible Dictionary*
ABR	*Australian Biblical Review*
AnBib	Analecta biblica
ANET	*Ancient Near Eastern Texts Relating to the Old Testament*
APSP	*American Philosophical Society Proceedings*
ATANT	Abhandlungen zur Theologie des Alten und Neuen Testaments
BASOR	*Bulletin of the American Schools of Oriental Research*
BBB	Bonner biblische Beiträge
BET	Beiträge zur evangelischen Theologie
Bib	*Biblica*
BJRL	*Bulletin of the John Rylands University Library*
BWANT	Beiträge zur Wissenschaft vom Alten und Neuen Testament
BZAW	Beihefte zur *ZAW*
CBC	Cambridge Bible Commentary
CBQ	*Catholic Biblical Quarterly*
CBQMS	Catholic Biblical Quarterly Monograph Series
DH	Martin Noth, *The Deuteronomistic History*. 2nd ed. Sheffield: Sheffield Academic, 1991
ETL	*Ephemerides theologicae lovanienses*
FAT	*Forschungen zum Alten Testament*
FB	Forschung zur Bibel
FOTL	Forms of the Old Testament Literature
FRLANT	Forschungen zur Religion und Literatur des Alten und Neuen Testaments
HAT	Handbuch zum Alten Testament
HSM	Harvard Semitic Monographs
HUCA	Hebrew Union College Annual
ICC	International Critical Commentary
JBL	*Journal of Biblical Literature*
JNSL	*Journal of Northwest Semitic Languages*
JPS	Jewish Publication Society, The Holy Scriptures (1917)
JQR	*Jewish Quarterly Review*
JSOT	*Journal for the Study of the Old Testament*
JSOTSup	Journal for the Study of the Old Testament Supplement
JTS	*Journal of Theological Studies*
KHC	Kurzer Hand-Commentar zum Alten Testament
NAB	New American Bible
NRSV	New Revised Standard Version
OBO	Orbis biblicus et orientalis
OTL	Old Testament Library
RB	*Revue biblique*
RSV	Revised Standard Version
SBLDS	Society of Biblical Literature Dissertation Series

SBLMS   Society of Biblical Literature Monograph Series
SBLSCS   Society of Biblical Literature Septuagint and Cognate Studies
SBS   Stuttgarter Bibelstudien
TB   Theologische Bücherei
ThZ   Theologische Zeitschrift
VT   *Vetus Testamentum*
WBC   Word Biblical Commentary
WMANT   Wissenschaftliche Monographien zum Alten und Neuen
           Testament
ZAW   *Zeitschrift für die alttestamentliche Wissenschaft*
ZThK   *Zeitschrift für Theologie und Kirche*

Editors' Foreword

This volume by Professor Antony F. Campbell, S.J., represents the first of his two commentaries on the books of Samuel and the fourteenth appearance in the commentary series of The Forms of the Old Testament Literature. It follows the basic design by which all contributions to this commentary have been guided from its inception a generation ago. This design was described in each of the previously published volumes. These repeated descriptions may be read and kept in mind also for the present volume and the forthcoming volume on *2 Samuel* by the same author. Nevertheless, it should be helpful to highlight some aspects concerning the distinctive focus in this commentary series and also at least one modification by Professor Campbell to it.

As an established part of the tasks of exegesis, the entire commentary series has been and continues to be preoccupied with what has been known as the form-critical interpretation of the Old Testament (Hebrew Bible). Within the tradition of this form-critical interpretation, however, the method pursued in this commentary represents not only an addition to the original method of form criticism but also a shift in the approach to it.

Original form criticism explains the texts in light of their societal background. It focused — and focuses — on such patterns in the texts that reveal that these patterns have their origin in typical conventions in the settings and traditions of actual societal life, and are typically structured and intended to function according to these conventions. The reference to — societal — "setting" *(Sitz im Leben)* is, of course, not to be confused with the reference to, or question of — historical — "situation" *(historische Situation)*. However, since the aspect of the settings of these conventions is inseparably connected with the aspect of their traditions, form criticism has from its outset been connected with the study of the history of traditions, or tradition history, and also — in due course — with the study of the history of the transmission of the traditions, or transmission history.

While the interest in the societal background reflected in the texts remains acknowledged and pursued, the present commentary series focuses first of all on the conditions of the texts themselves as they are before us, their readers. This focus rests on the insight that the texts are also shaped according to the conditions of their own present, which are reflected in their own structure and setting and are indicative also of the genres at work in that present identity. In whatever sense the texts before us reflect societal conventions underneath, or refer to past events or conditions, or rest on orally transmitted traditions, they not only presuppose, reflect, and even represent and often directly refer to their own reality, instead of those other realities; they are before us only as written literature. The genuine nature of the texts, as literature in its own right, especially in antiquity, cannot be emphasized enough. And the fact that we encounter this literary reality before any other is also important at the initial stage of the study of the texts in form criticism. The current commentary starts therefore with the interpretation of the written nature of the texts in their own socio-historical reality and as a part of it — which is what the title of the commentary has always meant: The Forms of the Old Testament Literature — as literature.

As many years of experience of what is involved in this direction of exegesis have shown, the study of the structure of each text in its own right, of what is meant by a text's structure, and of the laborious and penetrating processes toward discerning its inherent structure, has taken an ever more prominent place in the work. The discovery of the systemically structured texts amounts to a kind of experience of the contents and concepts of their views that for many involved in this sort of study is without parallel and comparison. These experiences are possible for students of all levels and fields of study, for ministers, priests, rabbis, and for lay-people as well as for scholars.

The structured network in a text, concisely presented at the beginning of the discussion of each unit, is indeed the result of such intensive study. And without becoming personally involved in the process of such study of each text-unit, the reader of these results may scarcely fully understand how deeply the presentations of these structures are derived from the learning of the heightened spirit and intellectuality in the texts, and how significantly they advance the reader's own fuller perception of the texts' wealth.

It is for these reasons that the contributors have begun to expand more and more their explanations that follow their presentation of each text's structure. Even so, it has always been clear that any commentary must be read after its user's own initial reading of a text, during and along with such reading, and that it must lead back to its — hopefully — more informed and understanding reading.

Special attention is necessary to a modification by Professor Campbell of the expression "intention" which has been used as the superscription for the last of the four foci in interpretation in the past volumes. Instead of saying "intention," Campbell prefers to speak about "meaning," and the reader may pay special attention to his explanation in the section on Genre, Setting, and Meaning on pp. 5-7 in his INTRODUCTION. Suffice it to quote his opening statement to his explanation: "Intention, as used in this FOTL series, relates not to the intention of an author but to the intention of the text itself and is the meaning that we can make today of the text as we best understand it in its own time, emerging out of our encounter as interpreters with the text as text. To avoid misunderstanding, in these two Samuel volumes the subhead Meaning is used here in place of Intention" (p. 6).

As always, the editors acknowledge with appreciation the cooperation of the Eerdmans Publishing Company and their association with the Institute for Antiquity and Christianity at the Claremont Graduate University.

ROLF P. KNIERIM
MARVIN A. SWEENEY

AUTHOR'S PREFACE

The invitation to contribute 1-2 Samuel within this series, The Forms of the Old Testament Literature, was accepted long ago in 1976, following on the grave ill-health of the late Fr. Dennis McCarthy, S.J. The writing was begun with an extensive handwritten draft in 1977 (that was in pre-computer days). Since then, much has happened for me, some directly affecting this Samuel volume. *Of Prophets and Kings* was published in 1986, followed by *The Study Companion to Old Testament Literature* in 1989; articles after that included "1 Samuel" for *The New Jerome Biblical Commentary* in 1990 and, with Mark O'Brien, O.P., "Samuel-Kings" in *The International Bible Commentary* in 1998. Perhaps most significant for the present work was the publication, again with Mark O'Brien, of *Unfolding the Deuteronomistic History* in 2000. As a result, instead of these 1 and 2 Samuel volumes being the start of a young man's publishing career they are far closer to an older man's retirement years.

Since this work began, major developments have occurred in understanding the task of interpreting biblical literature. The uncertainty and infertility of some biblical analysis have been more widely recognized; the final text has come to be more appropriately valued. Two convictions have come to the fore for me. First, in matters of biblical analysis, what is possible need not be necessary; if some editorial activity is merely possible, it need not have happened. Second, experience of the biblical text has led to the conviction that it has been produced by skilled and intelligent editors, rather than the "inept redactors" often assumed in the past. The first of these views may argue against implausible fragmentation of the text. The second puts a premium on the issue of meaning in the final text. Analysis that does not generate meaning is unlikely to have lasting impact. At the same time, the text on occasion reveals that skilled editors and copyists can sometimes act like collection-building librarians rather than unity-creating authors.

Over recent years it has become clear that the range of biblical interpreters is spread across a spectrum that extends from "process" people at one end to "product" people at the other — and the range will remain (see, for example, Mowinckel's 1946 *Prophecy and Tradition*). Process people prefer to, or are

xv

disposed to, or find themselves compelled by the present biblical text as end product to explore the process of the text's production. Product people prefer to, or are disposed to, or find themselves compelled to stay with the present biblical text as end product and to explore the meaning a dialogue with it may generate. Both process and product readings are legitimate and both are necessary (see *Unfolding,* 4-7); neither reading ought be presented as though the other was not part of a legitimate reading of the Bible. A treatment of the product that is incompatible with the nature of the process is likely to be flawed. A treatment of the process that invalidates the product is equally suspect. For many people, what might be called an inflated view of biblical text can be helpfully modified by reflection on the process that produced the text. For many others, the meaning and significance generated by reflection on the text as it now stands needs a priority. History and present reality indicate that not only is the range or spectrum with us but it will and should stay with us.

Some find more meaning and satisfaction in exploring the process that produced the text while others find more meaning and satisfaction in engaging with the final product. Among the many influences that bear on the choice of approaches to the text, the possibility exists of favor toward incarnation or fear of it. To simplify outrageously — and with strong emphasis on the "some" and "others" in what follows, which mean "by no means all" — for some, the "this-worldliness" of the process producing the biblical text is important, for it may point to the incarnation of the divine and the ambiguity of the human; for others, the "other-worldliness" of the final biblical text is important, for it may point to the revelation of the divine and a clarity in the human. To each their needs.

An important civilizing and uplifting activity, whether intellectual or emotional, needs to be distinguished from both these. It is the weaving of a discourse that takes as its point of departure aspects of the biblical text, and that may integrate further aspects of the text into the discourse, but that is focused on the meaning of the discourse itself rather than on the meaning of the biblical text. The worth of what is said is derived from or measured against the value of the discourse as a whole and not by the light it throws on the understanding of the text. Many a sermon and many a literary piece fans the spark of spirit for its hearers or its readers. Rather than as an exacting interpretation of this particular biblical text, the value of the discourse is to be found in itself, as an interpretation of life or an unfolding of thought.

What is sought here is an understanding of the present biblical text that takes into account a couple of centuries of scholarship that, for all its errors, has succeeded in making the case that the biblical text has a history of past development. Not all present-text interpretation makes appropriate allowance for this past development. If, in the practicalities of interpretation, the history of past development is to all intents and purposes denied, then the flat surface of the present text becomes a hypothesis — odd though that may sound. The hypothesis: this present text is of such a nature that it can be interpreted as though it did not have a history of development — as though the text were somehow "disinherited," artificially rootless, without forebears we may call upon (characterized and castigated by K. Noll as "either impervious to, or antithetical to, historical considerations," *Faces of David,* 12). Such a text is one-dimensional; the multi-dimensional past is excluded. Such a "flat text" is a hypothesis, as is a "flat earth"; in the light of the evidence, both are unacceptable. If the biblical text is treated in this fashion, some present-text interpretation may be reduced to a certain kind of reader response. It may not hold the interest of adherents to the biblical tradition who place a high value on the humanness of the text in its past history — the biblical word's "incarnational" aspect.

Some yearn for simplicity in their scriptures. Alas, that yearning has to go unsatisfied. The scriptures are no less complex than most of us human beings.

Interpretation is a work of art. Art seeks to be expressive, not definitive. It is beyond the reach of a Michelangelo to sculpt the definitive David or of a Fra Angelico to paint the definitive Madonna. There is often more than one way in which a text may be structured and named. The definitive interpretation of a text is out of reach because interpretation needs to take account of the experience of each generation and engage with the needs of particular individuals. It is unhelpful to ask whether an interpretation is the right one; it is usually helpful to ask whether an interpretation is adequate and responsible. Responsible: an interpretation that pays attention to the signals in the text that need to be interpreted. Adequate: an interpretation that integrates all or most of these signals into a single interpretative horizon.

With the passing years, the practice of noting scholarly argument has been subordinated here to the need for an uncluttered text. As a result, academic references have been severely restricted in this final version of the book. The aim has been to let the text tell its story. The inclusion or omission of a reference has often been judged in this light. If any feel overlooked, I offer my regrets and apologies.

Bibliography of Works Cited Above

Campbell, Antony F. *Of Prophets and Kings: A Late Ninth-Century Document (1 Samuel 1–2 Kings 10).* CBQMS 17. Washington: CBA of America, 1986.
———. *The Study Companion to Old Testament Literature: An Approach to the Writings of Pre-Exilic and Exilic Israel.* Wilmington: Glazier, 1989; Collegeville: The Liturgical Press, 1992.
———. "1 Samuel." In *The New Jerome Biblical Commentary.* Edited by R. E. Brown, J. A. Fitzmyer, and R. E. Murphy. Englewood Cliffs, NJ: Prentice Hall, 1990.
Campbell, Antony F., and Mark A. O'Brien. "1-2 Samuel." In *The International Bible Commentary.* Collegeville: The Liturgical Press, 1998.
———. *Unfolding the Deuteronomistic History: Origins, Upgrades, Present Text.* Minneapolis: Fortress, 2000.
Mowinckel, Sigmund. *Prophecy and Tradition: The Prophetic Books in the Light of the Study of the Growth and History of the Tradition.* Oslo: Jacob Dybwad, 1946.
Noll, K. L. *The Faces of David.* JSOTSup 242. Sheffield: Sheffield Academic Press, 1997.

Bibliography of Frequently Cited Works

In the text that follows, the following works will be cited by author's name only; bibliographical details provided here will not be repeated within the relevant sections. Other studies by these scholars will be referenced in the usual way.

Alter, Robert. *The David Story: A Translation with Commentary of 1 and 2 Samuel.* New York: Norton, 1999.

Barthélemy, Dominique. *Critique textuelle de l'Ancien Testament.* Vol. 1. OBO 50/1. Fribourg, Switz.: Éditions Universitaires, 1982.

Brueggemann, Walter. *First and Second Samuel.* Interpretation. Louisville: John Knox, 1990.

Driver, S. R. *Notes on the Hebrew Text and the Topography of the Books of Samuel.* 2nd ed. Oxford: Clarendon, 1913.

Hertzberg, Hans Wilhelm. *I & II Samuel.* OTL. London: SCM, 1964.

Klein, Ralph W. *1 Samuel.* WBC 10. Waco: Word Books, 1983.

McCarter, P. Kyle, Jr. *I Samuel.* AB 8. Garden City: Doubleday, 1980.

Pisano, Stephen, S.J. *Additions or Omissions in the Books of Samuel: The Significant Pluses and Minuses in the Massoretic, LXX and Qumran Texts.* OBO 57. Freiburg, Switz.: Universitätsverlag, 1984.

Stoebe, Hans Joachim. *Das erste Buch Samuelis.* KAT VIII/1. Gütersloh: Mohn, 1973.

Note

It should be said that the completed manuscript of this volume went to the editors and the publisher in June 2001. Around the same year, four books were published that are significant for the study of 1-2 Samuel:

William G. Dever, *What Did the Biblical Writers Know and When Did They Know It?* Grand Rapids: Wm. B. Eerdmans, 2001.

Israel Finkelstein and Noel Asher Silberman, *The Bible Unearthed: Archaeology's New Vision of Ancient Israel and the Origin of Its Sacred Texts.* New York: Free Press, 2001.

Baruch Halpern, *David's Secret Demons: Messiah, Murderer, Traitor, King.* Grand Rapids: Wm. B. Eerdmans, 2001.

Steven L. McKenzie, *King David: A Biography.* New York: Oxford, 2000.

Careful reading reveals that changes to what is here are not required. Further comment can wait for the forthcoming publication of *2 Samuel.*

INTRODUCTION

This volume sets out to build on some of the best insights from recent biblical interpretation. These show up in the concern for close attention to the present text, in the concern to show due respect for the text's past, and in the concern to focus on the fundamental questions of the text's form and meaning.

At present, we can no longer be satisfied with the old patterns of biblical exegesis. Ways are needed to combine appropriately the insights of literary analysis with those of developmental analysis in the service of meaning. This book, coming out of the form-critical stable, is an attempt to explore new patterns. Two aspects facilitate the literary process. First, the text is not atomized. It is dealt with in its larger units, whether of sense or story, where meaning is to be found. Second, the text is not fragmented into a hypothetical past. It is dealt with substantially as it now exists, as present text. At the same time, a couple of centuries of modern research are not ignored; they have uncovered a history of the text that no postmodern should want to claim as non-existent. The opening to union between present and past is the recognition of the high level of intelligence and skill used by the editors who shaped the past traditions into the present text. Finally, the basic questions of form criticism are constantly asked: What sort of a text is this? What is its shape or structure? What does it mean?

1-2 SAMUEL

In the experience of many, no narrative texts in the Older Testament are more stirring and more challenging than those in the books of Samuel.

In the person of Samuel, they deal with the emergence of the figure of the prophet, so significant in the religion, politics, and literature of Israel. In the person of David, they deal with the emergence of the figure of the king, the head of central government in ancient Israel, both north and south.

The overall structure of the books is centered in the monarchy, begun with Saul and established with David. The role of the prophet is central to the establishment of the monarchy; but the prophetic role goes beyond establishment, claiming the right not only to designate and dismiss certain kings but also to exercise ultimate control over the conscience of the king. The preeminent prophetic figures in these books are Samuel and Nathan.

For the twenty-five years or so that I have been concerned with 1-2 Samuel, like everyone else, I have taken for granted that Samuel was brought on the scene for the inauguration of the monarchy in Israel. It has only dawned on me in recent years that Samuel's prime task in the narrative presentation was to anoint David as Israel's future king. The inauguration of the monarchy and the rejection of Saul are merely steps along the way to the major task: the anointing of David. Brueggemann is right: "the first fifteen chapters are a preparation for him [David]" (p. 2). This is not to argue against distilling a history of Saulide Israel, challenging as that might be; it is a corrective to the understanding of 1 Samuel as "this narrative about Saul" (Edelman, *King Saul,* 11).

Once this has been seen, a number of things fall into place. It explains, above all, why Saul gets such a rotten press from the prophets — rejected as soon as he is king, and rejected on what really must be reckoned an unfair charge (13:7b-15a). Saul's reign is wrapped up and summarized almost before it has got under way (14:47-52). Saul's definitive rejection in favor of David follows at once (15:1-35). For the Elisha circle (or whoever was interested in inserting these texts in which prophets anoint or designate kings and dismiss kings), the inauguration of the monarchy and the anointing and dismissal of Saul were merely steps leading toward the anointing of David, the king over Israel who mattered and who set matters to rights.

So we have first the *prophetic* moves to establish David as king (1 Sam 1:1–16:13) to be followed then by the *political* moves to establish David as king (1 Sam 16:14–2 Sam 8:18). Why has the world of biblical scholarship taken for granted for so many years that Samuel's major task, after resisting kingship first, is portrayed as presiding over the installation of Saul as king in Israel and pronouncing his rejection — and only then proceeding to the anointing of David? The obvious answer: because that is how it is presented in the present text, with Saul preceding David, and Samuel's death reported well before David's accession to the throne. But there is reason to pause. Samuel's emergence in Israel is treated as an event of great significance; after three chapters, it is said that "all Israel from Dan to Beer-sheba knew that Samuel was a trustworthy prophet of the LORD" (3:20). Samuel and Saul receive some seven chapters in the Samuel text (about one and a half chapters for the anointing and about the same for the rejecting); after that, "Samuel did not see Saul again until the day of his death" (15:35). David is anointed by Samuel in 1 Sam 16:1-13; Samuel's death is reported in 25:1; David's accession to power in Judah and Israel is completed in 2 Sam 5:3. On the other hand, David's line ruled in Judah until the very end; David's name was held up as the model for Judah's kings (cf. 1 Kgs 15:11; 2 Kgs 14:3; 16:2; 18:3). The figure of David bulks far larger than that of Saul.

Without question, kings are of central importance in the text of Deuteronomy through Second Kings, and for the most part they are not looked on kindly. Almost all kings are judged as doing what was right or doing what was evil "in

2

the sight of the LORD." Solomon set Israel on a downward course (1 Kgs 11:9-13, esp. when read in the light of 1 Kgs 9:1-9). Jeroboam caused northern Israel to sin (1 Kgs 12:30; 13:34); all the northern kings from Jehu to Hoshea are noted as not departing "from the sins of Jeroboam the son of Nebat." Manasseh in his turn "caused Judah to sin" (2 Kgs 21:16). Only three are noted without reserve as doing what was right in the sight of the LORD: David, Hezekiah, and Josiah. It is hardly surprising that Samuel's role was viewed as both crucial and complex: to resist the monarchy at first; to yield when appropriate and inaugurate the monarchy; finally to give the guidelines by which monarchy could function positively in Israel (1 Sam 12:14-15, 20-24) and to warn against the dangers of infidelity (12:25). Once this monitory role is highlighted for Samuel, the attention given to Saul's kingship and Samuel's initial resistance to it can easily be allowed undue importance.

The perception of a Josianic Deuteronomistic History, followed in the time of exile by a fully revised version, changes all this (see below under Diachronic Dimension; also Campbell and O'Brien, *Unfolding*). A positive attitude toward the monarchy is not at odds with a Josianic DH; the History is understood to have been put together initially in support of King Josiah's reform. In a Josianic DH, the role of Samuel in establishing the kingship begins with 1 Sam 9:1–10:16. Attention is freed to focus on the enormous importance of David for Israel's future. A reading becomes possible, even reasonable, in which — despite 1 Sam 7–8 and 10:17-27, as well as 1 Sam 12 — the *prophetic* moves in 1 Sam 1:1–16:13 are seen as directed toward establishing David as king, followed by the *political* moves to establish David as king (1 Sam 16:14–2 Sam 8:18). This cannot be claimed as a mandatory reading; it can be claimed as a reasonable one. This reading facilitates understanding the texts as efforts to articulate the experience of the institution of monarchy among God's people.

FORM CRITICISM

Form criticism is for many a "red rag" word. "Red rag" words bring with them an association of universes of ideas, strong emotions, deeply felt experiences. For many Americans, "socialized medicine" is a red rag word. For many biblical scholars, form criticism is another.

Ironically, form criticism is as unavoidable as breathing. We practice both all the time. Clearly there are connotations to form criticism that turn an essential human activity into a red rag word. These connotations we need to explore.

First, the claim that we practice form criticism all the time. "How are you?" has a totally different meaning if asked by a friend in the supermarket or a doctor in a surgery. Both answers may begin with "Fine," but in most cases a friend does not expect to hear a follow-up list of symptoms and a doctor does. The newspaper placards "President seduces space alien" or "President vetoes Congress bill" tell us instantly whether we are looking at sensationalist or serious journalism.

In our newspapers, we expect to know the difference between news reports, editorial opinion, and columnists' views or humor. In our books, we differentiate between textbooks and entertainment, between history and fiction, between literature and pulp. As cultures move from the readable toward the visual, we automatically associate specific traits with sit-coms, sci-fi, horror shows, and action movies. All of these judgments are form-critical activities.

The variety of form criticism, practiced in this volume, seeks for meaning in a text and recognizes that all such search for meaning begins with an inquiry as to the sort of text that is under investigation. In this understanding, form criticism is the endeavor to identify the form of a text; the initial apprehension is usually intuitive, to be confirmed by more reflective and detailed observation. A form critic — like any reader, only maybe more so — needs to have some notion of what the literary genres (or types) are and some idea of the criteria by which they are identified. The use of "some" twice in the preceding sentence is not lazy writing but the result of painful observation.

This FOTL series goes beyond genre identification to the task of structural analysis — not to be confused with "structuralism" as such. The careful structural analysis undertaken in these volumes is as necessary to the full understanding of the text as anatomy is to a full understanding of the human body. It is not a substitute for reading, enjoying, pondering, and reveling in the text — just as anatomy and medical science are not a substitute for the erotic pleasure of the body (Barthes, *Plaisir,* 19ff.). Nor in reading a commentary such as this should we consider that we contemplate the sense and significance of the text at secondhand — the sense is in the text. Rather we perceive, at best, the interpreter's joy in encountering the text (Barthes, ibid., 30-31). The commentary should help appreciate the text; it should not replace the text.

The concept of setting was one of the elements of form criticism that held out the promise of moving from literature further into the life of Israel. The phrase itself, "setting in life" (German: *Sitz im Leben*), makes explicit the move from literature to life. The typical in a literary genre was believed to correlate with the institutional in the life of society. Just as the typical elements of a business letter might be expected to throw light on the institutions of business in a given society, so it was hoped the study of literary genres would throw light on the history of life in Israelite society. There was ground for this in the early form-critical study of the psalms. The typical in these prayers were correlated with what were believed to be typical situations in the religious life of Israel. Similar hopes could be held out for law and, to a lesser degree, for prophecy.

Where narrative and story are concerned, setting is a far less helpful concept. Of course, royal annals come from royal courts and temple records come from temples. But stories are a quite different kettle of fish. We can hazard an opinion as to whether particular stories are more likely to have originated at the family hearth, the local sanctuary, the military campfire, or the court of the king. That tells us remarkably little. We, in fact, know remarkably little about the industry of storytelling in ancient Israel. We have the story texts so we assume that there were storytellers. We do not know, in particular cases, whether they were men or women (but see below). We do not know whether they earned their living by their storytelling and whether they were organized into anything like a guild. They are not mentioned in our texts. In 2 Sam 14, a wise woman from Tekoa tells a story before the king. She improvises skillfully when David asks whether Joab is behind this storytelling. She had to come from outside Jerusalem, so as not to be recognized by David. A man would have been able to portray a situation even closer to David's than a mother could. But from one example only it is possible to draw only one conclusion: there were competent women storytellers in Israel. Who told stories, how the storytellers were trained, how the stories were told and preserved, and much more are simply unknown to us.

We may assume, however, that storytellers were often singers, that stories were often sung rather than prosaically narrated. Three obscure references to both male and female court singers — not to be confused with temple singers — allow us to assume that both men and women functioned ordinarily as storytellers in ancient Israel. These three are Barzillai's comment in 2 Sam 19:36 (NRSV, 19:35), Qohelet's in Qoh 2:8, and finally the narrator's in 2 Chron 35:25.

It is important to be aware that stories do not necessarily provide us with accurate information about details of life in ancient Israel. Then as now, we may assume, stories needed to be plausible; they did not need to be accurate in detail. A story of a legal action does not tell us with a lawyer's accuracy how such actions proceeded. It tells us what a storyteller considered an audience would find plausible. A story of behavior in the royal court does not tell us with accuracy about royal protocol. It tells us what an audience could be expected to find plausible.

For all this, the form-critical analysis of stories is extremely valuable. The emphasis on story as story brings an appropriate focus to bear on the point of a story. It was once all too easy to assume that stories recounted what happened, with the result that from stories the sequence of events could be recovered. Even today, scholars involved in biblical interpretation will be well aware of the popular passion for explaining details of the text by recourse to what might have happened. Stories are not driven by what happened, but by the plot around which the storyteller has chosen to weave the story. The task of form-critical interpretation, in recognizing a story, is to focus on how the story is told so as to squeeze from the text its meaning — the light with which the story illuminates human experience.

Today the setting of a story in the biblical text is a literary one; the story is enshrined in the present text. It may be part of the Pentateuch; it may have been part of the DH; it may belong within a prophetic book. It is no longer a story being told in a particular institutional or social setting. Reflections on the setting of a story, therefore, may need to be centered less institutionally and societally and turned more to the growth of literature and its impact for meaning.

GENRE, SETTING, AND MEANING

These three are central concepts within the history of form criticism and are central to an understanding of the intellectual activity that form criticism pursues. Literary genre (or type) relates to the attempt to express in words what can be known about the sort of text being studied. It focuses on the text itself. Setting (German: *Sitz im Leben* or setting in life) relates to the attempt to identify the institutional setting within the life of a community that can be seen as generating texts of this sort. Intention, as used in this FOTL series, relates not to the intention of an author but to the intention of the text itself and is the meaning that we can make today of the text as we best understand it in its own time, emerging out of our encounter as interpreters with the text as text. To avoid misunderstanding, in these two Samuel volumes the subhead Meaning is used here in place of Intention.

No change of significance is meant by this substitution. In the FOTL series, "Intention" has always meant the intention of the text. The change of rubric is aimed at avoiding possible misunderstanding by readers. Fairly or unfairly, historical-critical work is often associated with an outmoded quest for the intention of the hypothetical original author. Such a quest has always been impossible and today is widely recognized as absurd. Studies in hermeneutics recognize that the interpreter's subjectivity can never be isolated from the act of interpretation. What this series is concerned with is the "intention of the text" — what today's interpreter understands the text to communicate in the context of its time. Fearing that "intention" is susceptible of misunderstanding, I have in this volume (and its *2 Samuel* companion) used the rubric "meaning." Meaning can be legitimately understood in at least two ways. First, that meaning which today's interpreters can best articulate for a text in its ancient context, given the best understandings of contemporary scholarship regarding that ancient context. Second, that meaning which today's interpreters can best articulate for a text read in the contemporary context of today. Of these, the "meaning" rubric is primarily focused on the former, the meaning which today's interpreters can best articulate for a text in its ancient context.

The concept of genre has an in-built tension that drives its contribution to the interpretation of a text. Genre partakes of the universal, but it is embodied in the particular. There is a tension in every text between the universal and the particular. The emphasis on the "sort of text" being studied points toward the universal, toward all the characteristics shared by this sort of text. As an example, we may take the business letter. Almost all business letters share something in common, both in form and content, with almost all other business letters, and that "something" sets the business letter apart from love letters or letters between friends. But the universal business letter is never put on paper and put in an envelope and put in the mail. What ends up on paper, in an envelope, in the mail is always a particular business letter, to this particular firm, about this particular issue. The liveliness, interest, and individuality of any text emerge from its resolution of the tension generated by this interplay between the universal and the particular. The universal is expressed in the genre; the particular is expressed in the detail of the text; the interplay is between the genre chosen on this occasion and the text that it generates. In the concrete: I have chosen to write a business letter to this person (whom I may or may not know) about this issue (which may be new or ongoing) that results in this particular letter.

The German language has the potential, not always uniformly used, to differentiate between genre as universal *(Gattung)* and text as particular

(Form). This leads to the situation where the sequence of elements in a *Gattung* can be described, for example, as A-B-C-D, and the sequence of these elements in a particular text or *Form* will appear, for example, as D-B-A-C. What this reflects is accurate. We do have an idea in our heads (or our cultural memory) as to what is involved in a genre — a business letter, for example. When we come to write it, the finished product is likely to differ here and there from the idea.

The concept of setting also has an in-built tension that drives its contribution to the interpretation of a text. It is a different tension. It is tension between the text as words on paper and the non-verbal institutional world that has given rise to this text. The term itself, "setting in life," points to this tension. It is the setting of a text, but it is the setting in life of a text, and the life envisaged is outside the text. The text is marked by the institutional but it is a particular event. The setting is not particular; it is institutional. The business letter is marked by the practices and needs of the business world, but it is a particular piece of paper, addressed to a particular individual, about a particular issue. The business world, which generates letters like this, is an institutional element of society and is far bigger than any given letter on which it puts its stamp. Important cautions about the unwary use of "setting" are voiced by Burke Long ("Recent Field Studies").

The meaning of a text has its own tensions too that are of a different level again. Meaning involves the two-way encounter of an interpreter with a text. For a business letter, its meaning is the outcome of the recipient's reading of the letter; or it is the outcome of the writer's reading of the letter. The two need not be the same; the many need not be the one. Texts are written to be read or heard. They contain signals that guide the reader in shaping the meaning of the text. Signals can be overlooked or misinterpreted or experienced in different ways, so that the outcome of different interpreters' encounters with a text may be different. Among these different ways, there are the tensions between how we find meaning in a text as we read it for ourselves today and how we find meaning in the same text as we read it in close association with the setting or settings we believe we can assume for it. As I read this business letter today, it is dominated by class consciousness, male chauvinism, and a contempt for consumer rights; it is insulting and demeaning. As I look at the date of the letter and the impersonal size of the corporation, I recognize that it was a normal piece of correspondence for its time, concerned to deal sympathetically with the issues raised, and marked by the class consciousness, chauvinism, and contempt that, alas, were simply taken for granted in its time.

In a form-critical encounter with a biblical story, the tensions of genre, setting, and meaning need close attention. The literary genre is story. So there will be the tension between the universal characteristics of a story and the needs to be met in the telling of this particular story. The setting for this story text is the biblical text in which it is preserved and kept alive; it is also the institutional setting in which this story might have originated and been told. So there will be tension between the two. This tension will be complicated if we are forced to envisage several levels of biblical text in which, at different times, this story has been preserved and kept alive. Finally, there is the tension of meaning. We, the interpreters, make the meaning in our encounter with the texts we interpret. But we can make the meaning we believe to be appropriate for ourselves today or, within the limits of our knowledge, we can make the meanings we believe to be appropriate to the settings in which we believe this particular text may have functioned. So there may be acute tensions here too.

As part of a form-critical commentary, these volumes have specific benefits to offer. First, the structure analyses give a rapid overview of how the text is being understood. A glance at a structure analysis reveals what are seen as the major blocks within a text, what is seen as their meaning or function, and how they are seen to relate to each other. A text is treated as a whole, not as fragmented verses or passages. Where components are clustered in a group to form a larger whole, beyond the analyses for the component elements, a broader structure analysis seeks to make clear the meaning of the group as a whole. (When a more detailed structure analysis is provided for a component unit, the symbols identifying the parts are adjusted appropriately.) Second, the discussion reveals where this understanding is coming from and what it is based on in the text. Third, the classification of texts by literary genre affords the possibility of reviewing a text as a whole instead of its being fragmented into bits. Beyond this, there is the possibility of seeing how the text functions as a medium of communication, where it might be situated within society or literature, and above all what it might ultimately mean.

Among its roles, form criticism should count attention to the whole, to the gestalt. The question, "What literary type is present here?" or "What is the literary genre of this text?" invites us away from components to look at the whole. Many a "whole" is made up of many parts, but there is a grave risk of not seeing the whole if focus is directed primarily toward the parts. It would be a pity to miss the wood (or forest) for the trees.

A text like the first book of Samuel is made up of many parts, but their meaning will be missed if their compositional arrangement is not seen. The arrival of Samuel (chs. 1–3) and the departure of the ark (chs. 4–6) gain a depth of meaning if seen as presaging the emergence of something new in Israel. That something new turns out to be the monarchy and David's emergence as the first king to give stability to monarchy in Israel.

Northrop Frye, perhaps unfairly, divides biblical scholarship into two directions, the critical and the traditional. "The critical approach establishes the text and studies the historical and cultural background; the tradition interprets it in accordance with what a consensus of theological and ecclesiastical authorities have declared the meaning to be" (*Great Code,* xvii). This commentary follows neither approach. It hopes to be aware of historical and cultural matters and to be aware of theological and ecclesiastical traditions. The task of this commentary is to bring the text of 1 Samuel to life, to explore its skeletal structure, to follow the course of its vital fluids — so that the words may have breath and life and stand on their own feet (cf. Ezek 37:10). For this, history and culture are important. For this, the impact of tradition is inescapable. But this is not a work of cultural or religious history; it is not a work of theological or ecclesiastical tradition. It is a study of the text of 1 Samuel with the intention of entering as fully into the life of the text as is possible for this commentator.

I find a certain parallel in recent scientific discussion. "The triumph of science has come largely through the reductionist enterprise. It has always been accompanied by resynthesis. The ideal of much scientific research has been to take a complex process, to crack it apart into its component units . . . , to characterize those units as real units in such a way that they can be recombined according to certain algorithms, and hence to explain more fully the level at which you started. Reductionism works extremely well as a methodology, especially if combined with a resynthesis that takes into account position effects" (Prof. E. O. Wilson, in discussion; in Byers, *Search for Wisdom,* 128). Reductionism is, I take it, equivalent to what I am calling in biblical literature the process approach; resynthesis reflects the focus on the product. Reductionism and resynthesis are partners in science; process and product approaches are partners in biblical interpretation. Either approach disqualifies itself when it, somehow or other, invalidates the other. Biblical interpretation may or may not engage in studying the process of a text's development; it cannot dismiss the realities that such a process represents — that would be to invalidate the process approach. An understanding of process that assumes mindless editorial activity and a mindless final text that cannot be interpreted with integrity would equally be invalidating the product approach.

ISSUES OF A STORY OF DAVID'S RISE IN 1-2 SAMUEL

The greater part of 1 Samuel involves traditions associated with what has been called the Story of David's Rise, the possible narrative composition dealing with David's rise to power over all Israel. This narrative composition differs from other hypothetical ancient Israelite documents in that it is constituted by a series of largely independent stories; links to claim the existence of a single document are not obvious. We have the stories; we are less sure that we have evidence for the document. If there was such a document, we are unsure which stories might have belonged in it.

In the Stories of David's Middle Years — 2 Sam 11–20, also referred to as the Court History or the Succession Narrative; "middle years" reflects the reality that the story demands at least young adulthood for Amnon and Absalom, while leaving time for Solomon to achieve kingly age by 1 Kgs 1–2 — while its components may well have existed as independent stories, the current narrative sequence is demanded by the fact that independent beginnings and/or endings no longer exist for the major component stories. With or without Nathan's interpretation of his parable (2 Sam 12:7b-14), the story of David and Bathsheba sets a pattern for the sexual and homicidal violence to follow. The story of Amnon and Tamar opens with a classical editorial linking phrase, "some time passed" (13:1); it does not begin as might be expected of a classical Hebrew story. In the present text, it is necessary to motivate Absalom's killing of Amnon, David's heir. That story, in its turn, motivates Absalom's ill-fated return to Jerusalem and his botched reconciliation with David. It leads into the story of Absalom's revolt and David's flight and ultimate return to Jerusalem. The end of ch. 19 is hardly the end of a major narrative; ch. 20, the story of

Sheba's revolt, is less than perfect as an end — but it is better than ch. 19. So a text, the Stories of David's Middle Years, can be assumed. Whether it extends, around 2 Sam 21–24, into 1 Kgs 1–2 is open to discussion; that is not particularly likely. There is reason to see 1 Kgs 1–2 as an independent story about Solomon's accession.

The Prophetic Record (1 Sam 1:1–2 Kgs 10:28) is claimed as an ancient document. References back and forth — themes, concepts, or language — bind its various traditions into a coherent whole. The status of such a composition as a document is confirmed by examples of editorial overwriting. Early in the piece, prophetic overwriting, by the composing editors, is visible in 1 Sam 9:1–10:16 and 15:1-34, as also in 2 Sam 7:1-17. Later in the piece, overwriting by the composers of the DH is visible in passages such as the prophetic speeches to kings (e.g., 1 Kgs 14:4-13; 21:17-26; 2 Kgs 10:4-10). Editors used writing when they overwrote; of course, they overwrote written documents.

These factors are absent from the narrative of David's rise to power. The stories are there, but they could have been used in a variety of combinations and permutations. Mark O'Brien and I wrote: "the likely narrative organization around areas such as 1 Samuel 17–18, 23–26, and 28–31 points to the probability of such a text having existed" (*Unfolding*, 219). The density of this needs some unfolding itself. Before chs. 28–31 and before chs. 23–26, there are a couple of collections of information of the kind that would hardly have been gathered had a larger work not been in view (i.e., 27:1-7 and 22:1-5; cf. Rendtorff, "Beobachtungen," and below in the chapter on the diachronic dimension). 27:1-7 looks to Ziklag, but not beyond; it notes the sixteen months David was in Philistine territory, but no more. Together with the narrative organization of chs. 28–31, it is evidence for a composition dealing with David's time with the Philistines. It is not evidence for more. Together with the narrative organization of chs. 23–26, 1 Sam 22:1-5 is evidence for a composition dealing with David's time in the wilderness. It is not evidence for more.

Toward the end of chs. 17–18, there are three almost summary verses:

- David had success (18:14)
- Saul stood in awe of him (18:15)
- All Israel and Judah loved him (18:16)

Named are the three significant players in the events of David's rise to power: David, Saul, and all Israel and Judah. When "the tribes" came to David at Hebron to make him king over Israel, they are reported to have said: "it was you who led out Israel and brought it in" (2 Sam 5:2). The echo of 18:16's "it was he who marched out and came in leading them" is unmistakable, even in English; in Hebrew, it is more concise and closer. There may be a pointer here to an arc that understood the narrative of David's rise as extending from David's emergence at the court of Saul to David's emergence as Israel's king — from Philistine to throne. What such an understanding does not spell out is precisely what stories were included in any given version of the narrative, or whether all versions of the narrative shared this view of its appropriate extent.

The upshot of all this is the claim that the so-called Story of David's Rise is different from almost any of the hypothetical documents of ancient Israel. Its stories are preserved for us in largely independent form. Where links can be shown, the narrative extent is not great or not certain. Narrative compositions made up of such stories are likely to have existed. They may well have begun with early stories of Saul's becoming king; they may well have ended with David's capture of Jerusalem and the building of his palace, or they may have gone on even further to include early versions of the coming of the ark and Nathan's promise of a Davidic dynasty, with some acknowledgment of David's success as king. In the light of this, it is probably right to speak of a Story of David's Rise. It would not be right to be dogmatic about its beginning, its ending, or about details of its content. Given a certain overall unity and a thematic favoring of David, such a narrative composition could well have seen the light of day at different times, in different versions, and with varying component elements. We do not know. The present text we actually have has probably, substantially at least, been preserved for us by the Prophetic Record, putting on record the available traditions.

NATURE OF THE BIBLE

One paradigm for Bible users is rapidly losing favor as experience of the text overhauls tradition. The evident disparity of biblical witness argues against use of the Bible for the direct establishment of doctrine or policy. While few might admit to this practice, in practice many still do it. Most of the biblical text may well be a participant in dialogue that establishes doctrine or policy; but it participates, it does not establish.

The Bible, and 1 Samuel with it, is more important than the doctrine or policy that might be discussed today. It is needed by the biblical faith community. The nature of the need is, alas, not luminously clear and is clouded by areas of significant misuse.

The Bible is evidently enough the collection of texts associated with the development of faith communities. Whether Jewish or Christian, it is their foundation document. The Older Testament emerged along with the faith community of Israel; building on it, the Newer Testament did the same with the Christian community of faith. Some have quarried these foundational texts not so much for a rumor of angels but for the reality of God. Others have quarried them for history or piety. Fuller scrutiny of the text often provides little support for such searches — apart altogether from the significant roles of arousing feeling, fueling faith, and firing imagination.

The Bible can function as a mysterious glass, occasionally allowing its users glimpses of God. The Bible can function as a reflective glass, often allowing its users to see images of themselves. The modern scholar, within a faith community, may go further: the Bible can function as a pointer to the nature of part at least of God's communication with us and to the struggle of human faith to find expression. Articulating two extremes may help focus reflection. Faith may be understood as enlightenment to which God invites. Knowledge may be

11

understood as enlightenment that God reveals and, to that extent, imposes. Any position taken on the range between faith and knowledge needs ultimately to be based on experience of the biblical text. Minimal reflection is needed to realize that God can invite to faith and God can impose knowledge. At issue is not the source of either; at issue is the nature of the biblical text. Ultimately a faith position needs to be founded on experience of the biblical text. In my experience of the biblical text, the invitation to faith predominates.

Signposts may be vital to travelers on a journey. A single signpost that is pointing in the right direction and has not been tampered with can be invaluable. Several signposts, pointing in different directions to the same destination, invite reflection. Some may be misleading or have been interfered with by vandals, but it is not necessarily so. Several routes can lead to the same goal; on occasion, the longest way round (in distance) is the shortest way there (in time or effort). Reflection is invited. Experience of the biblical text suggests that reflection is being invited constantly.

What excites much critical interest in the Bible can be caught by naming three interwoven issues and can, in a paragraph, be no more than adumbrated at best. Three heavy-duty adjectives help in the naming: incarnational, foundational, and interpretational. The **incarnational** — not restricted to God's becoming one of us, but expanded to reflect our experience of God as unobtrusive and intangible, almost concealed from us in the ordinariness of life — may not, at first sight, be evidently applicable to the Bible. Many long to escape the ambiguity and uncertainty of so much human living, and the Bible often seems to offer an escape into the certainty and clarity of the divine. Closer acquaintance with it calls us back to explore, be reconciled with, and perhaps rejoice in the incarnational (involvement-in-the-human) uncertainty and ambiguity we find in our Bible and ourselves. The **foundational** issue — at the base of faith identity — arises where we quest for what is of ultimate concern to us in our lives. We need to know about the wellsprings in our past that are vital to our present. We yearn for foundations that rest in bedrock. We may need to examine the nature and the quality of the foundations on which major aspects of our faith-identity are built — just as people buying a house run checks on foundations and structural soundness, plumbing, roofing, and wiring, etc., or financial institutions contemplating takeovers run due diligence checks. In such a situation, adherents of biblical faith need to explore the Bible. The **interpretational** relates to that risky activity of exploring our present beings, of self-discovery, when we need to make meaning for ourselves of our living, when we need to interpret our lives to ourselves. For many, the exploration of the Bible — rooting around in the foundations of faith and even discovering there something of the incarnational — is an indispensable aid in interpreting life.

To simplify, the attraction exciting much critical engagement with the Bible can be spelled out in terms of three activities: being at home with my God, being at home with my faith, and being at home with myself.

It is above all at the level of communication and faith that my passion for the Bible, and the books of Samuel, is engaged. In these texts, God is constantly affirmed in events, and events are constantly required to unfold at an earthly level. The tension of affirmation and experience is intensified by the multiplication of affirmations and the plurality of experiences. In the process, God may be glimpsed. In the process, the images of humankind may be more deeply etched. But it is the process itself that speaks of the communication between God and humankind: affirmed, uncertain, in tension, and manifestly manifold. A researcher's paradise and a seedbed for faith.

Another aspect of the scrutiny of biblical texts that fascinates me is the discovery in them of what can attract or repel me in much modern society. In the composition of the text, there is the attraction of intelligence and integrity, of faith and skepticism. In the roles portrayed, there is much that can repel. For example: the arrogant claims of faith supporting self-righteousness or worse; the confident certainty that success denotes God's favor; the seesaw of motivation from self-interest to superstition.

In this context, Brueggemann's comment on the texts of Samuel is relevant.

> A "religious" reading is tempted to make the story of Israel in the books of Samuel excessively pious, to overlook the tension of factions, the reality of power, the seduction of sex, the temptation to alliances, the ignobility of motivations, and the reliance on brutality. . . . There is a long-established practice of an "innocent" religious reading of the Samuel narrative. These elements of power, seduction, brutality, and ignobility, however, are all there in the text. (p. 2)

The reality of life and politics, often sordid enough, needs to be balanced by awareness of the place of God in it all. Brueggemann again:

> If we try to reconstruct the transformation of Israel without serious reference to Yahweh, to Yahweh's words, deeds and purpose, we will have constructed a telling of the transformation that decisively departs from Israel's own recitation. (p. 3)

All of which leads directly to the issue of theology and history.

THEOLOGICAL WRITING OR HISTORIOGRAPHY

One participant in the current debate over different views of the monarchy and the pre-exilic period has written that "the appeal of the Hebrew Bible/Old Testament [to a wide constituency of scholars and students] . . . lies pre-eminently in its link with history and archaeology" (Davies, "Introduction," 14). From the point of view of this commentary, I can only hope that view of the Bible's appeal is wrong. The understanding of experience in relationship with God is more appealing. Another participant poses the question in an unfortunate formulation: "What is the early Jewish historiography that we call the Bible about?" (Thompson, "Historiography," 39). The Bible is much more than "early Jewish historiography"; it is difficult to assert that the Bible is about historiography at all. The practice of the Bible is generally to amalgamate compet-

13

ing traditions rather than to adjudicate between them. History as a rendering of account about the past tends to adjudicate rather than amalgamate; amalgamation without evaluation is an abdication of the historian's role.

If the books of Samuel were adjudged to be ancient historiography — which I do not believe they are — the criteria employed are such that the texts could be used by modern historians only very carefully and obliquely.

Three examples are enough.

1. The existence of significant and unacknowledged leaps.
   For example:
   • The leap from the boyish neophyte at the sanctuary to the nationally acknowledged prophet (1 Sam 3).
   • The leap from youngest son, handy with a sling, to the status of a senior commander among Saul's troops (1 Sam 16–18).
2. The presence of divine intervention, both highly visible and scarcely visible.
   For example:
   • The highly visible action of God in the Ark Narrative or during the deliverance of Israel mediated by Samuel (1 Sam 4–6; 7).
   • The scarcely visible action of God throughout the story of the struggle between Saul and David, noteworthy in the final campaign against the Philistines (1 Sam 16–31, note chs. 28–31).
3. The frequent practice in the biblical text of amalgamating conflicting evidence rather than offering any assessment of it.
   For example:
   • The traditions related to the emergence of kingship in Israel (1 Sam 7–8 amalgamated with 9:1–10:16 and 11).
   • The traditions of Saul's rejection (1 Sam 13:7b-15a and 15:1-35).
   • The traditions of David's sojourn with Achish at Gath (1 Sam 21:10-15 and 27:1-12).
   • The traditions concerning Goliath (amalgamated in 1 Sam 16:14–18:9; also 2 Sam 21:19).
   • The conviction that David's success was attributable to divine favor (e.g., 1 Sam 18:14) alongside the conviction that David's success was attributable to his being a murderous scoundrel (2 Sam 16:5-8).

Much biblical narrative is written to articulate experience. It may be the historian's role to identify or date the experience. It is the interpreter's role to explore the articulation. Much articulation is not naive reporting of experience; much experience is not easily identified within the articulation. When all of this is placed in the context of faith in the involvement of God with human experience, the result is much more theology than history.

For 1 Samuel, again three examples of this process will be illustration enough, looking at the portrayal of Samuel, Saul, and David. Samuel was envisaged as a prophet to all Israel ("from Dan to Beer-sheba," 1 Sam 3:20), who anointed and dismissed Saul and anointed David in his place. In particular, the association of the anointings of Saul, David, and Jehu places this portrayal in conjunction with the prophetic approval of Jehu's coup and eradication of Baal worship. The image of Jehu's coup provides the experience. The articulation of that experience calls for a particular view of the prophet, embodied above all in the figure of Samuel.

Saul is portrayed as a man designated by YHWH to be Israel's king, a success in the short term against Nahash and a failure in the long term against the Philistines. The experience is one of need that is unsatisfactorily met. The unsatisfactory can be accounted for by human fragility (Saul's disobedience) or by divine displeasure (God's withdrawal from Saul, cf. 1 Sam 16:14-15). The articulation of this experience blends the folly and the nobility of the human enmeshed in it.

David is presented as the king after God's own heart (1 Sam 13:14), who at the end of a long struggle attains to the throne of Judah and ultimately of Israel, benefiting from God's favor but without any sense of God's direct intervention on his behalf. The experience is presented as the transition from a premonarchic structure of existence (largely unknown to us) to a society with a degree of central government (the details of which are also largely unknown to us). The articulation lards David's success with affirmations of divine favor; the same articulation seldom overlooks the strategies and tactics that humanly bring such success.

The biblical text that engages with these issues situates itself at the beginning of a fragilely and temporarily united kingdom. What happens if the historian insists that the experiences generating these texts belong in a later and much different time? The experience changes; the articulation remains superficially the same. The portrayal of Samuel can serve as a model. The articulation is set in the time of Shiloh, Saul, and David; the experience that triggered this particular articulation may well be the interpretation of Jehu's coup in the late 9th century. Once we have said that 1-2 Samuel are not history and do not serve historiographical purposes, the questions that must be addressed are, What is the nature of 1-2 Samuel and what purposes do they serve?

Approached as neutrally as possible, the articulation of experience is a good model for understanding religious texts like 1-2 Samuel (I owe the model to Luke Timothy Johnson, *Writings,* esp. 10-16). Something triggers the drive to create what becomes text, whether remembered or written. Underlying that "something" may be found an experience. For stories of David's rise to power, the experience may be that David emerged as king — and an interpretation needed to be found to account for this emergence. God is appealed to in the interpretation; the text becomes theological. If ambition or the exercise of power or the issue of popular support was primary in the interpretation, it might well become political — and so on. It is possible that the historical reality of David's kingship was different from that portrayed in the text. The interpreter's challenge remains the same: to explore the articulation of the experience offered by the text.

What is the experience that provided the stimulus for 1-2 Samuel? At face value, it is that David has emerged as king in Israel, established in place by the institution of the monarchy. David's kingship was not an aberrant moment as might be said of any claim regarding Abimelech. David's kingship is por-

15

trayed as successful in the establishment of a monarchic institution in a way that Saul's was not.

As is evident from the biblical text, this new state of affairs demanded interpretation. For some voices, whether early or late, this action — the experience — was akin to apostasy: "they have rejected me [YHWH] from being king over them" (1 Sam 8:7); "how can this man save us?" (1 Sam 10:27). Clearly, for these, the development is not of God. For David's supporters — the originators, at one time or another, of the bulk of 1-2 Samuel — their interpretation of the experience was far from one of apostasy. It was indeed of God. For them, God was with David, and his kingship was God's will and God's doing. God was with him. Of course the working out of the divine will in the reality of human politics had to be done by David. David may have been far from perfect, but he ended up being Israel's model for God's ideal of a king.

If the overwriting of the image and activity of Samuel owes something to the prophetic circles associated with the legitimacy of Jehu's coup, it is appropriate — for simplicity's sake more than anything else — to identify the evidence for belief in God's endorsement of David's kingship. Samuel's anointing of Saul, as opposed to his commissioning by an anonymous prophet, as well as aspects of Saul's rejection and the anointing of David are all attributed to the Prophetic Record, the work of the late-9th-century prophetic circles associated to some degree with Jehu's coup. Some prophetic endorsement of Saul seems to have been in the tradition, along with some rebuke. Prophetic anointing of David (1 Sam 16:1-13) is attributed entirely to prophetic rewriting. The suggestion that Saul is in trouble with God comes with 1 Sam 16:14-23.

At this early stage, then, the belief that God is with David is founded on David's victory over the Philistine (cf. 1 Sam 17:47) and David's sustained success (1 Sam 18:14-16; 2 Sam 5:2). The Philistines posed a serious threat to Israel's independence. David's leadership and command, institutionalized in the monarchy, eliminated the threat and secured the independence. It must be of God. There is even a hint of this in David's comment on Solomon's accession: "Blessed be the LORD, the God of Israel, who today has granted one of my offspring to sit on my throne and permitted me to witness it" (1 Kgs 1:48). David gives twofold thanks to God. At a later stage (late 9th century), the belief in divine favor for David's kingship was expressed in terms of the prophetic endorsement and anointing.

In modern democracies, inundated by the media, subjected to the efforts of "spin doctors," we can become cynical about the interpretation put on events. We need to distinguish the inner-oriented from the outer-oriented. When interpretation is for the benefit of the inner being of those involved, whether as individuals or group, it can be a matter of conviction, morale, or indeed theology. When interpretation is oriented outward toward others, it can be concerned with persuasion, propaganda, or vindication (cf. Whitelam, "Defence of David," esp. 61-71). All theology that moves from the inner toward the outer becomes involved in the justification and/or propagation of the faith.

The conviction maintained here is that the origin of the bulk of the Davidic traditions is to be attributed to the interpretation of the experience of David's kingship. Such interpretation involves rehearsing the traditions of what

David did; otherwise the experience would be a void. It involves an understanding of David's activity such that it is not believed to be in conflict with the will of God or, in Israel's case, to demean the sovereignty of God. David is to be seen not as replacing God in Israel but as being God's instrument in the assuring of Israel's defense and independence. This is a theological endeavor; it is not history-writing.

If "the origin of the bulk of the Davidic traditions is to be attributed to the interpretation of the experience of David's kingship," we need to be aware of the subsequent experiences that demanded understanding and articulation and that are largely situated within the wider context of the DH. A full exploration is not possible in this Introduction, but an indication can be given as to where such an exploration might need to go. Its fragility and its hypothetical quality go without saying. The Prophetic Record, for example, presumably responds to the threat posed by Baalism, especially Baalism of foreign origin. The articulation of a response appeals to the guidance from God's prophets. The Josianic DH is a manifesto for reform. Presumably, elements in the context of its experience include the fall of the north, Sennacherib's siege of Jerusalem, and increasing anxiety in the face of imperial power. The response looks over the wider range of Israel's experience and concludes that fidelity to God will bring life and prosperity. The revised DH faces the experience that Josiah's fidelity, and that of his generation, did not bring life and prosperity. The articulation of this required revision of the Josianic texts, the introduction of threats and warnings, and so on. To sum up: Israel's experience that surfaces in one way or another in the books of Samuel runs the gamut from the emergence of prophets and kings in the mainstream of Israel's national structures through to the end of Israel's national independence. A lot of articulating needed to be done.

It would do no harm for devotees of 1-2 Samuel to steep themselves in the Arthurian legends, despite the fact that the gap between the two bodies of literature is vast — even making due allowance for the strong literary context of the lyric romanticism of the medieval troubadours. As is easily recognizable, within the Arthurian literature there are the barely legendary, the fully legendary, and the full flowering of faerie and myth (all represented in Ashley, *Arthurian Legends*). What such exploration will uncover is that, at times, the "barely legendary" — what is at the fringe of legend, touching on the historical — has echoes of 1-2 Samuel and its potential. The nature of the texts of 1-2 Samuel cannot be taken for granted; it must be explored.

ISSUES OF DEUTERONOMISTIC LANGUAGE

Deuteronomistic language, the language of the Deuteronomists or dtr editors, is marked by the particular theology and ways of expressing that theology which can be identified in the book of Deuteronomy and the Deuteronomistic History (cf. Weinfeld for a sound position and a valuable appendix identifying much dtr phraseology). The book of Deuteronomy, the deuteronomic reform based on it, and the circles inspired by it have had immense influence on the Older Testament text as we have it. If the growth of ideas and the development of theology in the Older Testament are to be taken seriously, it is important to be able to identify dtr passages. Since the question will come up quite often in 1 Samuel, it is worth considering more closely.

Not everything that a dtr editor wrote could possibly be couched in exclusively dtr language; it would be naive to expect that. But for proof of dtr editing, we have to start with the presence of demonstrably identifiable characteristics of dtr language and thought (language in the service of ideology), and we move out from there. That is the first level and it is a fairly sure one: we can identify, with a reasonable level of certainty, what is characteristic of the thought and language of the book of Deuteronomy or of the key structural passages of the DH. At the second level there are those sections of a text that, while not themselves expressed in dtr terms, are inseparable from other sections that are characterized by dtr expression. Here certainty will depend on just how inseparable the two parts are. There is a third level, where there is no clearly characteristic language or thought and no intrinsic link to such expression, but where it seems to make good sense to attribute a text to dtr sources. It may be a case of language or thought that one would expect the Deuteronomists to use, but that cannot be documented as characteristic of them; it may be a case of content that seems likely to have been of dtr origin. At this third level, there is considerable variation in the degree of probability that can be achieved.

HOW TO READ THIS BOOK

The structure analyses that are so central to this book and to this series are not glorified tables of contents. They bear a similar relation to the literary text as flow charts bear to projects or organizations: they seek to identify the component elements of the text and to indicate the interrelationships between them.

Good biblical commentaries invariably tempt their readers to succumb to reading the commentary rather than the biblical text. Precisely because it is good, the commentary is eminently readable and the biblical text can be bypassed — especially if found to be difficult. To benefit from both the structure analyses and the discussion in this book, the following steps are recommended.

- The first step has to be to read the biblical text under consideration. All too often, people pass this by, thinking they know the text or finding it too opaque and difficult. No commentary can open up a text for a reader if the text has not been read. It is rather like shaking hands with a person who is not there.
- The second step is basically to contemplate the structure analysis. What does it identify as major blocks in the text? How does it relate them to each other? How do the details fit in? What perception of the text — what grasp of what it is doing and what understanding of its meaning — does the structure analysis reveal?

- The third step is to read the text again in the light of the analysis, to see whether one finds the analysis verified in the text.
- The fourth step depends on whether the reader agrees or disagrees with the structure analysis. It involves reading the discussion in the commentary, with the reflections on genre, setting, and meaning. If the reader is in instinctive agreement with the analysis of the text, the discussion can be read for understanding and verification. If the reader disagrees with the analysis, then this fourth step is the time for comparing the text and the structure and evaluating them in the light of the discussion.
- As a fifth step, when all this has been done, readers are in a position to proceed to their own interpretation, for their own times, their own lives.

Ideally, interpretation proceeds from the signals in the text. Ideally, the structure analysis should articulate a perception of these signals that organizes them as coherently as the text allows or suggests. Assessing the perception of the text given in the structure analysis against the text itself and again in the light of the discussion should give as good grounds for the text's interpretation as a commentary can offer.

Finally, a particular methodological aspect needs to be underlined. For analysis, the text has been broken into larger narrative units. These are structural sections within the telling of the narrative; they do not constitute literary genres in themselves. No treatment is given of their genre, setting, and meaning. It is appropriate that this treatment should be kept until the section on the diachronic dimension; in this way, it has been possible to stay close to present-text analysis. Often enough, even within component elements of these larger narrative units more than one genre has been used to compile the narrative. For that reason, genre terms are not normally used in the superscriptions of units. Where, as often, a unit comprises several genres — for example, a story, a report or an account, and a notice or two — any overarching genre would be out of place in the unit's title. The text is narrative. The function that the various larger narratives perform is discussed under the rubric Diachronic Dimension.

AVOWAL

An avowal such as this should be taken for granted throughout biblical scholarship. But since it is not taken for granted, it needs to be said. The avowal is this: the interpretation of 1 Samuel presented in this volume is no more than that — an interpretation. It is not and does not attempt to be the definitive interpretation, simply because interpretation is an art and art does not attempt the definitive. The interpretation of 1 Samuel presented in this volume attempts to be both adequate and responsible. Adequate: accounting for as many of the signals seen in the text as possible within a coherent horizon. Responsible: alert to the claims of the text, proposing interpretations that are plausible within the canons of Israelite literature as we know it, and not passing over signals simply because they do not fit the presentation.

Two scholars do not have the place in this volume that the extent of their work would suggest. They are Jan Fokkelman and Robert Polzin. Fokkelman's study of the narrative art and poetry in the books of Samuel runs to four volumes (2,403 pages). Polzin has so far devoted three volumes to a literary study of the Deuteronomic History, with Part Two given to 1 Samuel. I have learned greatly from Polzin's concern for the present text, especially given his acceptance of the traditional processes belonging within the text. I disagree often enough with his conclusions about the present text. A thorough discussion of Polzin's work would need a book-length study. Scattered comments along the way would not do justice to his undertaking. So I have chosen to make this tribute and as a rule refrain from the scattered comments. However, his remark about Jeffrey Tigay's work might be turned back on his own: "both important and trivial" (*Samuel*, 229). Important for its emphasis on the present text; trivial, alas, for aspects of its interpretation of the same present text — despite many valuable insights. Fokkelman's aims in his massive study are significantly different from mine in this one. Again, scattered comments would not do justice to the matter, while a thorough discussion is out of the question in a study of this kind. Beyond these, David Jobling's *1 Samuel* is to be valued. It is not a commentary, but offers perceptive reflections on the impact for biblical interpretation of differing scholarly insights and viewpoints over a half-century. It is to be treasured.

Both this volume and the volume on 2 Samuel that will soon follow in this FOTL series owe much to the inspiration of Rolf Knierim and to the hospitality offered me over the years by the parish of Our Lady of the Assumption and by Claremont Graduate University's Institute for Antiquity and Christianity and the Claremont School of Theology, with especial thanks to its library staff. I am deeply grateful. Acknowledgment and profound gratitude are also due to my home institution, Jesuit Theological College, within the United Faculty of Theology, Parkville, and to its associated Joint Theological Library.

Finally, my gratitude to Allen Myers and his colleagues at Eerdmans for their care and competence in producing what I consider to be a splendid volume.

Bibliography of Works Cited Above

Ashley, M., ed. *The Mammoth Book of Arthurian Legends*. London: Robinson Publishing, 1998.

Barthes, Roland. *Le plaisir du texte*. Paris: Editions du Seuil, 1973.

Byers, David M., ed. *Religion, Science, and the Search for Wisdom: Proceedings of a Conference on Religion and Science, September 1986*. Washington, DC: United States Catholic Conference, 1987.

Campbell, Antony F., and Mark A. O'Brien. *Unfolding the Deuteronomistic History: Origins, Upgrades, Present Text*. Minneapolis: Fortress, 2000.

Davies, P. R. "Introduction." Pp. 11-21 in *The Origins of the Ancient Israelite States*. Edited by V. Fritz and P. R. Davies. JSOTSup 228. Sheffield: Sheffield Academic Press, 1996.

Edelman, Diana Vikander. *King Saul in the Historiography of Judah.* JSOTSup 121. Sheffield: Sheffield Academic Press, 1991.

Fokkelman, J. P. *Narrative Art and Poetry in the Books of Samuel: A Full Interpretation Based on Stylistic and Structural Analyses.* Vol. I: *King David (II Sam. 9–20 & I Kings 1–2).* Vol. II: *The Crossing Fates (I Sam. 13–31 & II Sam. 1).* Vol. III: *Throne and City (II Sam. 2–8 & 21–24).* Vol. IV: *Vow and Desire (I Sam. 1–12).* Assen/Maastricht, The Netherlands: Van Gorcum, 1981-93.

Frye, Northrop. *The Great Code: The Bible and Literature.* New York: Harcourt Brace Jovanovich, 1981-82.

Jobling, David. *1 Samuel.* Berit Olam: Studies in Hebrew Narrative & Poetry. A Michael Glazier Book. Collegeville: The Liturgical Press, 1998.

Johnson, Luke Timothy. *The Writings of the New Testament: An Interpretation.* Rev. ed. Minneapolis: Fortress, 1999.

Long, Burke O. "Recent Field Studies in Oral Literature and the Question of *Sitz im Leben.*" *Semeia* 5 (1976) 35-49.

Polzin, Robert. *A Literary Study of the Deuteronomic History.* Part One: *Moses and the Deuteronomist.* New York: Seabury, 1980. Part Two: *Samuel and the Deuteronomist.* San Francisco: Harper & Row, 1989. Part Three: *David and the Deuteronomist.* Bloomington: Indiana University Press, 1993.

Rendtorff, Rolf. "Beobachtungen zur altisraelitischen Geschichtsschreibung anhand der Geschichte vom Aufstieg Davids." Pp. 428-39 in *Probleme biblischer Theologie: Gerhard von Rad zum 70. Geburtstag.* Edited by H. W. Wolff. Munich: Chr. Kaiser, 1971.

Thompson, T. L. "Historiography of Ancient Palestine and Early Jewish Historiography: W. G. Dever and the Not So New Biblical Archaeology." Pp. 26-43 in *The Origins of the Ancient Israelite States.* Edited by V. Fritz and P. R. Davies. JSOTSup 228. Sheffield: Sheffield Academic Press, 1996.

Weinfeld, Moshe. *Deuteronomy and the Deuteronomic School.* Oxford: Clarendon, 1972.

Whitelam, Keith W. "The Defence of David." *JSOT* 29 (1984) 61-87.

Chapter 1

THE OVERALL SHAPE AND SCOPE OF 1-2 SAMUEL

The overall structuring of 1 Samuel alone is a task that wisely should not be attempted. It may be shortsighted to give an overall outline of pregnancy without reference to birth; it is imprudent to plan on earning ordinary income without thought of taxes; it is unwise to reflect on life without including death. 1-2 Samuel focuses on the figure of David. 1 Samuel speaks of the one after the LORD's own heart, who has been appointed to be ruler over Israel in place of Saul (13:14; cf. 15:28). The structural movement cannot end with the death of Saul. With the death of Saul, a page can be turned, a chapter ended; the book cannot be closed. So we are obliged to deal with 1-2 Samuel.

The books of Samuel (in Hebrew, the book of Samuel) move on two planes. At one level, events are unfolded in some form of chronological sequence. At another level, fundamental theological questions are raised by the text: in all the political turbulence associated with the names of Samuel, Saul, and David, what was God's role in the story of Israel? An attempt to conceptualize the structure of 1-2 Samuel needs to be aware of both these levels.

Any great work of literature, above all any attempt to enter into the mystery of God's dealings with humankind, is open to multiple understandings and susceptible of multiple interpretations. 1-2 Samuel is such a work. While the simple chronological sequences — from Samuel to Saul to David, from Shiloh to Jerusalem, and so on — are unlikely to invite challenge, the meaning to be derived from the texts and the reflection on the theological issues raised certainly invite multiple interpretation. It is not the place of this commentary to emphasize one interpretation of the texts as though it alone were right. It is the place of this commentary to propose at least one interpretation — as appropriate, as adequate and responsible.

Theological thinking in Israel was not divorced from the sequence of events in the life of the people. Israel's theology found its expression in the way that traditions about the sequence were formulated. Attention to detail is lavished on events that do not need such detail to be included in the sequence. Portrayals are shaped to provide an understanding that goes beyond the mere sequence. The text of 1-2 Samuel can be presented as follows.

The Beginnings of Stable Monarchy in Ancient Israel   **1-2 Samuel**

I. Preparations for David's emergence as king-to-be   1 Sam 1:1–16:13
  - A. Prophetic: arrival of Samuel on the national scene   1:1–4:1a
  - B. Liturgical: departure of the ark from the national scene   4:1b–7:1
  - C. Prophetic: emergence of monarchy   7:2–16:13
    1. Arrival of Saul and the new institution of monarchy   7:2–12:25
    2. Dismissal of Saul and beginning of David's arrival   13:1–16:13

II. Political moves to establish David as king   1 Sam 16:14- 2 Sam 8:18
  - A. Tension between Saul as king and David as anointed   1 Sam 16:14–31:13
    1. David at the court of Saul   16:14–21:1 (NRSV, 20:42)
    2. Open rupture between David and Saul   21:2 (NRSV, 21:1)–27:12
    3. Ultimate failure of Saul   28:1–31:13
  - B. Civil war in Israel   2 Sam 1–4
  - C. Establishment of David as king: completion of David's arrival   2 Sam 5–8
    1. Political establishment: arrival of David in Jerusalem   5:1-16
    2. Security of the kingdom I: from the Philistines   5:17-25
    3. Liturgical establishment: arrival of the ark in Jerusalem   6:1-23
    4. Prophetic establishment: dynasty of David in Jerusalem   7:1-29
    5. Security of the kingdom II: external relations generally   8:1-18
  - Appendix I: traditions associated with the following text   2 Sam 9–10

III. Stories of David's Middle Years: internal security threatened   2 Sam 11–20
  - A. David: the modeling of a king   11–12
  - B. The modeling within David's family   13–19
    1. Internal impact: without threat to David's rule   13–14
    2. External impact: with grave threat to David's rule   15–19
  - C. The modeling within David's kingdom   20
  - Appendix II: independent traditions about David   2 Sam 21–24

Within this structure, it is helpful to note the influences at work. Prophetic: Samuel arrives on the scene at the start — [= Structure Analysis: I.A] and departs after David's anointing; his job is done. A prophet, Samuel, anoints David — [I.C]; a prophet, Nathan, gives David God's promise of dynastic security in Jerusalem — [II.C.4]. Liturgical (we might say "cultic" but

24

the word evokes old-fashioned prejudices against ancient faith): Israel's central liturgical symbol, the ark, departs at the beginning — [I.B] and returns to the center of Israel's life only after David's possession of Jerusalem — [II.C.3]. There is the prophetic again. With the ark off the scene, the prophet Samuel is central to the traditions about the emergence of monarchy in ancient Israel — [I.C]. Political: constantly at work, alongside the divinely related realms of prophecy and liturgy, are the influences we call political — [II]. There is political tension between David and Saul — [II.A]; there is political struggle after Saul's death over succession to Saul's kingdom — [II.B]; and there is political struggle to establish David's kingdom securely — [II.C]. Within the books of Samuel, the stories of David's middle years are witness to the complexity of kingship and the reality of a stable monarchy in ancient Israel — [III]. David's kingdom was threatened by turbulence; David's dynasty was stable.

To report that Samuel was born and consecrated to the LORD at Shiloh does not require the detail of a barren woman's vow, the Lord's attention to her, and her fulfillment of her vow. Sequentially, the details of Elide failure and condemnation are less important than the details of what brought Samuel to the attention of "all Israel" (cf. 1 Sam 4:1a); these latter details are not given — just the bare report of 3:19–4:1a. Similarly, the move of the ark from Shiloh to Jerusalem, via Kiriath-jearim, is politically and historically significant. The details given serve another aim than the political and historical. Equally, the role of Samuel in Saul's kingship and David's emergence is important; the details provided reflect a concern with God's role in this new development. The many stories of the political struggle for power between Saul and David are fascinating for the sequence of events in Israel. As they are told, though, they reflect a concern for God's action and the realization of the prophetic word. The arrival of the ark in Jerusalem is told as an action under God's control. The assurance of David's dynastic security is given within a prophetic word associated with the royal proposal to build a temple. The stories of David's middle years have a characteristic dynamic that is peculiar to them alone. The detailed narrative goes far beyond the needs of any sequence of events. Divine action is present, but focus on it is restricted. The final collection (2 Sam 21–24) has a structural focus of its own; it scarcely contributes to the sequence of events — [Appendix II].

In Hebrew, the books of the Pentateuch are named from the first words of their text. The book of Samuel is named from the first major figure in its text. Samuel's life-work is finished by 1 Sam 16:13; he appears briefly in the text at 1 Sam 19:18-24; he is buried in 1 Sam 25:1. He had a job to do and he has done it; he has been God's instrument in inaugurating Israel's monarchy, and he has bestowed God's anointing on David who will be Israel's greatest king. Samuel occupies an extraordinarily dominant place in the biblical text. Since the ancestors and Moses, no one has had such attention paid to the story of their birth as Samuel. Since Moses, no one in Israel has established an office equal in significance to that of the king. Samuel could be dubbed the man born to make kings. The structural question is whether his fate is portrayed as first to anoint a failure and only then to anoint David, or whether, from the outset of the text, Samuel's destiny is to be seen as the anointing of David.

It is clear that Samuel had to emerge on the national scene as a recog-

25

nized prophet of YHWH before he could anoint a king in Israel. "All Israel . . .
knew that Samuel was a trustworthy prophet of the LORD" (1 Sam 3:20). Since
the biblical portrayal of Moses, there has been no prophetic figure of comparable stature until Samuel. Samuel starts a tradition of prophetic involvement
with the monarchy. It is not clear that the ark had to leave Shiloh for a king to be
established over Israel. What is clear in the text is that the ark as focal point for
God's action in Israel withdraws from the scene until its return to Jerusalem in
2 Sam 6. The way is clear for something new. It is clear in the text that God
would have acted differently had Saul been obedient to God's command —
communicated by the prophet. "The LORD would have established your kingdom over Israel forever, but now your kingdom will not continue" (1 Sam
13:13-14). What is not clear in the text is whether the anointings, first of Saul
and then of David, are portrayed in the text as the two peaks of Samuel's
achievement or whether the text's portrayal is better understood as oriented
from the outset toward David.

There is no certainty in the text, as to its structure; there are certain pointers. When God speaks to Samuel about sending Saul to him, Saul's mission is
to "save my people from the hand of the Philistines" (1 Sam 9:16). Saul does
not do this; David does. Other traditions of Saul's selection (1 Sam 8:1-22;
10:17-27) are tainted with overtones of displeasure and rejection. David alone
is the man after God's own heart (cf. 13:14). The moves recounted in 1 Sam 1–
12 to identify Saul as the man to be king are substantially religious. The moves
from 1 Sam 16:14 on are a more profound mingling of the political and the religious. Out of these moves emerge Saul's death (in 1 Sam 31:1-13) and David's
establishment as king over all Israel. Finally, in the biblical texts, the Davidic
dynasty is the one stable and enduring element in the story of the monarchy. I
do not believe that it can be affirmed with certainty as the structure of the text
but I do believe that it makes good sense of the text to see it as oriented toward
the Davidic monarchy, rather than toward a monarchy embodied first in Saul
and then in David.

It would be easy enough to make out a case for Saul's kingship that failed
through disobedience and David's that succeeded because of his fidelity. As
noted, 1 Sam 13:13-14 tries exactly that move for Saul. But in 13:7b-15a the
text hardly allows Saul the opportunity to repent. His repentance is emphatic in
15:24-25 and is accepted in 15:31. It is hard to make a convincing case that David is less disobedient to God in his dealings with Bathsheba and her husband.
It can be done; I doubt that it can be done convincingly.

Samuel's arrival on the Israelite scene then may be directed toward
founding the Davidic monarchy that will be an unshakable pillar in the traditions of Israel. Samuel's birth has to be portentous; his replacement of the
Elides has to happen. If something new is to happen in Israel, it is fitting for
God's traditional symbol of presence to be withdrawn, at least temporarily; so
the ark leaves Shiloh. There are conflicting traditions about the origins of Israel's monarchy. It is good to have these out of the way and the monarchy in
place before David is brought on the scene.

In these narrative books, Israel's prophetic claims are a mixture of the divinely absolute and the humanly realistic. Most of the time, prophets proclaim

God's word, and political activity is portrayed bringing it to realization. So Samuel is portrayed anointing Saul, dismissing Saul, anointing David; after this, the text spends more than twenty chapters portraying the political events that brought it to be. Once in being, the monarchy is a fascinating institution. It is subject to the quirks of human freedom; it is subject to the often unseen working of God's will. The Stories of David's Middle Years explore something of this fascination. The structure of 1-2 Samuel can be seen as remarkably unified: the portrayal of the arrival of the monarchy that will be given David — [I]; the portrayal of the political struggle that made this gift a reality — [II]; the portrayal of the workings of this institution in the life of David — [III]. Around these three bases, the traditions of 1-2 Samuel can be distributed.

Stories are told after events have happened. Prophecy ought to precede events; storytelling ought not. Israel's stories and traditions are based on the sequence of events that have happened, not that are foreseen for the future. The issue is not fact or fiction but past or future. Stories and traditions tell of the past. Story can be exclusively secular, without involving God, or story may be concerned with the role of God in the sequence of events. For the most part, the storytelling texts of 1-2 Samuel are about the role of God in the events of Israel's past. The events experienced are of major significance for Israel. Understanding is needed of the experience; stories provide the interpretation. Interest may be maintained by the storyteller's skill in weaving the sequence of events into a plot that arouses interest by raising tension and reaching resolution.

In one way or another, the narrative texts of 1-2 Samuel are involved with events that brought radical change for the people of Israel and their understanding of themselves. The old tribal era was replaced by the centralized government of a monarchy — all of this within a people who believed themselves chosen by their God and committed to their God. The religious implications of the experience are enormous. Interpretation of the experience is needed to grapple with these religious implications. Stories are one way of providing that interpretation. In this sense, the storytelling texts of 1-2 Samuel are religious texts; at their core, there is the need to interpret the experience of Israel in the events that produced a radically new institution within God's people.

Israel's experience, in these texts of 1-2 Samuel, is of the end of a period of tribes or tribal leadership, of the emergence of monarchy as the institutionalized leadership in Israel, and of the projection of this form of government into the foreseeable future. To the best of our knowledge, aspects of the interpretation of this experience are preserved for us from several stages in that future: early, middle, and late. Critical to an understanding of these texts is the realization that they offer an interpretation of the events of Israel's experience. Often the interpretation is religious: this was how God was acting or was not acting in our midst. Aspects of the interpretation come from various periods of time; they come also from various viewpoints in society. The interpretations reflect those viewpoints. Varying viewpoints should not surprise us; we should not be closed to the possibility of other viewpoints beyond those we have. Above all, we cannot let go of the realizations that these texts are, for the most part, the interpretation of experience and that, because the events are often experienced religiously, the interpretation generates religious texts.

27

One of the events may be that a prophetic figure, Samuel, replaced the priestly leadership in Israel, symbolized in the Elides, and exercised a dominant role in the establishment of a new form of government. In the interpretation of this event, Samuel's birth to a barren mother is seen as God's action in response to Hannah's vow; Samuel's presence in the sanctuary of Shiloh is seen as the fulfillment of a vow to God. The elimination of the Elides as a force in Israel is portrayed as God's doing, reflecting their failure as religious leaders within Israel.

Another of the events is the move of a major liturgical or cultic symbol, the ark, from traditional Shiloh to the newly established city of Jerusalem. Interpretation here removes this event from the realm of politics between peoples or within a people and portrays the move as the action of God disengaging from one moment in the trajectory of Israel and in due course committing to another.

Central to the events of 1-2 Samuel are the emergence of the monarchy and the domination of that institution in Israel by David. Interpretation places this in a securely religious context. Under God's instructions, Samuel — known to all Israel as a "trustworthy prophet," none of whose words God allowed to fall to the ground (cf. 1 Sam 3:19-20) — was involved in the appointment of Saul to the office of king, in announcing his dismissal to Saul, and in indicating that David was to be Israel's future king. The events may have seemed largely political; the texts interpreting them claim that these events were largely religious, that God was directly involved.

The names of Abimelech and Saul are reminders that monarchy, divinely willed or not, can be short-lived in Israel. A major event in the people's history is the enduring dominance of the Davidic dynasty in Jerusalem. The claim to this and the seeds for this are to be found in 2 Samuel. The interpretation of the events involves God intimately in this enormously significant structural achievement.

We have said above that aspects of the interpretation of this experience are, to the best of our knowledge, preserved for us from several stages in Israel's subsequent future — early, middle, and late. It is likely that many of the interpretative traditions come from a relatively early stage in the story of Israel's monarchy. Others may reflect prophetic concerns associated with prophetic support for Jehu's coup in the late 9th century. Others again may reflect enthusiasm for deuteronomic reform in the time of Josiah. Others, finally, may reflect the failure of that reform and the religious conviction that an autonomous monarchy led to the loss of Israel's independence as a people.

The texts in which these interpretations have first been incorporated, then preserved, and in various stages combined to form the present biblical text are discussed in the section called "Diachronic Dimension." It may be helpful to characterize them briefly here. Four cover the substantial bulk of 1-2 Samuel. First we meet the prophetic traditions about Samuel, preserved for us in the Prophetic Record (1 Sam 1–2 Kgs 10). Next comes the Ark Narrative (1 Sam 4–6 associated with 2 Sam 6). Stories of David's rise to power in Israel may have been selectively used to constitute various documents (in each case, the Story of David's Rise); as we have them, they are perhaps best envisaged as a relatively loose association of traditions. The beginnings of David's story may well go back to the beginning of Saul's (1 Sam 9:1); the end may well be traced

28

as far as David's establishment and success (2 Sam 8:15). Finally, what I term the Stories of David's Middle Years occupies a major block in 2 Samuel (2 Sam 11–20).

Some traditions from Saul's reign may be preserved independently in association with the core of 1 Sam 13–15; most come to us in Davidic clothing. Surprisingly independent Davidic traditions are preserved in a small four-chapter collection (2 Sam 21–24). Some other traditions may have been preserved in association with the larger Davidic texts (e.g., 2 Sam 9 and 10). Earlier units of tradition may be assumed to have been the raw materials for these narrative complexes. No attempt is made here to atomize raw materials to their origins. On the other hand, with these compiled traditions the substance of 1-2 Samuel is accounted for. (I regret that I do not find Langlamet's analyses helpful for interpreting the text we have [see the three studies listed in this section's bibliography]; hypotheses are possible, but frequent and selective fragmentation of passages in these narratives is suspect. The possible cannot be confused with the necessary.)

The narrative books of early Israel's traditions are rightly called "the former prophets"; apart from the almost-legendary status of Moses, Samuel begins a new era of prophetic activity in Israel. Textually, there are four references to a prophet before Moses (Gen 20:7; Exod 7:1; Num 11:29; 12:6); in the books of Samuel-Kings, there are around a hundred references. Along with Samuel, groups of prophets feature regularly in the texts; and, above all, significant individuals feature throughout the texts such as Gad, Nathan, Ahijah the Shilonite, Jehu ben Hanani, Elijah, and Elisha, Jonah ben Amittai, Isaiah ben Amoz, and Huldah, as well as the prophetic stories of 1 Kgs 13, 20, and 22. The DH conceptualizes all of these under the term God's servants the prophets.

It is appropriate that the first texts encountered in the books of Samuel should come from what may probably be regarded as a Prophetic Record, putting on record the prophetic claims to have guided the history of the monarchy in Israel from David to Jehu (cf. Campbell and O'Brien, *Unfolding*, passim). For such prophetic authority to be exercised, Samuel's position needed to be established, along with his having set in place the institution of monarchy and his having designated and dismissed the earliest kings, Saul and David. Later prophetic activity will claim to be effective for Jeroboam, Ahab, and Jehu; it is fitting that it begins with Saul and David.

The Ark Narrative (considered globally as 1 Sam 4–6 and 2 Sam 6) is the only substantial block of biblical text focused almost exclusively on the ark. It comes as a surprise to realize how little hard information we have about this apparently most important religious symbol in ancient Israel. According to the present biblical text, it and its accouterments were ordered and constructed in Exod 25–40; it was believed to have controlled Israel's journey from Sinai toward Canaan (Num 10:35), to have contained the law from Sinai (covenant: Exod 25:16, 21; 40:20; tablets: Deut 10:1-5), and to have been central to the Jordan crossing and the capture of Jericho (Josh 3–4; 6). Its presence is noted at Bethel (Judg 20:27), and more securely at Shiloh (1 Sam 3:3, etc.); it departed from Shiloh (1 Sam 4-6), sojourned at Kiriath-jearim (1 Sam 7:1), and ultimately came to Jerusalem (2 Sam 6), where in due course it was installed in the

Solomonic temple (1 Kgs 8:1-7); there it remains, virtually unnoticed in the biblical text, until it is dismissed in Jer 3:16. For all this, it is assumed — and surely rightly — that the ark was a central and significant symbol of God's presence in early Israel.

With the departure of the ark in 1 Sam 4–6, the portrayal prepares the way for something new. The God of the earlier tradition had withdrawn from Israel ("the glory has departed from Israel," 1 Sam 4:21, 22). Kiriath-jearim is unheard of in the mainstream of Israel's worship. The ark does not return to Israel's mainstream until it comes to Jerusalem (2 Sam 6). The absence of the old symbol allows free play to the new — the prophet Samuel. It is when the monarchy, inaugurated by Samuel, has been established in the new capital of Jerusalem that the ark comes there, as if it were confirming what had been achieved under Samuel's inspiration.

Much of 1-2 Samuel, from the beginnings of the monarchy with Saul to the success of the monarchy with David, is taken up with stories of David's rise to power. As was said earlier, the stories of David's rise to power in Israel may have been selectively used to constitute documents that were not necessarily identical (but in each case, the Story of David's Rise); as we have them, they are perhaps best envisaged as a relatively loose association of traditions. An interest in putting together the larger picture of David's rise to power is evidenced in the collections of otherwise unimportant detail (cf. Rendtorff, "Beobachtungen"). Beyond these, documentary status is suggested by the structural organization around chs. 17–18, 23–26, and 28–31; however, a variety of documents at different times cannot be excluded. What we have now is a relatively loose association of texts, preserving traditions about David's rise to power, in most cases shaped by the conviction that David's success came from the LORD's favor and that his rise to power was achieved without blameworthy bloodshed. When many of the texts are recognized as "reported stories" — providing an outline of stories that have been told and offering a base for the retelling of these stories — most of the Davidic traditions within 1 Sam 9 and 2 Sam 8 can be regarded as belonging among the stories of David's rise to power.

Readers need to bear in mind that these traditions have been shaped by two influences. One is religious: the conviction that David's success came from the LORD's favor — therefore a faith claim. The other is primarily political: the contention that David's rise to power was achieved without blameworthy bloodshed — therefore a matter of perception. The hermeneutics of suspicion are important but they cannot take us very far. It is quite possible that the denial of bloodshed was substantially propaganda (see, for example, the important studies of McCarter, "Apology," Levenson and Halpern, "Political Import," and VanderKam, "Davidic Complicity"); but what is possible is not necessary. The fact that Shimei ben Gera abuses David as "a man of blood" (2 Sam 16:8) decides nothing; it witnesses to two points of view in ancient Israel. It is equally possible that the claim of the LORD's favor was substantially propaganda; but, again, what is possible is not necessary. Contrasting judgments on a founding French king are illuminating. André Maurois writes: "A pitiless cynic, Clovis bettered his portion by trickery and assassination as much as by prowess. . . . By slaughtering friends and enemies, Clovis extended his kingdom to the Pyrenees." But he quotes Gregory of Tours: "Thus every day, God caused Clovis's enemies to fall under his hand and increased his kingdom, because he walked before the Lord with a righteous heart and did what was pleasing in His eyes" (Maurois, *History of France,* 30). Single sources often witness to a single point of view.

The experience of David's establishment of a monarchy in ancient Israel has ramifications for almost every aspect of Israelite life. The interpretation of such an experience is of necessity massively complex. Any single line of thought will be a simplification. The capacity of Israel's theologians to hold together the realities of political life and the claims of religious faith is remarkable. The texts we have are primarily religious texts, interpreting the events in the light of religious claims. We might be tempted to dispute these claims and portray David's rise to power in a different light. We are entitled to entertain the temptation. We are obliged to recognize that we do not have access to sources that give us an extensive coverage of differing convictions. We can imagine how Saul's supporters might have portrayed certain events. We have no evidence to take us beyond imaginings. We would be dilatory not to recognize that events of political impact with wide ramifications for the people have been provided with a strongly religious interpretation.

The final document in this quartet that has preserved the substance of the books of Samuel for us is 2 Sam 11–20. Probably the best approach to these stories of David's middle years, within the context of 1-2 Samuel, is to see them as a study in the phenomenon of monarchy. A king behaves badly in his private life. The evil spreads through his family to his kingdom, implicating the people of Israel. Order and unity are restored by a combination of good judgment and military power.

All in all, then, the books of Samuel can be unified around the interpretation of Israel's experience of monarchy: its preparation, its political realization, and inner aspects of its early functioning. Samuel is the figure used to put the religious stamp on the interpretation of this most significant change for Israel. David is the figure on whom the interpretation is focused. For Israel, as for us, the books are a marvelous source of reflection on the complex interplay of God's word and human realities.

As always, the discussion of setting is fraught with risk. Texts that appear to be associated with an early setting can be late products and vice versa. It does no harm, though, to take cognizance of the experiences that shook Israel deeply enough to have needed the sort of interpretation available in the texts of 1-2 Samuel. Whereas above we touched on these hypothetical texts in the sequence in which they are encountered, here it will be preferable to note the various settings chronologically.

The experience of the Davidic monarchy as a new institution in the life of Israel would have had profound impact for several generations. It involved major change, with implications for Israel's self-understanding. It would not have been easily absorbed. The traditions and stories we possess that have been described as associated with the Story of David's Rise are part of the endeavor to interpret this new institution in Israel. Involved in this vast change was the ark of the covenant. It had long been known as one of the symbols of traditional Israel, to be found in the traditional sanctuaries of Israel such as Bethel (Judg 20:27) or Shiloh. Now it was to be found in Jerusalem, a city with no significant roots in Israel's traditions. Such a move needed interpretation, and over generations the Ark Narrative sought to provide it.

Jehu's rebellion (2 Kgs 9–10) with its extensive bloodshed — involving the deaths of two kings, their numerous dependents, and all the prophets of Baal in the northern kingdom — was an experience with deep ramifications for Israel. The struggle for self-understanding expressed in the tension between commitment to YHWH and commitment to Baal was one aspect. The abiding threat to Israel's unity posed by the existence of two kingdoms was another. The PR appears as an attempt to interpret these events, organizing and expanding the traditions from Samuel, Saul, and David to its own day to situate the experience of profound change within the context of God's guidance and God's will, as well as within the ambit of prophetic guidance and prophetic power.

The deuteronomic movement, with its demand for radical reform, was an experience that had the potential to shake Israel to its core. The interpretation, not so much of the reform as of the demand for it, was provided by the Josianic DH. It selectively organized Israel's tradition from Moses to the time of Josiah to provide an interpretation of what it meant to the people of God and to situate the novelty of reform within the sweep of Israel's tradition. When Josiah's unexpected death in battle heralded the failure of this reform, circles associated with it faced, in the next few generations, the task of reinterpreting these traditions to explain the events that took Israel into exile. All of this involved the people and their monarchy, both so central to the books of Samuel. Not surprisingly, all of this left its mark on the books of Samuel, with the reform from Josiah's time and with the revision that struggled to account for its failure. In due course, from all of this, we have the present text of the books of Samuel.

Bibliography of Works Cited Above

Campbell, Antony F., and Mark A. O'Brien. *Unfolding the Deuteronomistic History: Origins, Upgrades, Present Text.* Minneapolis: Fortress, 2000.

Langlamet, F. "David, fils de Jessé: Une édition prédeutéronomiste de l' 'Histoire de la Succession.'" *RB* 89 (1982) 5-47.

———. "De 'David, fils de Jessé' au 'Livre de Jonathan': Deux éditions divergentes de l' 'Ascension de David' en 1 Sam 16 — 2 Sam 1?" *RB* 100 (1993) 321-57.

———. "'David — Jonathan — Saül' ou le 'Livre de Jonathan': *1 Sam* 16,14 — *2 Sam* 1,27*." *RB* 101 (1994) 326-54.

Levenson, Jon D., and Baruch Halpern. "The Political Import of David's Marriages." *JBL* 99 (1980) 507-18.

McCarter, P. Kyle, Jr. "The Apology of David." *JBL* 99 (1980) 489-504.

Maurois, André. *A History of France.* 3rd ed. London: University Paperbacks, 1960.

Rendtorff, Rolf. "Beobachtungen zur altisraelitischen Geschichtsschreibung anhand der Geschichte vom Aufstieg Davids." Pp. 428-39 in *Probleme biblischer Theologie:*

Gerhard von Rad zum 70. Geburtstag. Edited by H. W. Wolff. Munich: Chr. Kaiser, 1971.

VanderKam, James C. "Davidic Complicity in the Deaths of Abner and Eshbaal: A Historical and Redactional Study." *JBL* 99 (1980) 521-39.

Chapter 2

THE ARRIVAL OF SAMUEL ON THE NATIONAL SCENE (1 Samuel 1–3)

Set against the background of the preceding biblical text, the books of Samuel open by plotting a course for reform and radical national change in Israel; they end with doubts as to whether there is escape from the reality of the human condition. The Israel of the wilderness or Mosaic generation was portrayed as rebellious and unfaithful: they "have tested me these ten times and have not obeyed my voice" (Num 14:22). On the other hand, apart from the Achan incident (Josh 7), Joshua's generation is portrayed as obedient and faithful: "As the LORD had commanded his servant Moses, so Moses commanded Joshua, and so Joshua did; he left nothing undone of all that the LORD had commanded Moses" (Josh 11:15). After the death of Joshua, the book of Judges portrays a sharply downhill trajectory. The trajectory is traced from incomplete occupation of the land and consequent apostasy ("they abandoned the LORD the God of their ancestors," Judg 2:12), through an extended cycle of apostasy, punishment, and deliverance, to appalling stories of abduction, gruesome murder, and internecine tribal warfare: "In those days, there was no king in Israel; all the people did what was right in their own eyes" (Judg 21:25). "What was right in their own eyes" was not right at all. "Troubled Israel, as the books of Samuel begin, is waiting" (Brueggemann, 10).

So institutions are changed. A king is appointed and changed. The new king "administered justice and equity to all his people" (2 Sam 8:15) and then engaged in serious personal wrong, allowed serious wrongdoing into his family, and was almost overwhelmed by serious instability in the nation. Even the last chapters end on a note of royal folly and a costly breach with God (2 Sam 24). The reality of the human condition is not easily escaped.

With the books of Samuel, a major change is portrayed. Israel's national landscape is dominated by new figures: prophets and kings. Specifically, the prophet is Samuel and the king is David. The moves begin with the establishment of Samuel as prophet, the focal point for all that God is doing in Israel. The ark, the previous focal point for God's presence and symbol of God's power and purpose, is moved off the scene to end up in a peripheral backwater. The debate over Israel's central government is moderated by Samuel, who anoints Saul and inaugurates the era of monarchy. Prompted by two episodes of disobedience, Samuel announces to Saul his rejection by God (1 Sam 13–15). By the anointing of David, Samuel gives effect to God's designation of the son of Jesse as future king of Israel (1 Sam 16:1-13). It should not be at all surprising if — at some stage — Samuel, the prophet who anointed King David, was regarded as the prophet like Moses, promised in Deut 18:18 (cf. Jer 15:1; also 1 Sam 1:23; 3:20).

All this is in the realm of prophetic authority. To be effective, it has to become reality in the realm of political activity. The paradigm for this transfer from the prophetic to the political is in 1 Kgs 11–12. The prophet Ahijah designates Jeroboam as future king, the recipient of God's gift of ten tribes and "an enduring dynasty" as was promised David (11:26-40, see esp. vv. 31, 37, 38b). This becomes political reality in the popular support for Jeroboam against Solomon's son, King Rehoboam, over issues of tax reform (12:1-20).

For prophetic authority to be exercised, there must be a prophet. 1 Sam 1–3 establishes Samuel as a prophetic figure in Israel for the first time: "And the word of the LORD came to all Israel" (1 Sam 4:1a). Abraham and Moses may be seen as exercising prophetic functions (e.g., Deut 18:15) but, with the emergence of Samuel, something new is afoot in Israel. Samuel is the first of a series of forerunners leading to the phenomenon of classical prophecy in Israel. The role of prophets like Samuel, Ahijah of Shiloh, Elijah, and Elisha is unique in Israel's religious history. These prophets alone designate and dismiss kings. Nathan mediates the message of God's commitment to David's dynasty and plays a role as political agent in Solomon's succession to David's throne. Gad, by contrast, operates in the background. Samuel, Ahijah of Shiloh, Elijah, and Elisha alone of Israel's prophets designate and dismiss kings. Alone of these, Samuel and Elisha's anonymous disciple anointed kings or future kings; Samuel anointed Saul as king-designate *(nāgîd)* and David as king-to-be *(nāgîd* not used in 16:1-13), and Elisha's disciple anointed Jehu as king.

It is worth looking closely at the information we have about the emergence of Samuel as prophet to all Israel. Prophetic stories are not biographies. We have a story about how Samuel came to be born, more his mother's story than his (1:1–2:11). We have some scattered statements about his growing up (2:18, 21b, 26; 3:1a, 19a). We have the story of Samuel's first hearing of God's word, an embarrassing condemnation of the house of Eli (3:1-18). Finally we have the statement of Samuel's status as trustworthy prophet to all Israel (3:19–4:1a). Bluntly, the text moves from infant to acolyte to prophet of national stature. The bridges are brief: he grew up (2:21b, 26; 3:19a). Because this is not a biographical record, its elements will have been assembled for a purpose. They deserve our close scrutiny.

Before looking in close detail at the components of the text, it will help to have a picture in mind of the overall structure of these three chapters.

Emergence of Samuel on the National Scene	1 Sam 1:1–4:1a
I. Origins of Samuel	1:1–2:11
A. Introduction	1:1-2
B. Story of Samuel's birth and consecration	1:3–2:10
1. Samuel's birth	1:3-20
2. Samuel's consecration	1:21-28
3. Hannah's song	2:1-10
C. Conclusion	2:11
II. Contrast of Samuel and Elides	2:12–4:1a
A. Contrasting behavior: notices	2:12-26
1. First contrast	12-21
2. Second contrast	22-26
B. Contrasting destinies	2:27–4:1a
1. Elides: God's condemnation announced in prophecy	2:27–3:18
a. Through an anonymous man of God	2:27-36
b. Through Samuel	3:1-18
2. Samuel: approval as prophet to the nation	3:19–4:1a

What this structure makes immediately clear is the way that Samuel traditions have been sharply contrasted with Elide traditions. Samuel will increase; the Elides will decrease. The Elides are guilty of sinful behavior and come under repeated condemnation. Samuel is repeatedly approved and emerges as known to all Israel as a trustworthy prophet of the LORD.

In terms of national significance, Samuel is on the way in and the Elides are on the way out. This carefully arranged passage is a first intimation of national change in Israel. The second intimation is given in chs. 4–6, when the ark of God leaves the mainstream of Israel's religious life (Shiloh) and returns to an insignificant rural outpost (Kiriath-jearim).

We can look more closely at this passage under three heads: the origins of Samuel — [= Structure Analysis: I]; the contrasting behavior of Samuel and the Elides — [II.A]; the contrasting destinies of the Elides and Samuel — [II.B].

Origins of Samuel	1:1–2:11
I. Introduction: the persons and the problem	1:1-2
II. Story of Samuel's birth and consecration	1:3–2:10
A. Samuel's birth — in response to Hannah's vow	3-20
1. Situation of distress: need for a child	3-8
a. Occasion: annual Shiloh pilgrimage	3
b. Hannah's distress	4-7
1) Portrayed as habitual	4-7a
2) Portrayed on this particular occasion	7b
c. Elkanah's response: unhelpful	8
2. Appeal in distress: vow of consecration	9-18
a. Hannah's vow	9-11
b. Eli's response	12-17
1) Admonition from mistaken Eli	12-14
2) Blessing from admonished Eli	15-17

Textual Issues

1:11 The MT has only: "and I will give him to YHWH all the days of his life and no razor shall touch his head." This may be as close as the MT gets to describing Samuel as a nazirite (cf. Driver, 13; for the "naziritazion" of Samuel from MT to LXX to 4QSam[a], see Pisano especially, 19-24). The NRSV expands the verse with the LXX (cf. McCarter, 53-54).

1:20 Samuel is to be retained, probably without involvement of Saul traditions (cf. Driver, 13-19); despite McCarter, 62-66. Polzin insightfully sees here an anticipation of the later association with Saul (*Samuel,* 25). Note the associations made by Stanley Walters with Deut 18:18 ("Hanna and Anna," 405).

1:23 "His word" may be retained as possible (Barthélemy, 139-41). Elkanah wants YHWH to bring to fulfillment Hannah's promise to dedicate her son, as endorsed first by Eli (v. 17) and articulated for Elkanah by Hannah

(v. 22). Alternatively, with LXX and 4QSam[a]: May YHWH indeed establish that which goes forth from your mouth (cf. McCarter, 56). Walters reads the MT as "his word," understood as YHWH's word to raise up a prophet like Moses (Deut 18:18; "Hanna and Anna," 410-12).

1:24 The MT at the end of the verse is possible (see Barthélemy, 142-43; Pisano, 157-63); so the NRSV. Stoebe: and the lad was a nazirite (pp. 98-99). The LXX expands: . . . and the child with them. And they brought him before the Lord; and his father slew his offering which he offered from year to year to the Lord; and he brought near the child . . . (cf. McCarter, 57). As happens often with these mss., complexity is clearly present in the traditions; certainty is absent from the conclusions. The caution from Walters in 1982 is important: "the commentator risks replacing a group of nuanced narratives with one which has the distinctive features of none and cannot confidently be said to be the original text" . . . replacing "the actual with the hypothetical" (review of McCarter, 437).

1:28 "The textual confusion in all the witnesses may indicate that the Song of Hannah is secondary from a text-critical perspective" (Klein, 3). Pisano retains the MT, reads the verb "worship" as plural with Elkanah and Hannah as its subject (pp. 24-28).

2:1-10 For the textual base and linguistic aspects of the Song of Hannah, see Lewis, "Textual History."

Discussion

As should always be the case, the text controls its own interpretation. We, the interpreters, cannot impose on the text our own ideas about birth stories and consecration stories. Clearly these are in the context here, but how they are used is revealed to us by the signals implanted in the text. An analysis such as the one above emerges from close attention to these signals. Significant new sections need to open appropriately. They do not normally begin with pronouns or suffixed links back into the preceding section. Equally, sections need to be brought to an appropriate conclusion. Storytellers do not simply string together the elements of a story from beginning to end. Actors or action is focused in ways which hold a unity in diversity; normally, elements are grouped in twos and threes. Much more than this will be a pointer to our having overlooked the points of focus.

At the same time, it is good to remember that texts like this scarcely record the performance of a story's telling. They are story summaries (reported stories): the summary of an oral story, abbreviated for recording in an extensive composition such as this; the base from which a storyteller operated to create the oral performance of a story. As a base for performance, such texts may well derive from the experience of generations of storytelling. Our text records (in writing) either what was needed to record the gist of a story for a more extensive narrative or what a storyteller needed to hold in memory — i.e., the basic structure and elements that would be embodied in the telling of the story. A storyteller might deviate from or expand on what we now have as text. As interpreters of the text, we cannot do that. We interpret the text; it is all we have. We do not interpret the story as told; we do not have it.

The twos and threes of such an analysis (e.g., A-B or A-B-C, 1-2 or 1-2-3, etc.) are intrinsic to the structures of folklore and storytelling. The folkloric triad is well known; in folklore, things happen in threes (Olrik, "Epic Laws"). It is not for nothing that the French have a saying, "jamais deux sans trois" — never two without the third. In *The Poetics,* at the dawn of literary criticism, Aristotle remarked that all literature has to have a beginning, a middle, and an end. Hebrew poetic lines consist of two or, more rarely, three versets. The focus on two in storytelling would be reinforced by the habit in Hebrew poetry of taking what has been set out in the first verset and developing it differently in the second verset (Alter, *Art;* Kugel, *Idea*). It leads to an ability to see reality from two aspects, under two categories, and so on. The Greeks talk of essence and existence; instead, the Hebrew psalms hymn what God is and what God does. The poetic lines move from the broad to the focused, from the abstract to the concrete, from the simple to the heightened, and so on. Similarly, Hebrew narrative frequently moves from a general statement to its detailed unfolding, from a comprehensive statement to its detailed narration. Here, for example, the problem that will be unfolded in the story is told succinctly at the start: Peninnah had children but Hannah did not. At other times, Hebrew literature will balance the positive with the negative or give some other emphasis to balance or alternation — for example here, balancing the reversal of existing order (2:4-8) with the establishment of right order (2:9-10). This alternating emphasis finds expression in so many ways. There is no question that the use of language in literature affects the way both the inner and outer worlds are perceived. One way or the other, poetry and prose echo each other.

The clustering and focusing of material in twos and threes is almost certainly not merely a natural instinct but also a technique that helped storytellers in the remembering and weaving of stories. With the overall picture in mind of the elements that constitute a story or scene, a storyteller is then free to develop the details in the ways most appropriate to a given audience.

After the introduction — [I], the text is a story of Samuel's birth and consecration to God. Its structure, however, is built around a woman's distress — [II.A.1], her reaction to that distress in prayer and vow — [II.A.2], and the outcome of her prayer — [II.A.3]. The principal players are God and Hannah. God has closed her womb (v. 5). Hannah vows to God that if given a son she will consecrate him to God's service (v. 11). God remembers her (v. 19) and she conceives and bears a son (v. 20). Hannah fulfills her vow and consecrates Samuel to God's service (vv. 27-28). The concluding song sweeps from Hannah's joy to Israel's joy in its God and Israel's future security under its king — [II.C].

The story has a formal opening, identifying both the human players in the family drama and the problem that will be to the fore. The man is identified by locality, name, and lineage (v. 1). The treatment of the two wives is minimal: their names only, Hannah and Peninnah, and their status as mothers — Peninnah has children and Hannah does not (v. 2).

The first half of the story is to unfold within the context of the regular pilgrimage to Shiloh. A note on this pilgrimage (v. 3) opens the section on Hannah's distress — [II.A.1]; the section closes with Elkanah's ineffectual attempt to comfort Hannah with the thought that he is worth more to her than ten sons (v. 8). The second section, Hannah's prayer and vow — [II.A.2], opens with a blend of action and state: Hannah's action, leaving the celebrations (v. 9a); Eli's state, sitting at the door of the sanctuary (v. 9b); and Hannah's state, in bitterness of soul (v. 10). It closes with Hannah's acceptance in word and action of Eli's blessing, "Go in peace!" The third section — [II.A.3] — opens with a change of scene and situation: change of scene — the early rise to worship God and the return home; change of situation — the intercourse with her husband and the remembrance by God (v. 19). God remembers Hannah; she conceives and bears a son. Hannah remembers her vow; she prepares for its fulfillment. The section closes with Samuel at Shiloh. The song celebrates what that means, both for Hannah and for Israel — [II.C].

These three blocks are integral to the one story. The consecration of Samuel is not separate from his birth. It was promised in Hannah's vow before Samuel's conception; after his weaning, it is recalled and fulfilled in his consecration at Shiloh. The conclusion is provided by 2:11. It seems odd, since Elkanah has not been mentioned since 1:23, and the active figure at Shiloh has been Hannah; v. 21 is a reminder to us that of course Elkanah was there with his family. The story opened with Elkanah at Ramah; his return to his home at Ramah brings it to closure. Samuel remains at the Shiloh sanctuary, as expected; the final phrase, "in the presence of Eli the priest," facilitates the transition to the next section.

This text is a very classy piece of work, and it is fascinating to watch it unfold. Stories in the classical mode usually are driven by a need that has to be met somehow. The introduction to the story identifies Elkanah for us with full detail: place, genealogy over four generations, and tribal affiliation (Ephrathite/ Ephraimite; cf. 17:12!). Saul's father will get similar treatment (9:1). Hannah and Peninnah, the two women in the story, are simply identified by name and state; Peninnah has children and Hannah has not. It is a story that focuses on Hannah, but Elkanah is the anchor point for identity. The issue of need is present from the outset: Hannah's need for children.

Samuel is going to end up at Shiloh. The story of his birth and consecration will be told within the context of pilgrimages to Shiloh. It begins with the note of Elkanah's annual pilgrimage there. Well before Eli is mentioned, his two sons are named in relation to the sanctuary. Their deaths on the same day will be the sign to Eli that the hegemony of his priestly house is at an end (2:34). The narrative strand weaves closely the fate of prophet and priests.

In 1:4-7, the theme of childlessness is developed; the drama gets its detail. The regular ritual of the pilgrimage underscores Hannah's childlessness; her husband loves her; it is God who has closed her womb. The parallel with Rachel is unmistakable: loved by Jacob (Gen 29:18, 30) and kept barren by God (Gen 29:31; 30:2, 22). The provocation of the barren by the fertile evokes Sarah and Hagar (Gen 16:4-6) as well as Rachel and Leah. This pain had been happening year by year and it happened again this year. Is there an echo here of Israel's cycle of sin and deliverance that has never reached definitive solution?

Whatever may be said of Elkanah's attempt at consolation (v. 8), it does not help. Nothing is said in the text of Hannah's response or lack of it. Her move away comes after the meal (v. 9), in which presumably she has not participated. If the text is a story summary or a base for the storyteller to operate from, a skilled storyteller could do a lot with this scene of inner-family pain at Shiloh; or a storyteller might leave it as bare and as spare as it is in the text.

The text again invites a storyteller, or our imaginations, to paint the scene. Hannah rises (v. 9a). She will go to the Shiloh temple to pray. But first there is the scene: Eli the priest sitting on a chair by the entrance to the temple (v. 9b); Hannah herself, bitter of spirit (v. 10a). Praying to God, she weeps and makes her vow: three conditions and a promise (v. 11). The prayer is formal; three times she names herself "your servant": look on the misery of your servant; remember me and do not forget your servant; give to your servant a male child. The vow's commitment: he will be given to God for life and no razor will touch his head. Again the scene is there for our imaginations or the storyteller's skill: the woman intensifying her prayer to God, and Eli watching her mouth; she is praying silently in her heart with only her lips moving, and Eli thinks she is drunk (vv. 12-13). The initial image of the old priest is far from favorable.

He admonishes her; she protests to him. With no further comment, he sends her off with a benevolent wish for the outcome of her prayer (v. 17). A storyteller might leave it as bare and spare as here or might elaborate on this moment of priestly conversion and Hannah's consolation. In contrast to Elkanah's love, Eli's response proves helpful. Hannah is gracious to the priest and changes her own behavior; she eats and is no longer depressed.

The return home is beautifully sketched: they rise early and worship the LORD; they return home to Ramah; Elkanah has intercourse with Hannah; the LORD remembers her (v. 19). They remember the LORD; the LORD remembers her. So much for the general statement. The details are that she conceived, bore a son, and named him Samuel. The reason she gives for the name — "I have asked him of the LORD" — is not particularly illuminating, but it does not help to use it to claim the birth story as originally Saul's.

The personal distress has been Hannah's childlessness. With the birth of Samuel, that distress has been relieved. The relief was brought about by Hannah's vow. Now the vow's commitment must be fulfilled. In due course, Israel's distress will be relieved.

When the story turns to Samuel's consecration, however, it gives us a surprise. There is a reference to Elkanah's vow (v. 21b). This is the first we have heard of any vow by Elkanah; the only vow we know about has been Hannah's. It is probably unwise to adjust the text so that it is acceptable to us in our ignorance. Possibly cultural codes are at work of which we are unaware but which make a husband's concomitant vow perfectly intelligible to those in the culture. It is also possible, given the text as a story summary — a base for performance and not its record — that this phrase is a pointer to a version of the story in which Elkanah commits himself by vow in support of Hannah. If so, a storyteller would be free to use the motif or to pass over it.

Surprisingly again, there is reference in v. 23 to YHWH keeping his word. Again, this is the first we have heard of any word of YHWH. In antiquity, translators opted for Hannah's word, but why should God be invoked to keep Hannah's word, which Hannah is proposing to do anyway? Cultural patterns of speech may be involved; if so, they are unknown to us. Or again, is this phrase a pointer for a storyteller to the possibility of having a word of God earlier in the story, pronounced by Eli perhaps in association with v. 17, spelling out the destiny of the child to be born? Samson's destiny is revealed in similar circumstances: "It is he who shall begin to deliver Israel from the hand of the Philistines" (Judg 13:5b). If so, once again, a storyteller would be free to use the motif or to pass over it.

Hannah nurtured the child until she weaned him, possibly some three years (v. 23b). Hannah's care for her son continues into his early time at the sanctuary (2:19). To modern minds, the issue raises the question of child care at a major sanctuary. The text does not touch on it; either symbolically it is unimportant or culturally it is taken for granted.

When the child is presented to Eli, there is no mention of Hannah's vow (vv. 25-28). Hannah is identified simply as "the woman who was standing here in your presence, praying to the LORD" (v. 26). There is strong emphasis on Hannah's having asked for this son; as in the case of v. 20, the wordplay is closer to the name Saul than Samuel. Our understanding is not helped by assuming a clumsy transfer of a Saul story to Samuel (cf. Garsiel, *Biblical Names*, 244-45; also idem, *First Book of Samuel*, 72-74). Saul, in 1 Sam 9, is looking for donkeys not a kingdom. It would go against the direction of this story to have Saul singled out in any way from birth. It is Samuel who will single out Saul; the wordplay may be a delicately teasing reminder of what lies ahead.

The emphasis given to Hannah's prayer and Samuel's consecration is appropriate. Hannah's "visit to the Shiloh shrine where she interacts with the leading priestly figure of the day (Eli) and her behavior foreshadow her son's national significance. As such, the narrative is much more than a story of family life; it moves into the realm of national service" (Cook, *Hannah's Desire*, 39).

Hannah's song is scarcely the song of a mother just parted from her child. The song moves quickly from a first person focus (v. 1) to a third person focus on God. "The song has public, national dimensions" (Brueggemann, 16). The reference to the king, the LORD's anointed, points to a later time and an institution that Samuel will establish. The appropriateness of the song is precisely in its pointing to the change in Israel that is now begun with the birth and consecration of Samuel; the existing order will be reversed. A new era is beginning for Israel; Hannah's song celebrates it.

Genre

Two genres are involved here; one is (→) story, the other (→) hymn of praise (or thanksgiving song). The story is one of birth and consecration. A birth story is not a specific literary genre; rather it is a story with a specific content. Birth stories are rare in the Older Testament. Stories or notices are found for the ancestors — Isaac, Jacob, and Joseph. In the later literature, there are Samson and Samuel. The Moses story is not one of birth but of preservation of the newborn (Exod 2:1-10). Jeremiah's call narrative is not a birth story, although it has references to the time before birth (Jer 1:5).

Birth stories respond to need. Those in the Older Testament fall into two categories depending on whether the need is antecedent to the birth or is seen as something subsequent to the birth. In the majority of the cases of the ancestors, the need is developed as antecedent to the birth; elements and traditions are told, but they are not developed into full stories.

In the Yahwist narrative (or, for that matter, in the present Genesis text), Sarai is barren and the object of Hagar's contempt (cf. Gen 16:1b-2, 4-6). Offspring is needed for Abraham if the promise of Gen 12:1-3 is to be fulfilled. So Isaac's birth is promised (Gen 18:10-15) and noted (Gen 21:1a, 7). These are elements of a story; they are not united into a single story — not in the Yahwist and not in Genesis. Rebekah too is barren, and her conception is reported as a response to Isaac's prayer (Gen 25:21-26). Although two nations were in her womb (v. 23), the need implied is hers not theirs. Here too, the traditions could be actualized as a story, but they are not in story form in the text; they provide a context for the divine saying in v. 23. Joseph's birth responds to Rachel's need for children, expressed most sharply in the variant alleged as E: "Give me children or I shall die" (Gen 30:1). The tension is present from the beginning (Gen 29:31). Once more, these traditions are loosely integrated into the story line but they do not constitute a specific birth story.

These passages do not give us the base texts for birth stories. They give us the basic traditions that could easily be built up into the base texts for birth stories or into birth stories themselves. They hint at the stories that might have been told; they do not give the stories or even the base texts for them. They let us see the elements involved in such stories: portrayal of the need or distress, then assurance or promise of a child, and finally the birth and naming.

The situation is different in the Priestly traditions. Isaac's birth is promised with reference to future nations and the establishment of an everlasting covenant; Sarah's need is mentioned only in Abraham's expression of disbelief (Gen 17:15-21). The birth follows in Gen 21:1b-5. The births of Esau and Jacob and the sons of Jacob are not narrated in the extant Priestly tradition (cf. Campbell and O'Brien, *Sources,* 32-33; the sons of Jacob are listed in 35:22-26 — the births are not narrated). The divine speech within the Priestly theophany of Gen 17 promises a child but scarcely constitutes a birth story, even with 21:1-5 or 7.

The story of Samson's birth is different (Judg 13:2-25). The need portrayed is not antecedent to the birth but subsequent to it: "It is he who shall begin to deliver Israel from the hand of the Philistines" (13:5). The mother's barrenness is noted (v. 2b); it is not portrayed as a source of distress or need. It may well have been one; it is not portrayed as such. Within the present text, Israel is in need, under the oppression of the Philistines for a forty-year period (13:1). There is need for deliverance, and the son to be born will begin it. The focus of the story is on the mother and father and their encounters with God's messenger, not on the need for the child nor on the birth and consecration of the child.

The Samuel story straddles these two categories. The need is antecedent to the birth; the pain of Hannah is eloquently portrayed. Yet the need is possibly subsequent to the birth as well. At least three elements point to this as a significant presence in the story: (i) the consecration of the child; (ii) the potential of the comment "may the LORD establish his word" (v. 23); (iii) the reference in the concluding song to the king, God's anointed. All three point in the direction of significance subsequent to the birth of Samuel. The rivalry of two women, the one who is fertile and the one who is special but barren, echoes strongly the roles of Leah and Rachel in the Genesis narrative; and God remembers both Rachel and Hannah (Gen 30:22; 1 Sam 1:19). At the same time, Hannah's promise that "no razor shall touch his head" (v. 11) echoes the stipulation for Samson (Judg 13:5); there are no other occurrences.

The text in 1 Sam 1:1–2:11a is clearly in story form. There is a lack from the outset: Hannah's barrenness. Her distress is elaborately portrayed. The strategy of resolution is through her vow, which includes the commitment to Samuel's consecration. The plot must then move from birth to consecration in order to come to its resolution.

The universal elements of the genre include need or distress (whether before or after the birth), the promise of a child, and the birth, naming, etc. In this particular rendering of the typical, the need of the mother is portrayed before the birth of the child, but a possible later need of the nation might be introduced into the story. The promise of the child is in response to a vow that included the child's consecration to God. The birth and naming have to proceed further to the fulfillment of the vow in Samuel's consecration.

The (→) thanksgiving song or (→) hymn of praise is not situated outside the story. It is sung by Hannah before Elkanah returns to Ramah (2:1, 11a). It concludes Samuel's consecration at the sanctuary and it concludes the story as a whole. Hymns tend to celebrate who God is and what God does. The introductory focus is on the singer's cause for exultation (v. 1). The focus turns to God: first the incomparability of who God is (vv. 2-3), then the enumeration of what God does (vv. 4-10).

Setting

Birth stories are associated with famous figures and are propagated by those in some way allied with such figures. The Samuel who is born and consecrated in this story and who will become a trustworthy prophet of the LORD, known to all Israel, is the Samuel who will designate and dismiss kings, anointing Saul and dismissing him, then anointing David in Saul's stead. Samuel's initiative in Israel's history is followed by Ahijah, prophet of Shiloh, who designates Jeroboam and later dismisses him; by the great Elijah, who dismisses Ahab; and by the disciple of the prophet Elisha, who anoints Jehu and entrusts to him the elimination of the house of Ahab and of Baal worship from within Israel (2 Kgs 9–10).

A tradition binds together this claim for overwhelming prophetic authority and the claim to its exercise in the story of Israel, from the united kingdom of David to the divided kingdoms begun with Jeroboam. This claim may have been articulated within a single recoverable document, the Prophetic Record (so Campbell, *Of Prophets and Kings*), or it may be the result of editing of prophetic texts, by the Deuteronomists or others. Not all material about prophets has to be from prophets (so Wilson, "Former Prophets," 87-89). The Deuteronomists are interested in prophetic authority, but in my judgment the places where their distinctive language is present suggest they refined an existing text rather than created the text from whole cloth. The Elisha traditions are tied into those of the Elijah cycle, and it is a disciple of Elisha who anoints Jehu, holding together in one episode both the anointing traditions and the designation/dismissal traditions. We know that there was a circle around Elisha, no matter how loose it may have been. Superb and skillfully told stories about the prophet Elisha emanate from that circle (cf. 2 Kgs 2–8).

As likely as any a setting in society for the story of Samuel's birth and consecration is the circle of disciples associated with the names of Elijah and Elisha. As a literary setting, the opening of the PR is claimed by Campbell (see Introduction and the section below, "Diachronic Development"). Any search beyond these sources is questionable. Samuel was separated from his family in infancy; the sanctuary priesthood did not survive at Shiloh; Samuel's life at Ramah is shrouded in silence (cf. 1 Sam 7:16-17).

Meaning

The meaning of a story such as this is not bound to the story itself but stretches down to the traditions the story introduces. Within the story itself, there are indistinct pointers to a future; the future is delineated in the subsequent traditions.

The principal point of a birth story is to invest its hero with the distinction of being directly singled out by God, even from before birth. While Hannah's distress is resolved by Samuel's birth, Samuel is not singled out to be the progenitor of a hereditary line. Something of his future is hinted at in the elements noted earlier: his consecration, the possible word of God accompanying the promise of his birth (1:23), and the reference in Hannah's song to Israel's king, the LORD's anointed (2:10).

This story, with its emphasis on birth, consecration, and celebration, clothes the figure of Samuel with immense distinction. There is a passing reference to the priests of Shiloh (1:3b), soon to die. There is a possible reference to the name of Saul (esp. 1:27-28), soon to be anointed king. Down the trajectory of tradition lies the great prophet Samuel, sole dispenser of God's authority in Israel, exercising supreme power against which there is no appeal. In the Newer Testament, Moses is accompanied by Elijah, representing the prophets (Mark 9:4 and parallels); in the Older Testament, it is Samuel who is ranked along with Moses (Ps 99:6 and Jer 15:1). This story recounts the birth and consecration of a figure to be pre-eminent in Israel, of such stature as to be named in the same breath as Moses. The greatness to come is already intimated by God's in-

45

volvement in this birth. The story holds intimations of change for Israel; the hymn celebrates them.

Contrast of Samuel and Elides

After the birth of Samuel and his consecration at the Shiloh sanctuary, the narrative proceeds with a comparison between the old and the new, between the priesthood of Eli and his sons and the prophetic authority represented by Samuel. The comparison moves in two major stages: first, as to the past, the contrasting behavior of Samuel and the Elides (2:12-26); second, looking to the future, the contrasting destinies of the Elides and Samuel (2:27–4:1a). At the end of ch. 3, while the Elides are still on the scene, Samuel is portrayed as the preeminent authority for all Israel.

Contrasting Behavior of Samuel and the Elides: Past	1 Sam 2:12-26
I. First contrast	12-21
A. Concerning the Elides: sins of Eli's sons	12-17
1. General categorization of the Elides	12
2. Specific accusation of sacrificial abuse	13-16
a. Customary procedure at Shiloh	13-14
b. Contravention of this custom: sin	15-16
3. Conclusion: theological assessment	17
B. Concerning Samuel and his family	18-21
1. Concerning Samuel	18-19
a. His service before the LORD	18a
b. His attire	18b-19
2. Concerning Samuel's family	20-21a
a. Blessing by Eli: emphasis on Elkanah	20
b. Fulfillment by the LORD: emphasis on Hannah	21a
3. Concerning Samuel: his growth with the LORD	21b
II. Second contrast	22-26
A. Concerning the Elides: paternal admonition refused	22-25
1. Concerning the father	22-25a
a. His situation	22
1) His advanced age	22a
2) His awareness of his sons' sins	22b
b. His admonition	23-25a
1) Accusation expressed interrogatively	23
2) Weight of the admonition	24-25a
2. Concerning the sons: their refusal to listen	25b
a. Refusal	25bα
b. Reason	25bβ
B. Concerning Samuel: growth and favor, divine and human	26

Textual Issues

2:22b   The final clause of v. 22b is lacking in 4QSam[a] and LXX[B] (for discussion, see Pisano, 70-75).

Discussion

The compositional work involved in putting this passage together has been skillfully done. It establishes the contrast between the Elides and Samuel; the emphasis here is on the sinful behavior of the sons of Eli. The birth story has provided intimations of greatness to come. This section of the text, which comes between the birth story and the contrasting destinies of the Elides and Samuel, is carefully organized to depict the future prophetic figure against a background that is in need of change.

The text begins with contrasting images. The sons of Eli are responsible for great evil; they are bringing violence and lawlessness into the very sacrificial worship of the LORD which they are supposed to foster, the worship which is expressive of the bonds between God and people — [= Structure Analysis: I.A]. On the other hand, Samuel is serving the LORD (2:18) and growing in the LORD's presence (2:21b) — [I.B]. In a second contrast, the report of Eli admonishing his sons pictures them as incorrigible and doomed — [II.A]. Samuel, on the other hand, continues to grow in goodness before God and people (2:26) — [II.B].

The organization of this composite text serves its purpose perfectly: it places the Elide priesthood at Shiloh in deep shadow; it projects Samuel bathed in light. This is all the more remarkable when we reflect how little actual information about Samuel is provided, even including 2:11b and 3:1a and 19. Apart from the reference to his wearing the ephod (2:18b) and the details of his family history (2:19-21a), the information given on Samuel in 2:11b, 18, 21b, 26; 3:1a, and 19 is almost totally repetitive. This is evident from a comparison of the English text; it is even more striking in the Hebrew (the English below approximates to the Hebrew).

2:11b)	And the *boy* was in the presence of Eli the priest.	**ministering** to	*the LORD,*
2:18)	Samuel was *a boy* girded with a linen ephod.	**ministering** in the presence of	*the LORD,*
2:21b)	And *the boy* Samuel	**grew** with	*the LORD.*
2:26)	And *the boy* Samuel continued to and with people.	**grow** . . . in favor both with	*the LORD*

47

3:1a)	And *the boy* Samuel was before Eli.	**ministering** to	*the* LORD
3:19)	And Samuel was with him.	*grew*, and	*the* LORD

There is basically nothing here beyond the general themes of "ministering to the LORD" and "growth in the presence of the LORD." Of the six occurrences, ministering is central to three and growth is central to the other three; in all six, Samuel is brought into association with the LORD. The repetitive language suggests both the lack of available tradition to flesh out the picture and perhaps one and the same hand at work in composing the picture. Samuel is referred to as "the boy" *(hanna'ar)* in 2:11b, and as both "Samuel" and *na'ar* in 2:18; after that, the combined phrase "the boy Samuel" *(hanna'ar Šĕmû'ēl)* is used, until 3:19 reverts to Samuel. The usage *'et pĕnê* for "in the presence of" occurs four times in this narrative context (1:22; 2:11, 17, 18) and only four times in the rest of 1-2 Samuel. All in all, the passage alternates the traditions but has very little to work with where Samuel is concerned.

The general categorization of the sons of Eli is placed like a banner headline over all that is to follow: "Now the sons of Eli were scoundrels; they had no regard for the LORD" (v. 12). Right from the outset, there is no doubt as to the villains of the piece. There is already a subtle contrast with the conclusion of the previous section: Samuel ministers to the LORD; the sons of Eli have no regard for the LORD. Within the Elide camp, both contrasts are begun with verbless sentences. The first characterizes the sons; literally, it reads sharply: the sons of Eli were sons of Belial (v. 12). The second characterizes Eli: he is old (v. 22). The structural indicators of the narrative are ominous: the priest of Shiloh is old, his life drawing toward a close; his apparent successors are worthless.

The worthlessness of Eli's sons and their lack of regard for the LORD are vividly depicted. The traditional custom at the sacrificial meal was egalitarian: the priests took potluck with the worshippers; their servant stuck a fork into the pot and they took whatever came up. But the sons of Eli wanted the pick of the meat, apparently even before it was offered to the LORD (cf. v. 16a). Their demand was backed up with the threat of violence. As a result, instead of the sacrifice symbolizing and celebrating unity among the people, and between the people and their God, it became marked by inequality and injustice. Theologically assessed, the sin is very grave: they showed contempt for the offering of the LORD (v. 17).

We should be aware that this interpretation has to be tentative. It is not unambiguously clear whether we are in fact presented with the rightful procedure (vv. 13-14) and its abuse (vv. 15-16). The custom described in v. 13 could itself be understood as abusive; the beginning of v. 15 would normally be translated "furthermore, before . . . ," indicating a second abuse (so Hertzberg, 34-35). But the understanding "even before" cannot be excluded. In the context, the interpretation adopted is the more likely (so McCarter, 82-83; cf. Stoebe, 110-13). A generalized statement of the prevailing rightful custom is given in

vv. 13-14 (cf. vv. 13a and 14b); the specific abuse is detailed in vv. 15-16, and described as grave sin (v. 17). Our lack of precise knowledge of the customs prevailing at the time complicates the interpretation. But the fact that these customs do not correspond with the later extant sacrificial laws may witness to the age of the tradition. The prescriptions for the portions allotted to the priests are in Lev 7:28-36; Num 18:17-18; Deut 18:3; references to the boiling of sacrificial meat occur also in Exod 29:31; Lev 8:31; Deut 16:7 (cf. Exod 12:8-9); Ezek 46:20-24; Zech 14:21; and 2 Chron 35:13.

Samuel and his family stand in sharp contrast. Samuel is in the service of the LORD. The little robe, renewed each year, is a pointer to the child's growth; the reference to the repeated visits and the birth of five more children evokes the passage of time. But, above all, it is symbolic of the blessing and favor bestowed on the family, in direct connection with Samuel (v. 20). While Eli blesses Elkanah and his wife, the weight of his blessing seems to fall on the man; when its fulfillment is reported, the emphasis is on the LORD's visiting the woman. And Samuel grew in the presence of the LORD (v. 21b), while the sons of Eli were growing in contempt of the LORD (v. 17). Eli is gently treated (v. 20); the reproach is reserved for his sons.

The second contrast between the Elides and Samuel uses Eli's admonition to depict the evil of his sons — [II.A]. It probably continues the tradition of the first passage; "to all Israel" in v. 22a echoes the same words in v. 14b, and v. 25a reflects v. 17. The reference to sexual transgression may be an expansion of the older accusation; it goes beyond the rituals of sacrifice to sexual abuse with the servants of the sanctuary. Eli is again treated gently (in contrast to 2:29 and 3:13b). There is a distance maintained between him and his sons; their sins are known to him only by report. The theology of mediation in v. 25a is unusual. Normally, it is a human being who intercedes with God, a role frequently exercised by Moses, exemplified in Abraham (Gen 18:17-32), and implied for the prophets (cf. Jer 7:16; 15:1). Here it is God who is proposed as mediating in human affairs, with no possibility envisaged of an intercessor for sin against God. Here it is used to put emphasis on the gravity of the sin, for it is a sin against the LORD.

The sons ignored their father's admonition, "for it was the will of the LORD to kill them" (v. 25b). The theological claim sounds appalling to modern ears. In the context, it emphasizes what has been latent: what is happening in Israel is God's doing. Samuel's birth has been God's doing; now the Elides' demise is to be God's doing. We will see below that the loss of the ark is portrayed as God's doing. Involved in all this is the sign to be announced in 2:34 and fulfilled in 4:11. Within the narrative composition, not only is the end of the Elide priesthood at Shiloh foreshadowed; it is specifically placed under the sign of the LORD's will. In contrast with the doomed Elides, Samuel's growth in favor is emphasized. The contrast of the two highlights the understanding that the coming change in leadership is a matter of the LORD's will.

Genre

The text from 2:12-26 is scarcely a literary genre in its own right. At best, it is a composite (→) account, built up from a series of notices and establishing contrasts between the Elides and Samuel.

The material involved in these contrasts comes to us in the form of (→) notices, for the most part; some of the Samuel texts hardly constitute even a notice. The fundamental quality of a notice is the communication of information, without concern for the movement of plot within the communication. Interest is aroused either by the information itself or, as particularly here, by its juxtaposition with contrasting information. Within the notices, there is no concern for plot or the creation of narrative tension and its resolution. The difference between (→) account and (→) notice is often no more than a matter of length; the passages here are brief enough for notice to suffice.

Setting

The present setting is literary: the composition in which this material is embedded. There is no particular cultural or institutional setting to which any of the traditions are intrinsically related. One may ask where or in what settings such traditions might have been preserved, or whether they have to be regarded as resulting from memory or imagination. The answer to such a question is highly speculative; there is almost no evidence available to us on which it can be based.

Some diversity between the anti-Elide traditions here and later might well suggest some diversity in the setting where these traditions have been preserved. Eli's admonition to his sons (2:22-25) is in implicit tension with 2:29 and in explicit tension with 3:13. At the least, it is highly unlikely that these differing passages were the work of one imagination. It is possible that the material here (vv. 12-17 and 22-25) derives from one source (perhaps with an interest in appropriate ritual and behavior at a sanctuary) and the material attributed to the man of God and to Samuel derives from another. The Samuel material, if it derives from memory at all, is too homogeneous and too limited to come from more than one source.

If the anti-Elide material comes from memory rather than imagination, it is most likely to have come from those with an interest in remembering why the Elides fell from favor. Bethel, Mizpah, and Ramah were sanctuaries associated with Samuel (7:16-17); Gilgal was a sanctuary with links to Samuel and to the Elisha circle. Any of these could be source for the sanctuary-related traditions of 2:12-17 and 22-25, for example, or other material. Shiloh's fate after the loss of the ark is not detailed in biblical text; 1 Sam 4 does not say, Ps 78:60-64 is too poetically vague, Jer 7:12-15 and 26:6, 9 would be more apt associated with the destruction of the north in 722 B.C.E. (Nicholson, *Jeremiah*, 78). Archeology's verdict is not hugely helpful: "The buildings of the western slope [apparently not the shrine which, according to the data from the excavations, was

probably at the badly eroded summit of the tell] were destroyed by a fierce con-
flagration. As suggested by Albright and Kjaer, this was probably the work of
the Philistines in the aftermath of the battle of Ebenezer in the mid-11th century
B.C.E." (Finkelstein, "Seilun," 1072). "The site lay in ruins for some time. The
resumption of settlement in Iron II is represented by scanty village-type remains" (ibid.). Nevertheless, Ahijah, the prophet who designated Jeroboam to
be king and later dismissed him, is called "the Shilonite" (e.g., 1 Kgs 11:29).
The preservation of traditions at Shiloh has to be reckoned a possibility. To go
beyond this would be to go beyond the evidence we have.

Meaning

This composite text sits between the story of Samuel's birth and consecration
and the texts in which the elimination of the Elides is to be announced. This text
performs a bridging function between these two points. After the birth of the
new and before announcing the elimination of the old, it contrasts old and new
in no uncertain terms: the old is evil and the new is good; the old is marked by
God's disfavor and the new by God's favor. Both pictures of the Elides are grim
in the extreme: the evil was great, since the offering of the LORD was treated
with contempt (2:17); there was no apparent possibility of mediation, and it
was the LORD's will to kill them (2:25). It is right that spiritual leadership in Israel will pass to Samuel.

Contrasting Destinies of the Elides and Samuel: Prophecy	**2:27–4:1a**
I. Elides: God's condemnation announced twice in prophecy	2:27–3:18
A. Through judgment speech from an anonymous	
man of God	2:27-36
1. Reproach	27-29
a. Recall of past favors	27-28
b. Reproach	29
2. Announcement of judgment	30-36
a. Revocation of past promise	30
b. Announcement of future consequences	31-36
1) Punishment	31-33
2) Sign	34
3) Establishment of a new priesthood	35-36
B. Through Samuel's first experience of God's word	3:1-18
1. The situation	1-3
a. In general: Samuel's service and rarity of God's word	1
b. In particular: Eli; the lamp of God; Samuel	2-3
2. The experience itself	4-14
a. Recognition of the speaker as God	4-9
1) 1st call from God	4-5
a) Non-recognition by Samuel	4-5aα
b) Non-recognition by Eli	5aβ-b

Textual Issues

4:1a   Considerable textual uncertainty exists here. As the MT text and chapter and verse division stand, 4:1a is "a call to arms addressed by Samuel to the Israelites" (Pisano, 34). By contrast, the LXX ends the previous passage with a reference to Eli and his sons: "And Eli was very old and his sons kept advancing and their way was evil before the Lord" (3:21, end). The LXX then goes on to attribute the initiative in the war that follows to the Philistines (see next chapter). Samuel has no place in chs. 4–6, so 4:1a probably belongs with what precedes. The changes are complex and need not concern us further here (cf. Barthélemy, 151-52, Pisano, 29-34).

Discussion

The use of prophecy in the title to this passage catches its concerns. The Elides' rejection by God is pronounced in two prophecies, one from an anonymous man of God — [= Structure Analysis: I.A], the other from Samuel — [I.B]. Samuel is not approved by a prophecy; he is approved as a prophet, a trustworthy prophet to all the nation. The behavior of the Elides and Samuel has been contrasted, with the Elides found wanting. Now it is the destinies of the Elides and Samuel that are contrasted. Two prophecies spell out the downfall of the house of Eli, rejected by God — [I]; by contrast, Samuel is in position as God's trustworthy prophet to all Israel — [II]. The change for Israel intimated in the story of Samuel's birth is now ready to be effected.

For simplicity's sake, the structure analysis has been foreshortened at the start of the man of God's judgment speech — [I.A]. First, the man of God is introduced (v. 27a). He comes to Eli. We are told nothing about him: not where he is from; nothing about his identity. The "man of God" figure functions in such circumstances as a convenient bringer of a message from God; such figures drop into the scene from nowhere, deliver God's message, and usually drop out of the scene into nowhere again. His speech begins with an introduction, the classic messenger formula used to identify the source of a message: "Thus the LORD has said" (v. 27b*). The condemnation of the Elides is no human judgment; it is the word of God.

The judgment speech has two main parts: the reproach or accusation leveled against Eli and his family (— [I.A.1]; vv. 27b-29); the announcement of judgment itself, proclaiming the consequences that flow from the accusation (— [I.A.2]; vv. 30-36). The reproach looks to the past, before turning to the present; it reaches farther afield than anything else in the context. In Egypt, God chose Eli's ancestral house out of all of the tribes of Israel, to be priest, to perform the duties and receive the benefits of that office. The bestowal of such privilege should call forth a response of fidelity. Instead, Eli is reproached with predatory greed for the sacrifices of Israel and with honoring his sons above his God. While the reference to skimming the sacrifices tallies with 2:12-17, the personal attack on Eli comes as a surprise and disagrees with 2:22-25.

The announcement looks first to the past, then to the future. The promise made in the past (v. 30), a promise which is otherwise unknown to us, is solemnly revoked. The future consequences are outlined in three stages. First, the punishment itself: the days are coming when there will not be an old man in the house of Eli (v. 31). This is a punishment known in Israel as *kareth;* it refers to the dishonor involved when the members of a house are cut off before they reach old age (cf. Tsevat, "Studies"). In the midst of Israel's prosperity, the Elides will look on in bitterness (v. 32); grief and early death are to be their lot (v. 33). Second, the sign to Eli by which he will be able to recognize the announcement as true prophecy: his two sons will die on the same day (v. 34). Third, the dishonored Elides will be replaced: a faithful priestly line will be established (the Zadokites) and the remaining Elides will turn to them as supplicants (vv. 35-36).

This is a fearful judgment passed on an ancient priestly house — the antecedents of the house are not traced in detail (cf. Cross, "Priestly Houses"). Historically, the sign is fulfilled at the battle of Ebenezer-Aphek (cf. 4:11). The "cutting off" of Eli's house can be correlated with the slaughter of the priests at Nob under Saul (22:6-19). The replacement of Elides by Zadokites is effective with the banishment of Abiathar from the court of Solomon (1 Kgs 2:27; cf. 2:35). It is possible that the supplicant status of Eli's descendants (1 Sam 2:36) relates to the relegation of the levitical priests to secondary status, during Josiah's reform (cf. 2 Kgs 23:5, 9).

With so much of subsequent history involved, it would not be surprising if the text were reworked as later generations saw items of relevance to their own situations. There are strong enough links to suggest a unity within vv. 27-33 (see Tsevat, "Studies," 212-13). The weight these links give to the potential unity of the text is reinforced by the structure of the text on a broader scale: "thus the LORD has said" (v. 27), "why then" (v. 29), "therefore" (v. 30a), "but now" (v. 30b), and "see, a time is coming" (v. 31). Verse 34 may have originally been the concluding sign, certainly its function in the present text. As the first mention of Hophni and Phineas by name, it was possibly added to tie in with 1 Sam 4. The specific usages noted by Tsevat do not extend into vv. 34-36.

On the other hand, in v. 35, "a sure house" (cf. 1 Sam 25:28; 2 Sam 7:16; and 1 Kgs 11:38) and "my anointed" both point beyond the present context to the Davidic dynasty and the Zadokite priesthood. There is a subtle shift in outlook from "before me" (v. 28) to "before my anointed" (v. 35). Although v. 36 contains a reference to "your house," the verse is clearly dependent on v. 35, through the reference back to the faithful priest. The temptation to see Samuel as this faithful priest has to be resisted; Samuel is established as prophet, not priest (3:20). It is very doubtful that the speech as a whole can be attributed to the Deuteronomists (despite Hertzberg, 39). Close scrutiny reveals nothing that is clearly a cliché characteristic of the dtr style (despite McCarter, 92). The most one can say is that v. 35 is quite close to characteristically dtr language, and that v. 36 may well reflect dtr concerns; it is possible that both verses were added by the Deuteronomists (cf. Miller and Roberts, *Hand of the Lord*, 20-21, 30-31).

After God's rejection of the Elides has been announced so brutally by the man of God, the text proceeds to pile insult on injury. Next the fate of the Elides is to be prophesied by Samuel, the one who is now replacing them as God's authority in Israel — [I.B]. It is a cruel irony: Samuel's first experience of God's word is directed against the Elides whose place he is taking on the national scene. N.B.: as already noted, this is not to be confused with the replacement of the Elide house by a "faithful priest" (2:35); this "faithful priest" is in the prophesied future, while Samuel's authority — as prophet not priest — is in the now of Israel's immediate situation.

The story is carefully presented. Samuel is in God's service under Eli; the changeover has not happened yet. "The word of the LORD was rare in those days" (3:1); this reflects poorly on the Elide time, even though they were priests not prophets, and it throws light on Samuel's failure to recognize God's word immediately. Word and vision are mentioned as though almost synonymous; here, God's word is received in visionary experience. The staging of the drama to come is equally carefully done (vv. 2-3). As we know from v. 15, it is night. Eli lies in his own room, apparently apart from the temple; his eyesight is failing — symbolic of the man and his time. Samuel lies in the temple, where the ark is; he is close to God, plausibly within earshot of Eli, but distant enough that Eli will not hear what Samuel hears and Samuel will have to run to the old man when he hears his name called. Between these two observations, it is noted that "the lamp of God had not yet gone out" (3:3). We do not know what this lamp of God is that had not yet gone out, but the reference is ominous for the Elides.

The story of the experience is focused in two stages: first, the identity of the speaker (vv. 4-9); second, the message from this speaker (vv. 10-14). The structure in the first part follows a typical narrative pattern, the folkloric triad — self-consciously, see "a third time" (v. 8). Three times God summons Samuel; three times Samuel mistakenly runs to Eli, and only at the third time does Eli realize that it is the LORD. On the fourth time that God calls, Samuel responds appropriately. For the proverbial sequence of "three plus a fourth," see Prov 30:15b, 18, 21, 29.

The narrative style is impeccable. In the first call, all the details of the exchanges are given, but with studied conciseness. There are three moments. God to Samuel; Samuel to Eli; Eli to Samuel. This first time, everything is spelled out. The second time, specified as God called "again," some details can be taken for granted. Samuel's failure to recognize God's speaking is explained by his inexperience (v. 7). The third time God calls, Samuel still does not recognize the speaker — but Eli does. There is deep irony in the old rejected priest instructing the inexperienced young man who will replace him how to receive God's word announcing evil against Eli's own house. In the fourth call, the emphasis shifts to God: he came, he stood, and he called as before; and this time the summons is doubled for solemnity (in the MT), "Samuel, Samuel!" Samuel replies almost as Eli had instructed him. These subtle shifts of variation and emphasis are part of good Israelite storytelling. Here and there, LXX and 4QSam[a] have leveled out these differences (cf. McCarter, 95-96). They should not be erased by textual emendation, particularly if this short text is story summary or a base for storytelling.

With God's identity as the speaker now certain, the message is communicated. The judgment is introduced as a chilling message. The image of an "ear-tingling" oracle occurs elsewhere only in 2 Kgs 21:12 and Jer 19:3 (with very slight variations); it is too natural to be in itself a justification for asserting dtr authorship (against Veijola, *Ewige Dynastie,* 38-39, and McCarter, 98). Verse 12 contains a clear reference to the oracle in 2:27-36*, which need indicate no more than the compositional nature of the overall text. The announcement itself is followed by the reason for it (v. 13), and sworn confirmation of it as beyond atonement (v. 14). The reason, implicating Eli for his failure to restrain his sons, contrasts with 2:22-25, and is a further pointer to the compositional nature of the text.

The story concludes with the report of the announcement to Eli. It is delicately told. Samuel is no eager harbinger of bad tidings. Eli has to wring it out of him, under threat of a curse (v. 17). So Samuel is freed from any trace of vindictiveness; correspondingly, Eli's acquiescence lends to the old man an element of nobility in the face of his destiny.

Contrasted with this fateful destiny of the Elides is the destiny of Samuel. Samuel has God's approval as prophet to the nation now. The notice about Samuel involves all three players: Samuel, Israel, and YHWH God of Israel. "Israel must now heed Samuel. . . . He is the one in whom Israel's destiny for the future is vested" (Brueggemann, 26). Where Samuel is concerned, it is necessary to create room for the youth serving at Shiloh to become the prophet to all Israel. The reference to growth (3:19a, continuing the trajectory of 2:21b, 26) provides the bare minimum required; four words in English translation (NRSV), two words in Hebrew. The experience just recounted of Samuel (3:1-18) was not to be unique; it was the beginning of a continuing process. Where Israel is concerned, the implications are spelled out. From the traditional extremities of Dan to Beer-sheba, all Israel knew that Samuel was established as a trustworthy prophet of God (v. 20; is there a relationship with Deut 18:15-18?). This is an immense step and an immense claim; but the narrative provides no evidence for it beyond this bald statement, which is probably derived from the subsequent traditions it serves to introduce. Where God is concerned, revelation continued at Shiloh, but it took place through the word and through Samuel. That too is an immense step and an immense claim; it effectively sidelines the Elides. The focus swings back to Samuel: his word reached to all Israel. There is no mention of Shiloh in the rest of the Samuel traditions. After this, the narrative focus will turn elsewhere.

The last word here can be given to Brueggemann.

There is a chance for newness, and that chance is rooted in Hannah's piety, in Israel's daring doxology, in Eli's yielding, in Samuel's availability, in God's resolve to do a new thing. (p. 27)

Above all, in God's resolve to do a new thing.

Genre

The man of God speech is an (→) account of a (→) prophetic judgment speech. It covers the two basic concerns that are present in such speeches: an (→) accusation, which provides the reason for the punishment; an (→) announcement of the judgment or punishment. Here the accusation is couched in the form of a (→) reproach: the brief review of God's favors to the house of Eli leads to the expression of displeasure (v. 29). The announcement parallels this structure: the review of God's favor has as its corresponding element the revocation of God's promise; the displeasing behavior has as its consequence the future punishment.

The nocturnal revelation to Samuel, with its announcement of judgment on the house of Eli, is in the form of a (→) story. The sketch of the situation arouses interest: the drought of God's word is about to break. With the LORD's call, this begins to happen; the complication is introduced of how to bring the inexperienced Samuel to recognize the speaker and to know how to respond. Although, as audience, we know from the outset that it is the LORD (v. 4), the narrative proceeds through the tension of Samuel's process of discovery,

56

through Eli's recognition, to Samuel's "Speak, for your servant hears." The tension is then transferred to a new level. What is about to be said will be such as to make ears tingle (v. 11). And so the story reaches its climax: past word to be fulfilled, punishment to be exacted, and no expiation to be possible. Even then, the storyteller is not done. "Samuel lay until morning" hints at what is made explicit a moment later: Samuel was afraid to tell Eli. Between these two lies the perfunctory ordinariness of opening the temple doors in the morning. The initiative is then given to Eli, and the focus of interest moves to his reaction. The story comes to rest with his acceptance.

It is important to recognize that this is not a prophetic call narrative; there is no call. It may serve in place of a call narrative, since after this first experience of God's word Samuel continues as a trustworthy prophet of the LORD. For all that, it is not a call narrative.

Contrasting with the fate of the Elides, Samuel's destiny is spelled out less in terms of what he will be as rather in (→) notices about what he is. Briefly and without plot, the information is conveyed: he grows; he is favored by God; he brings God's word to all Israel.

Setting

The present setting is that of a literary compilation, where Elide condemnation — conveyed in the account of a prophetic judgment speech and the story of Samuel's first reception of God's word — is contrasted with notices favoring Samuel. We have noted earlier that Eli's admonition to his sons (2:22-25) is in implicit tension with 2:29 and in explicit tension with 3:13. Such tensions militate against any hypothesis of imaginative creation at the compiler's level; it would also point toward preservation in different places.

It is likely that the judgment speech of the anonymous man of God was remembered in circles interested in the fall of the Elides, while the story of Samuel's first prophetic experience might have been remembered in circles interested in the reception of prophecy; nothing prevents these circles from overlapping. The present formulation has a degree of correlation; "all that I have spoken concerning his house" (cf. 3:12-13) may but need not refer to the announcement of the man of God. It might reflect memory; it might be a compiler's tribute to continuity. We have no certainty. Possible places have been noted in relation to the setting of 2:12-16; the matter is too speculative to repeat here. It is likely that vv. 35-36 are a later and probably dtr addition to the prophetic speech. It is very doubtful that the speech as a whole can be attributed to the Deuteronomists, despite Hertzberg ("We have here, then, generally speaking, a speech constructed by the deuteronomistic compiler," 39) and McCarter ("This passage is replete with the devices and clichés of the Josianic historian," 92). Close scrutiny reveals nothing that is clearly a cliché characteristic of the dtr style.

The notices about Samuel may reflect overall tradition in prophetic circles or may express the conviction of what must have been. To go beyond this would be to go beyond the evidence we have.

Meaning

The passage as it stands reflects the stark contrast between the future of the Elides and Samuel. The previous contrast was between their behavior. Now the balance is between downfall and favor — the downfall of the Elides and the favor of Samuel. Even at Shiloh the Elides are now seen as replaced by Samuel. Not only have the intimations of change been realized at Shiloh; there are now intimations for change in Israel itself. The new figure of Samuel the prophet has been established as a significant bearer of God's word to all Israel.

Such changes at the national helm are not remembered and recorded unless they have significance for the nation. Now that the destinies of Elides and Samuel are known, the question remains: what lies in the future for the destiny of Israel?

Bibliography of Works Cited Above

Alter, Robert. *The Art of Biblical Poetry*. New York: Basic Books, 1985.

Campbell, Antony F. *Of Prophets and Kings: A Late Ninth-Century Document (1 Samuel 1–2 Kings 10)*. CBQMS 17. Washington: CBA of America, 1986.

Campbell, Antony F., and Mark A. O'Brien. *Sources of the Pentateuch: Texts, Introductions, Annotations*. Minneapolis: Fortress, 1993.

Cook, Joan E. *Hannah's Desire, God's Design: Early Interpretations of the Story of Hannah*. JSOTSup 282. Sheffield: Sheffield Academic Press, 1999.

Cross, Frank Moore. "The Priestly Houses of Early Israel." Pp. 195-215 in F. M. Cross, *Canaanite Myth and Hebrew Epic: Essays in the History of the Religion of Israel*. Cambridge: Harvard University Press, 1973.

Finkelstein, Israel. "Seilun, Khirbet." Pp. 1069-72 in *ABD*, vol. 5.

Garsiel, Moshe. *The First Book of Samuel: A Literary Study of Comparative Structures, Analogies and Parallels*. Ramat Gan: Revivim, 1985.

————. *Biblical Names: A Literary Study of Midrashic Derivations and Puns*. Ramat Gan: Bar-Ilan University Press, 1991.

Kugel, James L. *The Idea of Biblical Poetry*. New Haven: Yale University Press, 1981.

Lewis, Theodore J. "The Textual History of the Song of Hannah: 1 Samuel II 1-10." *VT* 44 (1994) 18-46.

Miller, Patrick D., Jr., and J. J. M. Roberts. *The Hand of the Lord: A Reassessment of the "Ark Narrative" of 1 Samuel*. Baltimore: The Johns Hopkins University Press, 1977.

Nicholson, Ernest W. *Jeremiah 1–25*. CBC. Cambridge: Cambridge University Press, 1973.

Olrik, A. "Epic Laws of Folk Narrative." Pp. 129-41 in *The Study of Folklore*. Edited by A. Dundes. Englewood Cliffs: Prentice-Hall, 1965. German original: 1909.

Polzin, Robert. *A Literary Study of the Deuteronomic History*. Part Two: *Samuel and the Deuteronomist*. San Francisco: Harper & Row, 1989.

Tsevat, Matitiahu. "Studies in the Book of Samuel." *HUCA* 32 (1961) 191-216.

Veijola, Timo. *Die Ewige Dynastie: David und die Entstehung seiner Dynastie nach der deuteronomistischen Darstellung.* AASF B 193. Helsinki: Suomalainen Tiedeakatemia, 1975.

Walters, Stanley D. Review of P. Kyle McCarter, *I Samuel: A New Translation with Introduction, Notes and Commentary. JBL* 101 (1982) 435-38.

————. "Hanna and Anna: The Greek and Hebrew Texts of 1 Samuel 1." *JBL* 107 (1988) 385-412.

Wilson, Robert R. "The Former Prophets: Reading the Books of Kings." Pp. 83-96 in *Old Testament Interpretation: Past, Present, and Future. Essays in Honor of Gene M. Tucker.* Edited by J. L. Mays, D. L. Petersen, and K. H. Richards. Nashville: Abingdon, 1995.

Chapter 3

THE DEPARTURE OF THE ARK FROM THE NATIONAL SCENE (1 Samuel 4–6)

The preparations for a transition in national authority (1 Sam 1:1–7:1) are presented on two fronts. First, the emergence of Samuel on the national scene as a trustworthy prophet of the LORD, the effective replacement of the Elide priesthood at Shiloh (1:1–4:1a). Second, the departure of the ark from the national scene, leaving the sanctuary of Shiloh bereft of the symbols of its past (4:1b–7:1).

We know almost nothing about the significance and symbolism of the ark at Shiloh. It is often thought of as a national shrine, but we have no clear affirmation to this effect. It would be clear, if there was only one ark of God among Israel's religious symbols; but this is not immediately clear. Psalm 78 speaks as if there were only Shiloh: "God . . . utterly rejected Israel. He abandoned his dwelling at Shiloh, the tent where he dwelt among mortals" (78:59-60). The idea of an amphictyony was entertained, a twelve-tribe federation in which each tribe served the central sanctuary for a month of the twelve-month lunar year; but the idea has rightly been abandoned. Psalm 78 offers guidance that is consonant with the Samuel text; we may accept it, aware of the limits of our knowledge. Karel Van der Toorn and Cees Houtman describe the ark as "a Deuteronomic phantom, produced by the projection of a late theological ideal upon Israel's prehistory" ("David and the Ark," 231). What matters is the significance claimed for the ark in the narrative texts; it is far from proven that blame should be laid on some Deuteronomist.

The ark of God, then, is portrayed as the symbol of God's presence to Israel. Its withdrawal from Shiloh is a significant change in the status quo. Its failure to return to Shiloh raises questions about God's purpose with regard to Israel. The ark eventually returns to Jerusalem (2 Sam 6); a major change in the national institutions of Israel is confirmed (cf. Ps 78:67-69).

No theology could leave the ark of God in obscurity without adequately accounting for the absence of God from Israel. Departure is a correlative either of abandonment or return. Once the presence of the ark in Jerusalem is acknowledged, its departure from Shiloh is a correlative of its return to Jerusalem. Until the presence of the ark in Jerusalem is acknowledged, for those for whom the ark is the exclusive symbol of God's presence in Israel, its departure from Shiloh is shrouded in uncertainty. It is a departure that may be a correlative of abandonment or of return. There is no weightier theological issue for Israel.

The Departure of the Ark from the National Scene	1 Sam 4:1b–7:1
I. Departure of the ark from Israel: Israel's loss of God's favor	4:1b-22
A. Military loss	1b-11
1. 1st report of battle: initial defeat of Israel	1b-2
2. Account of hopes and fears raised	3-9
3. 2nd report of battle: definitive defeat of Israel	10-11
B. Significance of the loss	12-22
1. As fatal: death of Eli	12-18
2. As abandonment: naming of Ichabod	19-22
II. Reversal of the situation of defeat	5:1-12
A. Introduction: Philistines bring the ark to Ashdod	1
B. Demonstration of YHWH's supremacy and disfavor	2-12
1. Toward the Philistine god: in the temple of Dagon	2-5
2. Toward the Philistine people: in the cities of the Philistines	6-12
III. Return of the ark to Israel: without Israel's return to God's favor	6:1–7:1
A. Return of the ark from Philistine territory	1-18
1. Consultation of diviners by the Philistines	1-9
2. Compliance with the diviners' instructions	10-18
B. Departure of ark: no bestowal of God's favor	6:19–7:1
1. Disaster: sudden death associated with the ark	19a
2. Consequences: departure of the ark to Kiriath-jearim	19b-7:1

The structure outlines a short narrative of immense significance (despite Nadav Na'aman's view that "it was never an independent entity," "Pre-Deuteronomistic Story," 654). The discussion of the extent of this narrative will be taken up below. For now, we may notice that with 1 Sam 4:1b there is a change of scene. Two new actors take center stage: Israel and the Philistines. The story is no longer restricted to the narrow confines of a sanctuary in the central hills of Ephraim and the contrasts between individuals there. Now the narrative unfolds on the broad plain that sweeps from the base of those hills to the Mediterranean and toward the territory of the Philistines, and now the narrative features contrast and conflict between nations. The fate of individuals — Hophni, Phinehas, Eli, the wife of Phinehas, Ichabod — is symbolic but not central. Samuel, the newly emerged and established prophet at Shiloh, is not mentioned; he does not reappear until 1 Sam 7:3. The central actor in this drama is the ark of God. Only when the ark is no longer central, but is lodged at Kiriath-jearim, does the focus move back to Samuel — but not until then. To discover the full significance of these chapters, one must begin by realizing that they are unique in the entire Older Testament. Nowhere else, with the exception of 2 Sam 6 — which in the later discussion will be associated with these chapters — is there such concentrated focus on the ark of YHWH. Nowhere else is what YHWH is doing in the story of Israel expressed, to so sustained a degree, through the symbolic actions of the ark. It has been aptly said:

> The subject of the narrative is *Yahweh,* and not the ark. The issue is not what happens to the ark, but what Yahweh is doing among his people. Not the ark, but Yahweh's power and purpose is what the story is about. It is a thoroughly theological narrative at its very core. (Miller and Roberts, *Hand of the Lord,* 60)

What makes this narrative unique in the Older Testament is that this expression of YHWH's power and purpose is focused exclusively through the ark. The ark leaves the sanctuary at Shiloh and leaves the territory of Israel; while it returns to the territory of Israel, it does not return to a central position of honor or to a major sanctuary in Israel. Yet all of this is expressive of "what Yahweh is doing among his people." To determine what it is that the narrative says YHWH is doing, one must pay close attention to the structure and composition of this remarkably dense text.

We can review it under the heads of its three major moments: the departure of the ark from Israel, expressing the loss of God's favor — [= Structure Analysis: I]; the reversal — [II]; and the return of the ark to Israel, without Israel's return to God's favor — [III].

Departure of the Ark from Israel: 1 Sam 4:1b-22
Israel's Loss of God's Favor

I. Military loss	1b-11
A. 1st report of battle: initial defeat of Israel	1b-2
1. Gathering of opposing forces	1b
2. Battle, defeat, casualties	2
B. Account of hopes and fears raised	3-9
1. Israel's hopes raised	3-5
a. Theological question asked	3a
b. Proposal made and implemented: bringing the ark	3b-4
c. Israel's exultation	5
2. Philistine fears raised	6-9
a. Awareness of arrival of the ark	6
b. Fear and lamentation	7-8
c. Exhortation to courage	9
C. 2nd report of battle: definitive defeat of Israel	10-11
1. Military aspect: battle, defeat and flight, worse casualties	10
2. Religious aspect: ark captured, two priest sons of Eli dead	11
II. Significance of the loss	12-22
A. As fatal: expressed by an anecdote — death of Eli	12-18

1. Prelude: the Benjaminite runner and the anxious Eli 12-13a
2. Bringing of the news of defeat 13b-17
   a. Intimation 13b-14a
     1) The man tells the town: outcry 13b
     2) Eli inquires about the outcry 14a
   b. Announcement to Eli 14b-17
     1) The man comes before Eli 14b
     2) Eli's state 15
     3) The man's identification 16a
     4) Eli's inquiry 16b
     5) The messenger's response: the announcement 17
3. Consequence: the death of Eli 18
   a. Description of Eli's death on hearing of the ark 18a
   b. Statement of the length of his period of judgeship 18b
B. As abandonment: expressed by an anecdote —
naming of Ichabod 19-22
1. Reception of the news by Eli's daughter-in-law 19a
2. Reaction to the news by Eli's daughter-in-law 19b-22
   a. Birth of a son 19b
   b. Death of a mother 20-22
     1) Her refusal to be comforted as she dies 20
     2) Her naming of the son 21-22
       a) His name 21aα
       b) Interpretation of the name 21aβb-22
         (1) With reference to the ark, Eli, and
           her husband 21aβb
         (2) With specific reference to the capture
           of the ark 22

Textual Issues

4:1b As was noted for 4:1a in the preceding chapter, there is considerable textual uncertainty here with complex changes involved. The present text of the MT (4:1a) suggests that Samuel's word to all Israel is a call to arms — highly unlikely in the light of what follows. Without 4:1a, the initiative for conflict with the Philistines is Israel's. Among its changes, the LXX has transferred the initiative, and so the responsibility, for the conflict from Israel to the Philistines (cf. Pisano, 33-34). The issue may be less between textual versions or translations than between traditions or theologies. LXX is accepted by McCarter (pp. 97, 103) and Klein (pp. 36-37), perhaps unwisely.

Discussion

The extent of the unit is established by the focus on Israel's defeat in battle. The military loss is held within the frame of the two reports of battle — [I.A & C]. The reflection on its significance is bound into the narrative of the loss by the man who "ran from the battle line, and came to Shiloh the same day" (4:12). The effect of his news on Eli and on Eli's daughter-in-law is held together (cf. "his daughter-in-law," 4:19) as two reflections on the significance of the loss of the ark — [II.A & B].

Given that this is no ordinary story of war, as any audience will discover, who took the initiative in the hostilities may be important. MT gives the initiative to Israel; the LXX, followed by the NRSV, gives it to the Philistines. Given that this is a story of God's abandoning Israel, it may be that the MT is right to give Israel the initiative in these fateful hostilities. The idiom translated "went out" *(wayyēṣē' liqra't)* is usually used in situations of response; but one or two cases of its use with the initiating party are found (e.g., Judg 7:2-4; 2 Sam 18:6). The gathering of the forces (v. 1b) sets the scene for both battles; it is not repeated before vv. 10-11. The opposing camps are located at Ebenezer and Aphek, situated where the coastal plain meets the rising foothills. The beginning is abrupt, but both battle reports are taut and concise, with no leaders mentioned beyond the elders of Israel.

The battle itself is reported in the barest possible fashion: the Philistines ranged against Israel, the battle spread, Israel was defeated. Then the number of the dead is given, as some measure of the gravity of the defeat. The numbers may be of a proportional nature, relating to military units. Israelite military units are described as tens, fifties, hundreds, and thousands (cf. Deut 1:15). As with modern military units — such as platoons, companies, battalions, regiments, and divisions — there is no assurance that these were up to full strength at any particular time; the numbers do not always correspond with the names. Following George Mendenhall's analysis of Numbers 1–2, McCarter suggests a range of from 20 to 56 for the four thousand in v. 2, and from 150 to 420 for the thirty thousand in v. 10 (pp. 105, 107); however the proportions might vary considerably at different times. What matters in this narrative is not the precise number but the more than sevenfold increase in casualties from v. 2 to v. 10.

This first battle is an initial engagement. There is no mention of rout or flight; instead there is a return to the camp (v. 3). Whether historically accurate or not, this is totally within the historical realm — it is a battle between armies, with victors and vanquished, and a body count for the dead. The narrative promptly moves out of the historical into the theological realm. With the elders' deliberation — at least in the present context — the tone changes completely: this is no longer bare reporting of an event, but interpretative narration, bringing the interpretation to expression through the understanding and the utterances of the participants. As the text now stands, the deliberation begins with the question posed by the elders of Israel: "Why has the LORD put us to rout today before the Philistines?" (4:3). In the text, it is not an offhand question from some disconsolate soldier; it is asked by the elders of Israel. With many, Robert Alter unfairly denigrates the elders. His comment that they conceive the ark "magically or fetishistically" reflects a modern prejudice that is not in the text; a check of biblical usage shows the "to us" (Hebrew: bring to us; NRSV: bring here) is not superfluous — Alter's prejudicial comment is (p. 22). It is important to note that the story is told at the level of Israel: it is Israel that goes out, Israel that is defeated, Israel's elders that deliberate in council — no commanders or military figures are named at all.

The question may not be meant to be answered at once. Certainly, it is to be taken seriously and not answered facilely. We cannot attribute the defeat to the absence of the ark. Although it may be portrayed as the thought of the elders, it would render inexplicable the second defeat where the ark is present. To attribute the second defeat to God's punishment of Israel for their blind trust in a cultic object smacks of an inappropriate and anachronistic polemic against sacramentalism (against Hertzberg, 51), while still failing to explain the first defeat. To see the first defeat as God's means of bringing Hophni and Phinehas on the scene with the ark, in order that they might die in the disastrous second battle, overlooks the rest of the narrative and has God employ means that are totally disproportionate to the end. To find the explanation of the defeats in the sins of the Elides (detailed in 1 Sam 2:12-17, 22-25, 27-36) is open to serious objection (against Miller and Roberts, *Hand of the Lord*). First, there is the inconsistency within this anti-Elide material, discussed above; there is also inconsistency with ch. 4 — in 2:34, for example, there is no reference to Eli's own death, or to the loss of the ark, or to the defeats suffered by Israel. Second, the narrative of ch. 4 is of national significance; the concerns of the anti-Elide material in ch. 2 are not formulated so as to go beyond the priestly family. Third, the death of Eli's two sons is given in 2:34 as the sign for Eli, but a sign always points forward to something beyond itself (for details, see Campbell, "Yahweh and the Ark"). The question in 4:3 is left open; only the narrative as a whole will provide an answer. According to the text, the answer here is not a simple one of crime and punishment.

At the beginning of the narrative, the elders speak of "the ark of the covenant of the LORD (= YHWH)" (4:3); the text then has the full solemn title, "the ark of the covenant of the LORD of hosts [= YHWH ṣĕbāʾôt], who is enthroned on the cherubim" (4:4). Similar solemn nomenclature is used again in 2 Sam 6:2. Titles are notoriously difficult to pin down. They can be traditional; they can be added at any time when judged appropriate. Context and other criteria are sometimes helpful, sometimes not.

For example, the alternation of "David" and "the king" in Samuel texts has been compared with the alternation of YHWH and ʾĕlōhîm in the Pentateuch. Not so. Even the crudest statistics for the use of the proper name "David" (D) and the common noun or title "the king" (K) in 2 Sam 6–24 are worth noting ("King David" is counted as one of each):

2S	6	7	8	9	10	11	12	13	14	15	16	17	18	19	20	21	22	23	24
D	22	6	21	7	12	23	17	8	0	10	9	9	5	5	7	12	2	9	15
K	3	4	3	11	1	8	1	24	39	21	13	4	24	61	5	6	1	0	15

The huge range in these figures (from 15/15 in ch. 24 to 39/0 in ch. 14 or 61/5 in ch. 19, across a total of 199 for D and 244 for K) is evidence that the distribution is not random; but the factors controlling the distribution are apparently multiple and certainly difficult to identify. Tradition has its role, preference has its role, what is appropriate can have its role, editorial work can have its role. There is no suggestion of the equivalent of pentateuchal narrative strands; there is no suggestion that the distribution regularly reflects the difference of personal name and public office.

Similarly, in the ark narrative the use of titles for the ark of God must be approached with care. Variations may reflect narrative strands or editorial layers (see Diachronic Dimension, below). The full titles ("LORD of hosts" coupled with "enthroned on the cherubim") in 1 Sam 4:4 and 2 Sam 6:2, occurring at the start of major sections of the text (and only here in the books of Samuel), suggest a need for weighty solemnity. "LORD of hosts" alone is also used in 1 Sam 1:3, 11; 15:2; 17:45 and 2 Sam 6:18; 7:8, 26, 27 — all solemn moments. The "enthroned" image is different from the protective cherubim above the ark in Solomon's temple (1 Kgs 8:6-7) and from their incorporation into the lid of the ark in the priestly tradition (Exod 25:18-22); for the literature, see McCarter (pp. 105-6, 108). Reference to the covenant may easily have been inserted by dtr editors, expressing their particular understanding of the ark's theological function. All seven references to the "ark of the God of Israel" relate to utterances of the Philistines.

The proposal to bring the ark from Shiloh to the camp is motivated by the hope of God's presence (v. 3bβ) and of deliverance (v. 3bγ). So the ark is brought. The two sons of Eli are mentioned as being with the ark (v. 4b); it is difficult to see that their mention is more than an appendix to the verse, preparing the ground for their death, which in turn prepares for the two anecdotes. The significance given to the coming of the ark is expressed by the reaction of both Israelites (v. 5) and Philistines (vv. 6-9). Both are portrayed as convinced that, with the arrival of the ark, the outcome is now heavily weighted in favor of the Israelites.

We moderns are used to instant communication, and we can easily read such a text as reporting the sequence of events as they occur. We must resist the temptation to conclude that the Israelite army was over-confident and the Philistine army over-anxious, or to be sidetracked into questions about how the Philistines managed to be so well-informed about Israelite theology. This is not on-the-spot reporting; it is narrative, concerning an event that is past. If we fail to recognize this as narrative, put together after the events, well aware that definitive defeat looms ahead in vv. 10-11, we will fail to recognize the strangeness of vv. 3-9. It is an account of hopes and fears raised. The text has the Israelite elders place the initial defeat in the context of their God and propose to bring the icon of their God to the field of battle. Now victory will surely be theirs, and a "mighty shout" echoes from the Israelite camp. Hopes are unquestionably raised — in a text that knows they will certainly be dashed. The Philistines are portrayed as fearful. More than half of this account is given to their anticipation of defeat; in the context, even the exhortation is tinged with despair (v. 9). The references to the Exodus aptly introduce a theme that will return in chs. 5–6. Fears are unquestionably raised — in a text that knows they are certainly unfounded.

What meaning do we give to a text that sandwiches an account of the false hopes of the soon-to-be vanquished and the false fears of the soon-to-be victors between reports of a defeat that may be only initial and a subsequent defeat that is indeed definitive? Both hopes and fears are based in the text on the presence and action of God. The only conclusion from the text is that God did not act as expected. The text sets up its audience to expect God's gift of victory to the Israelites; the Israelites hope for it and the Philistines fear it. When it does not happen, the question of v. 3, "Why has the LORD put us to rout today before the Philistines?" acquires new meaning and urgency.

The report of the second defeat completely reverses the movement of expectation that has been built up in the preceding verses. The intensification of the consequences over against those of the first defeat should be noted: (i) it is final — defeated Israel has fled for home; (ii) it is described as "a very great slaughter"; (iii) the number of dead is increased more than sevenfold. There is no description of pursuit or plunder. Instead, there is the laconic statement of the loss of the ark and the death of Eli's sons. Explanations are not given; "a closely disciplined narrative strategy is being employed. . . . The defeat can be understood only as the will of Yahweh" (Brueggemann, 31-32).

At the level of the larger narrative, this opening section takes what might have been an almost banal incident in the fortunes of Israel and transforms it into an episode of national importance. As a simple incident in the military and religious story of Israel, it would have meant no more than that the ark was carried into battle and lost, only to be recovered within the year. Granted, the occurrence is unique in the biblical record. Yet on many occasions, the temple was looted and sacred vessels were lost (e.g., 1 Kgs 14:25-27; 15:18; 2 Kgs 12:18-19 [NRSV 17-18]; 14:14; 16:8; 18:15-16; 24:13; 25:9, 13-18). Most of these cases concern the treasury, and even in those where vessels are named the ark is not mentioned (not even in Jer 27:16-22). Yet it could hardly have always escaped (cf. Jer 3:16). The art of this text has been to take a potentially banal incident and make it a matter of key significance for the theological story of Israel.

The significance of the loss is the focus of the text that follows. The first anecdote is a masterpiece of storytelling. It is carefully constructed, alternating between the messenger, bearer of fateful tidings, and Eli, priest of the sanctuary that has been deserted by its God. There is a skillful blend of anticipation and retardation: Eli is introduced before the runner reaches the townsfolk, yet the runner's arrival before Eli is delayed two verses; Eli is actually reported as being told in v. 14b ("and the man came quickly and told Eli"), yet the content of the announcement is withheld until v. 17.

The prelude sets a tone of ominous foreboding for what is to come. The condition of the runner — his clothing torn and his head sprinkled with earth — intimates the nature of his news (v. 12b). Similarly, the waiting of Eli is also anxious — because of the ark (v. 13a). For a storyteller, 4:1b-11 would be more than adequate grounds for describing Eli as anxious.

The portrayal of the runner creating an uproar in the town before coming to Eli reflects the demands of narrative art. The text is most likely the base from which the story is told or the summary of such a story. The storyteller can elaborate on why Eli was not told first or later what circumstances contributed to his broken neck; the summary or base text need not — and does not. The story's goal is so near: the runner has come; Eli is at hand anxiously waiting — but the text retards the disclosure. We are not told what the messenger told the town, because we already know; within the narrative, the outcry in the town can only mean a lamentable disaster (cf. 4:6). This first intimation must reinforce Eli's anxiety. The movement toward the announcement proceeds inevitably. From the town, the messenger hastens to Eli. The messenger's haste contrasts with the text's delaying tactics. It is said that the messenger tells Eli (v. 14b), but no announcement is disclosed. It is delayed by the description of Eli, which explains his immobility and his inability to perceive what is happening, but which also prepares for his death; and it is delayed by the self-presentation of the messenger, which also ends with foreboding — "from the battle I fled today" (v. 16a).

Finally, the announcement is made (v. 17). Even here, the suspense is maintained to the end. The basic statement that Israel fled before the Philistines is extended, first by reference to the great slaughter, then by reference to the death of Eli's sons, and finally the capture of the ark is told. In both Hebrew and the NRSV, the fateful word "captured" is withheld until last. The text specifies that it was at the mention of the ark that Eli fell and died (v. 18a). The sanctuary of Shiloh has lost its ark and its principal priest; Israel has lost the ark of its God.

The note of Eli's forty-year judgeship is considered a post-dtr addition (cf. Noth, *Deuteronomistic History,* 39-40); according to Noth, Eli does not function within the schema of the judges. Eli is not portrayed as a deliverer-judge. Judg 13:1 speaks of a forty-year oppression by the Philistines. Samson is said to "begin to deliver Israel" (Judg 13:5); his "judgeship" is given as twenty years (Judg 15:20; 16:31). "Some twenty years" is reported to have passed from the time the ark came to Kiriath-jearim (1 Sam 7:2), before Samuel is portrayed as the intercessor who brought about deliverance by YHWH and the rout of the Philistines, so that "the hand of the LORD was against the Philistines all the days of Samuel" (1 Sam 7:13). In this context, competing with Samson and 1 Sam 7:2, it is hard to find meaning for Eli's forty years. At this point in the text, however, it contributes to the note of finality.

The structure of the second anecdote is simpler. The principal action is narrated immediately, and what follows is the reaction to it. The woman is presented as daughter-in-law of Eli and wife of Phinehas, and her pregnancy is near to term. She hears the news (v. 19a). Both here and in v. 21, the capture of the ark is mentioned before the fate of her father-in-law and her husband. On hearing the news, the woman goes into labor and gives birth. The name of the child is to be the climax of the story, and yet the tension is heightened by retardation. That she is dying is noted, as those in attendance offer comfort; this disaster is not one where comfort is in order. The exhortation "Do not be afraid" (v. 20) is usually accompanied by the assertion of God's presence or support. Not so here; the name to be given her child implies the opposite conviction.

A dying mother in Israel names her child and interprets the name she has given: literally, the glory has gone into exile from Israel (v. 21a; NRSV: has departed from). The interpretation follows a sacral sequence rather than a personal one: "because the ark of God had been captured and because of her father-in-law and her husband" (v. 21b). The repetition in v. 22 focuses exclusively on the capture of the ark. Here, for the first time, the meaning of the military loss is expressly named: God has gone into exile from Israel.

The archetypal quality of the moment is echoed in the West's great myth of romantic love, the myth of Tristan and Iseult. Tristan's symbolic naming is placed in that moment of his mother Blanchefleur's dying (taken from: Johnson, *Psychology of Romantic Love*, 9-10).

> She abided three days in sorrow and longing for death. And on the fourth day she brought forth a child and said:
> *"Little son, I have longed a while to see you, . . . the fairest thing ever a woman bore. In sadness came I hither, in sadness did I bring forth, in sadness has your first feast day gone. And as by sadness you came into the world, your name shall be called Tristan; that is, the child of sadness."*
> This did she name her child, and kissed him, and then she died.

It is not by chance that the myth of Tristan and Iseult should echo not only this moment but also the storm at sea in Jonah 1 and the single combat of David and Goliath in 1 Sam 17 (cf. ibid., pp. 9-15).

Genre

This narrative section is built up from a selection of genres. There are (→) two reports in the passage. They are a good example of the genre, responding to the need to convey information about the battles, but subordinating it to the overall needs of the narrative. Between them is an (→) account in which both the hopes of Israel are raised and the fears of the Philistines are equally raised.

The significance of the loss is expressed in two brief stories probably best described as (→) anecdotes. An anecdote is a short narrative of an interesting or amusing episode, often biographical, and often told to illustrate a point. Both the passages here, about Eli's death and about Ichabod's naming, are biographical, and both are told to illustrate a point — the theological significance of the defeats. Neither is intended to be amusing; their interest is deeply serious.

The question remains: what sort of a narrative is this chapter? If it is (→) report, then the interpretative work of theology has yet to be done. If it is (→) story, then the work of interpretation may have already been begun. There is no reason why options should not be left open at this point. For our purposes, they may be more clearly seen in the context of the whole, under the rubric of the Diachronic Dimension. A little earlier, however, Miller and Roberts have been quoted with approval: "It is a thoroughly theological narrative at its very core."

Setting

The setting is literary. This is evident for the account of raised hopes and fears; it can have no function outside the literary setting of the narrative. While the facts of the battles at Ebenezer-Aphek may have been well known and often repeated, the precise formulation given them here, as reports of battle, is tailored to the needs of the literary context, which thus becomes their setting. The two anecdotes may also have been well known. Now they form a single unit within the text, illustrating the significance of 4:1b-11.

The focus of all these elements is less on military or family matters and more on the ark. Before being taken into the narrative, it is not unlikely that these traditions would have been kept alive within the circles of those responsible for the ark of God, at first perhaps at Kiriath-jearim, certainly later in Jerusalem.

Meaning

This narrative passage is a setting of the question, "Why has the LORD put us to rout today before the Philistines?" (4:3). It is not an abstract asking of the question. It is set in concrete circumstance of defeat and death. It is utterly inadequate to describe the story of the ark as "aimed to satisfy the audience's curiosity" (Gitay, "Reflection," 226).

Resumed briefly, it presents two successive military defeats in such a way that central theological questions must necessarily be asked about them. This is achieved in two ways. The first is the introduction of the question: "Why has the LORD put us to rout today before the Philistines?" Attention is focused on God's responsibility for Israel's success and failure in battle. The second is the intervening account, which creates a general expectation of imminent victory for the Israelites and defeat for the Philistines. The second disaster, in shattering this expectation, brings into question the fundamental assumption on which it was based: that God is fighting on the side of Israel. The question that then stands out sharply is: Was it indeed God who defeated Israel, and, if so, to what purpose?

The two anecdotes reflect the significance of the loss: Is it grave or is it one of the momentary happenstances of history? The loss of the ark is fatal and death bringing; the loss of the ark signifies abandonment for Israel. Within the narrative, the anecdotes highlight the significance of the military defeats. Far from being a couple of temporary setbacks, these defeats are portrayed as fatal (Eli) and as signifying God's departure from Israel (Ichabod).

The chapter as a whole sets the question, "Why has the LORD put us to rout today before the Philistines?" fairly and squarely in the text. It is not allowed to be passed over as a rhetorical throwaway. It has fatal overtones. It is associated with statements of God's exile from Israel. It cries out for exploration and explanation. The narrative will continue.

Textual Issues

There are considerable differences between the MT and the LXX^B in 1 Sam 5. The MT provides, as a rule, the more concise and more artistically constructed text, over against the expanded LXX^B. While some of the differences may be due to scribal error, the major part seem more likely to stem from a different version of the tradition. Many versions of these stories apparently circulated in oral form, and the Hebrew text being translated for LXX^B probably reflected such versions. The mice, for example, appear in the LXX^B at 5:6, but not in the MT until ch. 6; they appear to have been integral to the LXX^B, rather than omitted from the MT (see, however, the discussion in McCarter, 118-20). It seems probable that in the written versions of stories — as reported stories or the base for performance — a key detail from a different version was included, as a reminder of another way of telling the story.

    5:4 An emendation may be needed to specify the trunk of the headless and handless Dagon (cf. Driver, 50-51). Stoebe retains the sense, but cautions about reconstructing an original text (p. 139).

Discussion

The transfer to Philistine territory separates this part of the narrative from what precedes it. 6:1, since it stipulates the length of the stay, looks on it as completed; it provides a new beginning and leads into a new set of concerns. So chapter 5 may be treated as a unit, within the larger narrative.

In the present text, the introductory transfer of the ark to the Philistine city of Ashdod — [I] is followed by two accounts demonstrating YHWH's supremacy over and disfavor toward the Philistine god, Dagon — [II.A], and the Philistine people themselves — [II.B]. Two moves are extremely important here. First, the issue of YHWH's supremacy over the Philistine god. This responds to the question whether YHWH defeated Israel before the Philistines (4:3). If Dagon were to prove the stronger god, YHWH did not defeat Israel but Dagon defeated YHWH. If YHWH is stronger than Dagon, then the question arises whether YHWH has chosen to leave Israel in favor of the Philistines. The demonstration of YHWH's disfavor toward the Philistine people provides a resounding response to this question. There is no comedy here; the issues are deadly serious for Israel. No Israelite, listening to this narrative, could fail to draw the conclusion: YHWH was not compelled to go into exile from Israel; YHWH went into exile freely. While the Israelite listeners might rejoice at the Philistines' discomfiture, inevitably they must be disturbed by the question the narrative puts before them. If YHWH has freely departed from Israel, what does the future hold? What is the state of YHWH's relationship with Israel?

In 5:1-2, the term "the ark of God" is used; in 5:3-4, the term is "the ark of YHWH." This could reflect a growth in the text, with a factual tradition in vv. 1-2 and an interpretative tradition in vv. 3-4 (cf. Fohrer, "Ladeerzählung"). Alternatively, "ark of YHWH" could be used in vv. 3-4 because the direct confrontation with another god, Dagon, required the proper name of Israel's God. This could be accommodated within a single text or as a "stylistic expansion within a single literary unit" (Miller and Roberts, Hand of the Lord, 41).

The Philistines bring the ark to Ashdod and install it in Dagon's temple. After that, it is left in the care of the people of Ashdod. In the ancient Near East, it was normal that the captured symbol of a foreign god should be placed in the temple of the victors (see, for example, the Moabite stone, ANET, 320; Miller and Roberts, Hand of the Lord, 43; for a discussion of Assyrian practice, see Cogan, Imperialism and Religion, 22-34). The surprise in v. 2 is that the ark was placed "beside" Dagon ('ēṣel), instead of "before" him (lipnê), as might have been expected. The rabbis saw the problem. Rabbi Jonathan said that the Philistines did YHWH honor, placing a god beside a god. Rabbi Shimeon saw it as indicating submission, with the vanquished god placed in worship of the victor (Midrash Samuel, from Segal, "Studies," 424-25; cf. also Wünsche, Midrasch Samuel, 71). It is possible that the text literally sets the stage for what is to come; if Dagon is to fall forward "on his face," the ark could not be placed before the statue of Dagon. It is also possible that care was taken to set up a situation of contest and not of homage. Verses 3-4 present a "staging" problem: Dagon falls "on his face" (lĕpānāyw) both times and is prostrate "before the ark of YHWH" (lipnê) both times. This suggests the ark is somewhere to the front

72

of and at some distance from Dagon's statue. Accepting the text as a basis for performance, we can assume a storyteller's skill to make such actions as plausible as necessary.

The people of Ashdod rose early the next day *(wayyaškimû)*. In the context, the verb suggests eager anticipation of an outcome: hardly the case for a liturgical or cultic practice, but quite in order for a cultic contest — not of course the Philistines' intention, but certainly in the text! Dagon is found, fallen forward on the ground before the ark of YHWH — note the irony of worshipful language. But where the interpretation of divine action is concerned, whether in reality or in story, one must always consider the possibility of chance (cf. 1 Sam 6:9). So Dagon is restored to his place. The second phase unfolds: again the early rise, and again Dagon is found prostrate before YHWH. But this time, a further and definitive note is added: Dagon's head and his two hands, severed, were lying on the threshold; only his trunk was left on the ground. It is an image of defeat: Assyrian murals delight to display the piles of heads and hands being heaped before the victorious king. They can serve as trophies of victory: there are the heads of Goliath (1 Sam 17:54) and Saul (1 Sam 31: 9); or the grisly trophies of the Ugaritic goddess, Anath, under her, over her, and bound around her (cf. V AB, ii, 9-13, translated in *ANET,* 136). Headless and handless, Dagon is powerless to think or act (Budde, *Bücher Samuel,* 39). Beyond this, there is the symbolism of death, with the body fallen forward on the ground (Miller and Roberts, *Hand of the Lord,* 44-46). The symbolism is harsh but striking: the superiority of YHWH is established, beyond a shadow of doubt. In what is to come, the hand of YHWH will rest heavily on the Philistines (cf. 1 Sam 5:6, 7, 9, 11; 6:3, 5, 9); here the hand of Dagon has been rendered lifeless and powerless. The double defeat of Dagon in his temple parallels the narrative movement of the double defeat of Israel at Ebenezer-Aphek — and the outcome is equally significant. In Brueggemann's words, we have here "the decisive inversion that is at the heart of the entire narrative. . . . The only ground for understanding the reversal is to discern the distinctive character of Yahweh" (pp. 34-35).

The etiology in v. 5 supposedly derives the threshold-leaping practice of the priests of Dagon in Ashdod from this episode. Such practices are quite well known and would not be unique to this temple (cf. Zeph 1:8-9). It is likely that the point of including the etiology is not an antiquarian interest in the origin of the custom, but a desire to provide an apparent corroboration of the story of YHWH and Dagon.

YHWH's supremacy over Dagon has been demonstrated; headless and handless on his own temple floor, Dagon scarcely enjoys YHWH's favor. In vv. 6-12, attention turns from the Philistines' god to the Philistines themselves. The scene changes from the temple to the cities and their inhabitants. The actors change too. The "hand of YHWH" is now the predominant force (vv. 6, 7, 9, 11); its force is felt by the Philistines of Ashdod, Gath, and Ekron. Chapter 6 depicts a situation in which the plagues affected all five cities of the Philistine pentapolis — the other two were Gaza and Ashkelon (cf. 6:4, 17). At the level of the present text, the Philistines went to war, the Philistines captured the ark, and so the Philistines as a whole are responsible in ch. 6. Perhaps originally two different traditions were drawn on. Perhaps originally ch. 5 had its own view of the return of the ark: from Ashdod on the coast, inland to Gath, and then to Ekron in the direction of Beth-shemesh. On the other hand, ch. 6 may have had a longer stay in view (cf. 6:1) with more interest in the interpretation of the events than in their description.

The account is structured on the itinerary of the ark, with considerable repetition within the section for each of the three towns. Yet there is a progressive intensification as the narrative advances. The structure is similar in all three cases. With the coming of the ark to the city, there is a report of the affliction of the inhabitants by the hand of YHWH; then the reaction of the Philistine people. The structure is present in full at Ashdod. At Gath, the reaction of the people is very briefly treated. Convocations of the leaders of the Philistines are held at Ashdod and at Ekron, perhaps because they are the beginning and the end of the journey; at Gath, the ark is simply sent on its way (v. 10a). At Ekron, the report of the affliction is replaced by the people's complaint, which takes the imminent affliction for granted (v. 10b). The description of the affliction there is given by the narrator after the convocation (vv. 11b-12). The intensification is evident from a comparison of the two convocations: at Ashdod, the leaders are asked, "What shall we do with the ark?" (v. 8); at Ekron, they are told, "Send away the ark" (v. 11). The ark has become an intolerable burden to the Philistines.

Genre

In the overall structure of the narrative, this section functions as a reversal of fortune. In the opening scenes, the victims were Israel; here suddenly, the victims have become the Philistine god and the Philistines themselves. The first section (vv. 1-5) is an (→) account of the events in the temple of Dagon. What is recounted is best described as a combat of the gods. True, there is no description of weapons or battle; there are none of the gruesome details of the cosmogonic myths or the cyclic annual fertility rites (so, correctly, Schicklberger, *Ladeerzählungen,* 194). But the emblems or symbols of two gods are juxtaposed, and the issue of superiority between them is settled beyond all doubt. It is not set in the context of myth and mythic time; it is set in the context of historical events, although it takes place within the sacred space of a temple. The symbolism of combat is expressed through the images or cult objects of the respective gods, ark and statue; the outcome is determined when one falls helpless to the ground before the other, headless and handless. The account stands midway between those myths in which gods battle one another directly (cf. Isa 51:9) and the much less direct demonstrations of comparative power (cf. the Mt. Carmel confrontation, 1 Kgs 18:20-40). It would be scarcely correct to call this a combat of the gods story. It is reported, rather than told as a story. It is not a narrative of combat. It is an account of events that embody and symbolize a combat of the gods. It is eminently possible that the text could serve as a base for storytelling or is a summary of storytelling.

Similarly, the (→) accounts of the plagues in the Philistine cities are not narrated as stories and so do not really come under the category of plague stories. They provide a bare account of the events, structured around the itinerary of the ark from city to city, on its way toward Beth-shemesh. There is no attempt to tell a story, as in the Exodus where a demand is made and refused and then submission is enforced through the infliction of a plague, or in the desert wandering where disobedience will be portrayed and then punished by a plague. Here, there is the simple account of what happened, and what happened was a succession of plagues. As for the temple of Dagon episode, so here the text could serve as a base for some wonderful storytelling.

Setting

These disparate elements, with the etiology, have been brought together under the same rubric: the reversal of fortune that befell the Philistines and their god. There is practically nothing to point to specific settings in which they might have originated or been preserved. The period of the ark's "retirement" at Kiriath-jearim does not seem a likely time for their extensive propagation; more probable is the period after the ark had been brought to Jerusalem, and when its presence there was seen as a sign of God's blessing and approval for the Davidic monarchy. While there is nothing in the accounts to point to particular priestly interests, the custodians of the ark sanctuary would still be the most likely setting for the preservation of such traditions. The formation of the accounts will have been in close association with the composition of the Ark Narrative.

Meaning

This passage reflects the impact of the captured ark on Dagon, the Philistine god, and on the Philistine people. As noted at the start of the discussion, it responds to two questions. First, was Dagon the stronger god? The answer is negative, but the question had to be asked. Second, are the Philistines favored? Again the answer is negative, but again the question had to be asked.

5:1-5 demonstrate the patent superiority of YHWH over Dagon (see Delcor, "Jahweh et Dagon"). According to the ancient Near Eastern understanding, the defeats at Ebenezer were not merely military successes — the gods were also involved. Delcor quotes Pedersen with approval: wars between peoples were wars between gods (ibid., 143). For the Philistines, the position was clear: at Ebenezer-Aphek, on the field of battle, Dagon had triumphed over the mighty god of Israel. For the Israelites, two interpretations of the events were open: (1) YHWH, their god, had succumbed to the superior might of Dagon; (2) YHWH, their god, was himself responsible for their defeat. The narrative itself, with the question in 4:3, has already raised this second option; but the first, too, was not to be neglected (cf. Deut 32:26-27; 1 Kgs 20:22-30).

If YHWH was supremely and definitively victorious in Dagon's own temple, then he was hardly vanquished by Dagon on the distant field of battle. The juxtaposition of traditions forces the conclusion that YHWH, the God of Israel, was responsible for Israel's defeats at Ebenezer-Aphek, and for the capture and departure of the ark — the exile of his glory from Israel. Without the return of the ark and the events of 2 Sam 6, such a conclusion might have been unthinkable. In their traditions, however, Israel's theologians were not afraid to articulate the possibility that YHWH might forsake his people (cf. Exod 32:7-14; Num 14:11-23; Deut 9:7-29; Ezek 8-11; 20:13; see also Childs, *Exodus,* 567-68). Such reflection on the possibility of abandonment is the correlative of faith in God's unconditional commitment.

The meaning of the etiology, as noted, would most probably be to authenticate the story (cf. Miller and Roberts, *Hand of the Lord,* 46). The logic is that since the Philistines do indeed avoid treading on the threshold of the Ashdod temple, these events did indeed take place.

The account of the plagues and the ark's journey through the Philistine cities, inspiring deathly panic, removes any possibility of God's favor having been transferred from Israel to the Philistines. The ark of God did not depart in exile from Israel to reside among a newly chosen people, the Philistines. This much is clear; the future remains ahead. The glory *(kābôd)* that departed from Israel is echoed in the hand of YHWH which has been heavy (root: *KBD*) upon the Philistines (5:6, 11). This culminates in the subsequent Philistine recognition of their need to give glory *(kābôd)* to the god of Israel (6:5).

Textual Issues

Chapter 6   It would seem clear from 6:17-18 that traditions of a plague experience involving both tumors and mice were associated with the events of ch. 6, and perhaps also ch. 5. They are partially preserved in the MT and more fully in the LXX. Reconstruction of the process by which the two texts (MT and LXX) came to their present state is extremely difficult; fortunately it does not affect the sense of the chapter (cf. Driver, 60-61; Stoebe, 150-51; McCarter, 128-31; Pisano, 249-57). Again, as in ch. 5, it seems likely that numerous versions of these stories circulated, and that some of these variant options are either noted in the text or have contaminated it. Pisano refers to Schicklberger's complaint: "it is probably impossible to unravel the textual problems surrounding the tumors and mice in these two chapters" (p. 252). Pisano's own conclusion: "at least to a certain extent, the variations in Greek are explicable through editorial activity on the part of the Greek translator" (p. 256).

6:3 LXX and 4QSam^a have "ransomed/reconciled" (so McCarter, 129; Klein, 53-54). On the other hand, the MT's "it will be known to you why his hand does not turn away from you [RSV]" in 6:3 is consonant with the remarkable statement in 6:9, "then we shall know that it is not his hand that struck us; it happened to us by chance."

6:19 Like the case of Uzzah in 2 Sam 6:6-7, the event behind the text is highly mysterious. The possibility has to be envisaged that the LXX tried to provide an explanation for the basically inexplicable. Barthélemy appeals to the possibility of haggadah (p. 155); Driver comments, with British understatement, that "it is not possible to restore the text with entire certainty" (p. 58). McCarter opts for "the sons of the priests" (p. 131); Klein stays with the LXX's "the sons of Jeconiah" (p. 54). What all explanations must grapple with is why many should die for the infractions of few and/or why the ark should be sent away if the infractions can be identified.

Discussion

The passage is basically concerned with the implementation of the Philistines' demand: "Send away the ark of the God of Israel, and let it return to its own place, that it may not kill us and our people" (5:11). This demand is formulated with confident certainty that the deaths are due to the God of Israel. In ch. 6, this certainty is replaced by uncertainty (6:9). In the light of this replacement, the possibility suggested by the titles for the ark that 6:1–7:1 has taken the place of an earlier version gains a certain plausibility — it is not totally unthinkable (cf. Diachronic Dimension). 6:1 looks back on the ark's stay in Philistine territory as complete: seven months — a sacred number — [I.A]. 6:2 introduces the question of sending back the ark. So a new section is under way. Its ending is less clear. The ark's journey ends with v. 16 — [I.B]; the offering is part of the whole and involves vv. 17-18a; the "great stone" witnesses to the ark's return (v. 18b) — [I.C]. Verse 18 would make a good ending if the beginning of v. 19 were not so difficult and uncertain. As it is in the text, or as it is reconstructed, v. 19 can hardly begin anything. The present text is best followed through to 7:1 — [II].

Some see this passage as the weirder section of a crazy sequence: falling idols, ghastly plagues, soothsaying cows, and unexpected deaths that should push even the credulous into incredulity. Others marvel at the divine power revealed in these events, exploring the association of bubonic plague with tumors and mice. Many miss the intensely modern interest of the chapter: Was God responsible or was it chance? "And watch: if it goes up on the way to its own land, to Beth-shemesh, then it is he who has done us this great harm; but if not, then we shall know that it is not his hand that struck us: it happened to us by chance" (6:9). God or chance? Believers, atheist or theist, must ask this often. Only closed minds give quick answers.

The complexity of the chapter lies in its grappling with this unexpressed question. The two questions — "What shall we do with the ark?" and "Tell us what we should send with it to its place" — reflect the complexity of the unexpressed. It would have been easy to write: if we should send it back, tell us what we should send with it to its place. But that is not the text. The alternative expressed in 6:9, God or chance, suggests that behind the question "What shall we do with the ark?" lies the further question: What is going on with the ark; is the ark responsible for these catastrophes or is it chance?

The chapter is admirable as a summary of storytelling or a base for storytelling. The storyteller can focus the story on the journey of return or on the discernment by divination involving the journey, or on the accompanying guilt offering by which the Philistines give glory to the God of Israel (v. 5). The text avoids such clarity of focus and so leaves the way open to a variety of stories that can be developed from it.

The consultation involves priests and diviners. If these are Philistines, in vv. (3-4) 5-6 they show a remarkable capacity for distancing themselves from their clients; in v. 9, solidarity returns. There may be traditio-historical growth in the text. Leonhard Rost avoided the problem by omitting 6:5-9 from his text; the reasons do not appear convincing (cf. Rost, *Succession,* 12; against his view, Campbell, *Ark Narrative,* 166-68; Miller and Roberts, *Hand of the Lord,* 103-4). Two questions are asked: what to do with the ark and what to send it back with.

The diviners take up the second question first: the issue of the offering that is to accompany the ark (vv. 3-6). The offering is characterized as an 'āšām, an offering made in reparation for the profanation of the sacred (cf. Anderson, "Sacrifice," 880-81, for the reparation offering within the P system). Later understandings of the 'āšām offering need not be true of this Samuel text; the meaning of such terms can vary with time. Clearly, reparation is involved; as the tumors and mice are associated with God's punishment, their images in gold are intended as appeasement of God's anger. For the issues of reparation or restitution, see the prayer of the Hittite sovereign Mursilis (*ANET,* 394-96; Campbell, *Ark Narrative,* 103, n. 2; Miller and Roberts, *Hand of the Lord,* 52-54, also 56). The Samuel text is remarkable. There is no certainty available; only when the cure is experienced will the Philistines know that the remedy was right (v. 3b, MT). The extent of the reversal is evident in the diviners' exhortation: "give glory to the God of Israel" (v. 5a). Instead of certainty, there is hope ("perhaps," v. 5b) and the lesson of history (v. 6). Twice now in this narrative there has been reference to the exodus (4:8b; 6:6).

Concerning the ark, the first question, the diviners answer indirectly by a series of instructions that set up a divination procedure to discern whether what has happened was from God or by chance (vv. 7-9). Verse 9 does not transform a simple journey home into a discernment by divination. New cart or not, untrained cows with their calves tied up back home were never going to provide a simple journey home.

The instructions for this divination, structured on the actions to be performed, are expressed predominantly with verbs in the perfect tense, 2nd masculine plural. The sequence begins with a pair of imperatives: "take" relating to both cart and cows, and "make" relating just to the cart. At the end of v. 8a, however, there is a change of word order and a verb in the imperfect tense, 2nd masculine plural ("and put in a box at its side" etc.); otherwise, differing forms are in subordinate clauses. The change in syntax may be a signal indicating an addition. In the execution of the instructions, the offering is mentioned only in v. 11b, with both the ark and the box (or pouch, cf. McCarter, 135) subsumed under the one verb. We, the audience, may be being told that the offering has been blended into a text that previously was concerned only with the journey and divination. A storyteller may be being alerted to variations in the way the story can be told. It could be told with full incorporation of the *'āšām* offering, or with partial or implied reference to the offering, or with no reference to the offering at all. In this last case, the traditions of vv. 2b-6, 11b, and 17-18a would offer a variant version that need not be utilized. The variant tradition would account for the differences of involvement and concern; for example, in v. 3b, the concern is to know *why* his hand has not turned from *you;* in v. 9, it is to know *who* has done this evil to *us.*

The compliance with the diviners' instructions (vv. 10-16) does not recount the carrying out of the instructions for the accompanying offering (vv. 3-6); it is concerned with the journey of the ark and its reception in Beth-shemesh. In vv. 10-11, the text moves from the general ("the men did so") to the particular details. In vv. 14-16, there is a similar move from the impersonal (v. 14) to the personal (vv. 15-16) — possibly with greater implications for meaning. The cart stops the journey in the field of Joshua (v. 14a); the cart is chopped up and the cows offered in sacrifice (v. 14b). The destruction of the cart and the sacrifice of the cows symbolize a definitive end to the journey; the ark will wander no more. The event is narrated impersonally — no one is given the credit beyond "they." Verses 15-16 allocate the various roles: the Levites unloaded the ark and the offering; the people of Beth-shemesh offered the sacrifice; the Philistine leaders observed to the end and then returned home to Ekron. It is puzzling why the Levites should be mentioned here and nowhere else in the chapters concerned with the ark; v. 15 may have had the role of expressing with precision what a later age saw as implicit in v. 14. The Philistine leaders had accompanied the ark in v. 12; it may have been felt necessary for them to stay until the journey's definitive end had been celebrated.

The two entries in the list of the offering have a common structure. There is an identification of the objects constituting the entry, followed by their enumeration. The enumeration of the mice presumes a larger number than specified in 6:4, reflecting something of the complexity of these traditions. The stone was resting place to the ark and so is witness to the journey's end. With 6:1, it brackets the story.

The story of the ark's return could end with 6:18. But the text does not end there. Somehow, the story of the ark's return is not complete without reference to what happened to it and why. A story that ended with v. 18 would have a happy ending. God went into exile but God returned; we rejoice. Verse 19 disposes of any happy ending.

The text of 6:19 defies satisfactory reconstruction; no reconstruction should eliminate its mystery. Some texts are not for sanitizing. As a beginning, it is inadequate: it has no subject. As a logical statement, it is inadequate: the reason given for the disaster is not appropriate. The MT, literally translated, reads: because they looked at the ark; it provides no cause for the slaughter. The RSV rendering (NRSV margin) "because they looked *into* the ark" is unique to this occasion, trying to provide a reason. The NRSV and others reconstruct from the LXX: "The descendants of Jeconiah did not rejoice with the inhabitants of Beth-shemesh when they greeted the ark of the LORD." The difficulty with any rendering that makes the disaster intelligible is that it then nullifies the question in v. 20: "Who is able to stand before the LORD, this holy God?" The traditional liturgical reply is given in Psalm 15. If the answer is clear — those can stand before the ark who keep the liturgical or cultic rules about not looking into the ark or who have an appropriately worshipful attitude — then it would be the height of stupidity to banish the ark to Kiriath-jearim. But the ark is banished and the text is not about stupidity. With unintelligibility and mystery preserved, it becomes clear that the ark is not yet the occasion for blessing in Israel; it is dangerous to have it around. What cries out for explanation is the fact that the text includes so negative an episode in what is otherwise so positive a story for Israel. There has been a "great slaughter" (6:19); the last "great slaughter" we heard of was suffered by Israel in the second battle at Ebenezer-Aphek (4:10).

The MT has an alternation of subjects which is noteworthy (he — people — inhabitants): first "he struck" among the inhabitants of Beth-shemesh *('anšê bêt šemeš),* then among the people *(hā-'ām);* then the people mourn because of the slaughter among the people, and finally the inhabitants of Beth-shemesh raise the question of who can stand before this God. There may be more than one tradition behind this obscure episode. As it stands, the move may reflect a desire to extend the impact to the whole people. The mourning needs to have national perspective; the decision about the ark is local, because it is in Beth-shemesh. The cruel irony for the Israelites is unmistakable; they are as terrified before the afflicting hand of the Lord as the Philistines were (cf. 4:8 and 5:1-12). "To whom shall it go?" (6:20 = Where can we send it?) echoes the Philistines throughout 5:6-12. It is an ominous question now in Israel.

Nothing is said of why Kiriath-jearim should have been selected, or why its inhabitants should have accepted the ark. Speculation on the Philistines' motives or on the town's political affiliations is not part of the text's horizon. The ark was sent there, and there it remained in "cold storage" (Hertzberg, 61). The need for a man to be consecrated for the occasion, as the guardian of the ark *(lišmōr),* emphasizes that Kiriath-jearim was not a regular sanctuary with an established and functioning priesthood. The text is terse in the extreme — and should be left that way.

Genre

The material in 6:1-18 is on the borderline between (→) account and (→) story. The questions raised by the Philistines and the nature of the divination process used in their resolution create something like the semblance of a plot. But the text does not exploit the opportunity; instead, it remains at the level of simple recounting. As a base or summary, it is probably closer to a story than an account; it provides traditions of value to both genres.

A number of genres occur as elements in the text. Within the consultation, the answers are given as (→) instruction, here given by the Philistine priests. In vv. 7-9, the instruction concerns the carrying out of a (→) ritual; in vv. 17-18a, the text involved with the carrying out of the instruction comprises a (→) list of the items in the offering. Verse 18b is a (→) notice.

6:19–7:1, on the other hand, is an (→) account of the disaster and the consequences that followed it. It deals with a largely inexplicable outbreak of sudden death. What is certain and of central significance in the account is that sudden death occurred, in connection with the ark, of such magnitude that the people of Beth-shemesh wanted to be rid of it. There is no story, just the account of the episode and the consequences that followed it.

Setting

As a single text, concerned for the discernment of God's will by ritual divination, interest in the accompanying *'āšām* offering, and technical details of language and style make it likely that this account of divination and return was preserved in priestly circles, presumably those responsible for the care of the ark. Whether such circles existed before the installation of the ark in Jerusalem and whether they would have formulated the traditions of the ark while it was still on the isolated periphery of Israel are issues still open to reflection.

Meaning

Two questions are involved in the meaning of the passage. First, where is home for the ark? The divination journey, drawn by the two untrained cows, says clearly: home is Israel. Second, can we go on as we were? The slaughter says clearly: we cannot. The narrative thus far leaves us with questions, just as it opened with a question. We are left with the questions: "Who is able to stand before the LORD, this holy God? To whom shall he go from us?" (6:20; the NRSV's "so that we may be rid of him" is an unduly interpretative rendering). The immediate answer is: to Kiriath-jearim. As a long-term answer, that is the equivalent of abandonment. The long-term answer is provided in 2 Sam 6: the ark will go to David's Jerusalem. 2 Sam 6 also answers the question with which the entire narrative began: "Why has the LORD put us to rout today before the

Philistines?" (1 Sam 4:3). From the end-point of the ark's coming to Jerusalem we can see that the answer is: because God left the Israel of old, symbolized by Shiloh, in order to return to the new Israel, symbolized by Jerusalem. All that has taken place in between has been God's will, God's power and purpose at work in Israel. These aspects need to be seen from the point of view of 2 Sam 6.

The symbolism of the divination journey cannot be ignored. Although the text is couched in terms of Beth-shemesh or not (6:9), such a journey is in itself open to any direction. The direction taken is understood to be under the control of the god — and, here, the direction taken is back to Israel. Other forms of divination might have been employed which would not have had the expressive symbolism of the journey. But in the divination journey, the ark is placed on the wagon and, against all the natural forces, is driven by divine directive toward Israel. Over and above the issue of responsibility (God or chance), another issue is clear: the tradition expresses the free initiative of YHWH in the return of the ark to Israel. In short: the ark was not carried back by Philistines or Israelites — it came back.

The questions and traditions concerning the accompanying 'āšām offering display a different concern, and their inclusion relates to a different issue. They are concerned with the reparation to be made for offense given: not simply with the return of the ark, but with the honor of its god. And so, the Philistines are exhorted to give glory to the god of Israel; it is against this that they are not to harden their hearts. Even the mighty Philistines had to give glory to YHWH. The two great powers that had afflicted Israel, Egypt and Philistia (cf. Amos 3:9, MT), are coupled in giving glory to the God of Israel.

The list of tumors and mice and the reference to the stone, still standing as a witness, authenticate what has been said.

The implications of the concluding account (6:19–7:1), and its inclusion in the text, would appear to go beyond the simple demonstration that Israel is no more immune from the awesome power of its God than were the Philistines. The return to Israel was definitive; the ark was portrayed as home to stay. Yet its presence provoked a great slaughter among the people. The disaster has the same effect as the affliction of the Philistines, although death is specifically mentioned there only in 5:10-12. Wherever the figure of 50,000 dead was introduced from, it depicts a catastrophe far worse than the defeats at Ebenezer-Aphek (ch. 4). It is a counsel of despair to dismiss it as an independent tradition, a passage that does not cohere with the present context (cf. Schicklberger, *Ladeerzählungen*, 123-28; Stoebe, 153). "This small episode puts Israel on notice that Yahweh is no more easily at home in Israel than in Philistia" (Brueggemann, 43).

The ark does not return to the mainstream of Israel's religious life and history. It is put aside and left in a cultic backwater. One may invoke the political influence of the Philistines — but the narrative does not. The disaster at Beth-shemesh expresses the conviction that the ark's return to Israel does not imply Israel's return to YHWH's favor. The ark is relegated to the obscurity of "the house of Abinadab on the hill" in Kiriath-jearim. It is not just a fractious family that is chastised (Jeconiah), or a frontier village that is frightened (Beth-shemesh). It is the people of Israel who are depicted as deprived of a central symbol of the traditional and liturgical presence of their God (cf. Ps 78:59-69). The ark has departed from the national scene.

Bibliography of Works Cited Above

Anderson, Gary A. "Sacrifice and Sacrificial Offerings: Old Testament." Pp. 870-86 in *ABD*. Vol. 5.

ANET. Ancient Near Eastern Texts Relating to the Old Testament. 3rd ed. with Supplement. Edited by James B. Pritchard. Princeton: Princeton University Press, 1969.

Budde, Karl. *Die Bücher Samuel*. KHC 8. Tübingen: Mohr, 1902.

Campbell, Antony F. *The Ark Narrative (1 Sam 4–6; 2 Sam 6): A Form-Critical and Tradition-Historical Study*. SBLDS 16. Missoula: Scholars Press, 1975.

————. "Yahweh and the Ark: A Case Study in Narrative." *JBL* 98 (1979) 31-43.

Childs, Brevard S. *Exodus*. London: SCM, 1974.

Cogan, Morton. *Imperialism and Religion: Assyria, Judah and Israel in the Eighth and Seventh Centuries B.C.E.* SBLMS 19. Missoula: Scholars Press, 1974.

Delcor, M. "Jahweh et Dagon: Ou le Jahwisme face à la religion des Philistins, d'après 1 Sam. v." *VT* 14 (1964) 136-54.

Fohrer. Georg. "Die alttestamentliche Ladeerzählung." *JNSL* 1 (1971) 23-31.

Gitay, Yehoshua. "Reflection on the Poetics of the Samuel Narrative: The Question of the Ark Narrative." *CBQ* 54 (1992) 221-30.

Johnson, Robert A. *We: Understanding the Psychology of Romantic Love*. New York: Harper & Row, 1983. UK paperback publication used here, *The Psychology of Romantic Love*. London: Arkana, 1987.

Miller, Patrick D., Jr., and J. J. M. Roberts. *The Hand of the Lord: A Reassessment of the "Ark Narrative" of 1 Samuel*. Baltimore: The Johns Hopkins University Press, 1977.

Na'aman, Nadav. "The Pre-Deuteronomistic Story of King Saul and Its Historical Significance." *CBQ* 54 (1992) 638-58.

Noth, Martin. *The Deuteronomistic History*. 2nd ed. JSOTSup 15. Sheffield: Sheffield Academic Press, 1991. German original: 1943.

Rost, Leonhard. *The Succession to the Throne of David*. Sheffield: Almond, 1982. German original: 1926.

Schicklberger, Franz. *Die Ladeerzählungen des ersten Samuel-Buches: Eine literaturwissenschaftliche und theologiegeschichtliche Untersuchung*. FB 7. Würzburg: Echter, 1973.

Segal, M. H. "Studies in the Books of Samuel. IV: Ancient Jewish Exegesis and Modern Criticism." *JQR* 10 (1910) 421-33.

Van der Toorn, Karel, and Cees Houtman. "David and the Ark." *JBL* 113 (1994) 209-31.

Wünsche, August. *Aus Israels Lehrhallen*. Vol. 5: *Der Midrasch Samuel; Kleine Midraschim: Neue Pesikta und Midrasch Tadsche*. Hildesheim: Georg Olms, 1967.

Chapter 4

THE EMERGENCE OF THE MONARCHY: THE ARRIVAL OF SAUL AND THE NEW INSTITUTION OF MONARCHY (1 Samuel 7–12)

With Samuel on the national scene and the ark off the national scene, it is high time that something happened and that Samuel was at its center. The text will not disappoint us. In the next six chapters, Samuel is given several major roles, without conflict with his fundamental identity as prophet. The roles are intercessor (involving deliverance), intermediary between people and God, anointer of a king-designate, kingmaker, and national adjudicator. At the center of all this, Samuel is portrayed presiding over the emergence in Israel of a new form of central government: the monarchy. Despite some potential independence, the chapters form a loose, rather entangled unity. 8:1 and 9:1 could begin independent stories, but both stories require the continuation provided in 10:17ff. and 11:1ff., respectively; so they are entangled. The tradition in 7:5-14 could have been independent, but 7:15-17 now leads smoothly into 8:1ff. 12:1-25 needs the gathering at Gilgal. So there is a unity, and the whole is best looked at before the parts are examined in detail. The key that holds the composition together is the prophet Samuel, portrayed as the central figure of importance within Israel.

Monarchy erupted into Israel's life as a new phenomenon with widespread and deep impact. Israel's experience was in complete contrast with that of Mesopotamia, for example, where kingship had been a constant feature of society, as the Sumerian King List attests: "When kingship was lowered from heaven, kingship was (first) in Eridu. (In) Eridu, A-lulim (became) king and ruled 28,800 years. Alalgar ruled 36,000 years. Two kings (thus) ruled it for 64,800 years. . . . These are five cities, eight kings ruled them for 241,000 years. (Then) the Flood swept over (the earth)" (*ANET,* 265).

As an institution, monarchy was new in Israel. The one previous attempt had been a failure, Abimelech (Judg 9). According to the biblical account, at the beginning Israel was ruled by Moses. The transition to Joshua was smooth. After Joshua, the transition failed; the narrative offers no successor and "another generation grew up . . . who did not know the LORD or the work that he had done for Israel" (Judg 2:10). The pattern built into the narrative from this point has Israel do evil, suffer oppression, cry out to God, and be saved by a deliverer figure, called also a judge, who subdued the oppressor and gave quiet to the land for a generation. The picture is essentially cyclic, with apostasy followed by long periods of oppression — 18 years under Moab, 20 years under the Canaanites, 40 years under the Philistines — followed by deliverance and quiet for a generation.

Within 1 Sam 7–12, the initial chapter portrays Samuel as the intercessor for a repentant Israel; but early he is named as judge (7:6b) and it concludes with his activity as judge (7:15-17). The transition to his sons as national judges is portrayed as a failure. To replace them, Samuel is portrayed presiding over national processes by which the institution of monarchy is inaugurated in Israel. In his final role as adjudicator to "all Israel" (12:1), Samuel is portrayed remonstrating with the willfulness of the people and laying down constitutional guidelines for the successful operation of the new institution. In all of this, we have to say "is portrayed"; the text is complex and has come under many influences. We cannot hope to recover what actually happened; it is important to recognize what is actually said.

Conventional wisdom would have had it that establishing the monarchy was the high point of Samuel's career. Within in the books of Samuel, and possibly within the biblical text overall, the establishment of the monarchy is an important step along the way to the anointing of David as future king of Israel. I believe it is right to say that the anointing of David is presented in the books of Samuel as the high point of Samuel's career and the task for which he was elevated to be prophet to all Israel.

Interpretation of a complex text has been influenced by the experience of other biblical text. The success of source theory in the Pentateuch led to a perception of two sources in 1 Sam 7–12, one favoring monarchy and the other opposed to it. Alternative thinking suggested rather one stream openly favoring monarchy and the other advocating a more nuanced view. The hypothesis of an exilic Deuteronomistic History (DH) led to the belief that the basic trend would have been opposed to monarchy, supported by the conviction either that prophets opposed kings or that dtr circles opposed the monarchy. But because Samuel, as prophet and God's instrument, anointed Saul and David, there are complications within the approach assuming *prophetic* hostility. With the advance of the view that the DH was first composed before the exile, favoring a reform movement headed by King Josiah, there are further complications within the approach assuming fundamental *dtr* hostility. (For a wonderfully detailed and instructive assessment of the moves from Wellhausen to the late 1960s, see Langlamet, "Les récits.")

Our present task is to assess the text as accurately as we are able. The overall structure may be represented as follows.

Samuel's Establishment of the New Institution of Monarchy	7:2–12:25
I. Samuel as intercessor for repentant Israel	7:2-17
A. Israel's repentance of apostasy before Samuel	2-6
B. Israel's deliverance from Philistine threat: Samuel as intercessor	7-14
C. Samuel's subsequent activities	15-17
II. Samuel as intermediary, anointer, and kingmaker	8:1–11:15
A. The initiatives regarding a king	8:1–10:16
1. By popular demand (justice): Samuel as intermediary	8:1-22
2. By divine command (defense): Samuel as anointer	9:1–10:16
B. The outcomes regarding a king	10:17–11:15
1. Of popular demand: Samuel as kingmaker	10:17-27
2. Of divine command: Samuel as kingmaker	11:1-15
III. Samuel as adjudicator for "all Israel"	12:1-25
A. Assessment of Samuel's credentials	1-5
B. Assessment of Israel's present situation: evil but not hopeless	6-18
C. Assessment of Israel's future: hopeful but not threat free	19-25

Anyone familiar with the Samuel text will know at once that this broadly sketched overview has not highlighted the vociferous objections to the monarchy. They are present under the "evil but not hopeless" of ch. 12. They are also expressed emphatically in 8:7-21 and 10:18-19. They will be assessed in the detailed discussion; they cannot be adequately represented at the level of this overview. Similarly, the careful and correct repetition of the phrase "Samuel as kingmaker" (II.B.1 and B.2) is a pointer to duality, complexity, and composition in the text.

Before the big picture of the total composition can be discussed, it will be important first to assess the component elements (compare with McCarthy, "Inauguration"). There are six; four might be called "assembly" scenes, and two may be termed "prophetic." The four "assembly" scenes are 7:2-17 at Mizpah — [I], 8:1-22 at Ramah — [II.A.1], 10:17-25 at Mizpah again — [II.B.1], and 12:1-25 presumably at Gilgal — [III]. The two "prophetic" scenes are 9:1–10:16 — [II.A.2] and 11:1-15 — [II.B.2]. The terms "assembly" and "prophetic" are not chosen for their precision. The assembly in 7:2-17 hardly lasts beyond v. 6 and the prophetic in 11:1-15 hardly begins before v. 14; however, they can serve suitably as identification markers.

The monarchy was of immense significance to Israel in many ways; it was seen differently at different times by different groups. Under God, some saw it as Israel's hope of salvation, others as the seeds of Israel's destruction. These chapters portraying the establishment of the new institution of monarchy have been worked over by many of these groups at different times. As the detailed discussion will show, the chapters do not present a unified literary text. Some may have been reported stories and have served as the base for storytelling; others probably not. As they stand now, they are less the base for storytelling than the base for political and theological discussion. A modern analogy may well be the platforms of the Democratic and Republican parties in American presidential elections. As one presidential hopeful said of his party's platform: I am not bound by it and I have not read it. Such pronouncements do not stop the most intense engagement by those involved in writing the platforms. Similarly, the kings of Israel hardly pondered 1 Sam 7–12, but theologians and thinkers in Israel certainly did — and the text bears the marks of their involvement. Rather than a flowing text, these chapters present a variety of views, both for and against the monarchy, expressing different traditions of its origins in Israel. A broadly sketched overview highlights the basic flow of the narrative; the differing versions and contradictory opinions will be brought out in the discussion.

We can review the narrative appropriately if we focus Samuel's roles on three areas: intercessor, kingmaker, and adjudicator. Brief reflection on these roles will help. In their own way, they reflect the multiple roles gathered around the figure of Moses.

Samuel's role as the intercessor who delivers repentant Israel (1 Sam 7:2-17) needs to be viewed against the background of Judg 3–9 (see below). In this role, Samuel is closest to the figure of Deborah who is both prophet and judge in Israel before becoming engaged in the deliverance of Israel. Like Moses, Deborah is also a judge of the law, involved in settling issues Israelites brought for litigation (cf. Exod 18:13-27; Judg 4:5). This judicial role falls to Samuel in 7:15-17. Moses, of course, is an intercessor in Israel and deliverer par excellence, but the pattern imposed in Judg 3–9 does not apply either to Moses or Samuel. For Samuel, the *events* can be seen as similar; the *texts* are not (see below).

The kingmaker role is unheralded in Israel. No one had made kings in Israel before. Again, however, it is a Mosaic role. Moses stood before God and gave guidance to Israel about "the way they are to go and the things they are to do" (Exod 18:20; cf. 25:22). Throughout chs. 8–11, God is the guiding power, mediated by Samuel. God instructs Samuel to comply with the people's request (8:7a, 9, 22a), God identifies Saul and orders Samuel to anoint him (9:16-17), God operates through the divination processes of lot and oracle (10:20-24), Samuel is brought into Saul's action (11:7a), and it is "the dread of the LORD" that rallies the people behind Saul in the liberation of Jabesh-gilead (11:7b). As God's intermediary, Samuel is in the line of Moses (cf. Deut 18:15-19).

There is no such office in Israel as a national adjudicator. With the possible exception of Josh 24, there is no text elsewhere comparable with 1 Sam 12 unless we reckon with the book of Deuteronomy. Deuteronomy presents itself as the words of Moses to "all Israel" (Deut 1:1) at the end of his life, reminding them of their past and giving guidance as to how they must live in the future. Here too the aged Samuel is in the line of Moses. As these parallels unfold, the conjunction of Moses and Samuel as intermediaries before God becomes highly intelligible (cf. Jer 15:1).

It is important to look closely at the traditions involved in these chapters. According to the canons of Hebrew narrative, a new tradition clearly begins with 9:1. The full introduction with patronymics for Kish and the identification of his son, Saul, marks a new beginning in the narrative. In what follows it, as far as 10:16, there is no mention of apostasy on Israel's part; there is, however, mention of Philistine oppression and Israelite outcry (9:16). On the other hand, 7:2 also offers a new beginning, using terminology that is unlikely to be early. It introduces traditions of Israel's conversion from apostasy and of Samuel's elimination of the Philistine threat for his lifetime.

After ch. 7, there is the well-known issue of Israel's dissatisfaction with Samuel's sons and the demand for a king, a demand that is characterized by God as rejection: "they have rejected me from being king over them" (8:7). The contrast with 9:1–10:16 is evident.

The careful combination of contrasting traditions has long been recognized here. Numerous ways of accounting for this combination have been advanced. The acceptance of a Josianic DH allows for a relatively simple and satisfactory proposal (cf. Campbell and O'Brien, *Unfolding*). A DH composed in support of Josiah's reform had every reason to present the monarchy as God's gift to Israel, an institution enabling a good king to shape a faithful people, committed to their God. The traditions in 1 Sam 9:1–10:16 and 11:1-11, 15 adequately depict the emergence of that institution.

With Josiah's death and the failure of the reform, a revision of the DH was necessary. One point of focus was the impact of the evil kings (the "royal" focus); a second point of focus was the complicity of the people and the failure of fidelity (the "national" focus). The presence here of the traditions in 1 Sam 7:2–8:22 and 10:17-25 can make a lot of sense if their insertion is attributed to this post-Josianic revision of the DH.

To facilitate access to the present text, identifications can be noted here and then need not be treated extensively until the end of the section. The first point, to be heard loudly and clearly, is that the basic material used in this revision need not have been — and probably was not — composed at the time of the revision itself. On grounds of language, narrative independence, etc., it is probable that an alternative view of the emergence of monarchy in Israel was in circulation among those opposed to kings. Good reasons for such opposition were plentiful. What is suggested here is that the editors revising the DH had this material to hand and made good use of it.

The revision needed to make two moves. The justification for kingship on grounds of external (Philistine) threat had to be canceled out. The Samuel tradition of ch. 7 met that need. The perception of kingship as a gracious gift from God had to be opposed. The tradition of ch. 8 did that. By placing the bulk of these traditions in front of 9:1, leaving only 10:17-25 to follow, the revising editors skillfully introduced a competing understanding of the emergence of monarchy in Israel. A few touches were added here and there to highlight the picture, but the basic themes had been put in place.

The highlights are simple enough. The "royal" focus of revision was probably responsible for heightening Samuel's opposition to Israel's demand, his appeal to God, and God's warning to the people (cf. 8:7-21). The diatribe against royal demands (vv. 11-17) is likely to have been independent; it does not correlate with the complaint of the elders or the concerns of the surrounding context. It is not improbable that 10:25 comes from this "royal" focus of the revision.

The "national" focus of the DH revision was concerned with the people's apostasy and their failure in fidelity to the law of God. Its touches can be identified by these concerns and by the language used. As is clear, Samuel's address in 7:3 and Israel's actions in 7:4 precede the convening of the nation at Mizpah for a ceremony of repentance (7:5-6). Verse 6 admits to guilt: "We have sinned against the LORD." Samuel's address in v. 3 particularizes the sin as apostasy; the report of Israel's conversion in v. 4 admits it, naming the gods as "the Baals and the Astartes." Attribution of vv. 3-4 to the "national" focus of revision is likely. In 8:7b-8a, the intensification of the people's rejection of YHWH their god — by tracing rejection back to the exodus and including apostasy and the worship of foreign gods — bears all the marks of the "national" focus of revision. The same can be said of 8:18, with its focus on the people — their cry, their king, their choice, and their prayer being unheard. The theme of 8:7b-8a, popular rejection since the exodus, recurs in 10:18-19. The same "national" focus is probably responsible.

These editorial revisions to the DH do not so much provide a coherent text in 1 Sam 7–12; they provide alternatives to one account of the origin of kingship in Israel. Rather than a divine response to Israel's oppression by the Philistines, alternatives portray kingship in various possible guises: preceded by apostasy, unnecessary because Samuel's intercession had successfully eliminated the Philistine threat, triggered by injustice in Israel (Samuel's sons), undesirable because involving rejection of YHWH and relapse into apostasy.

The individual building blocks demand attention in detail. Discussion of the overall composition will be left until the end, after these components have been examined.

Samuel as Intercessor: Judge, Intercessor, Judge	**7:2-17**
I. Samuel as judge: presides over Israel's repentance	2-6
A. Initial situation	2-3
1. Lament: by all the house of Israel	2
2. Response by Samuel: to all the house of Israel	3
B. Repentance of people of Israel	4-6a
1. General: conversion of people	4
2. Special: repentance ceremony at Mizpah	5-6a
C. Activity of Samuel: judge	6b
II. Samuel as intercessor: Philistines subdued	7-14
A. Philistine threat	7
1. Philistine muster in response to Israel's gathering	7a
2. Israel's fear in response to Philistine muster	7b
B. Philistine defeat	8-12
1. Samuel's intercession	8-9
2. God's intervention	10
3. Israel's victory	11-12
C. Extent of Philistine defeat	13-14
1. In time: all the days of Samuel	13

Textual Issues

7:2 The key issue in the verse is the activity attributed to Israel. The root *NHH* is used as a verb in Mic 2:4 and Ezek 32:18 (both qal; niphal here only); as a substantive, it is found in Amos 5:16; Mic 2:4; Jer 9:10, 17, 18, 19; Ezek 27:32. There it refers to lamentation following death or disaster, a meaning that can be accepted here (with Stoebe, 168; Klein, 64). However even Barthélemy advocates caution (p. 158). Certainly there is nothing to suggest dtr usage.

The phrase, "all the house of Israel," is unlikely to be early. It occurs ten times in Ezekiel, twice here, twice in 2 Sam 6, twice in Jeremiah, and otherwise in Exod 40:38; Lev 10:6; and Num 20:29.

Discussion

The understanding of this chapter is muddied by the many roles given Samuel in these traditions. For ch. 7, Samuel's dominant role is expressed in vv. 8-9: it is intercession. The outcome of his intercession is Israel's deliverance by YHWH — [II]. A forerunner to that intercession is his role as judge (v. 6b — whatever precisely it may mean), presiding over the ceremony of Israel's repentance — [I]. A follow-up to his intercession and the deliverance of Israel is the peace in which Samuel's days are spent as judge in Israel, on circuit and at home (vv. 15-17) — [III]. If there is a dominant image of Samuel in this chapter, it is that of intercessor for Israel. "Judging" opens and closes the chapter; deliverance from the Philistines is central to it. That deliverance is achieved by Samuel's intercession; but it is YHWH who is the deliverer, who "thundered with a mighty voice that day" and routed the confused Philistines before Israel (cf. 7:10). Samuel is cast in the role of intercessor, as were Abraham (cf. Gen 18:17-32) and Moses (cf. Exod 32:7-14; Num 14:10b-25).

The concern with the ark is completed in 7:1; it has been taken to Kiriath-jearim and installed in the house of Abinadab, and Eleazar has been consecrated to have charge of it. Any Israelite theologian knew that it would be staying there for a while. It is possible that 7:2aα ("From the day that the ark was lodged at Kiriath-jearim, a long time passed") was once a coda to the ark narrative, offering a bridge to 2 Sam 6:2; if it was once a coda, it no longer has that function in the present text. The "twenty years" can be calculated from the 40 of Judg 13:1 and the 20 of Judg 15:20 and 16:31; alternatively, the 20 years of Judg 15:20 and 16:31 can be calculated from the 40 of Judg 13:1 and the 20 here in 1 Sam 7:2. Certainty is out of the question.

In the present text 7:2a has been blended with 7:2b to form the introduction to a new section of text, opening with Israel's reaction to the loss of the ark. The activity is best understood as lamentation (see "textual issues" above); the subject is "all the house of Israel" — a phrase that is unlikely to be early.

Samuel's address is directed to "all the house of Israel," named as such here for the last time; vv. 4 and 6 have "people of Israel" and v. 5 has "all Israel." Samuel's general address (v. 3) indicates what Israel must do. Conversion involves the elimination of foreign gods and an exclusive commitment to YHWH. The reference to deliverance from the Philistines (v. 3) links into what is to come and correlates well with the absence of the ark. Philistine power was evident in ch. 4; Philistine oppression can be traced back to Judg 13:1. A general response is reported in 7:4, before Samuel summons all Israel to Mizpah for a ceremony of repentance, involving libation, fast, and confession of sin.

In its context, the comment in v. 6b that "Samuel judged the people of Israel at Mizpah" must find its reference somehow in this ceremony of repentance. The role given Samuel in these verses is to set Israel on a right course; apostasy is implied and sin is admitted. Samuel presides over this action of Israel's repentance. His presidency is described as "judging" at Mizpah. There is no clear precedent for such activity to be described as judging. An echo may well be heard of the deliverer-judges in the preceding book; it is no more than an echo.

For Noth, the great Samuel was the last of the deliverer-judges. "Dtr. introduces Samuel as a 'judge' in the sense of the book of Judges" and in relation to 7:17; "for Dtr. this is the end of the last 'judges' story" (*DH*, 78 and 80). In this he was followed by Hertzberg (pp. 66, 70, 130). Subsequent commentators have been alert both to the similarity of the events to those in Judg 3–9 and to the dissimilarity of the texts (cf. Stoebe, 171-75; McCarter, 16-17, 19, 143, 150; Klein, 67, 70). As will be explored in detail below, while Samuel is called a judge in 7:6 and while as intercessor he brings about Israel's deliverance from the Philistine threat, the total text bears no resemblance to the patterns that are central to Judg 3–9.

The patterns in Judg 3–9 are relatively easily recovered (see in particular the table "Patterns and Judges" at the end of Campbell and O'Brien, *Unfolding*). Basically, Israel commits evil (three times specified as apostasy), God's anger is kindled, Israel is delivered over to oppressors, Israel cries out to God, God raises up a deliverer-judge, the oppressor is subdued before Israel, and the land was undisturbed for a generation. It is clear that an account of *the events* of 1 Sam 7 can be constructed to fit the basics of such a pattern. It is equally clear that *the text* of 1 Sam 7 does not fit the pattern of Judg 3–9.

Where the events are concerned: there has been apostasy; there has been oppression; there is repentance; Samuel achieves deliverance; the oppressor is subdued; there is peace for Samuel's generation.

Where the text of 1 Sam 7:2-17 is concerned, there is no statement of Israel's apostasy/evil (as for Judg 2:11; 3:7, 12a; 4:1a; 6:1a; 10:6); it can be found in Judg 13:1a. God's anger is not mentioned in the three core stories of Judges; its omission need not be significant. Israel's deliverance to Philistine oppression can be found in Judg 13:1b. (However, it is not easy to identify a stage of the text from Judges to Samuel in which an association with Judg 13:1 can be viewed as available.) There is no cry by Israel to God (as for Judg 3:9a, 15a; 4:3a; 6:6b; 10:10). The people fast and confess sin and Samuel cries out; the context and presentation are different. Samuel is not raised up as a deliverer; he has long been on the scene as a prophet (cf. 1 Sam 3:19-21). Any suggestion of military action or leadership on Samuel's part is lacking. The confusion and defeat of the Philistines is attributed exclusively to YHWH (7:10). The Philistines are described as subdued and the hand of the LORD was against them all the days of Samuel; there are subtle but notable differences from the expression in Judg 3:30a; 4:23-24; 8:28a; also 11:33b, to say nothing of 2:18 and 3:10. Finally the stereotyped language for the land being undisturbed for a generation (cf. Judg 3:11a, 30b; 5:31b; 8:28b) is absent; 1 Sam 7:13b may echo Judg 2:18a.

While the events can be marshaled into the pattern, the text presentation does not fit the pattern. The relocation of the "crying out" from an oppressed Israel to a leader figure, Samuel, the failure to portray Samuel as summoned by God for the occasion, Samuel's role as intercessor with YHWH as deliverer, and the numerous differences of detail deny any possibility of the framing elements of Judg 3–9 being transferred to this text. It is quite possible that the memory of the deliverer-judges is evoked by the 1 Sam 7 text or that the 1 Sam 7 text served as inspiration for the framers of Judg 3–9. It is quite clear that the same type of patterned text is not presented in 1 Sam 7.

The reference to Samuel as judging Israel at Mizpah (v. 6b) invites further reflection. It is to be understood from its immediate context, but syntactically it can belong with what precedes or with what follows. In the latter case, belonging with what follows, it would function as a headline statement. The episode is begun with the Philistine concern. Even in this case, what Samuel does is not to be confused with the role of the deliverer-judges earlier. This is an interesting application of the authorial fallacy: what a supposed editor may have meant is not known to us; what we can discover is revealed only by the context. In what precedes — the more likely context — Samuel convened and presided over the formal ceremony of Israel's repentance at Mizpah. While this is an unusual use of the verb "to judge," it is far from alien to it; Samuel presides over an action in which matters are set to rights. So Klein: "Samuel's leading Israel to repentance is interpreted as an example of his judging Israel" (p. 67).

The Philistine threat is presented straightforwardly. The Philistines heard of Israel's gathering and responded to it. As a liturgical ceremony, we know it is no threat to the Philistine hegemony. As a ceremony of repentance and renewal, we realize that it is indeed a threat to Philistine hegemony, if that hegemony derives from the Philistine role as oppressor appointed by YHWH. This confidence is not experienced in Israel; they heard and feared the Philistines. The people instruct Samuel not to stop interceding, so that YHWH might deliver them. Samuel's intercession is coupled with a burnt offering; YHWH's response is thunderous. The details are given of Israel's pursuit, of the commemorative stone, of the successful subduing of the Philistines for Samuel's lifetime. Even the return of towns and territory and the fact of peace with the Amorites (local inhabitants) are noted (v. 14). The deliverance from the Philistine threat is solidly established.

There is a sharp shift from this episode to vv. 15-17. There is a general statement that Samuel judged Israel all his life (v. 15). Within the echo of deliverance, this statement reflects the situation of v. 13b; inextricably linked to what follows, however, it has to take its meaning from its context (i.e., vv. 16-17 — "Samuel" from v. 15 is needed as subject). The manner of this judging is there spelled out: he went on an annual circuit to Bethel, Gilgal, and Mizpah, three towns in a relatively small area of Benjamin. His home was in Ramah; he had a house there, he exercised his function of judge there, and he built an altar there. While this smacks of old tradition, we know absolutely nothing about it. In fact, we have minimal information on Samuel's life. Up to this point, we have met him as a child, as a prophet (3:19-21; 4:1a), and as elder statesman on the brink of retirement (cf. 8:5; 12:2).

Genre

At first sight, this text hardly seems to be a (→) story. It seems more like a slightly disjointed recital of facts, dominated by (→) accounts and (→) notices. Closer inspection shows that it could be elaborated as a story. It moves from a situation of disturbed equilibrium to one of equilibrium regained. It does this along a trajectory which has the potential to arouse tension and expectation and then resolve them.

The initial situation of disturbed equilibrium is not described; rather, it is hinted at allusively, indicating that Israel is in a situation of oppression. The tension or expectation is created when Samuel assures Israel that their repentance and renunciation of the foreign gods will bring deliverance in its train (v. 3b). The tension becomes acute when the gathering for this ceremony of repentance precipitates an aggressive response from the Philistines — to the point where the lifting up of the intercessory offering and the charge of the Philistine forces are simultaneous (v. 10a). The tension is resolved when Samuel's intercession is successful and God's victorious intervention reduces the Philistines to defeat and flight. The equilibrium is fully restored with the details which give permanency to Israel's security from external foes and stability on the internal scene.

While the text is structured as a story, the impression of a somewhat disjointed recital is justified enough; it comes from the composite nature of the text, with its combination of (→) accounts and (→) notices. Rather than comparison with the "constructed story" ("konstruierte Erzählung," mentioned by Richter for Judges, *Untersuchungen,* 392-94) or the "imitated or factitious story" ("nachgeahmte Erzählung," discussed by Lohfink for Gen 15, *Land-*

verheißung, 31-34), it is more helpful to recognize that the text provides an example of (→) reported story, offering a base for storytelling.

Setting

We know nothing about the origins or historicity of the traditions assembled in 1 Sam 7. Any reflection on their setting must be restricted to the literary contexts in which they came to be expressed.

The great episode of deliverance (vv. 7-11) places Samuel in a similar role with Moses and the Amalekite battle (Exod 17:8-13) and Elijah and the prophets of Baal (1 Kgs 18:17-40); it is evocative of creative imagination in search of symbol. It is not to be confused with the exploits of Ehud, Deborah, Gideon, or Jephthah, despite similarities. There is nothing in vv. 7-11 or vv. 12-14 that signals dtr authorship.

The traditions of vv. 16-17, particularly when coupled with 8:1-3, appear to be old; it is difficult to point to a situation where they might derive from creative imagination rather than historical memory. Verse 15 belongs with vv. 16-17, although some have seen it reflecting the dtr concept of the judge; its reference is simply to "Israel," in common with vv. 16-17, not house of Israel (vv. 2-3) or people of Israel (vv. 4, 6b, 7, 8), or all Israel (v. 5).

The origin of vv. 2-6 is complex and has been adequately discussed above. Verses 3-4 are highly likely to have been part of the "national" focus of the dtr revision of the DH.

The picture drawn by Noth, in the first flush of enthusiasm for the DH, portrays 7:2-17 as very much the creation of the Deuteronomist: "But in Dtr.'s view, the major 'judges' had to save their country, and from this he inferred that the end of the Philistine oppression must be attributed to a decisive victory by Samuel" (Noth, *DH,* 78). As noted, clear evidence of dtr authorship in the chapter is restricted, so that subsequent views have not followed Noth's lead.

On the issue of dtr attribution, opinions differ: for Horst Seebass, 7:2a, 3-4, 14b are identifiable as dtr on grounds of style ("Vorgeschichte," 169); for Stoebe, the theme of separation from foreign gods is dtr (p. 172); Wolfgang Richter attributes 7:3-4, 6bβ [*sic*], 13, 15 to the Deuteronomist, understanding v. 14 as a pre-dtr expansion (*Bearbeitungen,* 123-25); Peter Weimar attributes vv. 3-4 (without "the Ashtaroth") to the Deuteronomist and also v. 2 ("Jahwekriegserzählungen," 63-69); McCarter regards vv. 2aα, 2b-4, 6b as new dtr material, and vv. 13-14, 15-16 as dtr summaries of original material (McCarter, 150). What is common to these positions is a conviction that at least vv. 5-6a, 7-12 belong to an older tradition, and that the dtr contribution has been made outside this core (except for v. 6b). Verses 5-6a, 7-12 form a natural unit, beginning with the account of the ceremony of repentance and ending with Samuel's action in setting up a memorial stone. As we have claimed, evidence is lacking for any dtr contribution within 7:2, 6, 12-17.

Meaning

In its context, the meaning is not easily described. In Samuel's lifetime still, the Philistines are going to be a major threat to Israel. In 1 Sam 9:16, God says to Samuel of the yet-to-be-anointed Saul: "He shall save my people from the hand of the Philistines; for I have seen the suffering of my people, because their out-cry has come to me." In the Davidic traditions before the death of Samuel (1 Sam 16–24), the Philistines are an active and aggressive threat to Israel. In this light, the pattern of Judg 3–9 has not come to much. Despite 7:13, the Philistines were not subdued "all the days of Samuel."

The hypothesis of a Josianic DH, initially favorable to the monarchy and subsequently revised, allows 1 Sam 7:2-17 to find its meaning within this final revision of the DH, with its negativity toward the monarchy. With regard to the following chapter, both Weiser ("Philister-Sieg," 270-71) and Stoebe (pp. 170-71) express reservations about the possibility of associating ch. 7 with ch. 8. Some tension is evident; there is no reference back in ch. 8. Association is made possible by the difference of concerns: deliverance in ch. 7; justice in ch. 8. At the end of ch. 7, Samuel's judging is affirmed generally in relation to Is-rael (v. 15) and is then restricted to Bethel, Gilgal, and Mizpah (v. 16) and Ramah (v. 17); his sons' judicial activity ("over Israel," 8:1) is located in far-off Beer-sheba. Whatever of fact and fiction, ch. 7 expresses a contrary view to the unchallenged conviction of the need for a king for national defense. Despite its trigger in social justice, the main impact of ch. 8 is the involvement of popular demand, God's acquiescence in that demand, and the characterization of the de-mand as rejection of God.

Kingship by Popular Demand: Samuel as Intermediary	8:1-22
I. Initial situation of need for justice	1-3
A. Samuel's age and action: appointment of his sons as judges	1
B. Samuel's sons	2-3
1. Their identity: names, role, and place	2
2. Their action: injustice — bribery, perversion of justice	3
II. Response to situation of need: request for a king	4-22a
A. Initial request	4-18
1. Elders assembled at Ramah request a king	4-5
2. Reaction to the request	6-18
a. Private	6-9
1) By Samuel: indignation and prayer	6
2) By God	7-9
a) Order: compliance with the request	7a
b) Characterization of the request: rejection and apostasy	7b-8
c) Order: compliance with the request — after warning	9
b. Public	10-18
1) General: the words of God	10
2) Specific: the warning of Samuel	11-18

Discussion

The beginning to this popular initiative is shrouded in mystery — [I]. What is stated in the text lies outside our knowledge of ancient Israel. First, what is stated in the text. Samuel made his sons judges over Israel (8:1); they were judges in Beer-sheba (8:2); they took bribes and perverted justice (8:3).

Second, what lies outside our knowledge. We have no knowledge of any office through which Samuel's sons might be judges over Israel; more importantly, we do not know of any right of Samuel's to make such appointments. Neither the deliverer-judges nor the minor judges were portrayed as holding hereditary offices. The similarities with Eli and Gideon are limited (cf. Hertzberg, 71-72; McCarter, 160). Eli is not portrayed as a leader of Israel; he is priest of the sanctuary at Shiloh. Rule over Israel was offered by the people of Israel and declined by Gideon (Judg 8:22-23); some sort of kingship was seized by his son, Abimelech, and was short-lived. There is, therefore, no precedent for Samuel's action. There is no authorization from God given for it (contrast Num 20:22-28 for Aaron and Eleazar and Num 27:18-23 for Moses and Joshua). We are not certain of the activity of Samuel depicted in 8:16-17. Therefore, we do not know whether Samuel is meant to be appointing his sons as his successors or whether they are appointed to an office separate from his own.

We have no knowledge of what office might be described as "judges over Israel." 7:15 and 17 describe Samuel as judging Israel, with 7:16 describing a judicial circuit through Bethel, Gilgal, and Mizpah. Verse 17 notes that, after the annual circuit, Samuel judged Israel at Ramah. The echo here is of Deborah, who judged Israel "under the palm of Deborah between Ramah and Bethel in the hill country of Ephraim; and the Israelites came up to her for judgment" (Judg 4:5). We have no echo of this office or function elsewhere in the Bible either, so we are left in the dark. Doubly puzzling is why Samuel's two sons should both be performing this office in Beer-sheba. Ramah, Bethel, Gilgal, and Mizpah are relatively central to Israel; Beer-sheba is not. It is not even central to Judah; it lies far to the south. What function, historically or imaginatively, do the two sons of Samuel perform as judges in Beer-sheba?

Finally, since we do not know the nature of their office, we also do not know how their greed could affect Israel nationally. Apparently, it is portrayed as doing just that.

The precise reference of the tradition is, therefore, uncertain; nor can we be sure, under these circumstances, that this is necessarily an independent and reliable tradition about Samuel (with Stoebe, 182-83; v. 2 is particularly doubt-ful; cf. Budde, *Bücher Samuel,* 53-54). What might be said is that it fits within the horizon revealed by the Gideon tradition (above): after the experience of de-liverance and during a period of stability, there would be a natural tendency among the people to seek to institutionalize this stability. Similarly, the two sons and their failure through greed may evoke an echo of the Elide tradition, especially being situated at a point of transition between epochs. The possibil-ity of mutual influence within the history of tradition cannot be ignored. What-ever its historical circumstances, the passage serves here to introduce the re-quest for a king.

The grounds for the request must be seen accurately. The complaint is that Samuel's sons do not follow in his ways but are greedy. Specifically, they take bribes and pervert justice (8:3). This complaint has to be measured against Samuel's response to the people. In his warning, Samuel points to conscription of sons and daughters (8:11-13), to taxes on produce (8:14-15), to levies on slaves and livestock (8:16-17a); with a final flourish, he describes Israel as slaves to the king (8:17b). Significant here is what Samuel has not said. He has not said a word about bribes and injustice, not even about greed. What Samuel has pictured vividly is the system of taxation to be expected under a royal re-gime. What Samuel has not addressed are the abuses reported in 8:3 — bribery and the perversion of justice. It would have been so easy to add at the end of the list: and the king will take bribes and pervert justice. But the text does not do so; it leaves a gap. Samuel's warning does not address the situation of need re-ported in 8:3. The gap cannot be denied its significance.

The issue of justice and injustice is immensely pertinent to the request for a king. "The establishment of a just society is the responsibility of the king" (Weinfeld, *Social Justice,* 45).

> Our interpretation of "justice and righteousness" does not exclude the juridi-cal sense of the expression. The judge, although subject to legal rules, cannot overlook considerations of fairness and equity, thus bringing about "true judgement." Our contention, however, is that "justice and righteousness" is not a concept that belongs to the jurisdiction alone, but is much more relevant for the social-political leaders who create the laws and are responsible for their execution. (ibid., 44)

Whether real or self-serving, the idea of the monarchy's responsibility for so-cial justice is about as old as the idea of kingship itself. The concern for social justice and the conviction that it is the responsibility of government under God long antedate the Bible and have their place within the community context of the ancient Near East. Two ancient texts help illustrate this.

> At that time Anum and Enlil named me to promote the welfare of the people, me, Hammurabi, the devout, god-fearing prince, to cause justice to prevail in the land, to destroy the wicked and the evil, that the strong might not oppress the weak. . . .
> The great gods called me . . . in order that the strong might not oppress

the weak, that justice might be dealt the orphan and the widow, . . . to pre-
scribe the ordinance of the land, to give justice to the oppressed.

> (from the prologue and epilogue to the Code of Hammurabi,
> 1728-1686 B.C.E.; translation: *ANET,* 164, 178)

> You have let your hand fall into mischief.
> You do not judge the cause of the widow,
> Nor do you adjudicate the case of the wretched;
> You do not drive out those that prey on the poor;
> You do not feed the fatherless before you,
> Nor the widow behind your back.
> Having become a brother of the sickbed,
> A companion of the bed of suffering,
> Descend from the kingship. . . .

> (from the Legend of King Keret, 14th-century B.C.E. copy;
> translation: *ANET,* 149)

In the ancient Near East and in Israel, the conviction existed that justice
and right order proceeded from God/the gods. In this, the king was their representative. As Ephraim Speiser expresses it:

> The basic premise of cuneiform law, the source to which the institution as a
> whole owed both its content and its vitality, may be summarized as follows:
> Law is an aspect of the cosmic order and hence ultimately the gift of the
> forces of the universe. The human ruler is but a temporary trustee who is re-
> sponsible to the gods for the implementation of the cosmic design. Because
> the king is thus answerable to powers outside himself, his subjects are auto-
> matically protected against autocracy, and the individual has the comfort and
> assurance of certain inalienable rights. ("Cuneiform Law," 537)

These reflections make clear the monarchy's responsibility for social justice. Understandably, then, failure of justice within society might trigger demand for a king. We have to admit, however, that the text of 1 Sam 8:1-3 hardly
does justice to or even evokes such weighty concerns. Maybe it is the art of
leaving the obvious unsaid; maybe it reflects a concern less for justice and more
for the obnoxiousness of monarchy.

Several of these features in the chapter are surprising and deserve to be
emphasized.

i. The unjust judges, Joel and Abijah, are at Beer-sheba, far away to the
south. What sort of power or sway was exercised from Beer-sheba? (Cf.
"like all the nations," vv. 5, 20.) Furthermore, important as justice may
be, if judges are unjust the appropriate remedy might be to replace them
with judges who were just. Why a king?

ii. The diatribe given Samuel against kings does not mention the issues of
bribery and injustice. Why the silence?

99

iii. The instruction from God to Samuel is to comply with the people's request, even though it is characterized as apostasy. This is indeed strange. Apostasy is considered to be evil. God's instruction to comply could be construed as complicity in evil. Why is such strange behavior attributed to God?

The text reports injustice: "they took bribes and perverted justice" (8:3) — [I]. The elders requested "a king to govern us, like other nations" (8:5) — [II.A.1]. When Samuel is portrayed warning against this request, he lists the burdens a king will impose but does not address the issue of injustice — [II.A.2]. The refusal to be swayed by this warning — "No! but we are determined to have a king over us" (8:19) — may express the willingness to pay the cost of monarchy if that is the price of justice. The defense issue is added to the justice issue at this point: "that we also may be like other nations, and that our king may govern us and go out before us and fight our battles" (8:20) — [II.B.1]. Politically, to govern us "like other nations" is appropriate, as kings in other nations were institutionally responsible for justice; theologically, it is inappropriate, as Israel is not like all the nations. Militarily, "go out before us and fight our battles" is appropriate, as it could be among a king's responsibilities to lead the people in battle; theologically, it calls for reflection.

There is another presupposition to be addressed: the modern, and especially Western, preference for democracy. A modern democrat reads Samuel's polemic (8:11-17) and feels in full agreement; kings belong in the same breath with oppressors. Today, monarchs are rare; monarchs who are loved may be rarer still. But in a thriving monarchy, citizens are honored to have sons serve in the military, especially in the officer corps, and privileged to have daughters serve at court. Of course taxes are a burden, but they are not too high a price to pay for a popular monarch and a just society. From the people's point of view, the issue is entirely one of popularity and popular well-being. From the vantage point of hindsight and national failure, an exilic generation might name monarchy apostasy. Without hindsight, a people in search of justice and security might well have thought the costs of monarchy a small price to bear.

There is a remarkable level of understatement in the text of ch. 8. It is often spoken of as the assembly at Ramah, but strictly it is not. There is no convocation of an assembly. "All the elders of Israel gathered together and came to Samuel at Ramah" (8:4). Whether in fact (elders only) or formality (no convocation), this is not the same as the earlier summons to a gathering of "all Israel" at Mizpah (7:5) or the summoning of "the people" to Mizpah (10:17), or the presence of "all the people" (11:15) invited to Gilgal. Samuel's interlocutors at Ramah vary slightly through the chapter: "all the elders" in 8:4-5, "the people *(hā'ām)* who were asking him for a king" in 8:10, and finally "the people" in 8:19, 21 *(hā'ām),* and 22 *('anšê yiśrā'ēl);* in 8:7, Samuel is told to "Listen to the voice of the people" *(hā'ām),* reflecting the language later in the chapter rather than 8:4-5. The nature of the need and the request both vary in their formulation. The narrator reports the situation as: "his sons did not follow in his ways, but turned aside after gain; they took bribes and perverted justice" (8:3); the elders repeat only the initial general statement: "your sons do not follow in your

ways" (8:5). The initial request (8:5) is for "a king to govern us, like other nations" (NRSV; Heb., like all the nations). Samuel's displeasure is focused simply on "a king to govern us" (8:6). After Samuel's warning, the request is expanded: "No! but we are determined to have a king over us, so that we also may
be like other nations, and that our king may govern us and go out before us and
fight our battles" (8:19-20).

It is not clear that all this is mere stylistic variation or even evidence that
the text is merely reported story — a story summary recording variations or a
base for the storyteller's performance in which such variations would be ironed
out. The elders can be claimed to reflect the people. Once reported, the full
statement of the need does not have to be repeated. Once triggered by the need
for justice, the request for a king can take into account the other functions of
kings. Perhaps there is no more than this. The impression remains that the text
is dancing with a certain delicacy around the topic.

Samuel's stance throughout may also be interpreted in various ways. At
base, perhaps there is the old man's resentment of the rejection of his sons and
the order he had set in place. Beyond that, there is the prophetic wisdom that in-
stinctively resists what will be deleterious to the people. The most all-
embracing portrait of the prophet would allow for the expression of prophetic
resistance to the monarchy and the desire to maintain a distance from it, reflecting traditions such as the Naboth story (1 Kgs 21). In the adjoining prophetic
tradition (9:1–10:16; 11:1-15), Samuel is a willing instrument in God's operation. The motive behind Samuel's displeasure (v. 6) is left unsaid.

The reason given by the elders for their request is discreetly phrased:
"Your sons do not follow in your ways" (8:5). When reported in the context of
Samuel's displeasure, there is an equally discreet shift: "when they said, 'Give
us a king to govern us'" (8:6). The text might have given an opening to Samuel's resentment over criticism of his sons by picking up "your sons do not follow in your ways"; it does not. The text might have given an opening to theological reflection behind Samuel's displeasure by picking up "like other
nations"; it does not. Instead the text focuses exclusively on the issue of a king
for Israel. We are left in the dark as to the reasons and context motivating Samuel's displeasure.

The text's difficulties are focused within vv. 7-21. Following on v. 6, "and
Samuel prayed to the LORD," a response is given in v. 22, "The LORD said to
Samuel, 'Listen to their voice. . . .'" In this context, there is no divine complicity in evil. God backs the wisdom of the elders against the resistance of Samuel,
and the people are to be given a king. Whether v. 22 reflects the narrative need
to replace the elders with a national gathering or whether it reflects a compiler's
need to insert 9:1–10:16 is largely immaterial. For a visually based presentation
of these traditions, see Campbell and O'Brien, *Unfolding.*

The difficulties start with v. 7; it can be seen as beginning to unfold what is
implicit in Samuel's displeasure (v. 6). There are two focuses in this unfolding:
first, warning for the people; second, rejection of God. Warning predominates:

v. 7a   God's order to comply with the people's request
v. 9b   God's order to warn the people beforehand

v. 10   Report of God's words to the people by Samuel (compliance but with warning)
vv. 11-17   Warning given to the people
vv. 19-20   Rejection of the warning by the people
v. 21   Report of the rejection

Before the warning is given, much less rejected, vv. 7b-8 explicitly affirm that the demand for a king is itself effectively rejection of YHWH as God of Israel. The same view is implicit in v. 18, echoing something of the thinking of Judg 10:14; why should YHWH assist those who have rejected him? If they choose a king, the burdens under which they groan will be burdens they have chosen.

With this understanding, the development of the present text falls into place. The emphasis on warning comes first. There can be no kingship without cost. The emphasis on rejection comes second, spliced into the warning. The cost is not just fiscal; it is also theological, the rejection of God.

A minor contradiction about whether Samuel is rejected or not ("so also they are doing to you" in v. 8) is intelligible enough. Its position at the end of the verse suggests addition by some careful pedant. Verse 7 says that it is not Samuel who is being rejected but God — which in the view of rejection theology is true enough. But of course you do not reject God without rejecting God's prophet — as the pedant of v. 8 is at pains to note.

Verses 11-17 and 18 are given as Samuel's warning to the people. They are carefully structured around four occurrences of "he will take," each time preceded by the object, preceded by what the king will take:

v. 11   Your sons he will take
v. 13   Your daughters he will take
v. 14   Your fields, your vineyards, your olive groves he will take
v. 16   Your slaves, male and female, your oxen and your donkeys he will take

In two other areas, tithes (levies of one-tenth) are indicated:

v. 15   Your seed-crops and vineyards he will tithe
v. 17   Your flocks he will tithe

The passage begins with the statement, "These will be the ways of the king" (v. 11a); it ends with the all-encompassing affirmation, "and you shall be his slaves" (v. 17b). It is a comprehensive assessment of the burdens involved in the support of a royal court (for provisions alone, see 1 Kgs 4:7-19, 22-28 [Heb. = 4:7-19; 5:2-8]; for the issue of tax burdens, see 1 Kgs 12:1-15). Such an assessment of royal burden could come from almost any period; what is surprising is that no mention is made of justice or injustice, of greed or the perversion of justice.

The text as we have it gives a most serious reading of Samuel's displeasure: the demand for a king is equivalent to the rejection of God, and Israel will be left to bear the burdens they have chosen. Despite this interpretation given to the monarchy, the order given Samuel initially ("Listen to the voice of the people," v. 7a) is repeated at the end ("Listen to their voice," v. 22a). The request has been made on grounds of social justice. Due warning has been given. The request has been accepted and is to be implemented. We may assume that the implementation lies ahead. The difficulties of the text as we have it need not be emphasized here. Brueggemann's comment, in its embarrassment, will be enough. "The way between the reservation [theological] and the brute fact [historical] is found in this grudging grant. Yahweh does not endorse but Yahweh also does not preclude. A settlement is found that does not entirely please any party" (p. 63). "The monarchy is left theologically doubtful by this 'permitted-but-disapproved' status" (p. 66).

Genre

This demand from the people (8:1-22) could be told in story form. As we have the traditions in the present text, they are not in story form. They are recounted without any signals suggesting the arousal of interest through plot or otherwise. The traditions are formulated as (→) accounts.

On the other hand, the density of the text is remarkable. With careful discussion of its potential development, it becomes clear that a much fuller unfolding of its presentation could be given. The tension aroused by plot could be used to hold the various elements together. Overall, there is the tension of a people suffering from injustice. Within that broad picture, there are the dangers raised by the demand for a king. There is the burden of taxation and service; there is the danger of apostasy, of rejection of their God. The text leaves open whether the people's last word — "No! but we are determined to have a king over us" (v. 19) — refers to burdens, or apostasy, or both. The text can leave issues open; a storyteller or a theologian might choose to unfold them. The genre of (→) reported story is a possibility.

Setting

Two issues have to be kept carefully apart here. The setting and time from which these traditions originated is one thing; the time at which they came into the present text is another.

We know of legal issues being settled at the royal court; we know of elders meeting at the city gate to enact justice; we know of the delegation of judicial authority authorized in the lawcodes. We may not always know of the precise periods when some of these procedures were in effect. We know nothing of a judicial authority, from Samuel's time or before, that could have implications for the welfare of Israel. We cannot therefore say much about the origins of traditions such as these, except that they may have been formulated well before the composition of the DH. This is equally true of the warning against the ways of a king (8:11-17). It could have come from early experience, Israel's or others' (cf. Mendelsohn, "Samuel's Denunciation"; for further literature, see O'Brien, *Deuteronomistic History Hypothesis,* 113); it could be later, reflecting the long history of Israel's experience. It can hardly be dated with any precision.

The introduction into the present text is a different matter. As has been adumbrated earlier and will be discussed after the treatment of ch. 12, a Josianic DH may well have used the traditions in 1 Sam 9:1–10:16 and 11:1-11, 15 to depict the emergence of monarchy in Israel. The post-Josianic revision of the DH is an appropriate setting for chs. 7–8 (also 10:17-25 and 12:1-25) to be introduced into the present text. The issues in vv. 7-21 related to warning bear marks and concerns that make attribution to the "royal" focus of the dtr revision likely; the issues relating to apostasy and rejection reflect the "national" focus. An older text may well have existed without these, or most of these, elements. Its existence and precise shape have to remain hypothetical.

Meaning

The present text of 1 Sam 8:1-22 reports a popular demand for a king and the order from God for implementation of that demand. Attention is given to Samuel's displeasure, to warnings about the burdens of monarchy, and to the issue of God's being rejected. The text moves from the situation of bribery and the perversion of justice with the consequent demand for a king, through these various issues, to the outcome in God's order to Samuel to comply with the demand.

As such, this text is one account of the initial stage in the process by which monarchy emerged in Israel. As we will see, 1 Sam 9:1–10:16 is another and different account of the initial stage in the process.

In this text, the reference to bribery and the perversion of justice (8:3) evokes the significance of monarchy for the maintenance of social justice. The displeasure of Samuel raises issues reflecting the darker side of monarchy. Samuel's displeasure is at first unfocused (v. 6). With the LORD's order to Samuel to comply, two issues are brought into focus: the rejection of God; the burden of monarchy.

The text portrays an initial stage in which the demand for a king came from the people, in the context of a situation of perverted justice. The demand was granted by God. Due warning was given to the people of the risks, both theological and political.

Textual Issues

9:25 The MT is possible (with Stoebe, 197, and Barthélemy, 162, appealing to Abravanel); the LXX offers an easier text (accepted by Driver, 77; McCarter, 171; Klein, 83, and the NRSV).

10:1 The LXX has a more expansive text, accepted by the NRSV. Opinions about the originality of the LXX expansion divide along customary lines (MT tentatively preferred: Barthélemy, 162-63; Pisano, 166-69; also Stoebe, 197; LXX preferred: Driver, 78; McCarter, 171; Klein, 83; also Hertzberg, 77). The sense is not affected.

Discussion

With the people off the scene, the narrative can turn to a second initiative about monarchy in Israel. This time it comes directly from God, is concerned with the defense of Israel against the Philistines, and involves an order from God to anoint Saul as future king.

The narrative begins with a classical opening for Hebrew storytelling — [I.A]: a four-generation identification of Saul's father, a Benjaminite and a man of wealth, certainly one of the landed gentry (9:1). His son was Saul, a young man of exceptional good looks and height. Only one son is mentioned, of fabled physique.

The story of the secret designation and anointing of Saul as king-designate begins with a young man's search for his father's asses (note: these are asses, more valuable and more significant than donkeys). There is no sign of ambition; on the human level, the outcome is pure chance. The young man wants to give up the unsuccessful search; it is his servant who suggests consulting the man of God. Far from being eager, the young man objects; it is the servant who surmounts his objections. And so the pair approach the man of God,

105

who will turn out to be Samuel — [I.B and C]. At a point when the encounter is about to happen, the present narrative — in a twenty-four-hour flashback — reports God's intervention with Samuel to designate the man who is to be made king (or, at this point "ruler," king-designate, Heb.: *nāgîd*). At the level of the present text, this could be understood as the consequence of God's order to Samuel in ch. 8. If Samuel is to "hearken to their voice, and make them a king" (8:22), he is not left without divine guidance in the matter. On the other hand, the reference to the Philistines as the foe from whose afflicting hand Israel is to be saved (9:16) is, of course, in contrast to 1 Sam 7. When Samuel is reported as seeing Saul, a second intervention by God makes the identification complete (v. 17) — [II.A].

Saul eats at the banquet as Samuel's guest of honor and spends the night in the town — [cf. II.B]. At crack of dawn the following day, dismissing even Saul's servant so that they are alone, Samuel anoints Saul as *nāgîd* over Israel, thereby executing the command given him in 9:16. Along with this private anointing, the present text has Samuel offer Saul three signs by which he will know that the LORD has indeed ordained his anointing, and the narrative has Samuel give him a commission to become operative when the signs are fulfilled (10:7). The encounter ends with Samuel's command to precede him to Gilgal and to wait for him there (v. 8) — [II.C].

As the conclusion of the journey is begun — [cf. III], it is reported that all these signs came to pass (10:9), but only the fulfillment of the third is reported in detail (vv. 10-13). The matter of Gilgal (10:8) does not recur until ch. 13. The episode of "Saul's uncle" (10:14-16) is odd and not easily understood. We do not know why an uncle might have asked questions that seem more likely to have come from Saul's father, who was still alive (cf. 9:5). Stoebe's rendering of a "trusted friend" is appropriate (pp. 211-12); it is within the word's semantic field, but we have no other occurrence in such a sense beyond this context. Despite the insistence on privacy evident in 9:27, no injunction to silence has been issued. The episode might be understood to account for Saul's "anonymity" in ch. 11. In the present text, it might be claimed to facilitate the transition to the report of the assembly at Mizpah and Saul's selection there. However, this latter would pose considerable problems in terms of the charade involved for Samuel and the tension for the Saul traditions between anointing and concealment.

The story is straightforward enough and can be read straightforwardly — as long as one foregrounds its unity. Once attention is paid to details, the unity is inevitably fragmented (details drawn from Schmidt, *Menschlicher Erfolg*, 58-102). The evidence points to the overwriting of an older story by prophetic interests. The older story concerns Saul's (chance) meeting with an anonymous man of God and his being commissioned for something special (10:7). The overwriting identifies the man of God as Samuel, is emphatic that rather than chance God is behind the meeting, and specifies the commissioning to be anointing as king-designate *(nāgîd)*. The principal details that point to this are:

1. The nameless man of God who finds things for a fee (9:6-8) contrasts with the established figure of Samuel, known to all Israel.

2. The chance nature of Saul's visit to the man of God contrasts with the invitations (9:13) that have been issued for a banquet in Saul's honor.
3. The search for lost asses contrasts with the anointing as *nāgîd* and deliverer (9:15-17).
4. Samuel's intention in 9:19b to pass the night before informing Saul of his concerns (possibly allowing for nocturnal revelation, cf. Num 22:8-13, 19-21) contrasts with his promptly telling Saul in 9:20 about the lost asses that have been found.
5. Telling Saul about the asses in 9:20 contrasts to some degree with the information about the asses as a sign in 10:2.
6. The banquet honoring Saul in 9:22-24 implies the dignity and status of the anointing commissioned in 9:15-17 and contrasts with the wealthy farmer's son in search of asses.
7. The name of God, *'ĕlōhîm*, in 9:9, 9:27, and 10:2-4, 7, and 9 (the older story) contrasts with the name of God, *YHWH*, in 9:15-17 and 10:1 (the prophetic overwriting).

The simplest way to see how these details signal the overwriting of an earlier story is to reproduce the text where it is most apparent, i.e., 9:13–10:1. The earlier story will be left in roman; the overwriting will be set in italic.

9:13 "As soon as you enter the town, you will find him, before he goes up to the shrine to eat. For the people will not eat until he comes, since he must bless the sacrifice; *afterward those eat who are invited.* Now go up, for you will meet him immediately." 14So they went up to the town. *As they were entering the town, they saw Samuel coming out toward them on his way up to the shrine.*

15*Now the day before Saul came, the Lord had revealed to Samuel:* 16*"Tomorrow about this time I will send to you a man from the land of Benjamin, and you shall anoint him to be ruler [nāgîd] over my people Israel. He shall save my people from the hand of the Philistines; for I have seen the suffering of my people, because their outcry has come to me."* 17*When Samuel saw Saul, the Lord told him, "Here is the man of whom I spoke to you. He it is who shall rule over my people."* 18Then Saul approached *Samuel* inside the gate, and said, "Tell me, please, where is the house of the seer?" 19*Samuel answered Saul, "I am the seer; go up before me to the shrine, for today you shall eat with me, and in the morning I will let you go and will tell you all that is on your mind. 20As for your asses that were lost three days ago, give no further thought to them, for they have been found. And on whom is all Israel's desire fixed, if not on you and on all your ancestral house?" 21Saul answered, "I am only a Benjaminite, from the least of the tribes of Israel, and my family is the humblest of all the families of the tribe of Benjamin. Why then have you spoken to me in this way?"*

22Then *Samuel* took Saul and his servant-boy and brought them into the hall, *and gave them a place at the head of those who had been invited, of whom there were about thirty. 23And Samuel said to the cook, "Bring the portion I gave you, the one I asked you to put aside." 24The cook took up the thigh and what went with it and set them before Saul. Samuel said, "See, what was kept is set before you. Eat; for it is set before you at the appointed time, so that you might eat with the guests."*

So Saul ate with *Samuel* that day. 25When they came down from the shrine into the town, a bed was spread for Saul on the roof, and he lay down to sleep. 26Then at the break of dawn *Samuel* called to Saul upon the roof, "Get up, so that I may send you on your way." Saul got up, and both he and *Samuel* went out into the street.

27As they were going down to the outskirts of the town, *Samuel* said to Saul, "Tell the boy to go on before us, and when he has passed on, stop here yourself for a while, that I may make known to you the word of God."

10:1*Samuel took a vial of oil and poured it on his head, and kissed him; he said, "The* Lord *has anointed you ruler [*nāgîd*] [LXX: over his people Israel. You shall reign over the people of the* Lord *and you will save them from the hand of their enemies all around. Now this shall be the sign to you that the* Lord *has anointed you ruler] over his heritage.*

The significance of this overwriting will be discussed under Meaning. The present text has a clear initiative coming from God to begin the process by which there will be a king in Israel to "save my people from the hand of the Philistines; for I have seen the suffering of my people, because their outcry has come to me" (9:16). This particular comment militates against an association of 9:1–10:16 with either chs. 7 or 8; in ch. 7, the Philistines have been subdued by Samuel for his lifetime and, in ch. 8, despite v. 20, the outcry is over the issue of justice. Attribution of 9:16b to a Deuteronomist is uncertain and not of much help (despite Veijola, *Königtum,* 73-79). The earlier overwritten text equally appears to have an initiative coming from God to begin the process by which there will be a king in Israel. On our best understanding, it ends with the commission in 10:7. A commission to do whatever you are able, for God is with you, may seem intolerably vague in its present context. We do not have an earlier context (see, however, Schmidt, *Menschlicher Erfolg,* 74-79). As a base for performance, such a text might allow for considerable expansion by a storyteller; for now, it is simply a reminder that older tradition was going in much the same direction as the present text.

Three other points need to be mentioned in connection with the story (cf. Schmidt, *Menschlicher Erfolg,* 97-98, 102). They constitute what we might call "signals" in the text.

1. 10:6 speaks of the coming of the spirit and Saul's becoming a different person in ways that do not correspond with either 10:9a or 11:6 in either circumstances or timing.
2. 10:8 issues precise instructions that take away the freedom given Saul in 10:7.
3. 10:9b reads like a conclusion, with "all these signs" being fulfilled that day, whereas 10:10-13a goes on to relate the fulfillment of only one of the signs, the one described in 10:5-6.

These three signals can be understood as pointers preparing the way for other traditions that have been attached to the story at this point.

1. 10:5-6 prepares for 10:10-13a, one of two stories explaining the saying "Is Saul also among the prophets?" (cf. also 19:18-24).
2. 10:8 prepares for 13:7b-15a, one of the versions of the reason for Saul's rejection.
3. 10:9b is indeed a conclusion, with 10:5-6 and 8 added before it and 10:10-13a added after it.

These are cases where flowing unity has not been attempted. Rather, traditions have been attached to this text as an appropriate place for their storage and recovery.

Genre

God's commission is conveyed in a (→) story (9:1–10:16). Taken at face value, the opening disequilibrium in the story is the loss of the asses. From the end of the story, it is clear that the real imbalance that drives the story is the need for a king in Israel. The term "king" is not used in the story, and one might think a deliverer would do; but deliverers were not anointed. Even at its earliest level, the story appears to have been moving in the direction of kingship. The older story ended with a commission (10:7). In the present context, it may hardly seem enough to bring the situation into equilibrium; its ultimate equilibrium is to be found in Saul's emergence as king. As a way station in this direction, it offers balance enough. At the level of the present text, the story moves from the lost asses to a specific commission of Saul as "ruler" *(nāgîd)*. This too is only a way station toward kingship.

Setting

The setting for a story of this kind is highly hypothetical. The most likely question that it might respond to would be: How did it happen that Saul came to be king over Israel? It is evident that the question might have been raised and the story told in a variety of settings, from the campfires of Saul's army to the surroundings of Saul's court.

The absence of ambition is not insignificant. Saul may cut up his oxen in 11:7; in 9:3 he was searching for his father's asses. The link between the two is God's commission, whether in the older 10:7 or in Samuel's anointing.

It would seem clear that the Prophetic Record made use of the overwritten Samuel version of the story. What is not clear is whether this was done as part of the composition of the PR or whether it was done independently beforehand. There is little chance of knowing.

109

Meaning

In the present text, as in either version, it is God who takes the initiative — whether through an anonymous seer or the well-known Samuel — to set in motion the process of a king's emergence in Israel.

In the older version, with the anonymous seer, there is the private conversation with Saul, to which the servant boy may not be privy. Saul is told of signs that will happen and is given an empowering commission. The understanding Ludwig Schmidt offers of 10:7 is related to the potential of the person involved: when these signs happen, do whatever you are able to as an empowered warrior (cf. *Menschlicher Erfolg,* 74-79). The privacy of the commissioning, under the four eyes of Samuel and Saul, allows for the absence of any action until 11:6.

The overwriting emphasizes God's intentionality and the implications of the commission. It was no act of chance that brought Saul to the prophet; it was God's doing in response to Israel's defense needs (cf. 9:15-16). It was no general commission that Saul was given, but a role (designated to be king) and a task (to save Israel from their enemies). With an eye to the more extensive narrative, we may note that the mention of the Philistines (in 9:16a) sets a signal pointing beyond Saul to David, the royal figure who ultimately will save Israel from the hand of the Philistines (2 Sam 5:17-25; 8:1).

Outcome to Kingship by Popular Demand:	**10:17-27**
Samuel as Kingmaker	
I. Account of a national assembly at Mizpah	17-25
A. Samuel's convocation and introductory address	17-19
1. Convocation	17
2. Samuel's speech: divine reproach	18-19a
3. Samuel's summons	19b
B. Business of the assembly	20-25a
1. Choice of the king by lot and oracle (divine will)	20-24a
2. Acclamation of the king	24b
3. Proclamation of rights and duties of the king	25a
C. Dismissal of the assembly	25b
II. Aftermath of the Mizpah convocation: orthodoxy now	26-27

Textual Issues

10:21 The MT omits specifying that Samuel brought the family of the Matrites near. Pisano's comment is apposite: "MT presents here a *lectio brevior et difficilior,* but one which nevertheless is understandable in the context. LXX had all the elements it needed . . . to supply what was seen as necessary to conform the text to the usual lot-casting process" (p. 172).

10:27 NRSV follows 4QSam^a and Josephus (*Antiquities,* VI, 68-71) which both preserve a further episode of Ammonite oppression, immediately preceding the present ch. 11. As reconstructed in the NRSV, it reads: "Now Nahash, king of the Ammonites, had been grievously oppressing the Gadites and the Reubenites. He would gouge out the right eye of each of them and would not grant Israel a deliverer. No one was left of the Israelites across the Jordan whose right eye Nahash, king of the Ammonites, had not gouged out. But there were seven thousand men who had escaped from the Ammonites and had entered Jabesh-gilead" (translation unchanged from Cross's original reconstruction, given in McCarter, 198-99). Subsequently, Cross opted for "and struck terror and dread in Israel" in place of "and would not grant Israel a deliverer" ("Ammonite Oppression," 107). Cross lists this particular restoration among several he describes as "problematical"; he appeals to texts such as Exod 15:16; 1 Chron 14:17; Deut 11:25 (p. 108). Cross notes that this was not his initial reading, but was pressed on him independently by several scholars, including McCarter, Rofé, and Greenberg (p. 116, n. 6).

The originality of this episode is defended by Cross of course, by his student Ulrich (*Qumran Text,* 166-70), and accepted by McCarter (above) and by Klein (pp. 102-3); it is vigorously contested by Barthélemy in a full discussion (pp. 166-72) and by his student Pisano (pp. 91-98). In a more recent study, Edward D. Herbert views the passage as an easily explained addition in a manuscript that has a couple of other pluses nearby. "It is thus almost certainly not original" ("4QSam[a]," 51).

The issues are complex, requiring fine judgments of syntax and style; consensus is improbable. The tradition of Nahash's brutality existed; if early, it is interesting for issues regarding the east-of-Jordan traditions. The question at issue, however, is whether this tradition originally formed part of the MT. Cross's argument that the full royal title, Nahash, king of the Ammonites, is the standard introduction for a foreign king carries weight; neither Barthélemy nor Pisano argue against it. But the issue has weight only if the text means Nahash to have the deference due a king. On the other hand, the first restoration (followed by the NRSV) notes Nahash's refusal to grant a deliverer, which is in tension with his apparent readiness to concede a seven-day search for a deliverer in 11:3. The 1980 restoration resolves this. Silence over the seven thousand refugees in 11:1-3 remains troublesome; Nahash treats the inhabitants of Jabesh-gilead without reference to the refugees. Caution points to the possibility of variant stories existing in the tradition rather than an omission from the MT. This view is supported by Pisano's judgment: "4QSam[a] seems clearly to witness to a textual tradition with expansionist tendencies" (p. 98; cf. Herbert, above). Zecharia Kallai sides with the anti-original camp: "a learned expansion . . . an amplification of a motif and not an additional datum . . . certainly secondary"; but the passage cannot be disqualified as a later interpolation (Kallai, "Samuel in Qumrān," 590-91). Originality is looking less likely.

Discussion

In the present text, as the structure analysis indicates, the choice and acclamation of a king in 10:17-27 are portrayed as a response to the people's request in 8:1-22.

Recognizing that 10:17-27 presently belongs with 8:1-22 is an appropriate moment to recall what is possible in terms of the present text and what is not. The compiling of the present text has been skillfully done and makes possible a reading that foregrounds its unity — that is, reading the text as a unity, without paying attention to the signals that militate against such unity. If we focus on unity in the foreground, a king is requested and God instructs Samuel to accede to the request (ch. 8), God then makes known to Samuel the identity of Saul as that future king (9:1–10:16), and God makes known to the people that the chosen king is Saul (10:17-27), and finally Saul demonstrates his power in delivering a town in Israel from tragic oppression (ch. 11). Signals set against such unity include the peace obtained for Samuel's lifetime (ch. 7), the request for a king motivated by a need for justice (ch. 8), the divine initiative for kingship to save Israel from the Philistines (9:1–10:16), the impropriety of Samuel's casting lots and seeking oracles to reveal to the people what God has already revealed to him — such is not the prophetic way of proceeding — as well as the tension between Saul anointed by Samuel and Saul hiding among the baggage (10:17-27), and finally the absence of any pointer to Saul as acclaimed king when the search is on for a deliverer of Jabesh-gilead (ch. 11). If we foreground plurality, it is not possible to read the text as a smooth unity; we even realize we have no assurance that 10:17-27 was in any sense an original continuation of 8:1-22 or, for that matter, that 11:1-15 was a continuation of 9:1–10:16. We can only say that in the present text they make best sense that way.

The convocation of an assembly at Mizpah is reported without any chronological specifications — [I]; nothing is said about the time that might have elapsed since the gathering at Ramah. Historical reporting is not the primary concern. Samuel's speech recalls the proceedings at Ramah in the two quotations: from God, v. 18, expanding part of 8:8; from the people, v. 19, expanding on 8:19. The language used in vv. 18-19 points to a late date and the dtr revision ("national" focus) of the history. The reference to "this day" (v. 19) is hardly to be taken as a chronological indicator (even at the level of an earlier text, against Hertzberg, 88, and Stoebe, 214-15). Rather, as in Deuteronomy, it has the sense of enduring validity; the rejection occurred at Ramah and it is still valid and actual at Mizpah (cf. von Rad, *Theology* 1.231).

The sequence is much the same as in ch. 8. Rejection of God is first addressed — [I.A]; then comes God's endorsement of the monarchy — [I.B]. No ceremony of coronation or enthronement is reported (cf. 2 Sam 5:3; 1 Kgs 1:39); on the other hand, 10:19, 24 and 11:14 leave no doubt that "the one whom the LORD has chosen" and whom all the people have acclaimed as king (10:24) has indeed become king in Israel.

The designation of the man to be king is achieved through a process of selection by lot. It appears that the use of the lot has been superimposed over another tradition in which the designation was expressed by an oracle such as, "He who is taller than any of the people from his shoulders upward will be king" (cf. vv. 23b-24a). The lot procedure requires presence; the oracle also requires it, though not in the same way. Adding the element of the choice by lot preserves an alternative tradition and may be felt to attribute the designation more directly to God. The oracle, based on physical attributes, might have seemed unduly naturalistic; the most imposing soldier makes the best king.

Such a view runs counter to a theological current in Israel that sought the least to be the evident instrument of God's power (e.g., Judg 6:14-16; 1 Sam 9:21). This tendency away from naturalism is visible in v. 22: it was not a question of selecting the tallest, most imposing man present, for the one designated by the oracular utterance was nowhere to be seen; his whereabouts, like his identity, is known only to God (cf. Hertzberg, 88-89; Stoebe, 217-18). The implication of this second appeal to the LORD, of course, is that when the men of Israel were lined up, in search of the one who was "taller than any of the people from his shoulders upward," it was found that the tallest were all approximately the same height. Appeals to Saul's modesty or timidity to explain his hiding among the baggage are, in this context, inappropriate for the anointed of God.

Saul is presented to the people, characterized as the one "whom the LORD has chosen." He is acclaimed by the people as king (cf. 1 Kgs 1:39b; 2 Kgs 11:12). So the action comprises two elements: designation or identification of the individual by God and acclamation or acceptance by the people. The continuity with ch. 8 is also maintained in at least two areas. First, in ch. 8, the people were warned about the ways of the king; now, in ch. 10, they are instructed in the rights and duties of the kingship. These are given the solemnity of written form, and preserved in the sanctuary, "before the LORD" (v. 25). No details are given. Second, the issue of the rejection of God is to the fore, again with reference to the exodus (cf. 8:7b-8; 10:18-19a). In this case, however, a significant difference is expressed. According to 8:8a, Israel has regularly rejected their God from the time of the exodus. There is an echo of the story of the golden calf and the pentateuchal traditions of repeated murmuring against God. But according to 10:19a, the rejection of God is to be situated in the present; it is not traced back into Israel's past history with God. 10:18 rehearses what God has done for Israel since the exodus; if awareness of Israel's past failure is intended here, it is not said.

The assembly Samuel had convoked (10:17) is now dismissed (10:25); a momentous act in the history of Israel has been concluded — [I.C]. In its aftermath, the tradition enshrined in a brief notice shows how orthodoxy has now changed in Israel (vv. 26-27) — [II]. The "warriors whose hearts God had touched" went with Saul, the newly chosen king. Those who said, "how can this man save us?" are characterized as "worthless fellows" *(bĕnê bĕliyya'al)*. By the standards of 10:19 — the request for a king is rejection of the God who saves — it should be precisely these "worthless fellows" whose hearts God had touched. It is in this paradox that the inauguration of a new situation is to be perceived: God has now chosen a king for Israel. The epochs have changed and the orthodoxy of yesterday has become the heresy of today (Boecker, *Beurteilung,* 56-59). This will be reinforced in 11:12-13.

Genre

As for the request from the people (8:1-22), so this response to the people's request (10:17-27) could be told in story form. Similar needs are being met in similar ways. As we have the tradition, it is not in story form. It is recounted without any signals suggesting the arousal of interest through plot or anything else. The traditions brought together in this assembly at Mizpah are formulated as an (→) account.

The negativity toward kingship is restricted to vv. 18-19; in ch. 8, it is given more extensive emphasis (cf. vv. 7-21). The traditions of 10:20-24 are positive, in the sense that they attribute to God the designation by lot or oracle of the man to be king. Hence Samuel's statement: "Do you see the one whom the LORD has chosen?" (v. 24).

The little traditions in 10:26-27 and 11:12-13 are (→) notices in the more traditional sense. They preserve brief unexpanded pieces of tradition. The significance of 10:26-27 comes from its location immediately after Saul's acclamation as king; in a different context the significance could be different. Its impact is heightened by the reprise in 11:12-13.

Setting

The settings for such traditions are uncertain. The literary setting is clear. It is the DH, probably in its revised form. As will be discussed at the end of this section, these traditions of ch. 8 and 10:17-25 (26-27) offer a view of the emergence of kingship in Israel that differs in tone from the portrayal in 9:1–10:16 and 11:1-11, 15. Such a revision of the DH is certainly to be dated after the death of Josiah (i.e., 609 B.C.E.), so probably in the 6th century.

What is far more difficult to assess is the period when such traditions might have originated. As noted in the discussion, two traditions of the identification of Saul appear to have been blended: a process or designation by lot and an identification by divine oracle. Such traditions might have circulated at almost any period after Saul had become Israel's king. Without more extensive context or evidence, it would be rash to try to narrow down either the time or the circles to which such traditions might be attributed.

Similarly, negative views of kingship do not have to wait for unfortunate experiences of monarchical rule. The language suggests that vv. 18-19 were formulated in association with the national focus of the DH revision. The antipathy can have existed well before its present formulation.

Meaning

The meaning of the passage is best seized from its outcome. After a national assembly at Mizpah, Israel has acclaimed its king: "Long live the king!" (10:24). The present text can hardly be dissociated from the traditions in 8:1-22. It would not be possible for Samuel to be given the negative sentiments of 10:18-19a without the preceding traditions of ch. 8. Similarly, without the divine command to set a king over Israel (cf. 8:22), Samuel could not utter 10:19b and proceed with a formal ceremony establishing a king.

114

The existence of a king is acclaimed. The context for this acclamation is shadowed; it is painted as Israel's rejection of their saving God. Yet the acclamation follows God's cooperation in the processes of divination by lot and oracle. Samuel's promulgation of "the rights and duties of the kingship" *(mišpaṭ hammělūkâ)* is noted without interpretation.

The two added verses, 10:26-27, indicate a change of epochs while recalling the reality of yesterday's orthodoxy. Those who went with the newly acclaimed king are characterized as "warriors whose hearts God had touched" (10:26). Those who clung to a now outdated orthodoxy are called "worthless fellows" (10:27, *běnê běliyya'al*). The rightness of the new is acknowledged; the radical nature of the change is given due expression.

Outcome to Kingship by Divine Command:	**11:1-15**
Samuel as Kingmaker	
I. Story of deliverance of Jabesh-gilead	1-11
A. Ammonite threat	1-3
B. Deliverance by Saul	4-11
1. Appeal for help: direct to Gibeah, indirect to Saul	4-5
2. Saul's reaction to the appeal	6-8
a. Empowerment by the spirit of God	6
b. Summons to Israel	7a
c. Gathering of a force, by fear of the LORD	7b-8
3. Deliverance of the town	9-11
a. Saul: reassures the inhabitants	9
b. Ruse: inhabitants deceive the besieging force	10
c. Saul: relief of siege by military victory	11
II. Aftermath of victory	12-15
A. Decree of amnesty by Saul	12-13
B. Renewal of the kingship at Gilgal	14-15
1. Suggested by Samuel	14
2. Done by all Israel	15

Textual Issues

For the issue of a brief fragment of text, found exclusively in 4QSam[a], preserving an associated tradition of Nahash's cruelty that might be judged to lead into this chapter, see the discussion above, under 10:27.

Discussion

In the present text, Samuel is kingmaker (cf. above all, 11:14). In the present text, this story of Saul's victory is the follow-up to God's initiative in 9:1–10:16. As we have seen, 9:16 had Samuel instructed to anoint Saul who would save Israel from the hand of the Philistines. In the present composition, 1 Sam 7 has eliminated the Philistine threat, at least as a short-term possibility. The words given Samuel in the actual anointing, whether in the Hebrew or the Greek, are not so specific (10:1). Space is created for the deliverance at Jabesh-gilead to be the occasion of Saul's charismatic demonstration of kingly power in Israel.

As noted, 4QSam^a has a significant expansion of the text here, as far as the activities of Nahash are concerned (following the NRSV, it has been discussed above, in relation to 10:27). Whatever decision is taken on textual grounds, the storyline in 11:1-11 is not substantially affected.

The Ammonite siege of Jabesh-gilead and its imminent fall provide the occasion for the demonstration of Saul's capacity as a leader in Israel — [I]. The story begins with the portrayal of need. The desperate urgency of the need is expressed in the exchange between the townspeople and the besieging king. The people of Jabesh-gilead sought for an honorable peace; the condition imposed upon them was that their right eyes be gouged out. What gives a special cachet to Saul's exploit is that not only was a town in Israel threatened with cruelly brutal treatment, but the disgrace was explicitly extended to all Israel (v. 2b). The concession of seven days respite, granted to the besieged citizens in order to summon help, is a narratively powerful expression of the contempt in which Nahash held Israel. On the text-critical issue, Nahash's challenge would seem the more striking, if it were the first gauntlet that he had thrown down before Israel, rather than the climax to his systematic mutilation of two tribes. Similarly, some of the luster is taken from Saul's victory, if he has been unable to prevent the horror of the humiliation of Gad and Reuben. However, these are subjective impressions that were not shared by those who incorporated the 4QSam^a fragment. Perhaps, as noted above, it is best understood as the preservation of a variant tradition.

It is worth noting here that the Ammonite threat on one side may possibly be regarded as matching the menace of the Philistine threat from the other. According to 1 Sam 9:16, Saul was anointed to save Israel from the hand of the Philistines. According to 2 Sam 8:12, it was David who subdued among others both Ammonites and Philistines (cf. 2 Sam 11–12). Fundamentally, our knowledge of the time derives from Davidic traditions; Saul's significance may have been downplayed. The story's expression of Ammonite contempt in allowing Jabesh-gilead a seven-day respite to seek help "through all the territory of Israel" (1 Sam 11:3) is as grave a pointer to the defenselessness of Israel as the isolated notice of its dependence on Philistine metallurgical skills (1 Sam 13:19-22).

Given the story's claim that the messengers were to be sent through all the territory of Israel (v. 3, however unreal this may be) and the narration of their reception at Gibeah of Saul, it is difficult to entertain the notion that they came to the publicly acclaimed king of the preceding story, publicly demanded before that (cf. Hertzberg, 92-93; Mauchline, *Samuel*, 104; Stoebe, 226-27; Klein, 104; McCarter, 205-7, speaks of king *de iure* and king *de facto* and develops the charismatic vs. dynastic line of argument — better abandoned [cf. Campbell, *Of Prophets and Kings*, 113]). The narrative can hardly follow on 10:17-27; the plowing farmer of 11:5 is not the acclaimed king of 10:24. It can follow on 9:1–10:16; the anointing was private and the gift of "another heart" in 10:9 discreetly leaves room for the onrush of the spirit in 11:6. (The onrush/possession of 10:6 and 10:10 belongs to another context and another tradition.) The reference to "all the territory of Israel" is part of the emphasis on Israel's defenselessness. On hearing the news, Saul is empowered by the spirit and, with the symbolic gesture of the cutting in pieces of his yoke of oxen, summons all Israel. In this, even at the level of the present text, he is fulfilling the commission given him in 10:7 (and before that in 10:1). Strategically, deceit plays its part in lulling the besieging forces (11:9-10), victory is won and deliverance gained. More to the point, a deliverer has emerged in Israel.

The concluding sentences of the chapter are burdened by the disparate nature of the traditions being brought into unity here (11:12-15) — [II]. Verse 14 harmonizes this story with the preceding one, through the change of a single word: "and there *renew* the kingdom" (v. 14). Samuel is portrayed recommending the Gilgal ceremony (v. 14); in the report of the celebrations at Gilgal, he is not mentioned. A difference of levels, as in 9:1–10:16, seems likely. Saul's coronation at the sanctuary of Gilgal brings the story to a close (v. 15). What God's initiative began in 9:1–10:16 is here completed. The defense of Israel is now assured. Samuel's work as kingmaker is complete.

However, before the story ends, vv. 12-13 return to the issue opened in 10:26-27. The question there, "How can this man save us?" (10:27), is rendered here, "Shall Saul reign over us?" (11:12). The substitution underlines the theological problem of kingship. The text also underlines the changed situation that has occurred. The question is brought to Samuel (v. 12); the decree of amnesty is handed down by Saul (v. 13). The portrayed transition of power is evident. The motive Saul gives for the exercise of his kingly power rebuts the accusation implied in 10:27 and reaches back into Israel's sacral traditions, reflecting favorably on the newly established institution: "for today the LORD has wrought deliverance in Israel" (v. 13). The saving victory is attributed to God; it is not claimed for himself by Saul (cf. 1 Sam 19:5; 2 Sam 23:10, 12). A new orthodoxy is assured.

Genre

The response to God's commissioning of Saul by Samuel relates to the deliverance of Jabesh-gilead (11:1-15). The text has the potential for a (→) story, but one would have to say that the potential has not been developed. The text begins with a situation of massive need: the town of Jabesh-gilead is portrayed in need of deliverance and Israel is portrayed as hugely humiliated in its inability to provide deliverance — even with seven days in which to organize it. The need is met by Saul's deliverance of the town. All the potential for a story is there, but the potential is not exploited. As it stands, the text is a bare (→) account. A (→) reported story is possible.

As with 10:26-27, the little tradition in 11:12-13 is a (→) notice in the more traditional sense. It preserves a brief unexpanded piece of tradition. The

117

significance of 11:12-13 comes from its location immediately after Saul's signal victory and from its reprise of 10:26-27.

Setting

The literary setting of the core of 11:1-15 would have originally been the PR. As it stands now, in the present text, its literary setting is that of the DH.

Any discussion of the original setting for the tradition of Saul's raising the siege at Jabesh-gilead is impossibly hypothetical. The option is there that the tradition was once independent, with no association with a prior prophetic commission; it is possible, but not certain. Under what circumstances such a tradition might have arisen and in what setting it might have been preserved cannot be more than a matter for conjecture.

The two traditions in 10:26-27 and 11:12-13 have their setting in literature no earlier than the revision of the DH. One is attached to 10:17-25 (in the present text, belonging to the revision of the DH); the other (attached now to PR tradition in the Josianic DH) can hardly have functioned alone. The timing for their insertion into the present text says nothing of the period from which they originate.

Meaning

As the text stands, its meaning is clear: in a time of Israel's apparent defenselessness, the spirit of God can empower a man to exercise leadership and deliver Israel. The signals in the text are more likely to evoke 9:1–10:16 than 10:17-25. Under the influence of this context, the meaning of the text can be more crisply focused: in a time of Israel's need, God has prepared someone whom the spirit of God can empower to exercise leadership and deliver Israel.

Samuel as National Adjudicator	**12:1-25**
I. Assessment of Samuel's credentials	1-5
A. Summary of situation: both present and past	1-2
B. Testimony of Samuel's stewardship	3-5
1. Invitation to testify against Samuel, before God and anointed	3
2. Testimony to Samuel's justice	4
3. Witness to this testimony: God and anointed	5
II. Assessment of Israel's present situation: evil but not hopeless	6-18
A. Witness: the God of Moses, Aaron, and the exodus	6
B. Assessment proper	7-18
1. Summary review of the past	7-12
a. Review of distant past: exodus	7-8
b. Review of recent past: rescuers	9-11

Textual Issues

12:6 Reading the Hebrew text, McCarthy's interpretation is as helpful as any: "a cult invocation or cry announcing the presence of the LORD on this solemn occasion" (*Treaty and Covenant*, 213-14).

12:8 The LXX adds "and his sons" to Jacob and goes further to say "and the Egyptians oppressed them." Either the MT allows for little leaps or the LXX smooths them over (e.g., cry for help without prior oppression). Scholarly opinion tends to divide in predictable directions (for the MT: Stoebe, 233; Barthélemy, 173; Pisano, 172-74; for the LXX: McCarter, 210; Klein, 111). A piecemeal approach can weaken the case for the LXX.

12:14 To be understood as a full conditional sentence: "both you and the king who rules over you will truly be followers of YHWH your God" (with Boecker, *Beurteilung*, 77-81; cf. Klein, 110-11; also McCarthy, *Treaty and Covenant*, 215-16).

12:15 Most read, with some form of the LXX, "against you and your king" (e.g., Driver, 94-95; Boecker, *Beurteilung*, 79; McCarter, 212; Klein, 111-12). R. Weiss suggests reading "and your houses" ("La Main du Seigneur"), a minor emendation but unsupported. The Hebrew text — "against you and your fathers" — is maintained, for example, by Stoebe (p. 234) and Barthélemy (pp. 174-75). Emendation is attractive; as it stands, the Hebrew requires improbable ingenuity.

Discussion

Martin Noth identified the dtr contribution in 1 Sam 7–12 as 7:2-17; 8:1-22; 10:17-27a; and 12:1-25 (*DH*, 78-84, esp. p. 83). Whatever the scholarship before him, after Noth, scholarship has been affected by this identification and has also struggled with it — for example: Hertzberg, 96-97; Stoebe, 171, 234-40, highly ambivalent (e.g., "in its core an independent piece of tradition" but also not to be set apart from ch. 8 and 10:17-27, "it [ch. 12] belongs in the Mizpah tradition" [p. 235]); McCarter, 219-21, "expanded by a Deuteronomistic hand"; Klein, 112-20, ambivalent (e.g., "access to an alternate tradition" [p. 114], but also "this chapter was used by the deuteronomistic historian to sum up his interpretation of the rise of kingship" [ibid.]). Credit for effectively separating ch. 12 from the core of the dtr work goes to Veijola, who claimed it for his DtrN (*Königtum*, 83-99); credit for establishing this conclusion on firmer ground goes to O'Brien (*Deuteronomistic History Hypothesis*, 120-28). A further reevaluation can be found in Campbell and O'Brien (*Unfolding*).

First Samuel 12 is undoubtedly an attempt to pull together both negative and positive views of kingship and reconcile them so that the history of Israel with YHWH could continue. In part, it does this thoroughly and well. Being appropriately located after the establishment of Saul as king (chs. 8–11), it is natural that it should have been thought to be from the compiler responsible for the composition of these chapters. Assuming the probability that some of the traditions in ch. 8–11 have old and different origins, the question is then thrown open as to the origin of the traditions in ch. 12.

The text-critical variations that began with the LXX and other ancient versions are a pointer to the likelihood that the historical traditions behind ch. 12 are different from those that precede it in the DH. In the preceding text (Judg 3:7–16:31), the oppressors are seven: Cushan-rishathaim, Eglon, Philistines (3:31), Jabin king of Canaan whose army commander was Sisera, Midianites, Ammonites, and Philistines; the deliverers are also seven: Othniel, Ehud, Shamgar, Deborah and Barak, Gideon, Jephthah, and Samson. The Hebrew of 1 Sam 12:9 lists three oppressors: Sisera (named as commander of the army of Hazor), Philistines, king of Moab; 12:11 lists four deliverers: Jerubbaal, Bedan, Jephthah, and Samuel. The LXX tradition agrees on the three oppressors of 1 Sam 12:9, but naming Sisera rather more correctly as commander to Jabin, king of Hazor. LXX traditions are not so agreed on the deliverers; some mss. have Jeroboam in place of Jerubbaal, Barak is preferred to Bedan (although Balak figures), Jephthah is uncontested, but some mss. prefer Samson to Samuel or include both. The Vulgate agrees fully with the Hebrew text in both v. 9 and v. 11.

The discrepancies between Judges and 1 Sam 12 are too great to encourage emendation and correction. It is not so much that a corrupted text has created difficulties for its interpreters but rather that a difficult (non-traditional) text has led to corrections and corruptions. By way of comparison: it would be imprudent to emend the non-traditional texts of 2 Sam 21:15-22 or 23:8-39 to bring them into closer conformity with the traditional Davidic texts. Prudence suggests that a non-traditional text is present in 1 Sam 12.

The identification of dtr thinking or language in a passage of this kind needs careful investigation and evaluation. For example, "the good and right way" of 12:23 is unique in the Hebrew Bible; one commentator describes it as "surely" dtr — it may be, but it is unique. There are surprises in store: to "serve YHWH" does not occur within the dtr contributions to the Josianic DH; "with all your hearts" (12:20, 24) evokes the national focus of the dtr revision (cf. Josh 23:14; 1 Sam 7:3), but there are also Jer 29:13 and Joel 2:12. Minor editorial touches are always possible. The margins can imitate the center; influence by the center on the margins is possible. Evaluation is important; what is not exclusive is unlikely to be demonstrative. The closer stereotyped language is to the system of dtr thinking, the more likely it is to be identifiably dtr.

Whether it makes good sense to correlate the oppressors with the deliverers listed is a question best left open. It could be that three of each have been chosen, with Samuel forming the link to the present. Sisera is local (Canaanite), the Philistines are to the west, the Moabites to the east. Except in Judg 9, the name Jerubbaal is rare for Gideon, Bedan as deliverer is unknown (cf. 1 Chron 7:17), and Jephthah figures as both deliverer-judge and minor judge. Features of the early verses of this chapter discourage any attempt at harmonization with what is traditionally known.

Among these features, we may note:

1. 12:1 surprises with a strong affirmation of what Samuel has done, "I have set a king over you"; it has no mention of God (cf. 8:22) — despite God's involvement throughout the preceding (thundering in ch. 7, warning in ch. 8, anointing in 9:1–10:16, identifying in 10:17-27, and empowering in ch. 11).
2. 12:2 surprises with no name for the king — despite Saul's presence from 9:1 on. No name is used in relation to the king throughout the chapter; Saul is not mentioned.
3. 12:2 also notes Samuel's old age and the presence of his sons, reminiscent of 8:1. But 12:3-5 are concerned with clearing Samuel of wrongdoing, including oppression and bribery (for defraud and oppress together, see Deut 28:33; Hos 5:11; and Amos 4:1). Similar accusations were made, in different language, against Samuel's sons in 8:3; but in 12:3-5, there is no mention of the accusations of bribery and injustice against these sons. Note: in these verses, the witnesses alleged are YHWH and "his anointed"; a tradition of the anointed is presumed — unless, as is possible, the references to the anointed are assumed to be additions.
4. 12:7 uses a rare term for "all the saving deeds of YHWH" (ṣidqôt yhwh), otherwise unparalleled in the dtr contributions to the DH; elsewhere, only Judg 5:11; Mic 6:5; and Ps 103:6. The clause, "that I may enter into judgment with you," is unique in the DH and otherwise late (McCarthy, *Treaty and Covenant*, 207).
5. 12:8 uses the "fathers/ancestors" to refer to the exodus generation. In its use of "you and your ancestors" (vv. 7, 15), it shares with dtr theology the idea of the availability of God's benevolence to the current generation as much as to the generation of the exodus (cf. von Rad, *Theology*, 1.231).

6. 12:9 has been discussed above. The clause "to forget YHWH" is relatively rare, with distribution wide enough to defy significance. McCarthy notes also Hos 2:13 (Heb., 2:15); 8:14; and 13:6 (*Treaty and Covenant,* 208).

7. 12:10 expresses strongly the theology of the "national" focus within the revision of the DH, found esp. in Judg 10:10-16 and 1 Sam 7:3-4 (for the comparison of Judg 10:10 with 1 Sam 12:10, see Veijola, *Königtum,* 87). The explicit confession of sin, the plea for deliverance, and the role of repentance as a condition before deliverance are not found in the Josianic Deuteronomist's contributions. They are found in either Judg 10:10-16 or 1 Sam 7:3-4 or both. The verb "to forsake" is not used of YHWH in the Josianic Deuteronomist's contributions; it is a feature of the national revision (cf. Judg 2:12). The emphasis in 12:23 on Samuel as instructor parallels the revision's view in Judg 2:17 and 2 Kgs 17:13; dependence (and, if any, the direction of dependence) has to remain uncertain.

8. 12:11 has been discussed above.

9. 12:12 surprises with the introduction of Nahash, king of Ammon, as a threatened menace that led to Israel's demand for a king. In chs. 8–11, Israel's demand for a king is motivated by the bribery and injustice attributed to Samuel's sons; victory over Nahash is preceded by Saul's kingship (10:24) and celebrated afterwards by the kingship's renewal (cf. 11:14). However the text is understood, neither the kingship nor its "renewal" is portrayed as a response to the threat posed by Nahash. The appeal to "an original feature of an older tradition" (Hertzberg, 99) is not to be restricted to this verse. However, in this verse and in aspects of what follows, there is an element of the rejection of God that would have appealed to the national focus of the revision.

10. 12:13 refers to the king "whom you have chosen," a description that does not fit with what precedes (despite 8:18), where the demand may come from the people but the choice comes from God. The additional "for whom you have asked" is much closer to what precedes; it is not attested in many of the LXX mss. Verse 13b, "see, the LORD has set a king over you," expresses a different emphasis from 12:1; there Samuel, here God.

McCarthy notes that, in 12:14-15, the apodoses — the second or main clauses — are untypical of Deuteronomy and dtr style, "which emphasize life and possession of the Land as the consequences of fidelity or their loss for infidelity" (*Treaty and Covenant,* 210). While the protases — the first or conditional clauses — have a "multiplication of phrases" (McCarthy), all of which can be found in dtr contexts, it is noteworthy that similar sequences are not found in the dtr literature. A close example is Deut 10:12. Like v. 14, it has four elements; only two of these are found in v. 14 and none of them in v. 15. The phrase "to rebel against the mouth of YHWH" has a remarkably limited distribution: Deut 1:26, 43; 9:23; 1 Sam 12:14, 15; 1 Kgs 13:21, 26. Overall, while the building blocks of vv. 14-15 can certainly be dtr, the construction built from them must be described as unique.

Verses 14-25 offer a constitutional settlement, expressing how Israel can live with its monarchy, though the LORD their God is their king. Fidelity will be fine; infidelity will be failure. God's power is demonstrated; the prophet's favor is assured; the future holds both hope and threat. As a constitutional settlement, vv. 14-25 form an attractive conclusion to chs. 7–12. As a reflection of Israel's prior history, vv. 1-13 are distinctly idiosyncratic. It is worth noting that, in a chapter devoted to the constitutional settlement of the monarchy, the activity of the prophet occupies two-thirds of the text (vv. 1-6 and 16-25). Verses 1-6 are concerned with clearing the prophet of any charge of self-interest or oppression. Verses 16-25 are bound up with the demonstration of prophetic authority and the assurance of prophetic intercession. The role of the prophet is closely involved with the role of the king.

It is tempting to see dtr editing at work in the latter part of the chapter at least — but in vain. Critical reading of the Hebrew does not evoke echoes of dtr composition; to the contrary, it is an unfamiliar style. Careful analysis of the Hebrew does not suggest dtr composition. Some examples: the "thunder" of vv. 17-18 is not dtr; the "we have added to our sins" of v. 19 is not dtr; the "turn aside after" of vv. 20-21 is not dtr; neither the "useless things" nor the expression of their unprofitability is dtr (v. 21); God's casting off or forsaking his people is not a dtr idiom (v. 22). The enigma of this chapter is how close it is to the complex of dtr thinking and how far away it is so often from dtr tradition and expression.

With this close examination completed, the last word can be given to Dennis McCarthy, although he may overemphasize the extent of dtr reworking: "To sum up: there is clear evidence for a solid mass of material in 1 Sam 12 which is not Dtistic but rather the remains of the tradition reworked to produce the chapter in its Dtistic form" (*Treaty and Covenant,* 212). This perception can be refined in the light of a Josianic DH with variant traditions being introduced and used by the dtr revision. 1 Sam 12 is most probably to be understood as a largely independent and highly idiosyncratic tradition that has been introduced by the dtr revision and adjusted to some degree, providing an appropriate conclusion to the revision's reorganization of traditions about the emergence of monarchy in Israel. Editorial impact on the text can be identified in the insertion of 12:10 by the "national" focus. Some further dtr editing cannot be excluded but is neither certain nor particularly significant. The attraction for the dtr revision would lie in the material's negativity toward the monarchy coupled with its insistence that nevertheless the monarchy could function in Israel if it was characterized by fidelity and obedience to YHWH (cf. 12:14-15). The emphasis on the people would have heightened its attractiveness to the national focus within the revision.

The conflicting evidence for autonomy and relationship is not easily assessed. O'Brien's comment is insightful: "The author made enough references to the history to establish a basic contextual relationship with it, but in doing so interpreted or adapted the reference points so that they would better serve the argument being developed" (*Deuteronomistic History Hypothesis,* 122). Beyond 12:10, the role played by the interaction of source and editing is difficult to determine with any precision. The meaning of the chapter is clear; its origin is enigmatic. It is based on traditions that are not identical with those of the preceding chapters of Samuel or Judges, but as a reflection it is grappling with the problems that are present in chs. 7–11. It is this paradox that allows ch. 12 to be so different from what precedes it and yet to be so apt as a reflection on the newly emerged monarchy.

If ch. 12 is a later insertion and not part of the Josianic DH, then at an earlier level the presentation of kingship ended with 11:15, followed by 13:1 (cf. Brueggemann, 97), making it easier to see Saul's kingship as a way station to the anointing of David — especially if 11:14 and Samuel's role are later harmonizations.

First Samuel 12 is structured around three major moments: the assessment of Samuel's credentials — [I], the assessment of Israel's present situation — [II], and the assessment of Israel's future — [III].

12:1-5 addresses the issue of credentials — [I]. It does not portray an assembly that Samuel has convoked. The people are at Gilgal for Saul's kingship; Samuel is portrayed seizing the opportunity to address "all Israel" (12:1). Samuel established the king at the people's demand, "I have listened to you in all that you have said to me" (v. 1) — echoes of ch. 8, but not a word about God's role or Saul's name. Samuel's sons are mentioned (v. 2); their names, offices, greed, and injustice are not. Samuel receives certification of his honesty from the people, before God and the king (vv. 3-5). God and the king form an envelope structure around this confirmation; they open v. 3 and return in v. 5.

At this point in the text we do not know why it is important for Samuel to have this public clearance from the people. It will become clear very shortly. Samuel's position stands in stark contrast with that of his sons in 8:1-3. He has not defrauded, oppressed, or wronged the people (12:4); his sons' greed and injustice have been felt as intolerable by the people (expressed by their elders). The contrast is not addressed.

12:6-18 addresses the issue of Israel's present situation — [II]. Verse 6 is difficult, and is often emended to include the sense of witnessing (e.g., McCarter, 210, 214; Klein, 111, 115-16). Even so it reads oddly. The bulk of the verse expresses praise of God, declaring what God has done (although without the usual participial form). It modulates from v. 5 (God as witness to Samuel's integrity) to v. 7 (God as the one before whom all Israel must stand and be judged). Its presence in the text and its syntax remain problematic. After textual adjustments in both vv. 6 and 8, v. 6 can be rendered: "It is YHWH who brought your fathers up out of the land of Egypt" (so Boecker, *Beurteilung,* 71-72). In the light of this fundamental constitutive basis of Israel's history, expressed in v. 6b, the rest of the discourse can be constructed. The outcome is attractive; the adjustments, however, are considerable. No solution is fully satisfactory (Stoebe brackets out v. 6b as foreign to its context, 233). Read as "a cult invocation or cry announcing the presence of the LORD on this solemn occasion" (McCarthy, *Treaty and Covenant,* 213-14), it would remain unadjusted: The LORD who appointed Moses and Aaron and brought your ancestors up out of the land of Egypt.

The structure of vv. 7-18 is of the 3 + 1 pattern known to us from Amos 1–2 and various proverbs (cf. Proverbs 30). There are a summary review of Israel's past, a statement of its present situation, and a summary review of the future, that is, the constitutional situation; and, beyond these three, there is the demonstration of God's power. Behind the past and present lurks lack of faith in God's power to deliver; hence the demonstration of God's power as a conclusion.

The review of Israel's past is broken up into three: the distant past, the recent past, and the immediate past. The distant past is unsurprising enough, although the theology is fascinating (vv. 7-8). The saving deeds (all salvation history, *'et kol ṣidqôt yhwh*, cf. Barthélemy, *Critique textuelle,* 172) were performed "for you and for your ancestors" (12:7). As noted, this is dtr theology where salvation reaches over centuries of failure to speak to the present day. The review touches simply on exodus and conquest (v. 8). The recent past is focused on oppression and deliverance (vv. 9-11). It is here, as we have seen, that ch. 12 differs markedly from the preceding traditions of the deliverer-judges. The immediate past, again as we have seen above, portrays the threat from Nahash as the trigger initiating the request for a king (v. 12); this is a quite different portrayal of the history from the preceding chapters.

These differences raise some substantial questions about our knowledge of Israel's past. Does ch. 12 preserve a variant tradition of Israel's experience of oppression and deliverance and kingship that has an equal claim to authenticity with the preceding traditions? For example, Jerubbaal (Gideon) is named first here, and the Gideon story in Judges opens without the "again" [*wayyōsipû*] found in the two before it (compare Judg 6:1 with 3:12 and 4:1, also 10:6; it is not in 3:7 of course). Alternatively, in either case are we looking at faulty recall of tradition or theologically influenced reshaping of tradition? We do not know. When we have one tradition, it is unchallenged; when we have more than one, we may have a challenge and no easy resolution.

The review of the constitutional situation (vv. 14-15) is the nub of the chapter. It offers a future that is positive, if there is fidelity from the people (v. 14). It offers a future that is negative, if there is infidelity from the people (v. 15). Many modern translations do not present a strict balance in the two verses. They treat the whole of v. 14 as being a conditional clause and add the equivalent of "it will be well" at the end — which is not in the Hebrew text. The constitutional balance is most easily seen when the parallel construction of the two sentences in Hebrew is clearly represented.

"*If* you will fear the LORD and serve him and heed his voice, and not rebel against the commandment of the LORD, *then* both you and the king who reigns over you will be loyal followers of the LORD your God." (v. 14)

"*If* you will not heed the voice of the LORD, but rebel against the commandment of the LORD, *then* the hand of the LORD will be against you and your ancestors." (v. 15; emphasis mine throughout)

This understanding of v. 14 is proposed by Boecker; it depends on the recognition that "following the LORD" (literally: being after) is a technical expression which, in the context of decision, expresses loyalty and fidelity (*Beurteilung,* 77-82, esp. p. 80; cf. 2 Sam 2:10; 15:13; 17:9; 1 Kgs 12:20; 16:21; so also Mc-Carthy, *Treaty and Covenant,* 215, and Klein, 110-11). Even in the traditional rendering of vv. 14-15, it is clear that two ways are being presented to Israel, one of which will bring weal, the other woe. Israel stood before blessing and curse at the end of Moses' exposition of the law, as it stood on the brink of life in the land (Deut 28). Israel stands now before blessing and curse, fidelity or infidelity to God, after the end of the period of the deliverer-judges, standing on the brink of life under the kings.

The demonstration of divine power which follows this central constitutional instruction as to how Israel can have their king and yet be loyal to their God resurrects the theme of the wickedness of the request for a king (v. 17). The miraculous exercise of divine power is further evidence of the needless nature of the request.

12:19-25 addresses the issue of Israel's future — [III]. The people's request for Samuel's intercession accepts his accusation of wickedness (v. 19). Samuel's response is a complex exhortation to fidelity, sandwiching assurance of God's fidelity and Samuel's own intercession and guidance between his initial call for the people's fidelity (vv. 20-21) and the final renewal of his exhortation to that fidelity (v. 24a). Only in the final sentence does the negative possibility of divine threat reemerge (v. 25).

Genre

The genre of 1 Sam 12 is close to indefinable. At a simply formal level, it is the report of a (→) speech by Samuel. At another level, its closest parallels are the book of Deuteronomy where Moses instructs Israel in "the good and right way" (1 Sam 12:23) and Josh 24 where Joshua does much the same — although, in both cases, without this language. While these might be seen as the testamentary activity of Moses and Joshua, putting their national legacies in order as their lives end, for Samuel there is much still ahead. Elijah's demand for Israel's choice on Mt. Carmel (1 Kgs 18) is another parallel, but a more remote one. A closer parallel may be found in Josiah's convocation of Judah and Jerusalem to commit the people to the covenant of renewal (2 Kgs 23:1-3). Alas, there is no speech by Josiah.

There is no genre of national adjudication and, yet, that is what Samuel does here. Israel's present situation is assessed in the light of its past and is found to be evil but not hopeless. What has been done is evil, but the new institution can be integrated into the people's relationship with God. Israel's future is assessed as hopeful, but threat lurks in the background. So there are reproach and condemnation for the past, constitutional guidance in the present, and both hope and instruction for the future. Samuel here is not principally in the role of prophet or deliverer-judge. Rather he takes the role of judge over all Israel and gives a judicial assessment of Israel's past, its present situation with the establishment of monarchy, and its future with God.

Setting

The setting for the chapter in its present form is a literary one and has to be within the national focus of the revision of the DH. The theology is in accord with this focus — the confession of sin (12:10a), the plea for deliverance (12:10b), with the confession and implied repentance preceding the plea for deliverance, as well as other features. The emphasis on the people is in accord with this revision, as are Samuel's role as national adjudicator and some traces of linguistic usage.

What escapes our understanding is why the dtr circles should adopt or produce a reflection on the emergence of the monarchy that is based on such widely different traditions from those portrayed in the text of the Josianic DH. Here, at least for the present, we have to admit our lack of knowledge.

Meaning

The meaning of the chapter is clear: the demand for kingship has been evil and unnecessary; nevertheless kingship is now an accepted fact in Israel; fruitful living in Israel under the monarchy is possible as long as fidelity and obedience to the God of Israel are maintained.

The chapter reflects on the issue of kingship as an evil that has nevertheless come about. Although based on a substantially different portrayal of the traditions, in this it mirrors the concern in chs. 8–11 once the rejection texts are in place. Prior to the insertion of these texts, both the initiative from the people (request) and the initiative from God (commission) were positive. With the insertion of the rejection texts, the initiative from God is overlooked and the initiative from the people is characterized as evil. It is this situation of tension between faithless demand and faithful response that ch. 12 grapples with.

It is not immediately clear what the sources of the ideological opposition to kingship might have been in Israel. It is not simply a question of an individual usurping God's place of leadership. Individuals, from Moses and Joshua to the judges, had been leaders in Israel before this; at least for the minor judges, there seems to have been some degree of institutionalization. The question has to be asked why kingship should have been considered, in some quarters, to be such a threat. From a theological point of view, it would appear that the institutional continuity of kingship and the development of supporting institutions, such as a standing army and a royal administration, were seen as eroding the sense of dependence on God. The drama of kingship in Israel is part of the constant drama of human faith. There is no reason why successful human institutions, providing security and an improved quality of life, should diminish faith in God. But it is one of the weaknesses of human nature to turn to God when confronted with the insuperable, but to turn a blind eye in times of human security (cf. Deut 6:10-12; Prov 30:7-9).

The danger that God is being made an accomplice in Israel's evil is not confronted in ch. 12 — possibly because the chapter was looking at another presentation of the tradition and does not contain sufficient specifics of its own to categorize God's response. The constitutional issue is solved in terms of fidelity and obedience. The institution of monarchy is not in itself intolerable. Coupled with fidelity and obedience, it will prove positive; without fidelity and obedience, it will be disastrous.

In this, 1 Sam 12 fits well into the present text. As a review of the present text of chs. 8–11, it grapples with the problem they address and it offers a solution. As a preview of what is to come, it is also appropriate. Saul will fail in fidelity and obedience, and will be dismissed as king. David will be portrayed as the model of fidelity and obedience and will succeed as king. What happens at the beginning of the monarchy reflects, alas, what will happen at its end.

The Overall Composition of 1 Samuel 7–12

It is not an understatement to say that 1 Sam 7–12 is a classic example of complex and controverted text. It is also a classic specimen of Israel's theological processes, expressing critical reflection in story, juxtaposing differing traditions, drawing on new material to update views, and often blending the whole into a final text of remarkable artistry and elegance (cf. Campbell and O'Brien, *Unfolding*). It is a mark of this complexity that the interpretation of chs. 7–12 can exploit several approaches and may construct a diversity of models. What will be advocated here involves one such approach and will construct one particular model; in my judgment, it is the simplest, the most economical, the most elegant, and the most faithful to the signals in the biblical text. It is certainly not the only approach to be taken or the only model to be constructed. To deny this would be to deny the complexity of the text.

At the Level of a Josianic Deuteronomistic History

Given the hypothesis that there was a Josianic DH, favorably disposed to the deuteronomic reform and favorably disposed to King Josiah in his implementation of the reform, a Josianic DH can be expected to have been favorably disposed to the idea of monarchy and to its emergence in Israel.

Such a history would be eminently well-served by the account of the emergence of kingship in Israel given by the combination of 1 Sam 9:1–10:16 with 11:1-11, 15. In such an account, kingship derives from God's initiative, with a view to succoring Israel's need, its value illustrated by Saul's successful relief of the siege of Jabesh-gilead.

Looked at as it stands, the independence of these two texts (9:1–10:16 and 11:1-11, 15) seems likely. Saul is not anointed king in 9:1–10:16; he is anointed "ruler," *nāgîd*. A fair assumption is that, when this text was composed, Saul was already firmly established in the tradition as having been king of Israel; this assumption would give an independent priority to 11:1-11, 15. It can, of course, be argued that the sequence is theologically determined: anointing precedes and makes possible the charismatic deed that leads to kingship. However, in the two other cases of prophetic anointing, this is not clear. David is anointed by Samuel (1 Sam 16:13); he not only has to evade Saul's onslaught to become king over Judah (2 Sam 2:4), but he must also win a long civil war (2 Sam 3:1) to become king over all Israel at Hebron (2 Sam 5:3). The LORD may be with him and David may be gifted with charisma; evidence of a charismatic deed is lacking, unless it is his single combat with the Philistine champion (Goliath) which marks the beginning of a long road (cf. 1 Sam 17 and context). Jehu is anointed king by Elisha's disciple and acclaimed by his army colleagues (2 Kgs 9:1-13); the only charismatic deed in the context is the successful and bloody execution of a brutal palace coup.

It is likely that the Josianic DH took over the combination of 1 Sam 9:1–10:16 and 11:1-11, 15 from the PR. In the hypothesis of a PR, prophetic anointing was needed for Saul and David, as for Jehu. The traditional story of Saul's encounter with an anonymous prophet who gave him a somewhat ambiguous commission (1 Sam 10:7) offered a core for the prophetic claim to have been the instrument of God in Saul's kingship. As noted, the knowledge of Saul as king may have been well established in the tradition and attested, for example, in 1 Sam 11:1-11, 15. Hence the concern in the text for privacy (1 Sam 9:27); privacy also makes sense for David and Jehu — David (some twenty chapters from the throne) and Jehu (no coup without the support of his fellow commanders).

At the Level of a Revised Deuteronomistic History

Josiah's unexpected death in battle and the abandonment of the deuteronomic reform called for a revision of the history. In fact, it should have called for a rethink of the entire dtr theology; the biblical text offers us only a revision of the history.

In the understanding offered here, the revising editors looked at the examples of evil kings in the south (above all, Ahaz and Manasseh) and the paradigms of royal evil in the north (above all, the Omrides) and drew the conclusion that monarchy had led Israel into apostasy and failure. In one tendency of the revision (the "royal" focus), emphasis was given to the evil done by the kings; in another (the "national" focus), the involvement of the people was emphasized.

The editors influenced by the "royal" focus had at their disposal other traditions about the emergence of kingship in Israel that were not so glowingly favorable as 9:1–10:16 and 11:1-11, 15. Note that "had at their disposal" presupposes that these traditions were not created from whole cloth by dtr editors; as Dennis McCarthy comments of these passages, "they are scarcely deuteronomistic compositions" ("Inauguration," 405). In the understanding offered here, these revising editors would have introduced much of 1 Sam 7:2–8:22 and 10:17-25 as a compensating balance to the enthusiastic account of the emergence of kingship in 9:1–10:16 and 11:1-11, 15. The traditions introduced in 1 Sam 7 undermined the notion that Israel needed a king, that kingship derived from God's initiative with a view to succoring Israel. With the peace achieved by Samuel's intercession lasting for Samuel's lifetime, any notion of need was eliminated — or at least downplayed and opened to discussion. The tradition introduced in 1 Sam 8 shifted the initiative away from God and placed it with the elders of Israel; added to it was the theme of warning from God. The traditions of 10:17, 20-25 could have been attractive to the revisers on two counts. First, Saul's hiding among the baggage could be construed as unkingly; second, the tradition did not involve a charismatic deed exalting Saul as deliverer and king. Having involved Samuel in the establishment of Saul as king (10:20-25), it would have been appropriate for these revisers to involve Samuel in the ceremony at Gilgal and have him call for a "renewal" of the kingship (11:14).

The editors influenced by the "national" focus took a more negative view of the emergence of monarchy. After all, it had proved the occasion for the people's apostasy and their failure to observe the laws of Deuteronomy, above all centralization of worship at Jerusalem and exclusive fidelity to YHWH. So they prefaced the account of Israel's repentance, presided over by Samuel, with a couple of verses to make clear from the outset that the trouble was apostasy and the worship of foreign gods (1 Sam 7:3-4). Then the demand for a king in ch. 8 needed to be modified so that it was not merely a shift of initiative but an active rejection of YHWH. Hence the additions of 8:7b-8 and also 10:18-19. Theological flexibility is evident in 12:1-25. In the adaptation of the negative texts, a fearful evil has been committed: Israel has needlessly rejected their God (cf. Jer 2:9-12). Less insightful theologians might have left it there, allowing subsequent generations to blame their forebears (cf. Jer 31:29). The insertion of 1 Sam 12:1-25 accepts the reality of sin in the emergence of monarchy and points the way for both king and people to remain faithful to YHWH — "both you and the king who reigns over you" will be loyal to YHWH (12:14). The blame lay with both parties; the option for fidelity was available (12:22-24), but it was not taken and so 12:25 came into force. The outcome is an effective envelope: Samuel is intercessor for Israel in ch. 7 (cf. esp. 7:8-9) and Samuel is again intercessor for Israel in ch. 12 (cf. esp. 12:19-23).

At some point, and it is hard to say when, the traditions of 10:26-27 and 11:12-13 were introduced into the text. They belong together; 11:12 needs 10:27 (or equivalent). In the present text, one is associated with the revision and the other with the Josianic DH. Other combinations might be possible. The point is clear: epochs have changed; yesterday's orthodoxy is no longer valid.

At the Level of the Present Text

The present text can be viewed in at least two different ways. If emphasis is laid on the differing traditions, the text of 1 Sam 7–12 is an excellent example of Israel's ability to hold on to and juxtapose conflicting traditions about its past. The believing community of Israel could hold together and treasure Genesis 1–3, or the composite text of Exodus 14 (with one tradition that has Israel remaining through the night on one side of the sea skillfully blended with another that has Israel passing through the sea with the waters parted to either side), or the different reasons for Moses' exclusion from the land (cf. Num 20:2-12 [sin of Moses, not others] and Deut 1:37 [sin of others, not Moses]). This same community apparently did not have difficulty holding, evaluating, and reflecting on the various views of significant events in their story. In relation to the emer-

130

gence of monarchy, Israel held together traditions that traced the origin back to issues of justice or to issues of defense, to divine initiative or to demand from the people, as well as to divine endorsement of the new institution alongside divine warning about monarchy and even its categorization as rejection of Israel's God, with final reflection on how monarchy could be incorporated into the faith community of Israel.

Alternatively, if emphasis is laid on the artful composition of these traditions, there is much to be noticed. The "prophetic" traditions (9:1–10:16 and 11:1-11, 15) have been framed by "assembly" traditions (chs. 7–8 [Mizpah and Ramah] at the beginning; 10:17-27 [Mizpah] in the middle; ch. 12 [Gilgal] at the end). The reevaluation of the overall setting of need and the emphasis on fidelity is placed at the beginning. God's involvement (cf. 8:7 and 22) and also God's warning (cf. 8:9-21) precede God's initiative. In its turn, God's initiative precedes the identification and acclamation of Saul as king. Saul's establishment as king precedes the demonstration of the power of his office in the relief of Jabesh-gilead. The conflicting traditions are held together in ch. 12 (cf. v. 13: "See, here is the king whom you have chosen, for whom you have asked; see, the LORD has set a king over you"); the conflict is resolved in favor of obedience and fidelity. More might be said.

It would be imprudent and misguided for emphasis on skillful composition to move to denial of the conflict between traditions. It would be just as imprudent and misguided for emphasis on the conflict between traditions to move to deny the skilled nature of the composition. Like ancient Israel, today's interpreters are confronted with both and must make the best of what they have.

It is important for the modern interpreter to be aware of the skilled composition of these texts. While independent traditions have been juxtaposed rather than blended, the main drift of two systems ("assembly" and "prophetic") have been interwoven rather than juxtaposed in sequence. In ancient Israel, two flood traditions were blended to form one narrative; since each tradition ends with God's promise never to destroy again, placed in sequence they would subvert each other (Gen 6:5–9:17). Two stories of deliverance at the Reed Sea were blended to form one; while mutually incompatible, combined they witness to a single origin of deliverance and faith in the story of Israel (Exod 13:17–14:31). Two traditions about the emergence of monarchy have been interwoven (the "prophetic": defense and divine initiative; the "assembly": justice and popular demand) with a result that reflects a single institution of monarchy in Israel (traced back for both Judah and northern Israel) and divided views about the appropriateness of monarchy. Samuel's presence throughout the traditions is a strongly unifying factor.

Genre

The genre of the present text, with its rich combination of traditions, can only be termed a (→) composite narrative, holding together in a single composition a variety of conflicting traditions.

Setting

The setting for the present text, taking into account the presence of the Josianic DH and its revision, is almost certainly exilic Israel. We know little of the dtr groups that engendered the DH and presumably undertook its revision. We would have to assume that such groups were the setting for this text.

Meaning

Whatever its origins, the last word on the meaning of these chapters can probably be given to 1 Sam 12. Monarchy in Israel emerged out of turbulent and troublesome times, with Israel torn between hope and fear, apostasy and fidelity. In the swirling mists of trouble, details of events and origins can be lost to view; differing convictions can be passed on to later generations. Like many institutions that emerge from troubled times, monarchy in Israel was heavily freighted with ambivalence. Holding to fidelity, Israel — people and king — could indeed be a people for YHWH (12:14, 22). Tempted by autonomy and lapsing into apostasy, Israel — people and king — could indeed be swept away (12:25).

Bibliography of Works Cited Above

ANET. Ancient Near Eastern Texts Relating to the Old Testament. 3rd ed. with Supplement. Edited by James B. Pritchard. Princeton: Princeton University Press, 1969.

Barthélemy, Dominique. *Critique textuelle de l'Ancien Testament.* Vol. 1. OBO 50/1. Fribourg, Switz.: Éditions Universitaires, 1982.

Boecker, Hans Jochen. *Die Beurteilung der Anfänge des Königtums in den deuteronomistischen Abschnitten des I. Samuelbuches.* WMANT 31. Neukirchen: Neukirchener Verlag, 1969.

Budde, Karl. *Die Bücher Samuel.* KHC 8. Tübingen: Mohr, 1902.

Campbell, Antony F. *Of Prophets and Kings: A Late Ninth-Century Document (1 Samuel 1–2 Kings 10).* CBQMS 17. Washington, DC: Catholic Biblical Association of America, 1986.

Campbell, Antony F., and Mark A. O'Brien. *Unfolding the Deuteronomistic History: Origins, Upgrades, Present Text.* Minneapolis: Fortress, 2000.

Cross, Frank Moore. "The Ammonite Oppression of the Tribes of Gad and Reuben: Missing Verses from 1 Samuel 11 Found in 4QSamuel[a]." Pp. 105-19 in *The Hebrew and Greek Texts of Samuel.* 1980 Proceedings IOSCS — Vienna. Edited by E. Tov. Jerusalem: Academon, 1980.

Herbert, Edward D. "4QSam[a] and Its Relationship to the LXX: An Exploration in Stemmatological Analysis." Pp. 37-55 in *IX Congress of the International Organization for Septuagint and Cognate Studies: Cambridge, 1955.* Edited by B. A. Taylor. SBLSCS 45. Atlanta: Scholars Press, 1997.

Josephus, Flavius. *Jewish Antiquities*. Books V-VIII. The Loeb Classical Library. London: Heinemann, 1934.

Kallai, Zecharia. "Samuel in Qumrān: Expansion of a Historiographical Pattern (4QSamª)." *RB* 103 (1996) 581-91.

Langlamet, F. "Les récits de l'institution de la royauté (I Sam., VII–XII): De Wellhausen aux travaux récents." *RB* 77 (1970) 161-200.

Lohfink, Norbert. *Die Landverheißung als Eid: Eine Studie zu Gn 15*. SBS 28. Stuttgart: Katholisches Bibelwerk, 1967.

Mauchline, John. *1 and 2 Samuel*. New Century Bible. London: Oliphants, 1971.

McCarthy, Dennis J. "The Inauguration of Monarchy in Israel. A Form-Critical Study of I Samuel 8–12." *Interpretation* 27 (1973) 401-12.

———. *Treaty and Covenant: A Study in Form in the Ancient Oriental Documents and in the Old Testament*. New ed., completely rewritten. AnBib 21A. Rome: Biblical Institute, 1978.

Mendelsohn, I. "Samuel's Denunciation of Kingship in the Light of the Akkadian Documents from Ugarit." *BASOR* 143 (1956) 17-22.

O'Brien, Mark A. *The Deuteronomistic History Hypothesis: A Reassessment*. OBO 92. Freiburg, Switzerland: Universitätsverlag, 1989.

Rad, Gerhard von. *Old Testament Theology*. 2 vols. Edinburgh: Oliver and Boyd, 1962, 1965.

Richter, Wolfgang. *Die Bearbeitungen des "Retterbuches" in der deuteronomischen Epoche*. BBB 21. Bonn: Peter Hanstein, 1964.

———. *Traditionsgeschichtliche Untersuchungen zum Richterbuch*. 2nd ed. BBB 18. Bonn: Peter Hanstein, 1966.

Schmidt, Ludwig. *Menschlicher Erfolg und Jahwes Initiative: Studien zu Tradition, Interpretation und Historie in Überlieferungen von Gideon, Saul und David*. WMANT 38. Neukirchen: Neukirchener Verlag, 1970.

Seebass, Horst. "Die Vorgeschichte der Königserhebung Sauls." *ZAW* 79 (1967) 155-71.

Speiser, E. A. "Cuneiform Law and the History of Civilization." *APSP* 107 (1963) 536-41.

Ulrich, Eugene C., Jr. *The Qumran Text of Samuel and Josephus*. HSM 19. Missoula: Scholars Press, 1978.

Veijola, Timo. *Das Königtum in der Beurteilung der deuteronomistischen Historiographie: Eine redaktionsgeschichtliche Untersuchung*. AASF B 198. Helsinki: Suomalainen Tiedeakatemia, 1977.

Weimar, Peter. "Die Jahwekriegserzählungen in Exodus 14, Josua 10, Richter 4 und 1 Samuel 7." *Bib* 57 (1976) 38-73.

Weinfeld, Moshe. *Social Justice in Ancient Israel and in the Ancient Near East*. Jerusalem: Magnes, 1995.

Weiser, Artur. "Samuel's 'Philister-Sieg': Die Überlieferungen in 1. Samuel 7." *ZThK* 56 (1959) 253-72.

Weiss, R. "'La Main du Seigneur sera contre vous et contre vos pères' (1 Samuel, XII,15)." *RB* 83 (1976) 51-54.

Chapter 5

THE EMERGENCE OF THE MONARCHY: THE DISMISSAL OF SAUL AND THE BEGINNING OF DAVID'S ARRIVAL (1 Samuel 13:1–16:13)

Samuel has presided over the establishment of the monarchy in Israel, but his work is not yet done. Almost immediately (it is built into the story of Saul's anointing, 10:8), Samuel will begin the process of Saul's dismissal (13:7b-15a). Rejection of Saul includes the mention of a successor; paradoxically, from the outset of Saul's reign, David is present as future king, clothed with the legitimacy of divine approbation. One story is then told, without giving much credit to Saul (14:1-46), and the text has a summarizing review of Saul's reign (14:47-52), followed by the story of Saul's final dismissal (15:1-35). Samuel is then portrayed anointing David. When Samuel returns to Ramah (16:13) his work is basically done. There is the tradition of 19:18-24; there is the report of Samuel's death in 25:1a; there is his return from the grave in ch. 28.

With the anointing of David (16:1-13), Samuel's prophetic task is done. He has prepared the way for David's establishment as king. From then on, the moves to establish David as king will be political. The text of Samuel's dismissal of Saul and anointing of David can be broadly structured as follows.

A. God's order to Samuel to anoint a king in place of Saul   1-3
B. Samuel's compliance with God's order   4-13

The complexity of the material concerning Saul can be seen first by the presence of the accession formula in 13:1 and a quasi formula of final review in 14:52 ("all the days of Saul"), second by the rejection of Saul in both 13:7b-15a and 15:1-35, and third by Saul's presence on the scene as king of all Israel until ch. 31. 13:1–15:35 are the only chapters where Saul is the unchallenged king of Israel, although 13:14 casts a shadow even on that — [I]. After David's anointing (16:1-13) — [II], David's presence is a constant challenge to Saul's crown. So there is a struggle between conflicting structural signals, an impression heightened by the summary notices in 14:47-51. They have much in common with the resumés for David's reign in 2 Sam 8:15-18 and 20:23-26. They would be clearly final, if they were not so oddly out of place; but 1 Kgs 4:1-6 is early in the account of Solomon's reign. Perhaps the only right place is where such information is felt to be appropriately located. For Saul, 14:47-52 may be just right. In terms of history, the reign of Saul is far from over; but this may be the end of the literature that has its primary focus on the achievements of Saul as king.

The Saul text — [I] is best treated according to the A.B.C of the structure analysis: the initial story of Saul's rejection (13:1-15a) — [I.A]; Saul's reign without a rival (13:15b–14:52) — [I.B]; and the final story of Saul's rejection (15:1-35) — [I.C].

Saul's Rejection: Initial   **13:1-15a**
  I. Setting of the scene for Saul's rejection by Samuel   1-7a
    A. Declaration of Saul's kingship   1
    B. Description of military situation   2-7a
      1. Israelite dispositions   2-4
      2. Philistine dispositions   5
      3. Israelite reaction   6-7a
 II. Story of Saul's rejection by Samuel   7b-15a
    A. Saul alone at Gilgal   7b-9
      1. Saul's presence at Gilgal asserted   7b
      2. Saul's seven-day wait for Samuel   8
      3. Saul's offering of sacrifice   9
    B. Samuel and Saul at Gilgal   10-14
      1. Samuel's arrival at Gilgal   10
      2. Samuel's rejection of Saul   11-14
        a. Samuel's question   11a
        b. Saul's response   11b-12
        c. Samuel's reply   13-14
          1) General judgment on Saul's action: folly   13a
          2) Specific unfolding of Saul's folly   13b-14
            a) Disobedience to God's command   13bα
            b) Consequences: Saul's rejection   13bβ-14bα
              (1) What might have been   13bβ

Textual Issues

13:1   The verse as a whole is missing from the LXX. "It is quite possible that it is only a late insertion in the Hebrew text"; certainly, "the [Hebrew] text as it stands is deficient" (Driver, 97). Barthélemy (with Wellhausen et al.): Saul's age may have been left blank and was simply never filled in (p. 176); the two-year reign, according to Noth, is a possible figure (*Deuteronomistic History,* 41-42; also *History of Israel,* 176-78) — with perhaps Saul's reign being considered to conclude with David's anointing, according to *Seder Olam,* one of Barthélemy's sources (p. 176).

13:3   The final clause has created difficulties. Emendation is possible (cf. Driver, 98). An understanding that Saul is calling a "third force" to revolt is endorsed by Barthélemy (p. 177) and Klein, citing Gottwald (pp. 122, 125-26).

13:5   The figure of 30,000 chariots is found in MT and most LXX mss. The boc^{2}e^2 manuscript group and the Syriac have 3,000. Most emend to agree with this (cf. Driver, 98). Barthélemy, retaining the text, points to the likelihood of the numbers being conventional and unrealistic (p. 178). Smith: "our author is prodigal of numbers" (*Samuel,* 95).

13:15   The LXX has more in this verse than the MT; it is followed by the NRSV. Most see the need to bring Saul from Gilgal to Geba and the grounds for haplography, therefore emending in the direction of the LXX (cf. Barthélemy, 179-80). Driver expresses the caution: "This [the LXX] may be accepted in substance, though not quite in the form in which it here appears" (p. 101). Stoebe resists the change, given the poor syntax of the LXX (p. 245). Pisano notes the insertion of vv. 7b-15a and concludes: "This combination of factors should at least make us hesitant to pronounce too quickly and too categorically in favor of the originality of this plus" (p. 183, cf. pp. 175-83).

Discussion

Saul's accession formula (13:1) bedevils the structuring of the beginning of this chapter. At one level, Saul's accession formula could introduce and stand outside his reign, but there is no concluding formula of assessment that can stand outside his reign at the end. At a pinch, 14:52 might serve, but even the rejection in 15:1-35 is evidence that Saul's reign goes beyond 14:52. After the abstract discourse of Samuel's adjudication in ch. 12, there is need for a declaration that Saul is the king in office. Following directly on 11:15, there might not have been the same narrative need for something like 13:1. Following on ch. 12, it can serve as part of the setting of the scene: in this scene, the king is Saul — [I.A].

The accession formula for kings of Judah, found in 13:1, is part of information usually provided in regnal resumés in 1-2 Kings associated with the start of a king's reign. The context here is not that of a regnal resumé. The age of the king at accession is normally given only for kings of Judah, throwing an interesting light on the understanding of Saul. Benjaminite though he was, the author of this regnal formula deemed or esteemed him a king of Judah. The omission of a number in the MT is most probably explained by the simple absence of any information on this point in the tradition available (cf. Stoebe, 242). The two years for his reign here may possibly refer to the period from his assumption of kingship until the designation of David. It may well be historically accurate; its form of expression in Hebrew and its historicity are defended by Stoebe (p. 243) and Barthélemy (pp. 175-76).

The setting of the scene is completed by a description of the military situation — [I.B]. The Israelite dispositions are noted first in terms of a general disposition of the troops (v. 2) and then in relation to a general mobilization prompted by a raid of Jonathan's and the expected Philistine reaction to it (vv. 3-4). The general disposition recounts what may be the establishment of a standing army: three thousand men are selected for service, the rest are sent home (cf. Hertzberg, 104). However, the division of forces between Saul (in the Michmash-Bethel area) and Jonathan (in Gibeah of Benjamin) suggests more than just the establishment of a standing army; on the other hand, the rest sent home suggests that no immediate danger is in view. We are confronted with the fact that we know very little about the historical reality of Saul's reign or about the degree to which the Saul traditions that have come down to us can be correlated with one another. Jonathan appears on the scene for the first time in the biblical narrative, in the role of a senior commander in Saul's forces. He is given no introduction, not even a note that he is a son of Saul (later supplied in the Syriac text; contrast 13:16; 14:1). Jonathan is presented as holding the fort at Saul's capital of Gibeah, while Saul himself with a larger force is placed farther north, without any indication of his precise activity there. Given the fragmentary state of these traditions, they need to be evaluated with caution.

The general mobilization, focused on Gilgal, is said to have been triggered by an aggressive military initiative by Jonathan (vv. 3-4). The Philistines are reported to have come out in massive force and established their camp at Michmash. The Israelite reaction is given as one of extreme fear — and in some cases (of "Hebrews"), flight across the Jordan. The stage is set for Saul's conflict with Samuel. The principal verbal forms *(qātal)* in vv. 4-7 indicate a setting of the scene rather than an advance of the narrative.

The geographical problems are complex and intricate (cf. 1 Sam 10:5, 10). Gibeah and Geba are names that are very similar, both in form and meaning. There is potential for confusion, especially as the two places are not geographically far apart. The textual witness of the versions provides considerable variation, and numerous suggestions have been made in the scholarly literature. Much of this is based on arguments from geography or military strategy. These overlook the fact that the text is compiled from different traditions and that, for all its detail in some sections, it is primarily storytelling rather than historical record. It is not a matter of veracity, measured against the realities of geography and strategy, but of verisimilitude, measured within the horizon of the story. To make matters worse, however, there is more than one story involved. Verses 3-7 fit well enough with the story of the Saul-Samuel conflict, associated with Gilgal and with an overwhelming Philistine force menacing from the north. Verse 2, on the other hand, deploying relatively small forces and locating the bulk with Saul in the Michmash-Bethel area, fits better with the story of ch. 14, in which the Philistine force must also be small. Stoebe's attempt to link Saul to an exploit at Gibeah and Jonathan to one at Geba has to be viewed with some reserve (p. 247 and "Zur Topographie").

For all the uncertainties of the traditions around the episode of Saul's conflict with Samuel, the story of rejection is brilliantly presented (vv. 7b-15a) — [II]. It has been prepared for by an Israelite mobilization at Gilgal and the massing of Philistine forces at Michmash to the north (vv. 3-5). Such is the Philistine superiority that the already meager Israelite forces are slipping from Saul's grasp (vv. 6-7a).

The text moves through three phases: Saul was still at Gilgal (v. 7b); and Samuel came (v. 10); and Samuel departed (v. 15a). In the present text, Saul's being "still at Gilgal" could be read as a statement of his standing fast while others slipped away. A storyteller would have had no trouble accounting for Saul's move from Michmash to Gilgal. However, "still at Gilgal" also evokes 10:8 where Saul was commanded to go to Gilgal and there wait seven days for Samuel. The scene of Saul alone at Gilgal is the story of that wait, of Samuel's failure to show up on schedule, and of the frittering away of Saul's forces. So Saul acts.

This is storytelling, so just at the moment when Saul completed the sacrifice Samuel makes his entrance. There is a taut sequence of question, answer, and judgment. Samuel's question: What have you done? Saul's answer will seem eminently reasonable to many moderns: the troops were taking flight, you were late, and the Philistines were gathering up there at Michmash. Samuel's judgment will seem eminently unreasonable to the same moderns: you have done foolishly!

This is storytelling. Its concern is with theology, not with social, political, and military issues. Obedience to God is primary; all else is secondary. The text does not raise any hermeneutical questions about whether Samuel's word is God's command. In the text, Samuel's word is God's command. In the text, Saul's responsibility is not to raise political or military issues but to obey.

The command to wait seven days can be assumed from 13:8; it is explicit only in 10:8. In 10:8, it is Samuel's command. Here it is explicitly God's command, opening and closing the unfolding of Saul's folly (vv. 13 and 14). Within this envelope structure, two moments are emphasized: what might have been and what will be. Under what will be, Samuel points to the termination of Saul's kingdom and to God's choice of another to be king-designate *(nāgîd)* in Israel. With this judgment delivered, Samuel departs.

Genre

The opening declaration of Saul's kingship, with its echoes of the (→) accession formula and the (→) regnal formula, is followed by (→) notices of the military situation. Whether they reflect memory or were put together to create a setting for the Saul-Samuel conflict we do not know. They certainly suit the latter admirably.

The text recounting the episode of Saul's rejection by Samuel could be thought of as a bare-bones (→) account. Closer inspection reveals the skeleton of a (→) story. Fear at the beginning is itself a factor of imbalance: "and all the people followed him trembling" (v. 7b). It is not a fear that will be allayed, but one that will be laid to rest by the reality of rejection. Similarly, the seven-day wait creates an unstable situation. On one side, the military threat of the Philistines; on the other, Saul's dwindling human resources. The moment Saul is committed to a course of action — the sacrifice — Samuel effects his grand entrance, Saul's defense vainly pleads human reason against divine command, and Samuel pronounces the judgment of rejection. For all its brevity, it encapsulates the tragedy of Saul, trapped between the logic of opposing perceptions.

The story contains the equivalent of a (→) prophetic announcement of judgment to an individual (Birch, *Israelite Monarchy*, 80-84; Westermann, *Basic Forms*, 129-63), with the substance of the accusation in vv. 7b-10 and the announcement in the core of vv. 13-14. There is no messenger formula. Despite its approximation to the announcement of judgment, it is best to recognize that here the genre is that of a (→) prophetic story.

Setting

The origins of the notices are unknown to us. Jonathan's defeat of a Philistine garrison at Geba (v. 3) is not out of keeping with his exploit in ch. 14. What is meant by Saul's proclamation, "Let the Hebrews hear!" escapes us — especially when followed by "And all Israel heard" (v. 4). The term "Hebrews" (עברים) occurs eight times in 1 Samuel. Five occurrences are in the mouths of Philistines (4:6, 9; 13:19; 14:11; 29:3); in three, the term is used by the narrator (13:3, 7; 14:21). Although in 13:3 the clause contributes nothing to the narrative, the content of 13:7 and 14:21 suggests that fragments of a specific tradition might be being preserved. For possible association with the ʿApiru, members of an ethnic or sociologically depressed group living in Canaan with close ties to the Israelites, see Stoebe, 247-50, and, more generally, Mendenhall, *Tenth Generation*, 122-41; Saul would then be summoning other potential allies for this struggle with the Philistines. The widely scattered cases of attribution to Philistine speakers may be based on some folk memory. Even if downsized to three thousand chariots, 13:5 is closer to poetry than to a military roll-call, suitable to inspire panic in Saul's forces that dwindle to a mere six hundred.

The story of Saul's rejection belongs to the same prophetic circles that overwrote 9:1–10:16 to emphasize Saul's anointing as king-designate *(nāgîd)*.

Here that role is already chosen for another (v. 14). Samuel has the prophetic authority to bestow and to withdraw the legitimacy of royalty. His command is God's, whether or not the claim is made fully explicit. The people may have acclaimed Saul king (10:24b; 11:15); it is the prophetic claim to designate and dismiss kings in God's name.

The secondary status of 10:8 within 9:1–10:16 points to the equally secondary status of this story here. "Secondary status" has nothing to do with date or reliability. It merely denotes a tradition that was not originally part of the narrative flow at this point. Jonathan's role in the tradition is tantalizing; see under Meaning.

It has been argued that the core of the judgment passed on Saul (i.e., vv. 13-14) is from a late dtr hand (Veijola, *Ewige Dynastie,* 55-57). To "keep the commandment of the LORD" is recognized as a dtr formula (Weinfeld, *Deuteronomic School,* 336, #16); nothing else in these verses demands attribution to the Deuteronomists. If the envelope — insisting that Samuel's word is indeed God's command — comes from the Deuteronomists, it is in full harmony with the prophetic thinking about prophetic authority. In the context, some judgment from Samuel is required; a core must be retained or assumed. If the envelope comes from the Deuteronomists, as seems probable, it casts a strong light on the theocratic aspect of dtr theology (see below).

Meaning

The meaning of this section on the initial story of Saul's rejection is clear. Although Saul will remain king of Israel until his death in 1 Sam 31, the texts covering his reign have him marked with the sign of rejection from the very beginning. It is brutal; and it is clear. Saul's kingdom will not continue. A successor has already been sought out by God — a king after God's own heart (v. 14).

A whole theology of authority and legitimacy is expressed here. Saul's kingdom over Israel would have been established by God forever (v. 13), but Saul failed in obedience to God. As the same circles will say later, "obedience is better than sacrifice" — שמע מזבח טוב *šĕmōʿa mizzebaḥ ṭôb* (15:22). It is a totally radical claim: kings must be subject to God, and the prophets are the bearers of God's will. It is the stuff of fanaticism or of martyrdom. If it is in the prophetic self-interest, however obscurely, unmellowed by experience or reflection, it will smack of fanaticism. If it is in the interest of the people and the nation, however confusedly, it shares in the values of martyrdom. The conflict with royal sin — David and Nathan, Ahab and Elijah — may be one of the roots of the experience. The power of Ahab and Jezebel to destroy the faith of Israel was surely another, if we correctly associate these prophetic circles with Jehu's revolt and the elimination of Baal worship from within Israel.

So radically theocratic a perception probably does not belong to the prophets alone. As v. 14 already hints, it is a perception that is not alien to the Davidic texts. The Davidic claim is that God was with David and that David was a man after God's own heart. Confronted with the gravest of sin, David's repentance is prompt and followed promptly by forgiveness (2 Sam 12:13). Nor is such a view far from the convictions of the DH. The whole history of Israel in the land, kings included, is judged by the strictures of the deuteronomic code. Deut 17:14-20 may be the extreme expression of this conviction but, like many an extreme position, it merely follows logic to its conclusion. The risk in Deuteronomy is that the king's "heart will turn away" (Deut 17:17). Here, the king God has chosen is a man after God's own heart (1 Sam 13:14).

Placed as it is at the start of kingship in Israel, Samuel's judgment does not fall on Saul alone but on kings as a whole. Rather than concerning a breach of sacral ritual, it concerns fear — failure of nerve because of fear (13:11-12). The king disobeyed the prophet because he saw his forces slipping away and he knew the Philistines were massing toward the north. Isaiah will say it to Ahaz: "If you do not stand firm in faith, you shall not stand at all" (Isa 7:9). In prophetic theology, obedience is based on faith and should not deviate because of fear. Shortly enough, David will be portrayed saying to Saul, "Let no one's heart fail because of him; your servant will go and fight with this Philistine" (1 Sam 17:32), and to the Philistine, "I come to you in the name of the LORD of hosts, the God of the armies of Israel" (17:45). Fear will paralyze Saul before the Philistine, Goliath (17:11). In the prophetic view, fear has already undone Saul at the very beginning of his reign.

All this raises a fascinating methodological issue. If, as we have said above, this passage on Saul's rejection is a secondary insertion here, did the editor who inserted it mean to make so far-reaching a statement? This is a question of authorial intention, and the answer is simple: we do not know. We can only speak of the impact of the passage given its present position in the text. Given its present position in the text, the impact of the passage is indeed far-reaching — as just outlined. It could be that an editor of Israel's texts and traditions wanted to store a variant tradition to ch. 15 in a place in the text where it could be easily recovered and where it would be appropriate — no more. It could be, but we have no way of knowing. Placed where it is in the text, its impact is not merely the rejection of Saul from the start of his reign but also a claim that the legitimacy of royal authority was dependent on obedience to God's will declared by a prophet.

One last issue needs to be raised; it can hardly be resolved. It is the role of Jonathan in these traditions. Saul's fear and failure occur in a context triggered by Jonathan. According to 13:3, Jonathan's defeat of a Philistine garrison at Geba (attributed to Saul in v. 4) made Israel "odious to the Philistines" (v. 4) and provoked the Philistine response. Bluntly, Jonathan put his father on the spot and his father failed. This would hardly be worth mentioning if it did not happen again in the next chapter. In 1 Sam 14, it is Jonathan's success against another Philistine garrison, this time at Michmash, that forces Saul to action (14:20), brings about victory for Israel (14:23), and involves Saul in folly again (14:24-46) — to the point where Saul passes sentence of death on his son and heir (v. 44). In the traditions of David's rise, Jonathan is increasingly portrayed as David's ally (cf. above all 1 Sam 23:15-18). The question begs for an answer: Who was keeping these ideas alive and why? We can understand that the Davidic tradition would keep alive the memory of Jonathan as allied to David.

141

But the raids on Philistine garrisons at Geba and Michmash? Michmash is a good story; Geba is the barest notice. Both episodes got Saul in trouble. Are they connected? Who was interested? Anyone can guess and no one will know.

Saul's Reign without a Rival   **13:15b–14:52**
    I. Portrayal of the Philistine menace   13:15b-23
      A. The opposing forces   15b-18
      B. Powerlessness of Israel   19-22
      C. Move of a Philistine garrison to the pass at Michmash   23
    II. Story of the Philistine defeat at Michmash   14:1-46
      A. Successful initiative: Jonathan's exploit   1-15
        1. Introductory   1-5
          a. Jonathan's proposal   1
          b. Parenthetic preparatory notices   2-5
        2. The exploit itself   6-15
          a. Preparatory planning   6-10
          b. Successful attack   11-15
      B. Consequence: Saul's involvement and victory   16-23a
        1. Introductory   16-19
          a. Observation of panic   16
          b. Absence of Jonathan and armor-bearer noted   17
          c. Divination process undertaken   18-19
        2. Engagement in the victorious battle   20-22
          a. Saul and those with him   20
          b. Hebrews from the Philistine side   21
          c. Israelites from their hiding places   22
        3. Deliverance for Israel given by God   23a
      C. Saul's failure to capitalize on the victory:
      story of the curse   23b-46
        1. Imposition of the curse   23b-24
        2. Effect of the curse: prevention of effective pursuit   25-45
          a. Physical effect of the curse   25-35
            1) Because of the curse: need (hunger) that is
            not satisfied   25-30
              a) Soldiers refrain from eating for fear of
              the curse   25-26
              b) Jonathan eats, unaware of the curse   27
              c) Unfolding: soldier; Jonathan   28-30
            2) Beyond the curse: need (hunger) that is satisfied   31-35
              a) Soldiers eat at evening, inattentive to the blood   31-32
              b) Saul remedies slaughter: eating without blood   33-34
              c) Notice: building of Saul's first altar   35
          b. Sacral effect of the curse   36-46
            1) Proposal to continue pursuit by night   36
            2) Response to the proposal   37-45
              a) Discovery of silence of God   37
              b) Discovery of the infraction of the curse   38-45

Textual Issues

14:7 The problem in this verse seems to be rather translational than textual.

14:18 With the LXX, emendation to "ephod" is usual (cf. Driver: "the ephod, not the ark, was the organ of divination," p. 110). Note 14:3. The possibility of a divergent tradition is raised by Hertzberg, 113-24; Stoebe, 260, 264; Davies, "Ark or Ephod" and "History of the Ark," 15-16; Barthélemy, 183; and Van der Toorn and Houtman, "David and the Ark."

14:23-24 The difficulty is highlighted by Pisano's note: "LXX contains a plus at the end of v. 23, after which its reading differs from MT. The majority of exegetes has accepted the originality of the plus, while others, along with most of the recent translations, have preferred the shorter MT" (p. 37). Note Klein: "no convincing explanation . . . has yet been offered" (p. 132). The sense is not gravely affected. Saul's "very rash act" (NRSV) is dubious; Driver: "agrees poorly with the context" (p. 112).

14:41 The MT and the LXX differ markedly. The NRSV note is misleading. If the MT is followed, the phrase translated with the LXX as "give Thummim" has to be rendered as "give a true decision" (Lindblom — from Pisano, 188). The MT is then intelligible but dense. The LXX expands informatively. Pisano's comment, after a thorough examination of the issues and views, is indicative: "This case, however, is highly uncertain and it does not seem possible to arrive at a definite decision either in favor of MT or of LXX here" (p. 199, cf. pp. 183-99). The distribution of views: for the LXX, with adjustments — Driver, 117-18; McCarter, 247-48; Barthélemy, 186; Klein, 132; for the MT — Hertzberg, 111; Stoebe, 269-70.

14:42 The LXX has here too a substantial expansion which is not in the MT and is not noted in the NRSV. After "and my son Jonathan," LXX reads: "whoever the Lord shall cause to be taken by lot, let him die; and the people said to Saul, This thing is not to be done. And Saul prevailed against the people, and they cast lots between him" and it continues with "and Jonathan his son. And Jonathan was taken" as in the MT. Homoioteleuton is clearly possible; however, nothing is provided that is not available in vv. 39 and 45. Pisano comments: "an examination of the textual witnesses is of no greater help in judging the plus" (p. 202). His own conclusion: "Considering, therefore, both the apparent superfluousness of the material contained in the plus, as well as the difficulty in providing a satisfying Hebrew retroversion, we can consider this plus not to have been original in the text" (p. 203, cf. pp. 199-204). Other views: Driver, "its originality is very doubtful" (p. 118); Hertzberg omits it, without comment (p. 111); Stoebe is against it (p. 270); McCarter (p. 248) and Klein (p. 132) accept it.

When these expansions in the LXX of vv. 41 and 42 are considered, it seems appropriate either to accept or reject the originality of both; a split judgment is difficult to justify. Either the MT was interested in these details and suffered loss, or the LXX was interested in such matters while the MT passed over them (cf. Stoebe, 270).

Discussion

The story of the battle of Michmash is among the most perplexing texts of the Samuel tradition. To aggravate matters, it is written in a terse and allusive Hebrew, with extensive textual difficulties. The condition of the text reflects the perplexity; it may be a result of the chapter's difficulties rather than their cause.

The chapter combines an audacious but minor exploit of Jonathan's with a major battle involving earthquake, great panic, and widespread forces. Yet very little is said of this battle in which God gave Israel victory. The ark features in a consultation where the ephod would be expected. In the aftermath of the battle, the details of victory are vague; instead the text interweaves a story of a disastrous curse, imposed by Saul, with an unprecedented story about breaches of ritual in the slaughter of spoil. Saul's forces are uncertain; he starts with six hundred but is joined by Hebrews and other Israelites. The Philistine forces are uncertain; Jonathan attacks a garrison outpost, but the panic spreads to camp, field, all the troops, even the raiders (14:15). The reference to raiders evokes the three raiding parties of 13:17-18; on the other hand, there is no mention of forces on the scale of the thousands of chariots and countless infantry of 13:5. The significance of the defeat inflicted on the Philistines is left unclear. Overall, what is said of the battle is true of the chapter: the confusion is very great (14:20).

The story of Saul's rejection by Samuel ends with Samuel's departure (13:15a). The MT has Samuel go up from Gilgal to Gibeah of Benjamin. We have no idea why Samuel should be presented as going to Gibeah. With the LXX, it makes more sense in the context for Saul and the troops with him to join forces with Jonathan at Gibeah (cf. 13:2, 16). It is a transitional move to shift the action from Gilgal to the Michmash area. The figure of six hundred troops given in 3:15 could be derived from 14:2. The information on the camps of the opposing forces implies a regrouping of Israel's forces around Jonathan at Gibeah of Benjamin (reflecting 13:2; emending 13:16), possibly under pressure of a Philistine move on Michmash. From Michmash, the Philistines send out raiding parties. Without a broader context, all this is difficult to interpret. We cannot write a history of Philistine incursions into Israel; we can be aware of the Philistines as a constant menace. Apart from the story of Saul's rejection and the traditions building up to that, the other traditions in ch. 13 are of little interest on their own, but serve to introduce the principal story in ch. 14 (cf. Birch, *Israelite Monarchy,* 78-79) — [I].

This is true of the snippet of tradition in 13:19-22, depicting the powerlessness of Israel in relation to the metal-working Philistines. It creates an image of Israel's weakness. It is not in harmony with the following story, where "every sword was against the other" (14:20). The great confusion suggests an image of intense hand-to-hand combat, and it is hardly to be supposed that the swords were only in the hands of the Philistines.

The move of a Philistine garrison to the pass at Michmash is the final setting of the scene. It implies that the pass is at some distance from the Philistine camp at Michmash. This sets the scene for Jonathan's skirmish — [II.A] and for the involvement of the nearby Philistine camp in a larger and more extensive battle — [II.B].

Jonathan's proposal in 14:1 is to be situated against the ominous background of Philistine power. Israel is in apparently hopeless straits, and Saul is not presented as performing any active leadership role to reverse this. The reference in v. 3 to Ahijah's presence with Saul — involving the names of Ichabod, Phineas, Eli, and Shiloh — recalls the disaster of Ebenezer (1 Sam 4). A second notice describes the exact topographical situation in Wadi Suweinit, which is to play a significant role in Jonathan's exploit (vv. 4-5).

After these preliminaries, Jonathan's proposal is repeated from v. 1 and filled out with a theological motivation. The Philistines become the "uncircumcised," a designation involving religious values. Faith, exemplified in the Gideon story, now comes to the fore. It is the LORD who saves, and the LORD can save "by many or by few" (v. 6). From the outset, Jonathan is presented as operating out of trust in God. This is stressed again in the decision on tactics. The pair will challenge the Philistine garrison by showing themselves to them. Instead of deciding whether the better tactic would be to wait for the Philistines on the lower ground or instead to climb the crags and fight them on the high ground, Jonathan proposes to let this be decided by the reaction of the Philistines to their appearance — for this will be a sign from God.

The association of the sign with the "climbing" alternative is probably due to the understanding that to climb the steep face toward the waiting garrison, after having shown themselves, would be the more difficult option — and so better fitted to a demonstration of God's power. In vv. 6-10, Jonathan's name is spelled in a fuller form, *yĕhônātān,* found otherwise only in 1 Sam 18–20 and 2 Samuel. The significance of this orthographic variation is not clear. It hardly indicates that the theological interpretation is an insertion into the text, since the idea is present in v. 12b, along with the usual spelling of Jonathan's name.

The climbing option is selected, and Jonathan and his armor-bearer emerge from their climb to achieve a remarkable victory. The narrative is brief and stark: the Philistines fell before Jonathan, and his armor-bearer behind him finished them off. There is no need to expand the MT, but a storyteller might well extend the portrayal. The two men are depicted slaying some twenty Philistines in a narrow space, perhaps about as many yards (see Driver, pp. 108-9). With the widespread panic among all the Philistine troops and the quaking of the earth, it becomes clear that all this is to be seen as God's doing. The text is storytelling, not historical report.

The effect of Jonathan's exploit is to bring to life the previously inert camp of Saul. The deed of one who trusts in God can inspire and mobilize the whole of frightened Israel. The storytelling is held back while Saul finds out what the listener or reader already knows: Jonathan and his armor-bearer are not there. A further delay in the narrative involves the ark, but its significance is most uncertain (vv. 18-19). Verse 3 associated Ahijah with the ephod, used elsewhere for divining God's purpose (and adopted in v. 18 by LXX and many commentators). We have no knowledge of the ark being used for divination. The text does not indicate why Saul called for the ark nor the meaning of the command, "Withdraw your hand" (v. 19). Where divination is involved, an answer from God is usually recorded. Not here. "Withdraw your hand" may be understood as Saul's having decided to go ahead without waiting for divine direction, given the development of events. If so, it echoes Saul's failure to wait for Samuel earlier. A storyteller might exploit it; it is too unclear for us to do so.

Saul and his troops join the battle — [II.B]. The Hebrews, who had been on the Philistine side, come over to the Israelites. The Israelites who had been in hiding throughout the hills of Ephraim also join in the battle. The disastrous and menacing situation so laboriously depicted in ch. 13 has been completely overturned. The section concludes with a further theological note: "the LORD delivered Israel that day" (v. 23a). The victory should be of enormous significance, yet it is practically passed over. The NRSV expands v. 23 from the Greek and Latin, adding: "and the troops with Saul numbered altogether about ten thousand men. The battle spread out over the hill country of Ephraim." While the expansion is attractive, it may not be justified. If the Hebrew is maintained in v. 24a, Saul's curse may be understood as an attempt to achieve sacrally what the weary troops were no longer able to achieve physically (cf. Driver, p. 112, without however emending the MT). The move failed sacrally; physically it backfired. However, both text and interpretation are uncertain. Whichever tradition is followed, the picture is not greatly changed; the significance of the victory is still ignored.

It may be a modern judgment that Saul committed a rash act, but Driver is right in noting that this view "agrees poorly with the context: in the sequel Saul is in no way condemned" (ibid.). However, the curse frustrates the pursuit, physically (v. 30) and sacrally (v. 46). This is the result of including vv. 24-46 here. V. 46 must be understood as a closing comment to both the whole of vv. 23-46 and the section on the sacral effect of the curse (vv. 36-46) — [II.C]; to this extent, the MT's paragraphing is correct. It is also drawn into the story as the ultimate response to Saul's proposal in v. 36, legitimating the paragraphing in the NRSV. Hence the unusual structural designation of 3. and 3); the verse does double duty in the narrative.

The story could well end at v. 23a. A statement about the defeat and the number of casualties is missing, but it is not adequately supplied later either (cf.

146

v. 46). Two further stories are involved here: one, the story of the curse (vv. 23b-30, 36-45); the other, inserted into the middle of the curse story, the story of the slaughter of the spoil (vv. 31-35). It may well be that neither belonged originally as a continuation of 14:1-23a (see Stoebe, 270-71; Jobling, "Saul's Fall," 272-73). Nevertheless, it is difficult to see how the components of the chapter might have made much sense except as fragmented traditions. Put together as they have been, there is a logic to the whole.

Jonathan's exploit has stirred Saul to a potentially major victory over the Philistines. Saul's curse on anyone who eats before evening and victory (v. 24b) prevents the revival of the troops so that their bringing about a major victory is out of the question (v. 30). The troops feast on the Philistine cattle and are ready to finish off the Philistines by night (v. 36). But Saul's curse is still active and it has to be explored to the end. At the end, the pursuit of the Philistines is abandoned (v. 46). A brilliant start to the day, a botched conclusion, and a lost opportunity to free Israel from the Philistine threat.

The components of the text may be puzzling enough in their independence from each other and in their incompleteness. However, together they form a whole. It is not a seamless whole, but it is a whole. A storyteller would have little trouble sorting out the seams. Others appear to have had troubles with the components, and the textual tradition is frayed around these seams.

Verses 23 and 24 belong to one of those frayed seams. In v. 23, the Greek tradition has a more extensive battle; it is followed by the NRSV (without a note to say so). The total text here requires a low-key victory and minimal follow-up; the MT is satisfactory. A battle that ranges from Michmash to Beth-aven (= Bethel) is not ranging very far. In v. 24, the NRSV again follows the Greek to pass judgment on Saul: "Now Saul committed a very rash act on that day." This leaves Saul's curse unmotivated. The MT's "The Israelites were distressed that day" opens the way to interpreting the curse as invoking the sacral and prohibiting natural means of relieving the fatigue and distress. Either option is possible and it may not be appropriate to decide between them.

The significance of the component elements of the text is established more from within the units than at their seams. The soldiers refrain from eating honey for fear of the curse. Jonathan, unaware of the curse, eats the honey and rallies his strength. The soldier telling Jonathan of Saul's curse adds that it is why the troops are faint. Jonathan characterizes Saul's action (as bringing trouble), points to his own being refreshed, and refers to the desirability of the troops' eating from the Philistine spoil — precisely what happens in vv. 31-35. Without Saul's curse, the slaughter of the Philistines would have been greater.

Verse 31 repeats that the troops were very faint; the battle ranged from Michmash to Aijalon. Two aspects of the verse are problematic. First, pursuit as far as Aijalon, on the coastal plain at the foot of the hills, would be a relatively successful outcome. So it is at odds with the tenor of the whole, with v. 30 in particular, and also with v. 46. Second, there is no specific subject to the verb "they struck down." It is scarcely a continuation of v. 30. Without its proper subject, it is a poor opening to a new section, much less a new tradition. Once again, the seams are frayed.

As Jonathan had thought desirable (v. 30), the troops slaughter and eat the spoil taken from the Philistines, without worrying about the appropriate blood-free ritual. The curse is no longer the issue; presumably evening has come (cf. "that night," v. 34). The issue has shifted to kosher slaughter; Saul provides the necessary remedy. An altar is built — oddly out of place in this battle story. For all their independence, there is a parallel between vv. 25-30 and 31-35. First, as noted in the analysis, the curse prohibits hunger being satisfied and the slaughtered spoil satisfies that hunger. Second, in vv. 25-30, the soldiers refrain and Jonathan eats; in vv. 31-35, the soldiers eat with the blood and Saul refrains. The parallel is not perfect, but there is an echo between the two passages.

Once the physical effect of Saul's curse has been alleviated, with the troops fed and refreshed, there is talk of resuming the pursuit by night. "Let us not leave one of them" (v. 36) suggests that total victory is still possible. Suddenly the sacral effect of the curse has its impact. The text is terse, but the drift is clear. God is silent, so not in support of Israel (v. 37). The cause has to be ascertained. Jonathan is identified as responsible; he confesses to having eaten the honey and accepts the death penalty (v. 43). Saul pronounces the penalty of death; the people (*hā'ām,* the army) repudiate it. "So the people ransomed Jonathan, and he did not die" (v. 45). The pursuit is abandoned and the Philistines make it safely home. It is an extraordinary passage; Saul's own actions nearly cost him the life of his heir and allow definitive victory to slip from his grasp.

The review of Saul's reign [III] comprises three sections. The first section (vv. 47-48) provides an extravagantly optimistic picture of Saul's kingship — [III.A]. The outcome of Saul's wars, as reported, has to be victory (with the NRSV; cf. Barthélemy, *Critique textuelle,* 187); Saul "fought against" five foes and the context clearly implies that his efforts were successful — "and rescued Israel out of the hands of those who plundered them" (v. 48). The picture portrayed fits the traditions about David better than it fits what we now have as traditions about Saul, and it has been suggested that there may have been some transference (see Stoebe, 277). It is difficult, however, to imagine what circles might have been responsible for modeling reports of Saul on those of David. The picture provided runs counter to all we know of Saul's kingdom. If there is any truth in it, then not only were Saul's descendants eliminated but also the record of his achievements.

The second section, the list of Saul's entourage, hardly reaches beyond his own family (vv. 49-51) — [III.B]. It is in marked contrast to the lists of David's officials (cf. 2 Sam 8:15-18; 20:23-26). While the absence or suppression of the relevant traditions is always a possibility to be taken into account, it would seem likely that this mirrors the difference in organizational and institutional complexity existing between the courts and kingdoms of Saul and David. It is closer to what we believe we know of Saul.

Finally, the third section, v. 52, depicts a situation in which fighting was constant throughout Saul's reign, despite the rosy picture of vv. 47-48 — [III.C]. The recruitment envisaged in this verse is another aspect of the standing army, encountered in 13:2. It also begins a practice which, like the kingdom itself, was to be brought to its full flowering under David. More than that, it prepares the way for David's recruitment by Saul — which is the beginning of Saul's replacement by David.

Genre

The composition in 13:15b–14:52 involves diverse traditions and several genres. The two major blocks are constituted by stories: the (→) hero story in 14:1-23a and the (→) curse story in 14:23b-45. Whether the hero story originally included vv. 16-23a is open to question; only v. 17 requires the preceding, while the references to "the priest" and the ark (vv. 18-19) do not accord perfectly with v. 3. But something like v. 23a is required to complete the deliverance. So, at the level of the present text, the hero story can be considered to include both elements: the heroic exploit and its successful consequences. The point is precisely that Israel was immobilized by fear until Jonathan's heroic deed inspired them. Jonathan's feat is similar to David's heroic deed in delivering and inspiring Israel by vanquishing the Philistine champion, Goliath. It is equally open to question whether vv. 31-35 belonged originally to the curse story. The transition at v. 31 is not completely smooth, and the unit is not really a story element. On the other hand, some rest and refreshment for the people is required between v. 30 and v. 36.

In both stories, the element of narrative tension and its resolution is clearly present. The unequal odds of two men against a garrison maintain the tension from v. 1 to its resolution in v. 13. The consequences could be considered concluded in v. 15, but that also provides the stimulus which extends the consequences into a wider battle and deliverance of Israel (v. 23a). In the curse story, the tension relates to the effectiveness of the curse and its ultimate impact. In both cases, we are dealing with texts that cry out to be extended by storytellers and appropriately exploited.

The earlier material leading up to these stories consists of two (→) short notices: 13:16-17, concerning the camps and raiding activity; and vv. 19-22, concerning the absence of smiths in Israel. These are pieces of information which, in themselves, are unlikely to have been important enough to find their way into official annals or chronicles and which are hardly substantial enough to have existed as independent traditions. But they are necessary for the telling of a story, and they are collected by the compiler or storyteller in order to provide the proper setting for the story (see Rendtorff, "Beobachtungen").

Finally, this section on Saul's reign concludes with a series of summary (→) notices. 14:47-48 purports to be a summary of Saul's reign, whatever its historical value. Verses 49-51 name Saul's family and immediate entourage. They are similar to the annalistic notices that listed the names of those who held important offices under the king (cf. 2 Sam 8:15-18; 20:23-26; 1 Kgs 4:1-6 [7-19]). 14:52 is another summary notice, in the same vein as vv. 47-48.

Setting

Beyond the literary setting of the present text, presumed to be that of the DH, interest lies in the circles where such traditions might have been preserved and such a composition put together. Three possibilities are evident: the court of

Ishbosheth (cf. 2 Sam 2–4), the associates of Mephibosheth (cf. 2 Sam 9), or the court of David. The Davidic court certainly cannot be excluded (despite Stoebe, 261). There are the powerful friendship between David and Jonathan and the affirmation of David's legitimacy through Jonathan's acknowledgment of his coming kingship; above all, the tendency to exalt Jonathan to the detriment of Saul would not be alien to Davidic admirers. However, other possibilities are not to be excluded. We simply do not know.

There is a parallel between Jonathan's daring behavior, through trust in God inspiring dispirited Israel, and David's deed of daring in challenging the Philistine Goliath. The fact that the legitimate heir outshines and outperforms Saul — just as David will later — would enhance the value of the story in the Davidic court. The respect shown for Saul is also typical of the Davidic tradition. Saul may be relegated to relative obscurity, but, in the tradition that was retained, despite the aberrances of his condition, he is still treated with the respect due to the king (cf. 1 Sam 24; 26; 2 Sam 1). It is possible to consider this respect as calculated and deliberate Davidic policy — after all, the respectful inviolability professed with regard to Saul would certainly have been a desirable attribute for David's own person.

Meaning

This is a text where it is easier to speak of impact than of meaning or intention. As a compositional piece, the meaning has not been articulated by the compiler. The impact depends substantially on what aspects of the text are attended to.

The text embraces remarkable levels of ambivalence. The impact of Jonathan's courage and trust in God is inescapable. But Jonathan is also a loose cannon who operates without clearance from his commander. Saul's curse seems like folly; it can be read as admirable trust in God. Saul's insistence on kosher slaughter may seem admirable; the episode can be read as emphasizing the troops' need for food.

The text comes after the previous chapter's account of the exploit of Jonathan at Geba (13:3) and its creation of a situation in which Saul failed miserably and lost his kingdom. Chapter 13 does not determine the meaning of ch. 14, but it affects the impact it has on those who read the present text. The story of the curse culminates in high praise of Jonathan: he has accomplished this great victory in Israel . . . he has worked with God this day (14:45). It is hard to escape the impression that this composition is put together in Jonathan's honor, perhaps in Jonathan's memory. Saul is overruled by the army and overshadowed by the story.

"Saul's reign without a rival" is an odd title to give a passage of biblical text. Yet the notices in 14:47-52 are those that come at the end of the account of a king's reign. When 2 Sam 8:15-18 was composed, 2 Sam 9–20 and 21–24 were probably not in view. In ch. 15, Saul will be rejected again; in chs. 16–18, David, Saul's rival, emerges on the national scene in Israel. It is accurate, then, to designate this passage as "Saul's reign without a rival." Despite its ambivalence, its overall impact as the account of Saul's reign is a sad one. The Philistine menace is real. Jonathan achieves a minor success; Saul, the king, is unable to convert it into a definitive victory. Is this passage of text symbolic of the reign of Saul? David will have significant successes against the Philistines; Saul will be unable to turn these to the advantage of Israel or of his kingdom.

Saul's Rejection: Final	**15:1-35**
I. Act by Saul of formal disobedience to God	1-9
A. Samuel's communication of a formal order from God	1-3
1. Call to obedience	1
a. Motivation: Saul's anointing as king	1a
b. Consequence: call to obedience	1b
2. Command from God: punish and destroy	2-3
B. Saul's response to this order	4-9
1. Saul's obedience	4-7
a. Expedition undertaken	4-5
b. Kenites dismissed	6
c. Amalekites defeated	7
2. Saul's disobedience	8-9
a. Solely Saul: ambiguous	8
b. Saul and the people: unambiguously disobedient	9
II. Consequences for Saul of formal disobedience to God	10-31
A. Communication from God to Samuel: *regret*	10-11
1. God's word: regret concerning Saul as disobedient king	10-11a
2. Samuel's reaction to this word: anger	11b
B. Communication from Samuel to Saul: *rebuke & rejection*	12-30
1. Meeting of Samuel and Saul	12-13
2. Accusation against Saul: *rebuke*	14-25
a. Samuel's question	14
b. Saul's excuse and Samuel's accusation	15-22(23)
1) 1st exchange: Saul's excuse and Samuel's accusation	15-19
2) 2nd exchange: Saul's excuse and Samuel's accusation	20-22(23)
c. Saul's confession of sin and plea for pardon & rehabilitation	24-25
3. Announcement of judgment: *rejection*	26-30
a. Samuel: denial of pardon	26
b. Symbolic action of the torn cloak	27-29
1) Action: the turning of Samuel and tearing of the cloak	27
2) Speech: Samuel's interpretation of the action	28-29
c. Saul: repetition of confession of sin & plea for rehabilitation	30
C. Conclusion: rehabilitation — Samuel returns with Saul	31
III. Conclusion	32-35
A. Completion of utter destruction: death of Agag	32-33

Textual Issues

15:29 The NRSV (with LXX and 4QSam[a]) opts for "will not recant"; McCarter, staying with MT "deceive," notes the possible confusion of the relevant letters in the 4th and 3rd centuries B.C.E. (p. 264).

   15:32 The word for Agag's situation is susceptible to various meanings. Stoebe (p. 292) and McCarter (p. 264) follow Kimchi to render "in fetters"; the NRSV, with LXX, Driver (p. 130), Hertzberg (p. 123), and Klein (pp. 145-46) follow Lagarde to render "haltingly." Equally, the MT version of Agag's statement can be read as "the liberating certainty of a sure death" or "the hope that . . . actions will be governed by mercy" (Hertzberg, p. 130). LXX opts for sure death.

Discussion

Seldom has a biblical text been so formal and at the same time explored so far into the ambiguity of human behavior.

   In this whole area, there is considerable conflict of traditions. In the preceding material the regnal accession formula (13:1) forms a potential envelope with the concluding notice of Saul's reign (14:52). The initial story of Saul's rejection naturally comes after the regnal formula; on the other hand, the final story follows the concluding notice. This second story of rejection has its own strong expression of closure. 15:34 closes off this story of a Samuel-Saul encounter; v. 35 closes off the Samuel-Saul relationship. The prophet who brought Saul to the throne now grieves over the rejected king. The final comment, reporting God's attitude, echoes the rejection announced as early as 13:7b-15a. The closure is confirmed in 16:1-13 where what was foreshadowed in 13:14 and 15:28 becomes actual: the prophet Samuel anoints David. There is a common signal in these traditions: this is where the focus on Saul's reign stops.

   The prophetic moves to establish David as king are now complete. What remains is for the political moves to have their effect — a long process. Saul will be on Israel's national stage until his death; but he will be playing second fiddle to David's stellar rise.

   The overall structure of the text is clear; it is act — [I] and consequence — [II], or more specifically crime and punishment. The will of God is behind the action of the entire narrative, echoed again in its last sentence. The formal tone is remarkable. The call to obedience is preceded by a recall of Saul's status and its origins. The Hebrew word order is unusual, with the personal pronoun thrown to the front of the sentence, "Me sent YHWH to anoint you king"; it is not unprecedented in these prophetic texts. The emphasis may be on the authority of Samuel (Birch, *Israelite Monarchy*, 96; Hertzberg, 124); more probably, the emphasis is on the origin of Saul's status. He owes his position absolutely to God and must therefore obey absolutely. The point is made again in v. 17. This is a closely knit text.

The punishment announced for the Amalekites is motivated from the beginnings of Israel's history after the exodus (Exod 17:8-16); this is no minor punitive expedition. The command is first expressed generally, "Go and smite Amalek" (v. 3); then it is spelled out in terms of the ban *(herem)*, the command for utter destruction. The emphasis on the ban can be seen from the formulation: *positively,* you will utterly destroy all that they have; *negatively,* do not spare them, followed by an enumeration. To our post-Holocaust generation, appalled by ethnic cleansing, the idea of such utter destruction (the ban) is intolerable. Without wanting to dilute this judgment, we will not understand this story if we do not recognize that the ban denied to a military campaign the major motivation for most military activity in the ancient world — plunder, the taking of captives and spoil.

There is one other aspect of this story of utter destruction modern readers need to know. As told, it did not happen. In 1 Sam 15, Agag is the last living Amalekite and he dies at the end of the chapter. In 1 Sam 27, the Amalekites are around to be raided by David (27:8). In 1 Sam 30, the Amalekites raid David's camp and, when David wages a victorious battle against them, there are still four hundred young men from the camel corps who escape (30:1-17). These traditions were almost certainly known to the authors of 1 Sam 15. 1 Sam 15 is a story of royal disobedience and its consequences; the Amalekites were not exterminated. The fact of being unreal, however, hardly renders the story attractive.

Given this formal command from God, the narrative has Saul move to comply — [I]. The troops are gathered at Telaim, in the south (cf. Josh 15:20-32). The numbers, as in 11:8, appear unnecessarily large, with minority participation from Judah. (LXX locates the scene of the muster at Gilgal and, again as in 11:8, considerably augments the numbers — 400,000 men and 30,000 from Judah.) While such variants in numbers and places may suggest that the story has been told many times, they do not detract from its central force. The mention of "the city of the Amalekites" (v. 5), out of place in reference to a Bedouin tribe (cf. Hertzberg, 124), may be an indication that the present formulation of the narrative derives from a period at some distance from the events. The dismissal of the Kenites (v. 6, cf. Judg 1:16) and the description of the Amalekite defeat (v. 7) fit better into the nomadic situation. The dismissal of the Kenites is not anticipated in the command; it may be a storyteller's option to ensure a high moral purpose for the campaign (cf. 1 Sam 27:10).

The defeat of the Amalekites follows in v. 7. So far the narrative has been straightforward: the story of an order and its execution, of Samuel's communication of God's command and Saul's compliance with it. The central exchange between Samuel and Saul will revolve around Saul's claim to have complied and the issue of his responsibility. The narrative prepares for this confrontation and opens up its ambiguities. Verse 7 is in clear compliance with the general order to smite the Amalekites. Verse 8 does not expressly affirm any infringement of the specifics of the order; Agag's being taken alive could be a matter of the fortunes of war and say nothing of his ultimate fate. Up to this point, Saul has been the sole subject of every action: Saul summoned, Saul came, Saul said, Saul defeated. With v. 9 and the explicit breach of the ban, the subject changes: "Saul and the people" spared Agag and the best of the booty, while "all that was despised and worthless they utterly destroyed" (v. 9). Here the text has Saul firmly among the guilty — but in emphatic association with "the people."

With v. 9, both Saul and the people are implicated in the act of disobedience. There is no suggestion that Saul was forced by the people and so no preparation for Saul's claim in v. 24. The verse also undermines Saul's other claim that the best of the beasts were spared for sacrifice (v. 15). According to v. 9, "they" were not willing (LXX: singular, "he was not willing") to destroy what was valuable. Unwillingness suggests more than setting aside for later sacrifice; the discrimination between "valuable" and "worthless" heightens the evil, evoking contempt for sacral ordinances. Explicit disobedience is kept to this final verse of Saul's response to the order (i.e., v. 9). The specific contrast between sparing what was valuable and destroying what was worthless leaves no room for Saul to escape the verdict that he himself will finally utter: "I have sinned" (v. 24). We have no evidence for assuming that Saul was trapped between God and the people, apart from Saul's excuse in v. 24 that emerges late in the discussion and is not supported by the narrative in v. 9 (against Weiser, "1 Samuel 15," 8, 18-19).

The second major stage of the story is exploration of the consequences for Saul of this disobedience — [II]. The position attributed to God is clear: "I regret that I made Saul king" (v. 11). The position attributed to Samuel is less clear; presumably Samuel's anger was directed against Saul and his failure in fidelity and obedience, but the nature of Samuel's "cry to the LORD" is not spelled out. The narrative pits Samuel against Saul; it is unlikely that a reader is invited to assume Samuel "cried to the LORD" for Saul. However, the bottom line is that it is not spelled out.

The precise significance of the brief tradition of the monument at Carmel is unclear. If the origin is an etiological concern (Hertzberg, 126; Stoebe, 293), there is no mention of a name nor any etiological notice. Perhaps the uncertainty, both as to significance and grammar, is responsible for the various readings in LXX and the versions (cf. Smith, *Samuel*, 137-38). What we know is that we do not know.

Samuel's communication of God's word to Saul takes place in an extended exchange (vv. 12-31). The confrontation begins with Saul's greeting and assertion of his compliance. In stark contrast to God's word to Samuel (v. 11), Saul affirms his compliance with the command. It is possible to juxtapose two conflicting statements as the evidence of witnesses might be juxtaposed in court. The juxtaposition of vv. 11 and 13 reflects pejoratively on Saul (cf. Amos 7:15b and 16b). Samuel's question raises the suspicion that Saul has not complied fully with the command; animals are alive and bleating. Saul's response appears directed toward placating Samuel; the animals were brought "to sacrifice to the LORD *your* God" (v. 15). There has also been a shift of responsibility: *they* brought them (3rd person plural), the people spared the best. The same shift that was noted in vv. 4-9 recurs here: in v. 13, Saul claims compliance; in v. 15, there is a shift to the plural and the people — with no mention of Saul. Israelite storytellers are skilled in portraying the evasion of responsibility, passing the buck. Adam does it to God: "the woman whom *you* gave to be with me" (Gen 3:12). God does it to Moses: "*Your* people, whom *you* brought up out of the land of Egypt" (Exod 32:7). So Saul tries to do it to Samuel: "to sacrifice to the LORD *your* God" (15:15).

Samuel injects a new element and a deeper seriousness into the exchange. The word of God is involved. Saul is portrayed, to his credit, as open to God's word. At stake is the office of the king. The reference to Saul as little in his own eyes may derive from 9:21; it also echoes 15:1. The reference to Saul's being anointed as king brings the royal office into conjunction with the obligation to obey. Samuel refuses to be placated and launches into an accusation of Saul (vv. 17-19). He ends with the accusation of disobedience and evildoing (v. 19).

In a second exchange, Saul's excuse drops all attempt at subtle shades; it is a blunt denial of responsibility. Four times the 1st person singular hammers home Saul's claim, "I have obeyed the voice of the LORD" (v. 20); the people alone bear the responsibility for bringing back the booty for sacrifice. Even Agag's survival is brought under this obedience! Only with v. 21 are the people involved, the disobedience admitted, without the reprehensible discrimination between valuable and worthless.

The evasion is brushed aside by Samuel's oracle, with its insistence on obedience, its denunciation of rebellion, equating disobedience with idolatry, and its culmination in the terrible word of rejection. Act is followed by consequence: disobedience is followed by rebuke; rejection of the word of God is followed by God's rejection. The balance of rebuke and rejection noted in the structure analysis is evident here. Verse 22, in itself, is a strong rebuke, expressing Samuel's accusation of Saul. Obedience is better than sacrifice; better to have obeyed the command than to have brought the best of the beasts back for sacrifice. Verse 23 moves from rebuke to rejection. The accusation ("you have rejected") sums up all that has gone before; the announcement ("he has rejected you") is the culmination of Samuel's intervention to this point.

The exchange continues; now it is Saul's penitent response to his rejection. He begins with the confession of sin; there can be no further dissimulation. And for the first time he claims fear of the people as the reason for his failure to obey. (Not so in LXX, where this motif is introduced at the beginning of v. 20, though without the explicit mention of fear.) Saul asks for pardon and for Samuel to return with him to restore him to community with God — and, although it is not said, presumably to honor before his own community (cf. v. 30).

Samuel's refusal is motivated in the narrative by a repetition of the word of rejection. While it is return that is spoken of, it is pardon that is refused. The narrative has Samuel turn away and, as he does so, his robe is torn. The MT does not name Saul as agent here. In ordinary Hebrew syntax, it is Samuel who grasped the edge of his own robe; however, LXX, 4QSam^a, and most commentators take it from the context to be Saul. It is possible that the MT attributes the act to Samuel as a deliberate symbolic action, considering such action to be undertaken by the prophets and not to be merely accidental (contrary view, Stoebe, 291; also McCarter, 260, 264, and 268; cf. Weiser, "1 Samuel 15," 4). With Jeroboam, Ahijah tears his new garment; there is no accident (1 Kgs 11:30). Storytellers may be left liberties.

The interpretation of the action goes beyond what has been said before. Not only is the kingdom torn from Saul, as the piece is torn from the garment; the kingdom is given to another. The advance on what has been said before permits vv. 24-31 to be retained (with Birch, *Israelite Monarchy*, 95; Hertzberg, apparently, 129; Stoebe, 295; against Weiser, "1 Samuel 15," 4). The decision is irrevocable, for "the Glory *(nēṣaḥ)* of Israel will not recant or change his mind" (v. 29). The contradiction between v. 29 and vv. 11 and 35 has long been seen; it is a reason for scholars to claim the section is an addition, and a problem even for some of those who retain the verses. It expresses, in close proximity, the tension that is found between Num 23:19 and Hos 11:9 (emendations notwithstanding). For all the distinctions between humanly and divinely speaking, it is one of the tensions theology will never escape.

There is no question of pardon for Saul, of revoking the rejection. In a repetition of his request (v. 30), he confesses his sin again and asks, not for pardon, but for honor and rehabilitation. Samuel accedes to the request and returns with him, and Saul worships the LORD. The precise implications of Samuel's honoring Saul and of Saul's worshipping the LORD are not clear. It is possible that behind these verses lies the recognition that, although rejected by the LORD, Saul continued to be king throughout his life and was honored by David as the LORD's anointed. Historically, it was not Samuel's task to depose Saul. Do we have here the tension between history and its interpretation, between the prophetic claim to perception of the divine will and its execution in the political sphere?

The story says nothing about the rest of the booty, but Agag is a king. Saul lays claim to Agag's presence as part of his compliance with God's will (v. 20); he is not included in the people's sin (v. 21). Technically, in this text, as long as Agag is alive, the Amalekites have not been utterly destroyed and God's command has not met with full compliance (v. 3). The compliance must be absolute and Samuel does not leave it to Saul — [III.A]; "Samuel hewed Agag in pieces before the LORD" (v. 33b). The manuscript traditions suggest uncertainty in ancient times about King Agag's forebodings. Samuel's act seems one of unparalleled savagery; today's equivalent: the prophet chopped the victim to pieces in church. Surprisingly, the text does not have Samuel appeal to the divine command but instead to the brutality of Agag himself — the Hebrew is a memorable line (v. 33a).

The narrative concludes with the definitive separation of Samuel and Saul, and the recall of the theme of the chapter: God was sorry that he had made Saul king over Israel — [III.B and C].

There is a fairly general consensus among scholars that 15:1-35 is a substantial unity (e.g., Birch, *Israelite Monarchy*, 95; Hertzberg, 123-30; Stoebe,

286-96; McCarter, who speaks of "prophetic reworking," 270; Weiser, "1 Samuel 15," except vv. 25-29, p. 4). The belief that the basic elements of the story go back to historical tradition is expressed by Weiser ("1 Samuel 15," 7, 16); 1 Sam 30:1-17 raises doubts for this belief. In recent years, the main voice raised against the unity of the chapter has been that of Horst Seebass, who argues from the observation of doublets and tensions between vv. 8 and 9, 15 and 23, 13bβ and 20a, 15a and 21, 15b and 20b, 25b and 30b, 23b and 26b, 11 and 29, and 24-28 and 31 ("I Samuel 15," 149-51). He concludes that there are three stages of growth in the chapter (ibid., 153-54). Despite the reworking to be discussed below, which will meet some of Seebass's concerns, this apparently impressive list of duplicates and inconsistencies reflects a failure to recognize the evident progress intended in the narrative of this confrontation between Samuel and Saul. Fragmentation of the whole is not justified. (The analyses by Foresti, *Rejection of Saul*, and Dietrich, *David, Saul und die Propheten*, which invoke the activity of DtrP and DtrN, I believe to be mistaken.)

However, in the light of our perception of the prophetic editing of these texts, and in the light of the prophetic reworking of 1 Sam 9:1–10:16, it is easy to see how an older story here has been given its present form through similar prophetic reworking.

The parts of the text expressing the concerns specific to the prophetic editors are easily recognized (15:1aβb, 10-12, 16, 17b, 23b, 26-30, 35b; for a visual presentation, see Campbell and O'Brien, *Unfolding*, 254-56); their concern is primarily the anointing of the king by God and God's rejection of the king in favor of another. There is 15:1aβb, "The LORD sent me to anoint you king over his people Israel; now therefore listen to the words of the LORD." Similarly, vv. 10-12 express God's word of regret that he had made Saul king, with Samuel's involvement. Verse 16 relates to this word from God. Verse 23b moves beyond rebuke for disobedience to Saul's rejection by God from being king. Verses 26-30, situated between Saul's plea (v. 25) and Samuel's response (v. 31), deal with this rejection of Saul, the tearing away of the kingdom from him and its being given to another — before a repetition of v. 25 to blend into v. 31. Finally, v. 35b returns to the theme of God's involvement and God's regret. The remainder (15:1aα, 2-9, 13-15, 17a, 18-22, 24-25, 31-35a) forms a continuous and relatively coherent story, with a slightly different point; Saul is rebuked rather than rejected.

Once the evidence for this prophetic rewriting of an earlier story has been clearly seen, the division between the earlier story and the prophetic overwriting can be identified more aesthetically. What has been listed in the preceding paragraph are the verses where the primary concern is clearly with the anointing of the king by God and God's rejection of the king in favor of another (so in *Unfolding*). What follows is a more hypothetical division and a more aesthetically satisfying one, based on the assumption that the evidence points to an older story having been overwritten. It incorporates the available evidence, but goes beyond it. The division in the preceding paragraph is closely restricted to the evidence itself.

On these grounds, it may be argued that the prophetic editors intervened to add three blocks of text: vv. 9-12 (God's communication of regret "that I made Saul king"), vv. 15-19 (the "1st exchange": the people blamed and the anointed Saul accused), and vv. 26-30 (the announcement of Saul's rejection). Beyond these, the shorter passages noted above complete the overwriting, namely: 15:1aβb, 23, and 35b. Apart from the inclusion of v. 9, the only difference from the more restricted identification (above, as in *Unfolding*) is the attribution of vv. 15-19 as a block to the prophetic overwriting. The aesthetics driving this identification relate to the repetition in the structure of the present text (cf. 1st and 2nd exchange). Uncertainty remains for vv. 1b and 35a.

As in 9:1–10:16, an older story has been overwritten by prophetic editing. Here the older story is complete; its concern is with Saul's rebuke for disobedience. "Obedience is better than sacrifice." The penitent Saul asks for acceptance (v. 25) and is given it (v. 31). The rewriting emphasizes Saul's anointing by God and his corresponding responsibility. The announcement of the consequences for Saul comes from God (vv. 10-11), not from Samuel. The consequences go far beyond a rebuke; they are Saul's rejection as king and his replacement by another, who will be David.

The elegance of the prophetic editorial work can be seen in a reproduction of the structure of the present text with the prophetic editing emphasized in italic. The outcome has been skillfully achieved by absorbing the earlier rebuke (v. 22) into the more emphatic accusation of vv. 17-19, creating room for the announcement of rejection (vv. 26-30). The analysis below reproduces the core of the text. It is a tribute to the editorial finesse involved that the only other retouches needed affected the first and last verses of the chapter — emphasizing the Lord's anointing of the king (in 15:1) and the Lord's change of heart about the king (in 15:35).

2. Saul's disobedience	8-9
a. Solely Saul: ambiguous	8
b. *Saul and the people: unambiguously disobedient*	9
II. Consequences for Saul of formal disobedience to God	10-31
A. *Communication from God to Samuel:* **regret**	10-11
1. *God's word: regret concerning Saul as disobedient king*	10-11a
2. *Samuel's reaction to this word: anger*	11b
B. Communication from Samuel to Saul: **rebuke &** *rejection*	12-31
1. Meeting of Samuel and Saul	12-13
2. Accusation against Saul: **rebuke**	14-25
a. Samuel's question	14
b. Saul's excuse and Samuel's accusation	15-22 *(23)*
1) *1st exchange: Saul's excuse and Samuel's accusation*	15-19
2) 2nd exchange: Saul's excuse and Samuel's accusation *(and rejection)*	20-22 *(23)*
c. Saul's confession of sin and plea for pardon & rehabilitation	24-25
3. *Announcement of judgment:* **rejection**	26-30
a. *Samuel: denial of pardon*	26
b. *Symbolic action of the torn cloak*	27-29

Genre

The genre here is that of (→) story. It is a story in which the prophet is a central figure and which contains both a prophetic word and a prophetic symbolic action; yet it is not simply restricted to these. The core of the story — an act of disobedience, including both the order from God and the disobedience by Saul; the emphasis given to Saul's kingship (vv. 1, 11, 17, 35b); the long development of the exchanges which probe to understand and interpret the situation; the repeated motivation of the rejection — shows clearly how this is a reflective presentation of the conflict between Samuel and Saul (Weiser, "1 Samuel 15," 16). The end is already hinted at in the beginning (cf. v. 11); what is being explored is the nature of the sin and the consequences. The consequences could be rebuke (cf. the assumed older story), punishment, or rejection. Not until the end of the story is it clear what form God's regret, in v. 11, will take.

There are a number of texts about prophetic intervention to announce judgment to kings which bear similarities to 1 Sam 15. We may note 2 Sam 12; 24; 1 Kgs 21; 22; also, of course, 1 Sam 13:7b-15a. Motifs appearing in 1 Sam 15 appear also in 1 Kgs 20:35-42 (sparing of a king devoted to destruction); 1 Kgs 11:29-39 (tearing of robe, removal of kingdom); 14:1-18 (contrast, tearing of kingdom, judgment, replacement); 16:1-4 (contrast and rejection); 2 Kgs 9:1-10 (anointing, replacement).

Within the story is the structure of the rejection of Saul (15:14-30), with its movement from accusation to announcement that is characteristic of the (→) prophetic speech of judgment (Westermann, *Basic Forms,* 129-68, esp. p. 130). Although the structure of the judgment speech, isolated by Westermann, is dissolved in the story, all of the elements are present: commission of the messenger (vv. 10-11, implicit); summons to hear (v. 16, equivalent); accusation (vv. 14, 17-19); messenger formula (v. 16, implicit); announcement (vv. 26-30). Further similarities are evident with regard to the contrast motif, the sign, and the correspondence of the announcement and the accusation (cf. Westermann, *Basic Forms,* 155-61). Any attempt to structure the whole chapter on the structure of the judgment speech (introduction: vv. 1-13; accusation: vv. 14-21; oracle: vv. 22-23; announcement: vv. 24-31) does not do justice to the much more complex narrative development of the passage. Nor are the correspondences of this chapter with similar passages precise enough to constitute clear evidence that 1 Sam 15 is at the late end of the range of the judgment speech to the individual. The primary point here has been made earlier. This is a story that includes a prophetic announcement of judgment. Generically, it is not a prophetic speech of judgment; it is a story.

It has been argued that the symbolic action of the torn robe is derived from the oral tradition of the Ahijah cycle in 1 Kgs 11 (so Grønbaek, *Aufstieg Davids,* 42-43, following Weiser). The stronger case favors dependence of 1 Kgs 11 in its somewhat artificial situation and presentation on the more naturally situated 1 Sam 15 (with Dietrich, *Prophetie und Geschichte,* 15-16).

Setting

The concern, the language, and the structure all point to a prophetic setting. Details such as the large numbers (v. 4) and the city of a nomadic group (v. 5) suggest a considerable distance in time from the period of the presumed events; also the conflicting tradition of 1 Sam 30:1-20. All this, and the doublet in 13:7b-15a, also located at Gilgal, caution against taking for granted that the story derives from an oral tradition going back to Samuel himself (against Weiser, "1 Samuel 15," 24). Naturally, some elements in the story may be older than the composition of the story itself.

The literary setting is practically the present text, before that the DH in its various editions, and before that the PR. All these are literary documents. Given the substantial reworking of so many of the prophetic traditions, we know very little about the operations of the early prophets. As far as we can judge, Gad in the desert (1 Sam 22:5) and Nathan at David's bedside (1 Kgs 1) have not been touched up. Beyond that, the literary terrain is most uncertain (cf. Campbell, *Of Prophets and Kings,* 114-15, 117-20).

Meaning

1 Sam 15 is a stark document. It is not about the divine right of kings; it is about the divine right over kings. From first to last, this is clear: God made you king, therefore obey! (v. 1); King Agag is the sole survivor; he too must die (vv. 32-33). The juxtaposition of the anointing and the call to obedience (v. 1) with the order (vv. 2-3), and the recall of both anointing and order (vv. 17-18) before the accusation of disobedience bring this strongly to the fore. Vested in the anointing as king is an obligation to obey the God who anoints. According to the text, Saul does not obey; he "has not carried out my commands" (v. 11). In the final text, disobedience is equated with rejection; rejection begets rejection. "Because you have rejected the word of the LORD, he has also rejected you from being king" (v. 23).

Rejection is the burden of vv. 10-11; it lurks in vv. 12-23, recurs and is intensified in vv. 24-30. Rejection is woven throughout the thread of the narrative (vv. 11, 19, 23, 24, 26). The basic statement of God's, justifying the rejection, is that Saul "has turned back from following me" — *kî šāb mē'aḥăray* (v. 11). In the present text, it is impossible for us not to hear an echo of 1 Sam 12:14 — if you listen to his voice, then both you and your king will follow the LORD your God *(wihyitem . . . 'aḥar yhwh)*. Both prophetic tradition and this dtr tradition are here singers of the same song.

There is no pardon; rejection begets rejection, and the rejection is irrevocable. There is nothing to show why this particular act of disobedience should constitute rejection, nor why it should be irrevocable. Yet the reference to the neighbor to whom the kingdom will be given, who is better than Saul (v. 28), brings into focus a theological problem which cannot be ignored. This neighbor, David, sinned — rape (or adultery) and murder — yet he confessed his sin and was promptly forgiven (2 Sam 12:13). Why the disparity of treatment? The prophecy claims to precede history; is it here condemned to follow history? Or were David's sins private in essence if not in effect, while Saul's sin was public from the outset? David in his prayer for his dying child has clearly not rejected God; but we are forced to ask why God has not rejected him. Or is it that Saul's story is not couched in the heat of human passion and weakness but in the chill formality of divine directive and human evasion? 1 Sam 15 does not offer an explicit answer, but the formal juxtaposition of royal office and royal obligation to obey points in that direction.

The prophetic conviction that God looks not on the outward appearance but on the heart (16:7) may lie behind the extended analysis of Saul's evasion of responsibility. The slow movement from Saul's initial avowal of obedience (v. 13), through an implicit involvement of the people (v. 15), to a claim of personal obedience while shifting the blame entirely to the people (vv. 20-21), before finally confessing sin because of fear of the people, is in its own way a study of the heart. Here Saul attributes his sin to fear of the people. In 1 Sam 13, Saul's sin was attributed to fear of the enemy. The narrative sweep of 1 Sam 13–15 stands at the beginning of the monarchy in ancient Israel. It portrays a thoroughly rejected king. It places him between two fears: fear of the enemy and fear of the people. In either case, the prophets stand with Isaiah: "If you do not stand firm in faith, you shall not stand at all" (Isa 7:9).

Theologically, this rejection is present as a necessary prerequisite for understanding the downfall of Saul, as well as the ultimate success of David. David will emerge, profiled against this shadow side of Saul. While the narrative leaves Saul respectfully and historically in place until his death, theologically the text places him under the sign of diminishment.

Samuel's Anointing of David

Textual Issues

16:4 The LXX makes explicit what can be derived from the MT (cf. Driver, 132-33).

  16:5 Instead of MT "come with me to the sacrifice" the LXX has "celebrate with me today" (followed by McCarter, 274); Stoebe (pp. 300-301) and Klein (pp. 157-58) retain MT. Opinions vary whether the MT might be clarifying an LXX original or the LXX easing a difficulty for the MT.

  16:7 The LXX makes explicit what can be derived from the MT. The verse would have a better balanced, more suitably proverbial form if it is expanded with LXX:

"For not as man sees, does YHWH see:
for man sees the appearance, but YHWH sees the heart."

Following LXX: Driver, 133; Stoebe, 301; McCarter, 274 (noting apparent support from 4QSam[b]); Klein, 157-58.

Discussion

This chapter, like 1 Sam 15, is structured around God's order — [I] — and the consequent compliance with it; only, in this case the compliance is complete — [II]. The rebuke to Samuel, with which the chapter begins, clearly links it to the conclusion of ch. 15. The grieving of Samuel and God's repentance there (15:35) are both picked up by the statement of Samuel's grief over Saul and God's rejection of Saul (16:1). The failure to name David in the order to anoint one of Jesse's sons may be a vestige of narrative tension; more probably, David's name is avoided in order not to forestall the aspect of divine choice on which such emphasis is laid (vv. 6-12).

Samuel's question, "How can I go? If Saul hears of it, he will kill me" (v. 2), throws an interesting light on the relationship between prophet and king. Chapter 15 portrayed Saul as submissive to Samuel, even after his disobedience; here, Samuel pleads Saul's readiness to kill him. This may be taken to reflect Israel's experience that the prophets did not have it all their own way (cf. Jer 26:8, 11, 20-23). Closer to hand, historically, may be the slaughter of the priests at Nob (1 Sam 22:6-19; with Hertzberg, 137; Stoebe, 303). It fits also with the violence and jealousy that surrounded the later Saul (cf. 18:10-11; 19:9-10; 20:33; 22:7-8, 13). We are left to surmise.

The sacrifice is the strategy by which Samuel is to get to Bethlehem safely. Why this should be acceptable to Saul we do not know. The elders and Jesse's family are invited to this sacrifice. There are echoes of the banquet in 1 Sam 9:22-24. The elders play no further role in the text; their fear remains unexplained. Perhaps here there is scope for storytellers to expand. The sacrifice was a strategy to get Samuel safely to Bethlehem; once this is achieved, the sacrifice has no further purpose. After the strategy has been imparted to Samuel, he is promised further instructions as to what to do and whom to anoint (v. 3). God's guiding hand is to be present throughout the proceedings. The action may be Samuel's; the direction of it is God's.

The choice is important, and it is important to see its structure. When Jesse's eldest, Eliab, comes on the scene, Samuel is immediately attracted to him: "Surely the LORD's anointed is now before the LORD" (v. 6). The LORD promptly disapproves, "for the LORD does not see as mortals see" (v. 7). Even the prophet is deficient in vision. With the rest, Samuel is much more cautious: "The Lord has not chosen this one/any of these" (cf. vv. 8, 9, 10). Even when the youngest is brought on the scene, Samuel does not venture an opinion; the text has the LORD take the initiative: "Rise and anoint him; for this is the one" (v. 12). His personal name, David, is mentioned only at the end, as the spirit of the LORD comes mightily upon him (v. 13).

There is an invitation to think that Eliab, the eldest, was in Saul's mold physically and so received Samuel's approval; it would seem he had "the outward appearance" of a king. David was handsome (specified here, but omitted in 17:42b); yet Samuel's question is needed before he is considered a candidate — perhaps more narrative style than anything else. There are echoes here of the pentateuchal traditions in which the unlikely is privileged; for example, Isaac over Ishmael, Jacob over Esau, Joseph over his brothers. The emphasis on God's choice is clear; even the prophet does not get it right.

Misreading of this text has led to misunderstanding of the traditions about David's coming to prominence in Israel. Certain points need to be noted here. First, David is the youngest of Jesse's sons; this says nothing about his age or size. He is younger than the other seven; that is all. Second, David's activity in keeping the sheep does not render him an unlikely contender for the kingship. Saul was looking for his father's asses in ch. 9, and in ch. 11 he was coming in from the field behind a yoke of oxen, presumably having finished plowing. There is no reason to believe plowboys outranked shepherds. Third, David's seven older brothers are described as "the young men/the youths" *(hanně'ārîm)* in v. 11; David is described by Saul as "a young man/a youth" *(na'ar)* in 17:33 (most unfortunately rendered "just a boy" by the NRSV and others). The meaning of *na'ar* is dependent on its context. It can range from an unweaned infant (1 Sam 1:22) to a king's minister for public works (1 Kgs 11:28); *ně'ārîm* can have sexual intercourse (1 Sam 21:2-5), can kill (2 Sam 2:12-17), and can head a major rebellion (2 Sam 18:5, 12). The meaning is dependent on the context. Here, Eliab, Abinadab, and Shammah are described as *ně'ārîm* and they can serve in Saul's army (17:13); David too is described as a *na'ar,* and this description in itself should be no bar to his serving in Saul's army as effectively as his brothers.

David is anointed in the midst of his brothers: there would appear to be no justification for harmonizing the text. The spirit of the LORD comes mightily upon him. There is no waiting here for the occasion to demonstrate charismatic power (as in 11:6; although cf. also 10:9); the possession is portrayed as being permanent — "from that day forward" (v. 13). This may indicate the need to understand 16:1-13 as closing a section in a larger composition.

Samuel went to Ramah. This is Samuel's last act on the national scene in his lifetime. The episode told in 1 Sam 19:18-24 is hardly portrayed as a matter of significance to all Israel. Samuel's words to Saul at En-dor (1 Sam 28:15-19) are of major significance, but they are after Samuel's death. Here his work is done. The prophetic moves to establish David as king are completed. The political moves lie ahead.

Genre

The text is best described as a prophetic (→) story, although it is a close call; it is near to an (→) account. The level of movement driven by the plot of a story is slight; but it is there. As the text stands, it is a good example of an abbreviated (→) story outline. With a little change, it could be an account; but as it is, it invites expansion into a story. There is the initial reference to providing a king from among Jesse's sons (v. 1). Fear of Saul, who might kill, is mentioned (v. 2); it is not mentioned again. Nevertheless, the potential for tension remains. The future king is to come from among Jesse's sons (v. 1). The name of David is not mentioned until the very end (v. 13). Again, there is potential for tension here. The eldest son meets with Samuel's immediate approval and is "rejected" by the LORD (vv. 6-7). David, the youngest, is not even present at this family muster. There is further potential for tension here.

At one level, the text as it stands, without expansion or modification, does a dexterous job of presenting David's anointing, after Saul's rejection and before David's demonstrations of charisma and leadership in Israel. At another level, so significant a moment in the Davidic and prophetic traditions is unlikely to have been restricted to a thirteen-verse pericope. The moment demands a story, and the text shows the potential for one. It is best classed as a story.

Setting

The setting is to be located in the prophetic circles responsible for the overwritten form of 9:1–10:16, with its emphasis on the secret anointing of Saul, as well as for 15:1-35 with its emphasis on Saul's rejection.

An attempt to situate these prophetic circles within the structures of Israel's institutions and cultural life belongs to the discussion of the PR and its origins, treated later under "Diachronic Dimension." At our present level, it is important and sufficient to have recognized the prophetic concerns that are likely to have made prophetic circles responsible for this passage. These are not the classical "writing prophets," but rather their predecessors — who may well have shaped the concept of what it was to be a prophet in Israel and have prepared the way for that vocation.

Meaning

The primary function of the passage is to bring to completion the shift in God's action in Israel. Saul has twice been noted as rejected and twice reference has been made to a successor determined by God (13:14; 15:28). Now the rejection has been moved into the past and God's order initiates something new: the anointing of the one who is to replace Saul (vv. 1 and 13).

When the whole sweep of the Samuel narrative is surveyed, we can see that the action of God, begun in the birth of Samuel, is here brought to fulfillment. What happens to David from now on will be the outcome largely of military and political forces. In the narrative, God is not distant from these forces; David succeeds in the narrative because God is with him. Samuel's work, however, is done. He has inaugurated the institution of monarchy in Israel; he has set the standards of obedience to God by which kings in Israel should be judged; and he has finally anointed David, the man to be king in place of the rejected Saul. He is entitled to retire to Ramah. The prophetic task has been accomplished. The political task lies ahead.

Bibliography of Works Cited Above

Birch, Bruce C. *The Rise of the Israelite Monarchy: The Growth and Development of 1 Samuel 7–15.* SBLDS 27. Missoula: Scholars Press, 1976.

Campbell, Antony F. *Of Prophets and Kings: A Late Ninth-Century Document (1 Samuel 1–2 Kings 10).* CBQMS 17. Washington, DC: Catholic Biblical Association of America, 1986.

Campbell, Antony F., and Mark A. O'Brien. *Unfolding the Deuteronomistic History: Origins, Upgrades, Present Text.* Minneapolis: Fortress, 2000.

Davies, P. R. "Ark or Ephod in 1 Sam xiv.18?" *JTS* 26 (1975) 82-87.

————, "The History of the Ark in the Books of Samuel." *JNSL* 5 (1977) 9-18.

Dietrich, Walter. *Prophetie und Geschichte: Eine redaktionsgeschichtliche Untersuchung zum deuteronomistischen Geschichtswerk.* FRLANT 108. Göttingen: Vandenhoeck & Ruprecht, 1972.

————. *David, Saul und die Propheten: Das Verhältnis von Religion und Politik nach den prophetischen Überlieferungen vom frühesten Königtum in Israel.* BWANT 122. Stuttgart: Kohlhammer, 1987.

Foresti, Fabrizio. *The Rejection of Saul in the Perspective of the Deuteronomistic School: A Study of 1 Sm 15 and Related Texts.* Rome: Teresianum, 1984.

Grønbaek, Jakob H. *Die Geschichte vom Aufstieg Davids (1. Sam. 15–2. Sam. 5): Tradition und Komposition.* Copenhagen: Munksgaard, 1971.

Jobling, David. "Saul's Fall and David's Rise: Tradition and Redaction in 1 Sam 14:1-46." *JBL* 95 (1976) 376-76.

Mendenhall, George E. *The Tenth Generation: The Origins of the Biblical Tradition.* Baltimore: The Johns Hopkins University Press, 1973.

Noth, Martin. *The History of Israel.* 2nd ed. London: Black, 1960.

————. *The Deuteronomistic History.* 2nd ed. JSOTSup 15. Sheffield: Sheffield Academic Press, 1991.

Rendtorff, Rolf. "Beobachtungen zur altisraelitischen Geschichtsschreibung anhand der Geschichte vom Aufstieg Davids." Pp. 428-39 in *Probleme biblischer Theologie.* Edited by H. W. Wolff. Munich: Chr. Kaiser, 1971.

Seebass, Horst. "I Samuel 15 als Schlüssel für das Verständnis der sogenannten königsfreundlichen Reihe I Sam 9:1–10:16; 11:1-15 und 13:2–14:52." *ZAW* 78 (1966) 148-79.

Smith, Henry Preserved. *The Books of Samuel.* ICC. Edinburgh: Clark, 1912.

Stoebe, Hans Joachim. "Zur Topographie und Überlieferung der Schlacht von Mikmas, 1. Sam. 13 und 14." *ThZ* 21 (1965) 269-80.

Van der Toorn, Karel, and Cees Houtman. "David and the Ark." *JBL* 113 (1994) 209-31.

Veijola, Timo. *Die Ewige Dynastie: David und die Entstehung seiner Dynastie nach der deuteronomistischen Darstellung.* AASF B 193. Helsinki: Suomalainen Tiedeakatemia, 1975.

Weinfeld, Moshe. *Deuteronomy and the Deuteronomic School.* Oxford: Clarendon, 1972.

Weiser, Artur. "1 Samuel 15." *ZAW* 54 (1936) 1-28.

Westermann, Claus. *Basic Forms of Prophetic Speech.* Philadelphia: Westminster, 1967.

Chapter 6

DAVID'S EMERGENCE IN ISRAEL
(1 Samuel 16:14–18:16)

So far, we have looked at the text concerned with the prophetic moves to establish David as king. In the initial structure analysis, this was as follows:

I. Preparations for David's emergence as king-to-be   1 Sam 1:1–16:13
   A. Prophetic: arrival of Samuel on the national scene   1:1–4:1a
   B. Liturgical: departure of the ark from the national scene   4:1b–7:1
   C. Prophetic: emergence of monarchy   7:2–16:13
      1. Arrival of Saul and the new institution of monarchy   7:2–12:25
      2. Dismissal of Saul and beginning of David's arrival   13:1–16:13

The next major section of the books of Samuel concerns the political moves to establish David as king, extending from 1 Sam 16:14 to 2 Sam 8:18. As this straddles both 1 and 2 Samuel, we need to look at it here, before going further. The structure analysis may be represented as follows:

II. The political moves to establish David
    as king   1 Sam 16:14–2 Sam 8:18
   A. Tension with Saul as king and David
      as anointed   1 Sam 16:14—31:13
      1. David at the court of Saul   16:14–21:1 (NRSV, 20:42)
        a. David's emergence in Israel   16:14–18:16
        b. Veiled conflict at the court   18:17–21:1 (NRSV, 20:42)
      2. Open rupture between David
      and Saul   21:2 (NRSV, 21:1)–27:12
        a. Within Israel: David as fugitive   21:2 (NRSV, 21:1)–26:25
          1) Flight and consequences   21:2 (NRSV, 21:1)–22:23
          2) Contrast of David and Saul,
            of fugitive and king   23:1-18
          3) David as innocent of murderous intent   23:19–26:25

The story of how David rose to power as king over all Israel is a rich compilation of traditions. A narrative is often referred to as the Story of David's Rise, encompassing at least the text of 1 Sam 16:14 to 2 Sam 5:10 or 12 (possibly beginning at 1 Sam 9:1 and equally possibly ending at 2 Sam 8:18 — see Diachronic Dimension). When it comes to structuring a compiled text like this, as we have just done, it is important for the reader to recognize and for the interpreter to avow that the structure analysis at this level is at times as much a matter of aesthetic satisfaction as of intellectual argument. In some cases, more than one analysis may adequately reflect the text; to be valid, any analysis must reflect the text and reflect it adequately.

In deciding how to present the structure of a text, issues of content, style, and syntax are all involved. For example, 28:1–31:13 is held together by the interlocking information of 28:1, 4, and 29:1, 11, and 31:1, by the fulfillment of ch. 28 in ch. 31, and by the association of ch. 29 with ch. 30. Chapter 27, however, gives the background for Achish's trust in David. As so often in narrative texts, some background knowledge must be presumed. On aesthetic and other grounds, I believe 28:1 is the better starting point for the final scene of Saul's failure, and ch. 27 is better as the culmination of the open rupture between David and Saul. Others may differ.

16:14–18:16 presents a microcosm of the story of David's rise to kingship over all Israel. It is summarized in 18:14-16 — David was successful, because the LORD was with him (v. 14); Saul was afraid of him (v. 15); and all Israel and Judah were loyal to him, because he provided leadership (v. 16). It is the perfect ending to the story of David's emergence in Israel. In the present text, however, the issue of marriage into Saul's family has been raised (17:25). So the narrative would flow on appropriately into the offers of first Merab then Michal in marriage to David (18:17-30). The added note of Saul's using his own daughters as bait to have David killed forms a satisfactory if ugly transition to the veiled conflict at the court. On the other hand, it is unlikely that the Story of David's Rise, extolling the David whose trust was in the LORD, would have made much space for ambitions on the scale of "What shall be done for the man who kills this Philistine?" (17:26). Without the theme of marriage to the king's daughter, 18:14-16 might be seen as a most satisfactory conclusion. Here the judgment of literary interpretation is being subtly swayed by the influences of tradition history — not by the text the way it is, but by the text the way it was. Judgments will differ. For an analysis of 1 Sam 17 alone in ethnopoetic terms, see Jason, "Story."

The veil is drawn aside from the conflict at court when Jonathan learns that his father wants David dead (20:30-34). The open rupture begins when David leaves for the life of a guerrilla leader in the wilderness. The content is clear. The syntax and style are satisfactory between the ending, "He [David] got up and left; and Jonathan went into the city," and the new beginning, "David came to Nob to the priest Ahimelech" (21:2; NRSV, 21:1). Others may differ and structure differently. The task of interpretation is to be adequate and responsible, not to be definitive.

The only thing that will not do is to bumble along from chapter to chapter. As will be evident, the narrative is skillfully composed and structured; it needs to be appreciated. Part of that appreciation is to notice where symbolism has taken over from reality. Honor and shame are surely significant themes underlying many of these narratives, but what chs. 16–17 do not reveal is "how David moves from an insignificant, unknown position . . . to one of relative status and prospect" (Stansell, "Honor and Shame," 95-96). David certainly does. But would one episode of courage and lateral thinking earn a senior command amongst Saul's military? How much is here concealed, subsumed under a symbolism that was of significance only later?

It is time to look more closely at the appropriate sections. From here to the end of 1 Samuel, the narrative grapples with the troublesome reality of Saul's presence as king and David's presence as anointed. A prophet has created the situation, making Saul king and anointing David as successor. Politicians or historians, who may know nothing of Saul's rejection or David's anointing, will have to resolve the situation. As narrative, this section begins with David at the court of Saul.

Stories of David's Emergence in Israel	16:14–18:16
I. Core story: opening	16:14–17:11
A. Introduction: coming of David to the court of Saul	16:14-23
1. Need: Saul's plight	14
2. Proposal: to seek out a lyre-player	15-16
3. Outcome: David's entry into Saul's service	17-23
B. Story of battle and single combat: David replaces Saul	17:1-54*
1. Introduction to the battle: confrontation of forces	1-3
2. Challenge and single combat	4-51a*
a. The challenge	4-40*
1) Challenge from the Philistine	4-10

The *variant story* is concluded in 18:17-19, 29b-30; see the following section.

Note: the asterisk (*) here, as elsewhere, serves notice that only the relevant parts of the verses cited are referred to. For example, in 17:1-54* the asterisk indicates that some of the verses are not relevant to the reference (i.e., vv. 12-31 and v. 50).

Textual Issues

17:32 The MT has "heart of man"; the LXX has "heart of my lord." Most emend with the LXX. The NRSV's understanding, "no one's heart," is possible and somewhat more respectful of the royal dignity that the text is about to demonstrate will, in due course, be David's. Alter appeals to insight into David's intention ("David uses a generalizing phrase") — unfortunately psychologizing (*David Story*, 106).

17:52 The structure of the text is such as to arouse caution about emendation (cf. Barthélemy, 192).

18:6-9 The MT can be read, as in the NRSV. The LXX offers a slightly shorter version. Emendation is, of course, possible; it is not necessary.

Discussion

A wide range of views exists on the nature of this text (see, for example, Barthélemy et al., *Story of David*). My approach to its structure analysis is discussed at greater length than is possible here in my article in the Rolf Knierim festschrift (Campbell, "Structure Analysis"). Space limits the possibility of extensive engagement with other interpretations (noted below, at the end of this chapter). Readers will often have to evaluate and judge. Once again, interpretation as an art attempts to be adequate and responsible but cannot be definitive.

To put matters in context, the interpretation to be offered here understands the present text as a composition, blending two narratives. The longer text (= MT) has come into existence through the addition of material (with De Vries, Hertzberg, Klein, Lust, McCarter, Stoebe, Tov); it is not the result of subtraction in search of harmonization and coherence (so Barthélemy, Gooding, Pisano). The concept of "reported story," assuming that not every known detail needs to be spelled out in text, allows the additional material to be understood as a base for a potential narrative (against Stoebe). The present interpretation avoids fragmentation and follows the process through to the end of ch. 18; in this, it goes beyond McCarter. In particular, the misunderstanding of "youth" *(na'ar)* has bedeviled too much interpretation, failing to take seriously the figure and faith of David. David is not portrayed as an ineffectual defenseless little shepherd boy. In addition, the nature of the sling as the ideal weapon in the circumstances has too often been overlooked.

The interpreter's task is to pick up the signals being sent by a text and to organize them to make the best possible sense of the text. There are signals aplenty to be found in this text; they do not allow themselves to be organized into a single flowing unitary text, nor do they allow themselves to be distributed across a couple of sources, as in the Pentateuch, nor do they give much support to the idea that a basic story has been supplemented here and there with variants of this or that aspect. According to my judgment, there is one story in the text, outlined from beginning to end, in which David as Saul's armor-bearer fights and kills the Philistine champion, Goliath, and so emerges as a leader figure in Israel and the target for Saul's jealousy. There is another story in the text, but it is not outlined from beginning to end. Enough of it is given for a storyteller to have no problem weaving a seamless narrative, but the text leaves significant gaps and its ending (18:17-19, 29b-30) belongs now in the following block of traditions. It is a story of David who comes to the battlefield almost by chance, hears the Philistine's challenge and sees the significance of the opportunity it offers, seizes the chance, and by killing the Philistine enters the court of King Saul, where his success leads to the offer of Saul's daughter in marriage, an offer that is not honored, reflecting Saul's enmity toward David, while David's success continues.

Three elements are integral to this approach. First, it assumes that at least two traditions circulated in ancient Israel about David's emerging to prominence. Second, it allows the MT to preserve both traditions, blending them intelligently into the semblance of a flowing narrative, while keeping the differences intact for those who want to see and exploit them. Third, it acknowledges the skill and discretion of storytellers and their responsibility for the actualization in story of the traditions preserved in written texts.

The otherwise attractive and insightful presentation of David's emergence in Israel by André Wénin, for example, fails to discuss significant signals (Wénin, "David roi," 76-89). Wénin's basic move is to contrast David the shepherd king with Saul the warrior king. While this may be a devotionally appealing approach, it does not reflect either this text itself or the subsequent stories of David's power struggle with Saul. Among other issues: the designation of David as small ("petit"), translating *haqqāṭān* in 1 Sam 16:11 and 17:14, exploits a potential overtone (in my judgment, incorrect), but it is irresponsible not to draw it into relation with the overwhelming meaning in such contexts of "younger" or "youngest"; the text's stumbling blocks need fuller comment in a scholarly study of the text as literature. For example, vv. 15-16, 31, 50-51, and 55-58 cannot be passed over without full discussion (note: Wénin's *David & Goliath* booklet was not available to me). For vv. 15-16: by returning to Jesse's flock David leaves Saul bereft of lyre-player and armor-bearer, while as narrative the Philistine's twice-daily appearance for forty days makes a mockery of what follows (cf. vv. 20b-24). For v. 31: in time of battle, the armor-bearer's place is by his king. For vv. 50-51: the Philistine is killed twice, once in each verse. For vv. 55-58: the issue of Saul's apparent non-recognition of David receives a paragraph that — despite the endeavors of Fokkelman, Gooding, Polzin, and Wénin — is too contrived to carry conviction. David's sling may well be a shepherd's sling, but the fact of the sling as a military weapon (2 Chron 26:14; Judg 20:16) needs more than a passing footnote reference, especially given the weapon's appropriateness in the present situation. The combined text offers a complexity of motivation (e.g., courage and ambition) that is diminished by appeal to the image of the little shepherd; the text's signals are not adequately identified by Wénin and cannot be appropriately organized under the image of the shepherd king.

There are signals constituting both major and minor tensions in the text. The major tensions are as follows.

1. David is twice introduced to the court of Saul, once at the beginning and once toward the end of the text. In 16:14-23, he is brought to Saul's court as lyre-player and is made Saul's armor-bearer; in 17:55-58, he is unknown to Saul and Abner, and in 18:1-5 he enters the court of Saul and is befriended by Jonathan. The double introduction to the court is superficially avoided if the story of David and the Philistine is begun at 17:1. Apart from ignoring the present text, this approach raises its own difficulties and the problems within the chapter remain unresolved.

2. David is twice introduced to the listener or reader, once in 16:18-23 and again in 17:12-14. In the present text, there is also 16:1-13; we may prescind from it in assessing the nature of ch. 17.

3. The conflict with the Philistines is twice introduced to the listener or reader, once in 17:1-3 and again in 17:19.

4. The Philistine champion is twice introduced to the listener or reader, by name and town, once in 17:4 and again in 17:23.

5. David is portrayed in a double light, both as ambitious and as faith-filled. In 17:25-30, David wants something, i.e., the rewards that come with killing the Philistine; in 17:32-37, David offers something, i.e., to fill the vacuum of Saul's fear with his own courage and trust in the LORD. Of course these two aspects of human nature and human discourse could be easily reconciled. The text does not reconcile them; the gaps are not filled. The full range of signals seems to be set against reconciling them.

6. David is twice reported killing the Philistine. In 17:50, he kills him and there was no sword in David's hand; with sling and stone he struck the Philistine and killed him. In 17:51, he kills him and the Philistine's sword was in David's hand; he drew the Philistine's sword, killed him, and cut off his head. The Hebrew verb "to strike" here can be ambiguous, involving either a blow or a killing; the Hebrew verb "to kill" here is unambiguous, unmistakably involving death.

The minor tensions may be enumerated briefly.

a. In 17:15, David's going back and forth from Saul to his father's sheepfold seems to try to harmonize two stories, or the two introductions. It conflicts with 16:21-22 which is as definitive as 18:2.

b. In 17:16, the Philistine is reported as taking his stand twice a day for forty days, which also seems to try to harmonize two stories or introductions.

c. In 17:23, the Philistine is reported speaking "the same words as before." 17:8-10 are implied. Verse 16 has had the Philistine "take his stand" twice a day for forty days. This may demand no more than a glowering menacing appearance on the scene. But then the storyteller must account for why, on this fortieth day, the Israelite army was "going forth to the battle, shouting the war cry" (v. 20) and why the Israelites panicked so precipitately (v. 24). On the other hand, it would be farcical to portray Israel as having performed like this twice a day for forty days.

d. In 17:31, Saul sends for David but has nothing to say to him and no offer to make him, beyond finally and grudgingly responding to David's courage and trust in the LORD. The issue of reward is not discussed.

e. In 17:55, Saul sees David going out against the Philistine; this is awkward alongside Saul's having sent for David (v. 31) and having sent him out to battle (v. 37b).

f. In 17:55, Saul inquires as to David's identity. With the first introduction, David is known to him as his lyre-player and armor-bearer. Without the first introduction, the question of David's identity is oddly missing from the encounter at 17:31.

g. In 17:57, David still has the head of the Philistine in his hand; in 17:54, the Philistine's head has been dispatched to Jerusalem — whatever that may mean.

None of these observations is contested by modern scholarship. Most attempts to reconcile them account for some while leaving others aside. I believe that the version of the two-story hypothesis presented here accounts for all the signals, with a core story complete with 18:14-16 and a variant story that is structurally incomplete until 18:17-19, 29b-30. It is regrettable that Alter's valuable reflection on variant traditions is here restricted to a comparison of ch. 16 with ch. 17, without being extended to the variants within ch. 17 (cf. pp. 110-11).

One more set of observations needs to be recorded: the textual tradition. There is a marked difference between the transmitted text of the MT and the LXX^B in chs. 17–18. The text in LXX^B is about 45 percent shorter than MT, some 49 verses to 88. The material not present in LXX^B consists of 17:12-31, 41, 48b, 50; 17:55–18:5; 18:6aα, 8a* ("Saul was very angry"), 8b, 10-11, 12b, 17-19, 21b, 29b-30 (note 18:17-19, 29b-30 for the conclusion of the variant story). This is not simply a matter of losses and omissions in a particular manuscript family. The verses are found in LXX^A and other Greek manuscripts. There, however, the translation style is different, and follows the MT more closely than elsewhere in the LXX of Samuel. These witnesses are supplying the gaps from the MT; the text translated by the LXX did not have them (cf. Driver, 140; Stoebe, 312-13). The shorter (or LXX) text approximates closely with the "core story" here; the longer (or MT) text includes both core and variant story outlines (including 18:17-19, 29b-30). It would appear that in the tradition represented by the LXX^B, only the core story was recorded. In the tradition represented by the MT, the significant passages of the variant story have been included, with the conclusion in 18:17-19, 29b-30. It may be helpful to consult Campbell and O'Brien, *Unfolding*, 258-65, for a visual presentation of this material.

In this presentation, the shorter text (LXX equivalent; i.e., the text common to both the LXX^B and the MT) is referred to as the core story; the material found *exclusively* in the longer text (MT equivalent; i.e, passages contained originally only in the MT) is referred to as the variant. The structure of the core story is:

A. Introduction: coming of David to the court of Saul   16:14-23
B. Story of battle and single combat   17:1-54*
C. Conclusion: emergence of David on the national scene   18:6-16

In the structure analysis of this particular passage, because of the distinctive nature of this text, the roman numerals (I-II-III) simply denote the sections of text belonging to the core story; similarly, the numbers IA and IIA denote the sections of text belonging to the variant story. Since the variant story is incomplete until 18:17-19, 29b-30, the divisions within these sections relate only to each individual section and not to the whole. The discussion will follow the sequence of the present biblical text (= MT).

The structure of the variant is worth identifying here. It could be given as follows:

A. David: arrival at Israel's battle — ambition   17:12-30
B. David: arrival at Saul's court — recognition   17:41, 48b, 50;
    17:55–18:5
C. David: a rival to Saul — reward denied: tension   18:17-19, 29b-30

Note: the final section of the variant story (18:17-19, 29b-30) will be discussed in its place where, in the present text, it belongs with the covert moves by Saul to kill David.

Methodologically, it is worth noting that the interpretation given here is a piece of source analysis, of reflection on origins; it is not an exercise in text criticism. Text-critically, 17:41, 48b and 18:6aα, 8a*, 8b, 10-11, 12b do not belong in the "core story"; they are not found in the shorter (LXX^B) text. Only 17:50 (also not found in the shorter LXX^B text) is singled out in the main analysis, because of its stark contradiction by v. 51a. If our aim was to reflect the history of the text's growth, as reflected in the textual tradition, 17:41, 48b and 18:6aα, 8a*, 8b, 10-11, 12b would need to be omitted from the core story; note the use of 17:41, 48b, 50 in the structure of the variant story above. 18:6aα, 8a*, 8b, 12b, and 21b are best described as fragments associated with the combination of the two stories. 18:10-11 is a special case. 17:41 and 48b are included in the core story here because our aim is to analyze the present text. The history of the text's growth is noted, but as subsidiary to the primary task of analysis.

Methodologically again, it is also worth noting that this is not a piece of strictly mechanistic source analysis. If it was, 17:41 and 48b, as well as 17:50, would be omitted from the "core story" because they would be judged doublets. While adding the note about the shield-bearer, 17:41 repeats information found in v. 48a; 17:48b repeats and expands on information found in v. 40b; 17:50 repeats and contradicts v. 51a. In source criticism, what can be done is not necessarily what must be done; "possible" is not the same as "necessary." It is in principle sound "not to assume literary disunity unless the occurrence of variants, of obvious seams and secondary connections, and the like, *compels* such an assumption" (Noth, *Pentateuchal Traditions,* 24). Source analysis that is flexible, moderate, and sensitive can look at possible divisions without being obligated to divide. So here, 17:41 and 48b need not be separate from the core story; 17:50 must be.

The core story is introduced by narrating the coming of David to the court of Saul — [I.A]. Its text begins with a remarkable piece of theological interpretation. Saul's courtiers note that "an evil spirit from God" torments him (16:15, 16, 23); this is an interpretation of observable events. The narrative goes a step further: the spirit of YHWH has departed from Saul, and the evil spirit that torments him is from YHWH (16:14). That the spirit of the LORD has departed from the king is a strong statement. That the king's torment is from the LORD has the makings of cruel irony. The spirit of the LORD has departed from Saul, yet the LORD is with David (16:18). An evil spirit has come upon Saul; yet when David is with Saul and plays for him, the evil spirit departs. At the end of the story, the irony becomes cruel when it is Saul who makes David depart from him (18:13).

The use of "the LORD" (YHWH) in v. 14 and of "God" in vv. 15-23 may reflect a traditio-historical process, pointing to different origins. The LXX, however, has "the LORD" in v. 15 as well, and simply "evil spirit" after that; it does not support the difference.

The movement of the narrative is clear. Saul is in need; he is tormented. A proposal is made that a lyre-player and music might soothe his torment. The proposal is adopted. David is put forward, summoned to the court, finds favor with Saul and is commissioned as his armor-bearer, and his playing brings about the desired outcome, relieving Saul of his torment. It has been noted that David's name is not given in v. 18 but is used by Saul in v. 19, along with his occupation; also that the qualities attributed to David and succinctly expressed in six Hebrew word pairs (v. 18) would have been more appropriate to the court of David than the court of Saul (cf. von Rad, *Old Testament Theology,* 1.430). It is possible that a less official description of David, and one which gave his name, once stood in the place of v. 18. But the story, as it was told for this context, came from the court of David; v. 18 would be quite satisfactory and proper (cf. Stoebe, 308). We should not put too much emphasis on gaps in a story outline (reported story), but the list is impressive enough to suggest David's court rather than Saul's. "The narrator is obviously presenting David's credentials for more than court musician" (Brueggemann, 126).

The first five qualities, and perhaps even the sixth, describe the requirements desired of a young man taking a place at court (cf. Stoebe, 307-10). "Skillful in playing" heads the list because of the present context. "Man of valor" refers probably to the possession of adequate means to bear arms and live at court. "Warrior" refers either to proper age for military service or to adequate general preparation. "Prudent in speech" may indicate training in rhetoric or the wisdom to give good counsel. "Man of good presence" or appearance expresses in abstract terms what is more impressionistically described in 16:12. Within such a listing of personal qualities, the statement "The LORD is with him" might have an almost secular sense — a well-favored young man.

The introduction has situated David at the court of Saul, as lyre-player to soothe the king in his tormented moments and as armor-bearer to be at the king's side in battle.

The text now moves into a story of battle and of single combat — [I.B]. It will be proposed by the Philistine that the outcome of the battle should depend on the outcome of the single combat (cf. 2 Sam 2:14, 17). The story begins with the opening elements of a battle report: the confrontation of two armies and the location of their camps. The geographical description is remarkably precise. The Philistine camp is located between Socoh and Azekah, located — if modern geographical identifications are correct — toward the western end of the valley of Elah. Israel is camped in the valley of Elah, presumably toward the eastern end and most likely on the northern side. The battle lines are then drawn toward the mountain ('el hāhār) at either end, with the broad level valley between them (cf. Stoebe, 316); hardly "on the mountain" (NRSV, in v. 3). The location is inside the first seaward range of the Judean hills, directly in the line of Philistine encroachment into Judah. Socoh is described as "which belongs to Judah" (v. 1).

The presentation of the Philistine champion and the description of his weapons are intended to inculcate awe and fear. His speech is a challenge to settle the battle by single combat: the fate of Israel will be riding on the outcome (v. 9). An introductory phrase stands both at the beginning (v. 8) and in the middle of his speech (v. 10). This phenomenon recurs again in one of David's speeches to Saul (vv. 34, 37), and in the Philistine's speech to David (vv. 43-44). There do not appear to be adequate grounds for considering these to indicate additions; rather, it appears to be a stylistic device, emphasizing or recapitulating elements of a speech (cf. Driver, 145). The Philistine's challenge has its effect. Saul and all Israel are afraid.

The name Goliath occurs twice in the chapter; the designation "Philistine" for the champion occurs twenty-seven times. The text's concern is not with a named individual, but with the representative who is symbolic of the Philistine threat as a whole (cf. 19:5). In 17:4, the name Goliath is mentioned naturally enough; in 17:23, the reference to the Philistine's name and origin seems awkwardly inserted into a phrase that otherwise reads, a "champion came up out of the ranks of the Philistines." It is well known that the killing of Goliath is attributed in 2 Sam 21:19 to "to Elhanan son of Jaare-oregim, the Bethlehemite." The frequencies just noted suggest that credit for the deed was later transferred to David and the name of Goliath inserted into the stories of David's legendary combat with a Philistine champion (cf. de Vaux, "Combats singuliers," 217; also McCarter, 291; against Stoebe, 317). 1 Sam 21:10 (NRSV, 21:9) and 22:10 presumably depend on this legendary identification.

The Philistine's challenge, as expressed in v. 9, has the future relationship of Philistines and Israelites hang on the outcome of this single combat. In these circumstances, a storyteller would not have a responsible king allow any self-opinionated young soldier to risk Israel's future in an unequal fight. An Israelite champion needs to be authorized. At the end of the combat story (v. 51b), this aspect of the single combat is ignored. Perhaps it was never meant to be more than the self-aggrandizement and pompous rhetoric of an arrogant and awesome warrior. It is appropriate for the story, because it symbolizes what is at stake in reality, whatever the rhetoric. In these chapters, the Philistines are presented as a life-threatening menace to Israel. If the Philistines were left unconquered, the Israelites would be left without autonomy and independence. That is what makes it so significant that Saul is powerless to provide and that David takes his place.

The text presents Saul's response to the Philistine challenge: "When Saul and all Israel heard these words of the Philistine, they were dismayed and greatly afraid" (v. 11). In the "core story," this is promptly followed by David's response, who as royal armor-bearer should be standing beside his king: "Let no one's heart fail because of him; your servant will go and fight with this Philistine" (v. 32). The contrast could not be starker. Saul is "dismayed and greatly afraid" — thoroughly unkingly behavior. David is courageous and ready to take up the challenge — he will deliver Israel from this threat. This is what the prophetic editing emphasized: Saul was anointed to deliver Israel from the Philistine threat (9:16). But Saul was rejected and David anointed. The working out of Saul's rejection and David's anointing is happening here before Israel's eyes — or before the storyteller's audience. J. P. Fokkelman's observation is à propos here; there is a chiastic structure either side of the intervening verses. The giant Philistine's arms are described, his challenge narrated, and the Israelite response noted (vv. 5-11); on the other side, David's response is given, his contempt narrated, and the theme of arms taken up (vv. 32-40). It is not perfect, but it emphasizes the contrasting presentations (*Crossing Fates*, 166-78, esp. 177).

In the present text, the dispirited Saul and the highly spirited David are separated by twenty verses. The interpretation favored here understands these intervening verses as the first part of the presentation of key moments in a variant story of David's coming to Saul's court — [*I.var*] — and there being singularly successful (18:5, 30). An introduction of David is necessary; the introduction here (17:12-14) draws on material shared with 16:1-13. The direction of derivation is uncertain, just as the age of the variant version is unknown. The use of the definite article for "the battle" in 17:13 might be taken as a reference to the scene already told in 17:1-11. That need not be so. Hebrew usage includes the article in cases where the meaning is simply "to battle/to war" (cf., for example, 1 Sam 4:1; 7:10; 17:1; 23:8 and most occurrences).

Verses 15 and 16 are best understood as bridge verses, introduced to allow the core story and the variant version to be presented in a single text. Verse 15 appears as a foreign body. If David was going back and forth between the army and the flock, he is likely to have been absent when needed to play the lyre for Saul and, in this time of war, he would have been needed as armor-bearer to his king. Over a forty-day period, it would be surprising that David had not heard of the Philistine's challenge earlier; yet v. 23b, "And David heard him," suggests that this is the first time. If David was going back and forth regularly, Eliab's anger in v. 28 is surprising. In its immediate context, Jesse's three eldest sons have followed Saul to war (vv. 13-14) so that David is going back and forth between the army and the flock (v. 15). As a bridge verse, it is not controlled by this immediate context; its role is to forge a link between David the armor-bearer of 16:14-23 and David the bearer of gifts and provisions in 17:17-22 — which it does with some incongruity.

Verse 16, with the round number 40, looks like legendary rather than historical detail. It serves to heighten the challenge: over forty days no response has been forthcoming from Israel. However, it is in tension with vv. 20b-24 — with the two armies drawn up in battle array, the challenge, and Israel's flight and fear. This appears to narrate a singular occurrence — and for the first time. Taken literally according to 17:16, this would have to be the seventy-ninth or eightieth time that the Philistine appeared. The verb "took his stand" leaves unspecified whether his challenge was regularly repeated or whether the armies faced off as before. The gathering of the armies for battle (vv. 20b-21) and the panicked flight/retreat of the Israelites (v. 24) twice a day for forty days would indeed be farcical. It may not be intended. The verse does forge a link between the Philistine of 17:4-10 and the Philistine of 17:23. A question remains: How do we understand the insertion of such a link verse by an intelligent editor? "A second time," inserted appropriately in a leaner v. 23, would have made for a smoother transition in a unified narrative. A twice-daily appearance by the menacing Philistine, without the gathering of the armies and without, even, the need for his challenge to be repeated in full, would also make for a smoother narrative. Alternatively, given the intelligence of the editor (which we have no right to deny), should we conclude that no smooth transition to a unified narrative is offered? We are expected to recognize that two stories are being presented in the same text. The "forty days" succeeds in keeping them apart while superficially bringing them together (see p. 187).

Once on the scene, David hears the Philistine's challenge (v. 23b). However, he is not portrayed as responding to it immediately. His response is prepared by the consternation of the men of Israel (v. 24) and their talk of the great reward awaiting the man who kills this Philistine (v. 25). David's response, when it comes, is directly in function of this reward: "What shall be done for the man who kills this Philistine, and takes away the reproach from Israel?" (v. 26a). The concern for the reward precedes the religion-weighted language of the uncircumcised Philistine who defies the armies of the living God. The exchange with Eliab fits awkwardly into the context. A storyteller may be invited to use it to show the younger David as undeterred or to emphasize his interest in the reward (vv. 28a and 30b). A reader may respond to it in the same way.

The classic reward in fairy tales and legends is half the kingdom and the hand of the king's daughter in marriage. The reward here comes close: great riches, the king's daughter in marriage, and freedom from taxes for his father's family (17:25). In the text, the reward is not promised by Saul; it is talked about by the troops. In the text, David does not make any claims; he listens to what is being offered. Saul does not make any promises; the rewards are proposed by the soldiery. Storytellers and readers are free to develop the theme appropriately. This theme also takes us beyond 18:16 to the third and concluding section from the variant story, now in 18:17-19, 29b-30, where Merab, the king's elder daughter, is offered to David in marriage. However, the plot has a brutal twist. What the soldiers promised as a reward Saul uses as a trap to eliminate his rival: "I will not raise a hand against him; let the Philistines deal with him" (18:17; cf.

v. 25, MT). It is in vain, of course; David was more successful than Saul (18:30).

As a bridge, 17:31 brings storyteller or reader back into the presence of Saul and David, the king and his armor-bearer. David's words, as noted in v. 29, have only been questions; developed a little, they can express readiness to fight the Philistine. Verse 31 does not belong in the core story; in the core story, as his armor-bearer David is at Saul's side. It does not belong in the variant story; in vv. 55-58, Saul does not know David's identity. The text from the variant story has a gap here, between David's ascertaining the probability of a reward and his venturing out against the Philistine. A storyteller might choose to keep this gap and could have David go into battle without a promise of reward from Saul and equally without authorization from Saul. A storyteller choosing to fill the gap and have Saul deal with the issues of reward and/or authorization would need to cater for or alter the presentation of vv. 55-58. Readers may do the same.

Saul has been seen "dismayed and greatly afraid" (v. 11). It is a position no man likes to be seen in, least of all a king leading his troops in battle — [II]. David speaks up with diplomatic discretion and no direct reference to the cowardice of the king (against LXX): "Let no one's heart fail because of him; your servant will go and fight with this Philistine" (v. 32).

Saul's reply has spawned more misunderstandings than any other verse in Samuel: "You cannot go against this Philistine to fight with him; for you are a youth [a na'ar], and he has been a warrior from his youth [minnĕ'urāyw = from the time he was a na'ar]" (v. 33). The meaning of the Hebrew, undistorted by translation, is clear: what you are now is what he was once at the beginning of his warrior's career. David is a recent recruit; the Philistine is a battle-tested veteran (cf. Stoebe, 335; Gooding, The Story, 56).

The range of meaning of the Hebrew term na'ar has been noted in the discussion of 16:1-13. Its basic meaning has been identified as dependence, either within the family or in service, i.e., within an institution such as the court (cf. Stähli, Knabe-Jüngling-Knecht). This is what allows the term to range from the suckling infant (1 Sam 1:22) to the royal overseer (1 Kgs 11:28). As we have seen, Jesse's sons are described as nĕ'ārîm (the plural, 16:11), and three of them are in Saul's army. The courtier who singles out David for Saul is one of the nĕ'ārîm (16:18); the soldiers allegedly picked for a special mission with David are nĕ'ārîm (21:3, 6; NRSV, vv. 2, 5); the twelve soldiers from each side who killed each other in hand-to-hand combat before Abner and Joab were nĕ'ārîm (2 Sam 2:14). The use of 'elem in 17:56 does not resolve anything; 'elem is used as a parallel to na'ar both here and in 1 Sam 20:22. Its feminine form means a young woman of marriageable age (cf. Prov 30:19).

One has to wonder why David's redheaded good looks, his status as youngest son, his being shepherd, Saul's doubts, and the Philistine's contempt should create among so many interpreters so strong an impression of his powerlessness before the powerful Philistine — the "small, apparently defenseless" shepherd boy (McCarter, 297) and the "half-grown youth" (Stähli, Knabe-Jüngling-Knecht, 91-92) against the invincible giant. It is often as if a "God of the gaps" theology is influential here and a "God of the guts" is ignored as unworthy. David has the physical attributes and the weaponry to do the job; all he needs is the courage and the nerve. He needs to be enabled to do what lies within his power — not to have done for him what lies beyond his grasp.

Physical attributes. The portrayal of David in his description of himself is revealing (17:34-37). He could chase down a lion or bear; so he is fast. He could strike it, rescuing its prey; so he is tough. If it turned on him, he could grab it around the jaw to kill it; so he is strong and his reflexes are very good. This is no little boy; whatever his physique, this young man is portrayed as fast, tough, and strong, with excellent reflexes. Of theological interest is the claim that David attributed these experiences to the supportive action of God. What David has done (vv. 34-35) has been done in conjunction with God (v. 37).

Weaponry: the sling. Judg 20:16 indicates that the sling could be considered a deadly accurate weapon; 2 Chron 26:14 indicates that the sling could be a standard military weapon, subject to normal procurement for stores — shields, spears, helmets, armor, bows, and stones for slinging. The ancient Israelite sling is not to be confused with a modern American slingshot. The sling was "whirled around to discharge its missile by centrifugal force" (Webster's), while the slingshot is "a forked stick with an elastic band attached for shooting small stones" (Webster's). Slingshots are for kids; slings were for killing.

As the Welsh longbow exposed the vulnerability of the heavily armored French cavalry to the British archers at Crecy and Agincourt, and as the crude muskets of mercenary German infantry shot the horses from under the aristocratic French knights at Pavia, and as a Molotov cocktail in the bare hands of a partisan could wipe out an armor-plated tank in World War II, so a sling in the hands of David could take out the massive Philistine. Two associated conditions would have been essential: (i) for David to get off his shot before the Philistine was on his guard; (ii) for David not to miss with his first shot. At close range, on his own terms, the Philistine was probably unbeatable. To win, David had to stay at long range. He had the weapon. He had the skill. As long as the Philistine's shield was being carried by his armor-bearer, he was vulnerable. A slingstone in the head would stun or kill. (Antiquarian details about Philistine helmets must yield to a storyteller's judgment of what will be accepted as plausible.)

David's status in this single combat can be measured by the role given him after the battle, without any narrative interval being suggested. In both core and variant stories, David is given a senior military command by Saul (18:13, 17). In this command, David is remarkably successful (18:16, 30). No kid gets this kind of kudos from the military. All the information we have points to David as a first-rate military strategist (cf. 2 Sam 17:8; 18:3). Saul offers to swap his gear with David (17:38-39); Jonathan effects a similar swap (18:4). If for nothing more than narrative plausibility, the image of David is likely to have been that of a big man.

The narrative has David decline Saul's armor. Two factors are at work in the text here: strategy and symbolism. Strategically, David must stay light. He has to be fast. He has to get close enough to be sure of not missing; he has to reach this range before the Philistine takes alarm and demands his shield. Strategically, Saul's armor would be an obstacle and most inappropriate. Symbolically, Saul's offer of armor is equivalent to trust in arms, and every Israelite storyteller knew that this was to be viewed with disfavor. In rejecting Saul's armor, David is portrayed putting his trust elsewhere — for "the LORD does not save by sword and spear; for the battle is the LORD's and he will give you into our hand" (17:47).

The pre-combat speeches are to be expected as part of the normal repertoire of battle stories. Again, two factors are at work: one strategic, the other theological. Strategically, David has to get within appropriate range of the Philistine without alarming him. Once the Philistine has taken his shield from his shield-bearer (cf. 17:7, as well as 41 [MT only]) and raised it before his face, he is immune to any slinger's attack. As long as he is speech-making, in pompous contempt for the unequipped peasant approaching him, he is vulnerable. So of course David picks up some stones from the brook and shoves them in his *yalqût* (glossed as shepherd's bag, v. 40). And of course David has his sling in his hand (v. 40), but any shrewd storyteller will locate that hand behind David's back, out of the Philistine's sight. And of course David has his stick in his hand (v. 40). The more the Philistine focuses indignantly on the stick (v. 43a), the less likely the Philistine is to wonder what David has in his other hand. Strategically, the speeches are a marvelous distraction allowing David to get within range without revealing his tactics and weapon. For storytellers, the speeches are a valuable delaying device, increasing tension. Theologically, the speeches transform a fight to the death between champions into a trial of strength between gods: the Philistine's gods (v. 43b) and the God of Israel (vv. 45-47; cf. 1 Sam 4:1-11, between armies; 1 Sam 5:1-5, between gods). The narrative presents us with an image for David's emergence in Israel: he courageously steps into the space vacated by a dejected king and delivers Israel through trust in "the name of the LORD of hosts, the God of the armies of Israel" (v. 45).

The description of the fight itself is brief. Verses 50 and 51a are, of course, in tension with one another. Verse 51a, with the beheading, is needed for v. 54. Verse 50 may be keeping a tradition alive and/or echoing v. 47 — not by sword or spear. The terms of the challenge (v. 9) are forgotten; perhaps they were never realistic anyway. They have served their function in heightening the narrative; now they can give place to pursuit and plunder. The pursuit is described as even to "the gates of Ekron" (v. 52; LXX, Ashkelon). The Philistines are portrayed as chased home to their city limits; it is questionable whether the story exceeds the reality, at least at this time.

Verse 54 has its problems. In the present text, David has no tent; he has come that day from Bethlehem. In the core story, as Saul's armor-bearer, there is no reason against his having a tent. The taking of the Philistine's head to Jerusalem is more of a problem. To speak of an anachronism is misleading since that would normally imply a retrojection of present conditions through ignorance of the past. The sequence from 1 Sam 17 to 2 Sam 5, however, was presumably as well known in ancient Israel as it is to modern commentators. So, for Josephus, the head went to David's tent and the sword was dedicated to God (*Antiquities,* VI, §192). No explanation is fully satisfactory, whether as threat to the Jebusites, or possibly because of Israel's short-term occupation of Jerusalem, or as relic or trophy. Perhaps rather than see David carrying the head to Jerusalem, we should hear in this statement an awareness that it was victory over the Philistine that carried David to Jerusalem — and to kingship there.

With v. 55, we reach the second section of the variant story — [*II.var*]. In the plain sense of the text, Saul is asking his army commander, Abner, the identity of the young soldier who is going out to fight the Philistine — and Abner does not know (v. 55). As the variant story is reported in v. 23, the Philistine's challenge was simply "as before," with no specification of the contract in the core story's v. 9. Readers and storytellers are free to emphasize the contract or not and, correspondingly, to have Saul authorize Israel's representative or not. If, as the narrative is actualized, Saul has ascertained David's identity and authorized him, the exchanges in vv. 55-58 will need modification. As they stand, either the issue of authorization has been played down or the whole contract theme is diminished. In my judgment, various suggestions that find a meaning for the question other than David's identity are too contrived and an unacceptable bending of the sense of the text in the exchange with Abner (vv. 55-56) as well as with David (v. 58). So, for example, Robert Polzin's suggestion (*Samuel*, 171-76) that Saul's "Whose son are you?" is to be understood in the present text as "Where does your loyalty lie?" ignores the force of 16:22. It is forced on Polzin by his chosen path of interpreting the present text as unified flowing text *at all costs*.

In the variant story, the encounter of Saul with David is not strictly a recognition scene; rather it is one of disclosure of identity. The text moves closer to something of the recognition scene with the instant bonding of Jonathan with David. Jonathan is Saul's heir presumptive (cf. 20:31) and he becomes involved in a scene of the most expressive bonding with David (18:1-4). "The action of Jonathan in giving David his robe and armor is a dramatic act that seems to transfer to David Jonathan's right to claim the throne" (Brueggemann, 136). In the variant story, it is at this point that David is accepted into the court of Saul. In the core story, David's position at the court of Saul precipitates his engagement with the Philistine. In the variant story, it is David's engagement with the Philistine that precipitates his entry into the court of Saul. Saul tries David as a commander; when he is successful, Saul gives him a senior command — with widespread approval among the military (18:5). Verse 5 requires a more extensive passage of time than its present context allows for. Within the variant story, it offers an appropriate transition to the offer of Merab in marriage.

The present text returns to the core story — [III]. David's emergence on the national scene is expressed in a variety of ways; the constant background is Saul's increasing fear of a rival. So David's prominence is portrayed in terms of Saul's jealousy (vv. 6-13) and by the narrative's concluding summary comment (vv. 14-16).

In the episode of the women's song (18:6-9), the MT has a bridging phrase that ties the moment to Saul and David's return from killing the Philistine, which conflicts with 18:5; among several differences, the LXX does not have this phrase, but has the women come out to meet David. All this means is that the song might have been sung at a later time; it is possible that the LXX tradition reflects a setting in which David alone was involved, after battles such as those reflected in 18:30. It does not matter; the text locates the episode appropriately enough here. The song speaks of Saul's thousands and David's ten thousands. It has been suggested that these terms must be heard poetically not mathematically; that a "thousand" and "ten thousand" are in parallelism and do not denote massive escalation (being the equivalent of x and x + 1; but cf. McCarter, 312). While this may be true poetically, here Saul is portrayed as judging it offensive and is angered. The Philistines will be portrayed remembering it (21:12 [NRSV, 11]; 29:5). In the MT, Saul's comment concludes with: "What more can he have but the kingdom?" (v. 8b); the phrase is lacking in the LXX. The MT is a sharper and more pointed expression of Saul's anguish; but the LXX is not radically different. Attention to Saul's jealousy begins here (v. 9). At this point, it is in Saul's mind.

Saul's jealousy promptly moves to action in vv. 10-11. The episode is attributed to an evil spirit from God. Saul seeks to pin David to the wall with a spear. We have no details of the action. We do not know the circumstances in which David eludes him twice (v. 11), implying that David may have stayed around long enough for Saul to have made a second attempt on his life. All the narrative tells us, and all we need to know, is that Saul's jealousy has moved from thought to action. The episode is repeated in 19:9-10 (an evil spirit from YHWH), where apparently David did not stay around for a second attempt by Saul; the seriousness of Saul's moods has to be evaluated against his doing the same to his son Jonathan (20:33).

The final reference to Saul's jealousy is a direct narrative comment: "Saul was afraid of David" (v. 12a). The MT has "because the LORD was with him but had departed from Saul" (v. 12b); the LXX does not have this bit of explicit interpretation. Verse 12b goes beyond 16:14; there the LORD had departed from Saul, here the LORD is now with David. "So they are contrasted, one the man 'with whom' the Lord is, and the other the man from whom the Lord has removed himself. And that is the meaning of the whole section" (Hertzberg, 158). As a result of his fear, Saul removes David from his presence and presumably from the court, putting him in command of a military unit. The cruelty of the irony here has already been mentioned. Saul is distancing himself from his own deliverer and the deliverer of Israel. At the same time, David's reputation as a military leader is being enhanced (v. 13b).

The narrative's final comment organizes all of this in terms of the players in the drama of leadership in Israel. The players are Saul, David, and the people. In three taut verses (18:14-16), the narrative sums up the situation of each. David, successful and the LORD with him; Saul, jealous; the people, loyal to David. It is not said explicitly; it does not need to be (cf. 2 Sam 5:2). These are the dynamics that will lead David to the throne of Judah, then to the throne of Israel, and finally to kingship over Israel and Judah in Jerusalem.

Genre

Generically, what we are looking at in 1 Sam 16:14–18:16 is a (→) composite narrative presenting the outlines of two (→) stories of David's emergence in Israel, one the core story and one the variant. Both stories have been expanded far beyond the traditions of heroism recounted in 2 Sam 21:15-22 and 23:8-39. The core story, in particular, is a masterpiece of succinct literary narrative; both, however, are candidates for consideration as (→) reported stories.

The core story moves from David's coming to the court of Saul, through his single combat with the Philistine, to his emergence on the national scene and Saul's corresponding jealousy. David is brought to Saul's court to free him from the torment of an evil spirit from God. Ironically, David's success on the battlefield leads a jealous Saul to remove him from his presence (18:13), so sending away the one who could liberate him from his torment. Saul was anointed king-designate in order to deliver Israel from the Philistines. Confronted with the Philistine challenge, Saul was afraid and David courageous. After the battle, maintenance of political power prevails over the national need for deliverance. Saul distanced the potential deliverer from his royal court. Ironically, his actions brought about the opposite of his intentions. "All Israel and Judah loved David" (18:16).

The variant story begins by bringing David to the battlefield almost by chance; he is bringing provisions for his brothers and gifts for their commander (17:17-18). While at the battlefield he hears the Philistine challenge. He hears the soldiers talking about the reward likely from the king for killing this Philistine champion. There is a gap, within which he kills the Philistine. The text resumes with Saul's inquiry about and ultimate discovery of David's identity, followed by David's entry into the court of Saul. This section ends on the note of David's position of military leadership and how "all the people, even the servants of Saul, approved" (18:5). As has already been noted, the variant version's ending (18:17-19, 29b-30) now belongs with the following section. The offer of Merab as wife is one of the covert moves that Saul makes to bring about David's destruction.

In both stories, core and variant, Israel's existence is threatened and David delivers Israel from the threat. In both, David emerges onto the national scene as a military leader. We can well ask whether either story incorporates a historical report. There are surely historical elements, but it is reasonable to reflect whether an unknown armor-bearer is thrust to a position of near-kingly eminence as it were almost overnight. What is involved here is a high level of reflection on the conditions surrounding David's emergence as a leading figure in Israel. The core story's reflection is steeped in theological tradition. YHWH's withdrawal from Saul brought David to the fore. David's trust in YHWH, in confrontation with the Philistine threat, brought David to leadership. David did not seek power, he exercised it when no one else would; David's power came in conjunction with the God who through him delivered Israel. This situates David within the tradition of charismatic leadership in Israel. Saul's anointing leads to initial success and ultimate failure. David's anointing leads to this initial success and sustained performance.

Setting

The setting of such a composite text can only be the present literary text. The operations involved in combining two such stories in just such a way are not what we find in oral tradition and presentation; the combination has been made at a literary level. Where issues of date are concerned, the question of whether material has been added to the MT or subtracted from it becomes central. For example, McCarter favors addition (cf. pp. 306-9) and Pisano favors subtraction (cf. pp. 78-86). Clearly, any issue of date will be affected by understandings of the composition of the text, and certainty is far from achieved.

The date of the composite text gives us no indication of the date when the two stories may have been formulated. The variant story gives the slight impression of being older, but that could result from either style or theme. The core story demonstrates a considerable degree of abstraction. It could well be associated with any Story of David's Rise to power; it exhibits in a microcosm the dynamics that brought David to the throne. As such, it could go back to a setting in the Davidic kingdom. It is also possible that the story of the slinger was told in military circles, as a source of inspiration or an example of tactics. The story in Judg 9:50-55 must have circulated as such an example (cf. 2 Sam 11:20-21). The song of the women (cf. Exod 15:21) shows the likelihood of camp followers and supporters who followed the army and helped in the preservation of its traditions (cf. 1 Sam 30).

Meaning

The meaning of the text as a composite text is clear. It is to preserve two stories, two traditions, of how David emerged as a power figure in Israel. Both deal with David's emergence in Israel. One, the core story, focuses on David's faith and courage; the other, the variant story, focuses on David's ambition and reward.

The core story, presenting David filling the vacant space left by Saul's failure, displays the forces that led David to be king of all Israel in place of Saul. "While Saul was king over us, it was you who led out Israel and brought it in" (2 Sam 5:2). It is a story of royal fear and failure on the part of Saul and of divine favor experienced by a courageous David.

The elements of the variant story present a story of singular chance swiftly seized. Given the chance of winning a significant reward, David seizes it and gains entry to the court of Saul, becomes a soul-mate of the crown prince, Jonathan, and is given a position of command. On its own, the culmination of this variant story comes in 18:17-19, 29b-30, with David victorious over the Philistines and more successful than the servants of Saul, "so that his fame became very great" (v. 30).

Both texts, though the core story more emphatically at this point, are concerned less with the killing of the Philistine champion than with the supplanting of Saul by David. Here David emerges on all-Israel's stage with the leadership capacity of one fit to be king.

Personal Reflection

For me, the text of David's combat with the Philistine raises a couple of questions that intrigue me and that I cannot answer. The first is why many experience a need to read the text as a single story. The second is why many experience the need to image David as small, the defenseless shepherd boy. These positions are scarcely a response to the demands of the text.

It is not uncommon in the interpretation of this text for it to be treated as a single story. Yet there are signals in the text that I read as clearly set against a single story. For the moment, I would like to discuss four of these signals; there are others.

- 17:15 has David go back and forth from Saul to his father's flocks at Bethlehem. Two warning bells sound about this statement as ordinary narrative. First, the person hired to be musician to the king in moments of royal distress does not abandon the king to play the shepherd back home; royal need is not in this case predictable. Second, when the troops are called to arms in time of war, the armor-bearer's place is at his king's side — not with his father's flocks in the fields. This is not ordinary narrative.
- 17:16 has the Philistine take his stand twice a day ("morning and evening") for forty days. This is not ordinary narrative. The armies do not file into the valley twice daily like spectators into an auditorium for the performances. They do not, twice a day, go forth to the battle line, "shouting the war cry" (v. 20). They hardly take flight (or simply retreat) and get very frightened (v. 24) twice a day for forty days. The challenge might be proclaimed morning and evening for forty days, but the text goes further and reports the massing of troops and the matching of "army against army" (v. 21). This is not ordinary narrative.
- 17:31 has David summoned to Saul's presence, yet when the moment of combat arrives, Saul is asking the question, "Whose son is this young man?" (v. 55). The future of Israel is to be decided by this single combat (v. 9, cf. v. 23). It would be remiss of a narrator not to have Saul identify the young man and check on his standing in Israel. Again the conclusion: this is not ordinary narrative. With the inclusion of 16:14-23, David is known to Saul and Saul's authorization is given in 17:37b. In a variant story, the gap can be left open, or a self-confident young man can be portrayed responding to the challenge without authorization, or the royal authorization may be given. It may be understood that the narrative has no more likelihood of observing the terms of the challenge than the Philistines demonstrate in vv. 51-53.
- 17:55-58 sits very oddly in the present text where it appears to be totally unnecessary. In 16:18-22, Saul has negotiated with Jesse the Bethlehem-

ite and enlisted Jesse's son, David, in his service permanently as his lyre-player and armor-bearer. Furthermore, as we have just noted for v. 31, David has been interviewed by Saul before being allowed to risk Israel's all in a single combat. The plain meaning of the text has Saul ask three times about David's identity and has David reply that he is the son of Jesse the Bethlehemite. To allow the chapter to be read as a single story, interpreters are forced to ignore the plain meaning and appeal to some inner meaning — in my judgment, tortuously contrived. Hebrew has succinct ways of asking such questions. Within the context of a single story, this is not ordinary narrative.

The question that baffles me in all this is why some interpreters — certainly as skilled and intelligent and knowledgeable as I am — feel obliged to read the text as a single story. I am tempted to paraphrase the gospel injunction, "what God has joined together, let no one separate" (Matt 19:6), to read: what the text has separated, let no interpreter join together. Clearly, not all interpreters read these signals as I read them. For some, consciously or not, the signals point to an association, however unrealistic, and therefore invite to the text's interpretation as a single story. For others (myself included), the signals point to the juxtaposition (or non-integrative amalgamation), most unrealistically, of two separate stories that are left separate. Different interpreters will pay attention to different signals in the same text; different interpreters will see even the same signals in a different light. I can be more at ease with a single-story interpretation if it emerges from a *reading* of the text for devotional purposes or whatever. I am uneasy if such an interpretation emerges from *study* of the text. When reading, we can treat the text as we treat friends, without fuss over details. When studying, we ought to treat the text as doctors treat patients, where attention to details can be very important.

Second, it is a matter of observation that many experience the need to image David as small (e.g., Wénin) or nearly powerless (e.g., McCarter, the apparently defenseless shepherd boy).

- Small. David is the youngest of Jesse's eight sons; we know from experience that this need not mean that he is the smallest. David's self-description (17:34-36) does not suggest smallness. Saul's armor is offered him (17:38-39), which is absurd if he were meant to be small. His declining it is a matter of symbolism and strategy; it need not be a matter of size. Jonathan gives David his robe and his armor (18:4). The role of crown prince does not designate Jonathan as the small one in the family; it would be unduly contrived to suggest that David draped these offerings over his arm. David is not small.
- Defenseless. The Philistine accuses David of coming to him "with sticks" (v. 43); apparently David's sling was out of sight. Wisely, David does not mention the shield when orating at the Philistine ("you come to me with sword and spear and javelin," v. 45). The mention of a shield might have reminded the Philistine to make use of his own. As has been emphasized above, the Philistine is presented as the sort of warrior who

was unquestionably unbeatable with ordinary weapons. Lateral thinking is needed and David's sling is the perfect military answer. Using a sling leaves David out of range of the Philistine's sword or spear or javelin. Using a sling leaves the unshielded Philistine fatally vulnerable. David is not defenseless.

I can only speak for Christians and I wonder what need is met by Christian interpretation of this story as an example of how the powerless bring the mighty low by the help of God. It is no such thing. Taken on its own terms, it is an example of how faith in God can enable people to do what in fact they can do but may be afraid to. Of course God's power is shown forth in the weak, but why not also in the courageous and the strong? What lies behind the need to interpret this text as a story of God's coming to the aid of the weak and helpless? Does the interpretation betray our own human inclination rather than any readiness to learn from the biblical text? It may not be out of place to quote a sentence from a completely different context. It is from Granville Henry, about Luther's calling Copernicus a fool for thinking the earth revolved around the sun. He writes: "Already 'knowing' the truth, Luther felt comfortable quoting a Bible example to confirm it" (Henry, *Christianity,* 22). There is enough in the sentence to justify a book; I will not attempt to justify its aptness here. We do tend to quote from the Bible what we already believe.

A Selection of Views from Scholarship

It will be helpful to outline a selection of recent views on these chapters; a consensus is not in sight. The differences among careful scholars appear to reflect more than simple attention to textual detail. After the discussion above, two matters in particular need to be kept in mind: (i) there is substantially less evidence available than has been assumed for David's "ineffectualness" — as opposed to being the redheaded youngest son, and good-looking to boot; (ii) the sling, as a standard military weapon, is appropriate, even ideal, for long-range use against a well-armed and experienced foot soldier. Beyond these, there is, above all, the need to acknowledge the skill and discretion of storytellers and their responsibility for the actualization in story of the traditions preserved in written texts. This brings new light to the understanding of the so-called "pluses" in the MT. Variations in how the prehistory of the various texts is understood counsel against organizing the following views under over-simple categories. The date of publication in each case is added in parentheses.

Auld and Ho (1992): the additions in the MT are "supplements, modelled by a redactor upon the story of Saul with the purpose of contrasting David and Saul" ("David and Goliath," 37-38). An original story about David and Goliath was remade so that "it conformed more fully to the patterns of an existing Saul story. The story as translated in the LXX is thus the more original, and that in the MT an embellishment" (ibid., 38).

Barthélemy (1986): regards the MT as the original text, with the LXX version representing an attempt at harmonization and coherence (cf. *The Story,* 54, 96, 98). It should not be overlooked, however, that Barthélemy considers that the person responsible for the "long" form (= the MT) integrated into the narrative several older and originally autonomous traditions (ibid., 98, 139).

Brueggemann (1990): "Though the narrative may have had a complex prehistory, it now is a powerful, well-crafted narrative capable of sustaining our interest and imagination through its long telling" (p. 127).

De Vries (1973): "It is very probable that the Hebrew recension on which the Greek text is based was created in an effort to improve by omission a confused and conflate *Vorlage* that was substantially the same as our present Hebrew text" ("David's Victory," 23). The later "hero saga" now found in the LXX "stands close to historical reality" (ibid., 31). The present MT has been heavily glossed and an editor has incorporated the LXX saga into it (ibid., 36).

Dietrich (1996): claims two earlier traditions combined editorially within ch. 17 of the MT, with the MT later abbreviated by the LXX. The strands are (i) David the unknown slinger: 17:1-9, 48b, 50, 51b-53; (ii) David the shepherd boy: 17:12-14a, 15b, 17-18, 20-23aα, 24-34a, 36, 40, 42abα, 43, 49, 51, 54-58. The editorial work to be assumed is extensive ("David und Goliat").

Gooding (1986): the LXX is "a self-evident wreck of the fuller scheme" of the MT (*The Story,* 154). Of this fuller scheme, Gooding writes: "we have found that the combined version as it stands is a highly-wrought, sophisticated, narrative-sequence, that everywhere makes excellent sense" (ibid., 75). "The combined version is the original version, which someone with a very literalistic, unimaginative mind has truncated, thinking thereby to improve it by removing doublets and discrepancies" (ibid., 82).

Grønbaek (1971): there are no convincing grounds for challenging the MT. One should not be overinfluenced by a one-sided emphasis on the differences between MT and LXX[B] (*Aufstieg Davids,* 83). There are two traditions within ch. 17, one of a victory of Saul's over the Philistines and the other of David's combat with Goliath; both have been so blended into a higher unity that separation can only be done along broad lines (ibid., 90-91).

Hertzberg (1964): "It was then the task of the compiler of the whole work to collect all these similar narratives and to adjust the detail to fit in with other material. . . . It is evident from the form of the LXX text how clearly it was remembered that originally two points of view were expressed here" (pp. 147-48). A little earlier: "We have such a story in 16.14-23; in the passages omitted by LXX we have another of a different kind" (p. 147).

Klein (1983): agrees with an increasing number of scholars "that LXX[B] represents the original text and that MT has been expanded"; some problems remain (p. 174).

van der Kooij (1992): "The shorter version . . . is best to be seen as the product of literary activity in later time. It may have been the work of a learned scribe on the basis of a Hebrew text, but I do not exclude the possibility that the author of the LXX shortened the story" ("David and Goliath," 129-30).

Lust (1999): reaffirmed his earlier published views (cf. 1986), first, that the text common to the Hebrew and the Septuagint reflects the original text and is not an abbreviation and, second, that the additions in the Hebrew reflect a variant story. The MT has two stories, while the LXX has only one ("David dans la Septante," 245; cf. 246-52).

McCarter (1980): "The materials missing from LXX[B], when collected by themselves as they are here, can be seen to form a more or less complete narrative of their own. This strongly suggests that they represent the bulk of a full alternative account of David's arrival and early days at court that was interpolated *in toto* into the primary narrative at some time subsequent to the divergence of the ancestral textual traditions that lie behind MT and LXX" (p. 307).

Pisano (1984): argues for 17:1–18:5 as an originally unified text with the conclusion that it seems "far more likely that the longer MT form of chapter 17-18 presents the earlier text, which was abbreviated by LXX" (p. 86). I would note that while setting ch. 16 aside eliminates a major difficulty within 17:1–18:5, it does not eliminate all the difficulties. More troubling is the process of accounting for the surrounding text.

Polzin (1989): makes a valiant — and, to my mind, unsuccessful — effort to read the material (from 16:1 to 19:24) as a unified literary piece (*Samuel,* 152-86).

Rofé (1987): "In my opinion, MT constitutes the primary source, while LXX represents a secondary, abridged version" ("David and Goliath," 119).

Stoebe (1973): the shorter text (i.e., common to MT and LXX) is a complete, independent, and original tradition, which has been expanded in the present MT (p. 313). The MT additional material scarcely constitutes an independent narrative (pp. 313-14). For further discussion of details, see pp. 325-28, 335-40.

Tov (1992): the LXX[B] translation unit here "reflects a literal method of translation, and, therefore, one cannot attribute to the translator the intention of abridging his source to such a great extent" (*Textual Criticism,* 335). According to some, this shorter (common) text was originally Hebrew, "created at an earlier stage as an abridgement of a longer Hebrew text" (ibid.). According to Tov, the additional material in the MT constitutes "a separate and parallel version" that has been added to the story common to both MT and LXX, "apparently with the intention of preserving a parallel ancient story" (ibid., pp. 335-36).

Wénin (1999): there are two stories, one mirrored within 16:1-13, 14-23 and the other in chs. 17–18, picking up these elements. Above all, David is small and a shepherd. Beyond this, Wénin is discreetly Gallic. The MT-LXX differences are not discussed.

Bibliography of Works Cited Above

Alter, Robert. *The David Story: A Translation with Commentary of 1 and 2 Samuel.* New York: Norton, 1999.

Auld, A. Graeme, and Craig Y. S. Ho. "The Making of David and Goliath." *JSOT* 56 (1992) 19-39.

Barthélemy, D., D. W. Gooding, J. Lust, and E. Tov. *The Story of David and Goliath: Textual and Literary Criticism.* OBO 73. Fribourg, Switz.: Editions Universitaires, 1986.

Campbell, Antony F. "Structure Analysis and the Art of Exegesis (1 Samuel 16:14–18:30)." Pp. 76-103 in *Problems in Biblical Theology: Essays in Honor of Rolf Knierim.* Edited by H. T. C. Sun et al. Grand Rapids: Eerdmans, 1997.

Campbell, Antony F., and Mark A. O'Brien. *Unfolding the Deuteronomistic History: Origins, Upgrades, Present Text.* Minneapolis: Fortress, 2000.

De Vries, Simon J. "David's Victory over the Philistine as Saga and as Legend." *JBL* 92 (1973) 23-36.

Dietrich, Walter. "Die Erzählungen von David und Goliat in I Sam 17." *ZAW* 108 (1996) 172-91.

Fokkelman, J. P. *Narrative Art and Poetry in the Books of Samuel.* Vol. 2: *The Crossing Fates (I Sam. 13–31 & II Sam. 1).* Studia Semitica Neerlandica 23. Assen-Maastricht: Van Gorcum, 1986.

Gooding, D. W. See under Barthélemy.

Grønbaek, Jakob H. *Die Geschichte vom Aufstieg Davids (1. Sam. 15–2. Sam. 5): Tradition und Komposition.* Copenhagen: Munksgaard, 1971.

Henry, Granville C. *Christianity and the Images of Science.* Macon, GA: Smyth & Helwys, 1998.

Jason, Heda. "The Story of David and Goliath: A Folk Epic." *Bib* 60 (1979) 36-70.

Josephus, Flavius. *Jewish Antiquities.* Books V-VIII. The Loeb Classical Library. London: Heinemann, 1934.

Kooij, Arie van der. "The Story of David and Goliath: The Early History of Its Text." *ETL* 68 (1992) 118-31.

Lust, J. "David dans la Septante." Pp. 243-63 in *Figures de David à travers la Bible: XVIIᵉ congrès de l'ACFEB* [= l'Association catholique française pour l'étude de la Bible] *(Lille, 1ᵉʳ-5 septembre 1997).* Edited by L. Desrousseaux and J. Vermeylen. Paris: Cerf, 1999.

Noth, Martin. *A History of Pentateuchal Traditions.* Translated by B. W. Anderson. Englewood Cliffs, NJ: Prentice-Hall, 1972. Reprint. Chico, CA: Scholars Press, 1981. German original, 1948.

Polzin, Robert. *Samuel and the Deuteronomist.* A Literary Study of the Deuteronomic History: Part Two. 1 Samuel. San Francisco: Harper & Row, 1989.

Rad, Gerhard von. *Old Testament Theology.* 2 vols. Edinburgh: Oliver and Boyd, 1962, 1965.

Rofé, Alexander. "The Battle of David and Goliath: Folklore, Theology, Eschatology." Pp. 117-51 in *Judaic Perspectives on Ancient Israel.* Edited by J. Neusner, B. A. Levine, and E. S. Frerichs. Philadelphia: Fortress, 1987.

Stähli, Hans-Peter. *Knabe-Jüngling-Knecht: Untersuchungen zum Begriff נער im Alten Testament.* BET 7. Frankfurt a.M.: Peter Lang, 1978.

Stansell, Gary. "Honor and Shame in the David Narratives." Pp. 94-114 in *Was ist der Mensch? Beiträge zur Anthropologie des Alten Testaments. Hans Walter Wolff zum 80. Geburtstag.* Edited by F. Crüsemann, C. Hardmeier, and R. Kessler. Munich: Kaiser, 1992.

Tov, Emanuel. *Textual Criticism of the Hebrew Bible.* Minneapolis: Fortress, 1992.

de Vaux, Roland. "Les Combats singuliers dans l'Ancien Testament." Pp. 217-30 in *Bibel et Orient.* Paris: Cerf, 1967.

Wénin, André. *David & Goliath: Le récit de 1 Samuel 16–18.* Connaître la Bible 3. Brussels: Lumen Vitae, 1997.

———. "David roi, de Goliath à Bethsabée: La figure de David dans les livres de Samuel." Pp. 75-112 in *Figures de David à travers la Bible: XVIIe congrès de l'ACFEB* [= l'Association catholique française pour l'étude de la Bible] *(Lille, 1er-5 septembre 1997).* Edited by L. Desrousseaux and J. Vermeylen. Paris: Cerf, 1999.

Chapter 7

VEILED CONFLICT AT THE COURT
(1 Samuel 18:17–21:1)

In this section of the narrative, conflict has arisen at the court between Saul and David. Saul is jealous of a suspected rival; in the narrative, David's intentions are unspecified. Saul is portrayed wanting to have David killed, but at the same time the conflict is not yet out in the open. The conflict will develop into open rupture with David's departure from the court of Saul. The narrative moves toward this development through a carefully structured series of stories.

In all these stories of Saul and David, it is important to be constantly aware that we are dealing with narrative. With Philip Esler, our focus needs to be "squarely on the narrative, rather than on any actual historical circumstances that arguably 'lie behind' the narrative" (Esler, "Madness of Saul," 221; cf. pp. 251-52). It is Saul's misfortune to have the stories about him told by those who supported David (ideological possibilities are valuably discussed by Brettler, *Creation of History,* 91-111). How different they might have been had they been told by those who supported and favorably remembered Saul. For David's people, the "evil spirit from the LORD" that tormented Saul ultimately drove him to destruction. The LORD was with David (16:18). These two convictions shape the narrative ahead.

Veiled Conflict at the Court of Saul	18:17–21:1 (NRSV, 20:42)
I. Covert moves by Saul to kill David	18:17-30
A. Through Merab	17-19
B. Through Michal	20-27
C. Narrative comment on these moves	28-30
II. Overt moves by Saul to kill David	19:1-10
A. Saul's instructions to his servants	1-7
B. Saul's attempt with his own spear	8-10
III. Moves to save David	19:11–21:1 (NRSV, 20:42)
A. By Michal	19:11-17

194

B. By Samuel	19:18-24
C. By Jonathan	20:1–21:1 (NRSV, 20:42)

The arrangement of the diverse traditions brought together here could be dictated by the sequence of events, or the traditions may have been marshaled to suit a perception of development. As they stand now, there is such a development. At the center sits the tradition of Saul's going public: he speaks to his son and his servants about having David killed; later, he attempts to do it himself with his spear — [II]. Before this, Saul is portrayed attempting to have the Philistines kill David for him, without revealing his own hand in it — [I]. After this, three significant figures are portrayed protecting David — [III].

There is no structuring principle imposed on the traditions within the text. They might be analyzed differently. For example: there are Saul's efforts to kill David, first through his daughters, second through his servants, third with his own spear; then there are efforts made by others to save David, first by Michal, second by Samuel, third by Jonathan. In my judgment the dual moves — from covert to overt attempts to kill on the part of Saul, and from Saul's attempts to kill to others' attempts to save — are best represented by the analysis given. The precise analysis is less important than the perception of the moves being made in the text. The component traditions may now be examined.

Covert Moves by Saul to Kill David	**18:17-30**
I. Through Merab	17-19
A. Saul's offer of Merab to David in marriage	17
1. Offer: the bait	17a
2. Purpose: the trap	17b
B. David's response	18
C. Saul's breach of promise	19
II. Through Michal	20-27
A. The occasion	20-21a
1. Michal's love for David	20
2. Saul's decision to use his daughter as bait for his trap	21a
B. The offer	21b-26
1. In general terms: a second offer	21b
2. In specific detail: the negotiations	22-26
a. Initial stage of negotiations	22-23
1) Offer concerning marriage: the bait	22-23a
2) Reluctance by David	23b
b. Final stage of negotiations	24-26
1) Offer concerning marriage present: the trap	24-26a
2) Acceptance by David	26b
C. The outcome	27
1. Marriage present given by David	27a
2. Michal given in marriage by Saul	27b
III. Narrative comment on these moves	28-30
A. Concerning Saul	28-29
1. His observation of David	28

Textual Issues

18:27   The MT here has 200 foreskins; 2 Sam 3:14 has 100. LXX here has 100. Emendation is possible but not necessary. Apart from the issue of various versions of the stories (see below), it is possible that 2 Sam 3:14 has David refer to the price asked (1 Sam 18:25) rather than the price paid. Driver correctly: "The change was no doubt made for the purpose of magnifying David's exploit" (p. 154). No doubt; the issue is whether such magnifying was part of the MT (corrected by the LXX) or whether it was a later change to the MT.

Discussion

As they stand in the present text, these traditions form a transition to Saul's open hostility. First he tries by covert means to eliminate David; when this fails, he moves overtly to have David killed. If taken with the "variant story" of ch. 17, these offers constitute the reward held out as likely by the soldiers: "and [the king] will give him his daughter" (17:25). The promised reward has been transformed into a potential trap. The final comment underscores the futility of Saul's treachery. His attempt to use his own daughters as bait in what are frankly sordid political moves has blown up in his face — [I and II]. Instead of having David dead, he has a live son-in-law whom he fears as an enemy and who is more successful than his own people — [III].

As was noted earlier, the verses 17-19, 21b, and 29b-30 are not in LXX^B. From a textual point of view, they belong with the "variant story" of ch. 17 — except for v. 21b, a bridge verse (cf. Talmon, "Textual Study," 363-64, esp. n. 175 for the possible understanding of v. 21b as referring to two daughters). At the level of the present text, both stories reflect the promise of a daughter's hand in marriage and both witness to David's transition from the hero whom Saul ought to reward to the rival whom Saul seeks to kill. Both stories might have been developed differently in different contexts; in the present context, Saul's desire for David's death is appropriate and vv. 17b, 21a, and 25b belong where they are (against Hertzberg, 159-60; Stoebe, 351, n. 33). Saul's behavior is comparable with David's later treatment of Uriah — only less ruthless and less successful.

The Merab story is given as the briefest possible outline: Saul's offer, David's response, and Saul's failure to keep his word — [I]. The core of Saul's offer is noted: what he said and what he thought. The core of David's response is given, as is the fact that when the time came Merab was given to another. The outline is there for a storyteller's art or a reader's imagination to develop; the text does not develop it. Saul gets a verse; David gets a verse; the outcome gets a verse. Merab does not get a word. The text mentions her by name twice — nothing more. It is a story outline; storyteller or reader may fill it out in detail so long as one remains within the twin parameters of Saul's hostility and breach of promise.

In Saul's offer, what he said constitutes the bait; what he thought depicts the trap. What he said includes "only be valiant for me and fight the LORD's battles" (v. 17a). There is no recognition that David has already done so in defeating the Philistine champion. The story looks to the future, where Saul's trap awaits David: "let the Philistines deal with him" (v. 17b). In the text, as we have it, David's reluctance is not followed up and Saul's offer is not followed through. Nor does the outline bother to address the tension that might be felt to arise between the David who has been removed from Saul's presence (18:13) and the David who is proposed as the king's son-in-law (18:18). Storytellers and readers will do so, if they have chosen to draw on this area of the context.

The Michal story is told differently — [II]. First, it begins with the fact of her love for David; second, it is structurally more developed. The basic theme is the same: Saul uses his daughter as bait for his fruitless trap. At one level, it is classic folktale: the suitor who has to pass a test, survive an ordeal, or perform some difficult task in order to win the hand of his bride (cf. Güttgemanns, "Introductory Remarks," 36, 90-91; Propp, *Morphology*, 60-61, 79-80). At another level, it has been twisted; the bride has become bait and the valiant exploit has become the trap in which the suitor is to die. But there is a double twist: David escapes the trap and Saul ends up trapped behind a better-performing rival.

As an alternative to the Merab story, this Michal story fits more comfortably in the context. While it may be appropriate protocol for messengers to be used, it is also necessary if David has been removed from Saul's presence. The present text sets it up as Saul's second attempt (v. 21b). A storyteller or reader drawing on both stories must account for a second round of David's innocent reactions. Within the present text, it helps that the initiative is Saul's in the case of Merab ("Here is my eldest daughter, Merab"), while in the case of Michal the initiative is hers ("Now Saul's daughter, Michal, loved David"). The offer of Michal as bait (vv. 20-23a) and the setting up of the marriage present as trap (vv. 23b-25) are much more extensive than in the Merab story (vv. 17-18). Traditions differ on the marriage present. Verse 25 has Saul ask for one hundred foreskins; v. 27 has David provide two hundred. LXX has only one hundred in v. 27, whereas in 2 Sam 3:14 both MT and LXX have one hundred. We may assume that the stories were told many times and in different versions. Here, the two hundred can be taken as an indication of overwhelming success. In 2 Sam 3:14, the tradition may be different or the reference may be to what was asked for rather than actually provided. Whatever of this, David is married to Michal (v. 27b).

The narrative comment focuses first on Saul and finally on David — [III]. Saul observes David's success (expressed as the LORD with him) and Michal's love (surprising here; LXX has "all Israel" in place of "Michal"), and Saul con-

197

tinues to fear David even more. This fear reflects a continuation of the observation in 18:12a and the comment in 18:15. Verses 29b-30 — wrapping up the variant tradition and not in LXX^B — express this continued fear in terms of continual hostility (v. 29b) and generalize David's success against the Philistines over that of Saul's followers (v. 30).

Genre

Three genres are involved in this passage: (→) story outline (or: reported story), (→) story, and (→) comment. Verses 17-19, concerning Merab, are clearly story outline. Many a story may well be regarded as a story outline; these three verses are too brief to be anything other than story outline — they cannot be a story. The briefest comparison with what follows shows how easily they could become a story. Verses 20-27, concerning Michal, are story in the classic mold. The king's daughter is in love; her beloved is willing and worthy. The king offers her hand. The beloved does valorous deeds and is rewarded with her love. Like so many stories in the texts, this one is too short to be called more than a story outline. Only respect for tradition suggests that nevertheless we call it story. Outside the compass of these stories, the narrator looks at events and comments on their outcome (vv. 28-30). Saul set out to destroy David and, at the end of two attempts, Saul is worse off than he was at the beginning.

Rendtorff has described a literary genre that he calls a (→) short communication (or: short notice; "kurze Mitteilung"). Such short communications are not fully fledged narratives or stories, nor do they appear to stem from annals or chronicles; instead they deal with events likely to have been known and handed down among the people and likely to have lapsed into insignificance if they had not been used to give color and background to larger narratives. He describes 18:17-19 as such a short communication. While the observation of this genre by Rendtorff is a major step in understanding the text of the Story of David's Rise, its application here is almost certainly wrong. First, 18:17-19 as belonging to the variant tradition were almost certainly not part of the Story of David's Rise. Second, Rendtorff has overlooked the possibility of a story outline. Verses 17-19 do not record details that become significant only in the context of a larger narrative. They record the core details necessary for telling a story of major significance.

Setting

The origin of the marriage traditions involved here would presumably lie in Davidic rather than Saulide circles. Saul's storytellers would hardly celebrate such failures; they would be perfectly to the point for David's apologists.

If the combined text belongs to a period after the translation of the LXX, the Merab story outline is very late. As the follow-on to the promised reward

(17:25) in the variant tradition, it would surely have been told as a full story, before the denouement of vv. 29b-30. It may well have been reduced to so skeletal a story outline at the time of the combination of the texts, especially given the presence in the main text of the fuller Michal story.

The Michal story belongs within the traditions of the story of David's rise to power and, now, within the DH. It is necessary for the following story of the "dummy in the bed" (19:11-17); as noted, it will reemerge in 2 Sam 3:14.

Meaning

The meaning of the two stories is made clear by the comment: Saul's failure nourished Saul's fear. Saul is portrayed as a man of intensifying hostility toward the deliverer who is becoming his rival. It is Saul's hope that David is to die and that it will appear an accident — the result of over-eager pursuit of military distinction and advancement at court. Alas for Saul, the LORD is with David and such a death is not to be David's fate. Saul's fear gets worse and his hostility more intense.

A dual theme begins here and continues through the narrative into ch. 20, until the separation of David from the court of Saul has been achieved. On the one hand, David escapes all Saul's attacks; not only are Michal and Jonathan with David, but the LORD is with David (18:28; 19:5; 20:13, 42). David's successful survival is a sign that the LORD is with him. On the other hand, these stories make clear that the responsibility for David's separation from Saul rests squarely on Saul's shoulders. David is protected against the possible accusation of disloyal rebellion against Saul, or of leaving Saul in the lurch so that he fails against the Philistines.

At this point in the narrative, the covert moves by Saul to kill David are ended. Saul has tried and failed. The intensifying narrative now turns to overt moves on Saul's part to have David killed.

Overt Moves by Saul to Kill David   19:1-10

  I. Acting through others: Saul's instructions to Jonathan and servants 1-7

     A. Peace in the kingdom disturbed: Saul gives orders to kill David 1a

     B. Peacemaking by Jonathan   1b-6

        1. Jonathan's basic attitude: delight in David   1b

        2. Peacemaking   2-6

          a. Spoke with David   2-3

            1) Warning to David   2a

            2) Proposals to David   2b-3

              a) Variant proposal: David to overhear   2b

              b) Main proposal: Jonathan to observe   3

          b. Spoke with Saul   4-6

            1) Intercession for David   4-5

            2) Acquiescence by Saul   6

     C. Peace in the kingdom restored: David in Saul's presence as before 7

Textual Issues

19:9 The MT's "evil spirit of YHWH" is unique. Emendation to the LXX's "evil spirit of God" (occurring three times in MT, i.e., 1 Sam 16:15, 16; 18:10) is common — but also the easier reading. Dealing here with a collection of traditions, rather than a single text, we should always be cautious about enforcing uniformity. LXX has an "evil spirit of the Lord" in 1 Sam 16:15 (against the MT).

Discussion

The movements in this area of the text relate to the portrayal of Saul. His hostility to David is clear, but it is to be explored through the attitudes of those around him — [I]. Jonathan will be the last to be convinced that his father is implacably opposed to David. In the story of 19:11-17, Michal knows it. After that, David knows it too. 20:30-34 will finally bring it home to Jonathan. In the present text, Jonathan's "delight in David" (v. 1) is simply a continuation of the bond expressed in 18:1-5. If this material is relegated to a variant tradition, introduced quite late, the emphasis here on Jonathan as Saul's son would be appropriate and the readiness of Jonathan to intercede for David would be quite striking. It is a common trait in Hebrew narrative to state something in general terms and unfold its consequences in detail. So here, Jonathan's friendship for David is stated first, as the premise from which the rest of his actions flow (v. 1b). At the same time, it is set in stark contrast to Saul's attitude. This opposition between father and son reaches a climax in 20:30-34.

The consequences of Jonathan's friendship with David move in two directions: first, he attends to David's safety; second, he intercedes with Saul. The intercession with Saul is skillfully portrayed. After another general statement in v. 4a, the fundamental move in v. 4b is: he has not done you evil; he has done you good. It is hard to be more basic than that. But Jonathan is looking to the past; Saul is looking to the future, "What more can he have but the king-dom?" (MT, 18:8). The second set of moves in v. 5 look back to David's single combat with the Philistine: David risked his life, and the LORD brought about deliverance (תשועה) in Israel, and Saul was pleased. Why should Saul now move against the innocent without cause? The rhetoric is convincing and brings about a change of Saul's heart. On the other hand, the words are now out there so that when Saul does turn definitively against David, he is condemned by the argument of his own son.

Jonathan's attention to David's safety takes the narrative in two directions. The main proposal is clear: Jonathan talks to Saul, observes his reaction, and informs David (v. 7a). A variant proposal is alluded to in just three words of v. 3a: "where you are." David will hide in a position known to Jonathan. Jonathan will go out at Saul's side and talk to him within earshot of David, who will then know how he stands. Alongside v. 7a, it is totally unnecessary. No storyteller would actualize both proposals; no reader should imagine both. The variant has potential for great storytelling: imagine telling of David safely ensconced in a leafy oak while Saul and Jonathan discuss his fate below. Similar story variants will recur in ch. 20.

With peace restored and David back in Saul's presence as before, the next episode casts Saul's instability in sharp relief — [II]. Jonathan argued on logical grounds and Saul agreed. Then "an evil spirit from the LORD" came upon Saul (v. 9) and he appears as the helpless creature of his impulses. In the present text, this is the second time that Saul has used his spear against David (cf. 18:10-11); before the advent of these variant traditions, 19:8-10 is the first example of this behavior. The evil spirit is "from the LORD"; poor Saul is fated (cf. 13:7b-15a; 15:1-35; and 16:14).

The text sets the little episode against a wider background. While Saul is preoccupied with his jealousy, war is again threatening Israel and it is David who puts the Philistines to flight (v. 8). Tightening the focus, the text brings the action to Saul's house where, possessed by his evil spirit, he is sitting with his spear in his hand and David is at his lyre — Saul's only source of relief. The scene is set for Saul to lunge at David. David is the deliverer of the people and the deliverer of the king — and Saul tries to eliminate him from both roles. It is an appalling portrayal of a troubled Saul.

Genre

The first piece has the makings of a (→) story. From the tension set up by Saul's intent to kill, it moves swiftly to the reconciliation, while offering some possibility for the diverting development of the plot. Brief and straightforward, it is probably better described as a (→) story outline (reported story). It cries out for a modicum of expansion, but none is given in the text. An example of a more developed form of this sort of story will be found in ch. 20.

The episode with Saul's spear (19:8-10) is left at the bare bones of a (→) short communication. It is possible that it could be developed into a full story, perhaps along the lines of chs. 24 or 26. Here, however, and in 18:10-11 it has been left as a short communication.

Setting

The origins of these traditions may have been among David's band of malcontents as they kept on the move in the wilderness of Judah. They would celebrate David the guerrilla leader, give a pointer to support for David in the court of Saul, and above all account for the presence of Saul's hostile troops hunting for David in the wilderness.

The literary setting is best placed within the Story of David's Rise. From there, the traditions have become part of the Prophetic Record and the DH.

Meaning

The meaning is clear: although David has support at court, his position there is becoming intolerable. Initially open to argument, Saul is portrayed falling under the influence of his evil spirit. Not only is Saul the aggressor, driving David from his presence, but David is portrayed as performing the function of leader in Israel contrasted with Saul who is caught up in his own jealousy. The theme will recur again in fuller narrative form in ch. 23, and there, too, with the same concern for contrast. David is portrayed as the successful deliverer; Saul as the unsuccessful destroyer.

Moves to Save David	19:11–21:1 (NRSV, 20:42)
I. By Michal, Saul's daughter	19:11-17
II. By Samuel, God's prophet	19:18-24
III. By Jonathan, Saul's son and heir	20:1–21:1 (NRSV, 20:42)

Before the breach between Saul and David comes out into the open, with David's flight from Jerusalem and gathering of a band of guerrillas on the one hand, and on the other Saul's address to his court and slaughter of the priests of Nob, suspected of supporting David, the narrative makes the brilliant move of gathering together three episodes. Each shows the intensity of Saul's hostility: David has no choice but flight.

Saul sets a guard over David's house so as to kill him in the morning — [I]. Saul pursues David even into the presence of Samuel and the prophets — [II]. In his determination to have David dead, Saul abuses his own heir and hurls his spear at him — [III]. Saul has decided to put David to death. The breach is out in the open and Saul's hostility is presented as its cause. The high level of David's support is also presented. He is saved by Michal, Saul's daughter. He is saved by Samuel, God's prophet. He is saved by Jonathan, Saul's son and heir. All three are portrayed acting as protectors of David. We can examine the episodes one at a time.

Textual Issues

19:11 The MT ends v. 10 with "and escaped that night." The LXX ends v. 10 without it and forms a temporal clause to begin v. 11, adding a verb: "And it happened that night. . . ." This may be correct in terms of the present text; it may not be the case for independent traditions. Caution is warranted.

Discussion

The differences between this anecdote and the context in which the narrator has placed it should not be overemphasized; the assumption of a wedding night and of association with 18:20-27 is unsupported (against Grønbaek, *Aufstieg Davids,* 108-9; Smith, 178-79; Stoebe, 360). Even if the MT is retained in v. 10 ("And David fled and escaped that night"), this would be no more than a further example of the narrator's habit of stating something generally first, before unfolding it in detail. Paraphrased: And David fled and escaped that night — and this was how it happened. As to the likelihood of David's returning to his house, it must be remembered that the criterion of verisimilitude lies within the level of the narrative, and not in some extrinsic criteria. In 18:10-11, the episode could be narrated without needing to have David take flight. In 20:33, Jonathan becomes the target, yet there is no indication that he quit the court (cf. 1 Sam 31). Nor is the story in contradiction with ch. 20, for there it is not David but Jonathan who needs convincing — although David may not be certain whether Saul's hostility will last (cf. 20:5-7).

The story has a dual impact: it shows the obstinacy of Saul's hostility in as extensive a manner as possible; it displays as broadly as possible the support David received from Saul's daughter. Even arranged within the larger narrative, the bounds of narrative credibility are not strained.

Stoebe is of the opinion that Michal was not married to David until after Saul's death (Stoebe, 352-53; also Stoebe, "David und Mikal," 228-29, where the argument rests heavily on an unwillingness to amend 2 Sam 21:8). Stoebe argues against 19:11-17 being old tradition. He would be better to argue against the unspoken assumption that vivid detail is a sign of historicity — this is not automatically the case. But it is unjustified to demand of the storyteller how Michal knew of Saul's intentions. A woman's intuition, a daughter's knowledge of her father, a warning from a servant, a glance at the guards — there are enough possibilities for plausibility. True, there is not a word about these in the text, but then it is an anecdote, very concisely told, and its principal interest is in the dummy in the bed. It is also true that there is nothing in the text about the position of the window. Was the house built into the city wall (cf. Josh 2:15; also Acts 9:25 & 2 Cor 11:33)? To argue, as Stoebe does, that such an under-standing cannot be silently presumed here, because, in the story of Rahab and the spies, the fact is explicitly stated (although not in the LXX), and so should be equally explicit here, is again unjustified. To go on to assert that 1 Sam 19:11-17 is modeled on the Rahab story can be justified only by special plead-ing (against Stoebe, 361). Stoebe's objections here are all added grounds for recognizing this passage as a "story outline" (see Genre below) rather than a record of the story as told by the storyteller.

The story begins with a reference to Saul's hostile intent — [I]. The need to introduce this at the beginning will account for the apparent duplication of the messengers (vv. 11, 14). Michal advises David of the menace to his life, and counsels flight — [II.A]. This is the fourth instance of Saul's hostility in these traditions, and there is a certain progression in the narrative. In the first, David is unaware of Saul's intention (18:20-29a); in the second, David is told of it by Jonathan, but a reconciliation is effected (19:1-7); in the third, David experi-ences it himself (19:8-10); in this fourth, David is convinced of it by Michal and permitted to escape; in the fifth instance, it is David who must convince Jonathan, and the flight is final (20:1-42*). There is another thematic element running here: this is the first of three moves to save David — by Michal, Saul's daughter; by Samuel, the prophet who anointed Saul; and finally by Jonathan, Saul's son and heir.

When David has disappeared out the window, the interest of the passage is concentrated on the deceitful ruse — [II.B]. The point is to make time for Da-vid, so Saul's messengers must come in the night (against Smith, 179). We know little about the *teraphim*. What is involved here must be larger than the *teraphim* of Gen 31:34-35; it is enough, along with some cloth (?) of goats' hair, to resemble the figure of a man. Its presence in the house reminds us how little we know of the details of ordinary life. K. D. Schunck has pointed to the association of the *teraphim* with the Benjaminites. Echoes of Jacob and Rachel may be seen here, but the differences make it unlikely that one is modeled on the other (against Stoebe, 362).

The ruse is successful, although in the present form of the story it plays a negligible role; the coming and going of the messengers creates the required delay, before the trick is discovered. The exchange with Saul is important less for Michal's lame excuse than for Saul's characterization of David as "my enemy" — [II.C]. The presentation of the hostility is intensified.

Genre

This text provides one of the clearest examples of a (→) story outline (or: reported story). Nothing is said of Michal's observations that lead her to conclude that tomorrow David will be dead. Has she seen the guards posted by Saul? Does she have a daughter's insight into her father's intentions? Are both factors or more in play? A storyteller can expand; a reader can imagine; the text does not say. No reasons are given why Saul sent messengers during the night instead of killing David in the morning. Perhaps the action took place early in the morning, as planned. Perhaps during the night the guards Saul had posted reported suspicious activity in the house. A storyteller can expand; a reader can imagine; the text does not say. In the present text, the dummy in the bed plays no part in the action; it is simply discovered. In a two-stage movement, the dummy can be used on the first visit; Michal demonstrates David's sickness and his presence by indicating the dummy in the bed. Saul then orders a second visit to have David brought before him, bed and all (so Josephus, *Antiquities,* VI. 217-18, locating the action at daybreak). Once the order has been given to bring David, bed and all, the dummy is of no use as a delaying tactic. A three-stage movement could be envisaged. On the first visit, Michal simply says that David is sick (as in v. 14). Note how the text moves from Saul's sending to Michal's saying; the messengers make no demand. On a second visit, the messengers are shown the dummy to convince them of David's sickness and his presence in the house and to allow David time to get well away. On the third visit, David is ordered to be brought, bed and all. A storyteller can expand; a reader can imagine; the text does not say. Did the messengers report their discovery to Saul? The text does not say. Did Saul come down to confront Michal or did he send for her? A storyteller can expand; a reader can imagine; the text does not say.

As the text stands, 1 Sam 19:11-17 has to be described as an (→) anecdote. "A short narrative detailing particulars of an interesting episode or event. In careful usage, the term most frequently refers to a narrated incident in the life of an important person and should lay claim to an element of truth" (Holman, *Handbook to Literature,* 25). This has to be balanced against the claims of a story outline.

While there can be deep seriousness in such a story, there is also room for considerable entertainment as Michal bluffs her father's messengers. A distinction then becomes significant. We may expect that the teller of the sacred or the traditional story was, to some degree at least, less free than the entertainment storyteller to expand or contract the material at will (cf. the similar distinction between a fixed text which is memorized and a fluid text which is re-created anew as noted by Lapointe, "Tradition and Language," 131).

Setting

Such an anecdote or story has its setting primarily in popular tradition. This one ranks as an example of entertainment from ancient Israel. Its presentation would be expected to be primarily oral. It would find acceptance in circles that were pro-Davidic and anti-Saul. It is likely that the written form we possess was put together specifically in the context of a Story of David's Rise. In this it resembles the short communication.

Meaning

While an oral telling might seek principally to amuse and entertain, the written version functions within a broader context. Saul is depicted as insistent in his pursuit of David — the spear throw was no caprice. The relationship between Saul and his erstwhile armor-bearer has become quite explicitly that of the king and his enemy (v. 17). On the other hand, the fidelity of Saul's family to David is intensified. In this particular aspect, 19:11-17 may prepare the way for the frustration of Saul's outburst in 20:30-33.

Second of the Moves to Save David: By Samuel	**19:18-24**
I. David's flight to Samuel	18
A. David comes to Samuel at Ramah	18a
1. He flees, escapes, and comes	18aα
2. He tells of Saul's treatment of him	18aβ
B. David and Samuel go together to Naioth	18b
II. Saul's pursuit of David	19-24
A. Saul is informed	19
B. Saul's efforts to take David	20-24a
1. Saul sends messengers to take David	20-21
a. First group	20
1) They are sent and see	20a
2) Seized by the spirit, they prophesy	20b
b. Second group	21a
1) Saul is told	21aα^1
2) More messengers are sent	21aα^2
3) They too prophesy	21aβ
c. Third group	21b
1) Saul continues	21bα^1
2) More messengers are sent	21bα^2
3) They too prophesy	21bβ

2. Saul goes himself to take David   22-24a
  a. He goes and asks after the whereabouts of
     Samuel and David   22-23a
  b. Seized by the spirit, he too prophesies   23b-24a
    1) While approaching Naioth   23b
    2) At Naioth: stripped before Samuel, naked
       all day and night   24a
C. Etiological note for the saying: Is Saul among the prophets?   24b

Textual Issues

19:18 The meaning of *naioth* is basically unknown. Driver considers some sort of dwelling as "just possible"; "more probably it is the name of some locality in Ramah, the signification of which is lost to us" (Driver, 159). Stoebe opts for some prophetic establishment (Stoebe, 365). McCarter and Klein translate "the camps" (p. 328 and p. 198 respectively); Klein: "probably not a proper noun . . . since it is always associated with another place name, Ramah" (ibid.). Cf. 2 Kgs 6:1-7.

19:20 The MT here has the unique *lahăqat;* most emend with LXX to *qĕhilat* (itself rare enough and late — Deut 33:4; Neh 5:7; Sir 7:7; 42:11 — and not used of the prophets), rendering the "company" of the prophets. Stoebe, however, favors a hapax legomenon meaning something along the lines of "leadership" (p. 366). Cf. Köhler-Baumgartner: "the seniors." The "band" of prophets in 1 Sam 10:5, 10 is *hebel;* elsewhere (10x) the "company of prophets" is literally "sons of the prophets." A hapax here is not unlikely.

Discussion

The principal concern of the passage is with Saul; David is only bait to bring Saul before the prophets. There is no mention of any word of Samuel to David. The marked parallel in the conceptualization of the story with 2 Kgs 1, coupled with the probable presumption of a tradition such as 16:1-13, suggests that the passage is from prophetic circles (cf. Hertzberg, 167; Stoebe, 369). It is unlikely that it was originally part of the Davidic traditions about David's rise to power.

In support of this, there is 1 Sam 15:35, although the two passages may not have been part of the same literary tradition. There is the interruption in David's flight (cf. 19:18 and 20:1) or its direction, although a narrator might have considered this reasonable. There is also the parallel etiology in 1 Sam 10:10-12. It is in all probability a prophetic story, reflecting the tradition of Saul's subordination before Samuel, the subordination of king before prophet (see under Genre below; also 1 Kgs 22).

In its place in the present text, the presence of David in the story (vv. 18,

19, 20a, 22a — even if not a significant presence) and the negative attitude evident toward Saul both fit the context and allow the passage to function as the second of the moves made to save David from Saul.

The story is carefully told. Three verbs — flee, escape, come — precede David's telling Samuel "all that Saul had done to him" (v. 18), so that once again Saul is cast in the role of the aggressor — [I]. The story is economically structured. The first group of messengers is sent out with an explicit purpose — to take David; their seizure by the spirit is noted as the cause of their prophesying. The sending of the second group is introduced with the note that Saul was told; the seizure by the spirit is not narrated, since it can now be presumed from their prophesying. For the final group, it is not even considered necessary to repeat that Saul was told; he simply continued, sent a third group and they too prophesied — [II.B.1].

When Saul moves, however, the narrative provides details. The story goes well beyond that of 10:10-12. Saul too strips off his clothes and lies before Samuel, held in the power of the prophetic phenomenon all through the day and through the night — [II.B.2]. LXX^B has "he too prophesied before them" instead of "before Samuel," possibly in view of 15:35 (Stoebe, 366). Secu and the great well there are unknown; but LXX "the cistern of the threshing floor which is on the height" is scarcely an improvement (with Stoebe, 366; against Driver, 159, and Smith, 182-83).

It is overall a massive demonstration of the prophetic power over the figure of the rejected king; in this it approaches 1 Sam 15.

Genre

The text has the potential for story, but is hardly in fully developed story form. David has fled to Samuel. The issue is: Will Saul pursue him and capture him from his prophet protector? Will the power of the soldier-king prevail over the power of the prophet? It is a storyline that is not unknown in ancient Israel. Ahaziah, king of Israel, three times sent a detachment of fifty men to bring in Elijah the Tishbite. Only when the superiority of prophetic power had been demonstrated by annihilating the first two detachments and bringing the captain of the third to his knees did the prophet receive divine permission to return with the military to the king. And the message he brought the king: "you shall surely die" (2 Kgs 1:9-16). A clear win for the prophets!

In the present case, three times messengers are sent to bring in David. This story has in view the saying about Saul and the prophets, so the messengers do not die; instead, they are overwhelmed by the spirit and prophesy (NRSV, fell into prophetic frenzy). Now it is Saul's turn. Samuel has dismissed Saul as king (1 Sam 15:23b, 26b, 28) and Saul is still in place as king. Will political power continue to override prophetic power? The story's answer is brutal. The messengers were overwhelmed by God's spirit in contact with the company of the prophets and Samuel at their head; it is explicit for the first ones, implicit for the second and third groups. Saul is overwhelmed by God's spirit and begins prophesying while still on the road; on arrival, he lay naked before Samuel "all that day and all that night." Another clear win for the prophets!

The genre here is (→) story outline. It is condensed from the fully developed telling of the story. The plot and necessary detail are provided: Samuel and David at Naioth and, on the other hand, the messengers and Saul and their fate. Storyteller and reader know all they need. Nothing is said of the outcome for David. But the story is not really about David. It ends, instead, with reference to the apparently popular saying: "Is Saul also among the prophets?" (cf. 1 Sam 10:12).

Setting

The setting is most probably to be sought in the same prophetic circles responsible for the Elijah and Elisha stories. From the contradiction with 15:35, it probably was not associated with the prophetic redaction we have seen in 1 Sam 1:1–16:13. The material in 1 Sam 10:5-6, 10-12 appears to be redactional, even in the prophetic context; the same may be true here. If the comment in 10:12a is correctly understood as derogatory, both episodes depict Saul pejoratively. They may be offshoots of the strong condemnation in 1 Sam 15; note also the redactional extension of this condemnation in 13:7b-15a.

On the other hand, both passages (10:5-6, 10-12 and 19:18-24), along with others such as 1 Kgs 22 and 2 Kgs 1, may derive from efforts to conceptualize the roles and priorities of prophets and kings.

Meaning

The minimal attention paid to David suggests that the meaning of this material is best sought in the context of portrayals of prophets and kings. As in 2 Kgs 1:9-16, so here the text shows prophetic power as clearly superior to kingly power. The king can send in the messengers or the troops; the prophet has superior means at his disposal. The rejected king is portrayed as subjugated by the prophetic force, rendered powerless by the spirit (cf. Stoebe, 368-69).

Within the present context, the story can be utilized to show that Samuel's superior prophetic power was on David's side to protect him from the sustained malevolence of Saul (cf. Hertzberg, 168). As such, it is the second of the moves to save David.

Third of the Moves to Save David: By Jonathan — 20:1–21:1 (NRSV, 20:42)

I. Dialogue establishing the problem of threat from Saul — 1-4
  A. 1st exchange — 1-2
    1. David's complaint to Jonathan about Saul's threat to his life — 1

209

Textual Issues

20:14 As Driver rightly comments: "Another difficult passage" (p. 164). Three negatives create problems. With a little creativity, the MT can be read to say: and if indeed I am still alive, show me loyalty as faithful as YHWH's; then I shall not die. Verse 15 goes on to look to the situation of Jonathan's house. The LXX takes the final clause of v. 14 to prepare for the transition to v. 15 and the concern for Jonathan's house: "but if I die." Certainty on details is out of reach.

20:16 Another dense and difficult verse. Jonathan's making a covenant with the house of David (NRSV) is possible (so Stoebe, 376; Barthélemy, 197; both refer to Noth, "Bundschliessen," 146-47). Stoebe abandons the second half of the verse as untranslatable (p. 376); the NRSV opts for an oath from Jonathan, "May the LORD seek out the enemies of David"; Barthélemy sees "enemies of David" as a euphemism for David himself, citing secondary euphemisms in 1 Sam 25:22 and 2 Sam 12:14, and assumes an unduly intricate oath (p. 197). On the LXX, see Driver, 165-66.

20:17 The LXX reads a nifal for the MT's hiphil of the verb "to swear," rendering: And Jonathan swore to David again (so Driver, 166; McCarter, 337; Klein, 203). The MT is retained by Stoebe (pp. 371, 376), Barthélemy (pp. 197-98), and the NRSV. The understanding here is largely controlled by the interpretation of what precedes.

20:19 and 41 A place is specified; its precise name eludes us and eluded the LXX (cf. Driver, 167-68; Barthélemy, 199).

211

Discussion

This is a complex chapter, textually, linguistically (the Hebrew often seems colloquial, cf. Stoebe, 382), and exegetically. The basic structure is clear. There is a problem — [I]. David is aware that his life is in danger, but this conviction is not shared by Jonathan. A plan is decided on to determine the matter with a promise to communicate the results to David — [II]. The plan is carried through, Saul's intention is clearly revealed, and David is warned to flee — [III]. The implication is that reconciliation through the good offices of Jonathan (cf. 19:1-7) is no longer possible. It may also be that David is unwilling to take flight without Jonathan's knowledge or consent; vv. 5-8 place David under Jonathan's orders.

The difficulties concern the story's place in its present context and its internal coherence. As to the present context, Jonathan's confidence in Saul's benevolence sits uncomfortably with Saul's will to kill in 19:1-7; David's being missed from table is not easily compatible with 19:8-10, 11-17; and we have no report of a covenant serious enough to involve life and death (v. 8). In the hypothesis of a collection of independent stories, these difficulties are not insurmountable. 19:1-7 shows not only Saul's hostility but the possibility of reconciliation. This can justify Jonathan's view; he has achieved a reconciliation once, and would know if it had broken down. The background of reconciliation and a presumption of Saul's fluctuating moods can permit the narrator/compiler to retain the absence-from-the-table motif. The covenant is presumed in the story, not reported; it is scarcely that of 18:2, at least in the present context.

Note that what is being suggested is not that 1 Sam 20 was originally continuous narrative with 19:1-7, 8-10, 11-17, but rather that these considerations would allow a compiler of the Davidic traditions to introduce it into the narrative without blatant contradiction.

The problems of internal coherence are another matter altogether; they are well known. There is one major problem and several minor ones. The major problem is that the text sets up or portrays both a personal meeting between David and Jonathan and also a carefully prearranged code that will communicate the necessary message without a personal meeting taking place. The problem is not so much at the end, where a storyteller might allow for Jonathan's change of heart and last-minute farewell. The problem lies in setting up the prearranged code to avoid a meeting (vv. 18-22) when the meeting has already been planned (v. 13). Harmonizations can be attempted, but in the end they are struggling to be faithful to the signals in the text.

The minor problems are: (1) the hiding place is referred to vaguely in v. 5 (cf. vv. 24 and 35; also 19:3a), but quite specifically in v. 19; (2) the passage of time is sketched broadly in vv. 5-7, while more detail is provided in vv. 18-19, as if envisaging vv. 24-27; (3) in v. 20, three arrows are to be shot before the boy is sent to find them, while in v. 36 the boy is sent ahead before an arrow is shot beyond him. The first two occur in vv. 18-19a's basic repetition of vv. 5-6a, with David as speaker in vv. 5-6a and Jonathan as speaker in vv. 18-19a. Beyond these, there is material concerning David's future loyalty to Jonathan and his house (vv. 16-17, 23, 42); in contrast with vv. 5-8, this material portrays Jonathan as subordinate.

These difficulties can be resolved once it is recognized (1) that this text provides a story outline or reported story rather than the record of events or the record of a particular telling of the story and (2) that at least one variant version is noted in the outline (with possibly a further minor variant, v. 38). Awareness of the variant version accounts for the major problem. The minor problems look more tractable when we are aware that we are dealing with a story outline, in which various details may be flagged at different points in the outline.

Any storyteller, any reader, has to face the difficulty that, if Saul is seriously intent on killing David, Jonathan may be suspect as David's friend and could be followed to discover David's whereabouts. A similar concern and another stratagem are present in 1 Sam 16:1-13, where Samuel is portrayed as afraid of Saul, and the LORD suggests a suitable pretext (16:2). However, if it is dangerous for Jonathan to tell David himself, it is also dangerous to have a messenger tell David. The messenger might always behave as Doeg does later (cf. 21:8 [NRSV, 7]; 22:9-10), winning Saul's favor by betraying both Jonathan and David — revealing Jonathan's sympathies and David's whereabouts. From this point of view, it is understandable that the story might be told with a pre-arranged code rather than a direct meeting between the two. A sympathetic reader and a good storyteller will recognize the need, in such a version, to have a farewell scene before David leaves for the hiding place.

A good storyteller will also be aware of the difficulty involved in this "no-meeting" version that, if the news is good and Saul's intentions are benign, David and Jonathan could walk in from the field hand-in-hand. The use of code for good news would need explanation; for example, Jonathan must not appear to be plotting with David. It is understandable, therefore, that a storyteller to avoid this issue might arrange for Jonathan to bring the bad news in person, with the possibility then of a full and satisfying farewell scene at the end of the story — where it most appropriately belongs. The storyteller would need to establish verisimilitude for Jonathan's not being followed. The text hints at a possibility for this in having "a little boy" (NRSV; or: young lad; Heb., *na'ar qāṭōn*) present in v. 35, before the variant is introduced with v. 36. This then allows for the interpretation that the two need not be followed because Jonathan was going out for routine archery practice (see below).

The possibility of a further minor variant is offered by the words in v. 38. It is possible, but not necessary, to understand them, while shouted overtly to the boy, as being addressed covertly to David in place of the coded message. "Hurry, be quick, do not linger"; there is no code; the instruction is direct and clear. The words are heard by the boy, but the message is meant for David. It is a possibility, but other interpretations are plausible (see below).

As represented in the structure analysis, the version taken as basic is the one encountered first in the text. The problem is posed: David is certain that Saul is determined to kill him — [I]; Jonathan, for any number of reasons, remains doubtful. How are they to find out (discovery)? — [II.A]; how is David to be told (disclosure)? — [II.B]. David suggests his absence from the festal meal as a way of provoking a reaction from Saul, and the details are worked out

213

(vv. 5-7; presumably the hiding place "in the field" is known, cf. 19:3). When the issue turns to disclosure ("Who will tell me if your father answers you harshly?" v. 10), they go out into open country (cf. 1 Kgs 11:29, "in the field"; against Hertzberg, 173). Jonathan will disobey his father's later command ("Now send and bring him to me, for he shall surely die," v. 31). So the plans laid in the country are strictly treasonable; security is important and storytelling tension is heightened (against Stoebe, 386).

In what follows in the text, Jonathan promises to send to David and tell him if the news is good (v. 12; there is no reason to attribute vv. 12-13 to dtr circles, against McCarter, Veijola, and Klein, see below). There are different understandings of this promise. Hertzberg emends the Hebrew to obtain the odd promise to send no one (p. 169). Stoebe obtains a similar but more diplomatic result by reading the latter part of v. 12 as: I will explore my father's intentions; certainly, they will be good news for David. If not, then I will send to you. . . . In this understanding, v. 13 unfolds the promise of v. 12b, exclusively concerning bad news (p. 371). If Stoebe's reading is accepted, the problem of good news is eliminated. There is tension with the code arranged in vv. 21-22 and executed in vv. 36-37, but there is no tension within this basic version of the story. The difficulty with Stoebe's reading is the presence of "I will send" in v. 12 and its absence in v. 13. Although there is no explicit first person pronoun in v. 13 to emphasize that "I myself will tell you," the sequence strongly suggests Jonathan's personal involvement: "disclose it to you, and send you away, so that you may go in safety" (NRSV, v. 13). The structure analysis in vv. 12-13a is based on this assumption. A prearranged code does not fit this context; a meeting is meant.

The promise, in this version then, is that Jonathan will tell David if the news is bad. There is no prearranged code or anything of the kind. Bypassing the variant material in vv. 18-23, the execution of the plan is unfolded in greater detail than was given in vv. 5-7. Once Jonathan is certain of his father's homicidal intentions for David, he goes out the following morning with his young attendant towards David's hiding place (v. 35). When in the area, he sends the attendant back with his gear, and there is the final farewell scene between David and Jonathan. By the time the attendant and Jonathan arrive separately at the city, it is too late to organize any pursuit of David. This is a story outline. Not every detail is provided for each version. No detail is absent from the total text, however, that could not be supplied from a storyteller's or a reader's imagination.

The attendant is needed in the variant version, with its plan outlined in vv. 18-22 — [II.B.var] — and executed in vv. 36-37 — [III.B.1.var], which will be discussed below. In the version where David and Jonathan meet, the attendant is not needed for any coded signal. Instead, the attendant's presence could be developed by the storyteller as the reason why Jonathan was not followed; he was going out with his servant for routine archery practice. This was apparently the view of Josephus: "But at daybreak he went out into the plain, before the city, seemingly for exercise, in reality to make known to his friend, in accordance with their agreement, the temper of his father" (*Antiquities,* VI, 239; the coded signal with the arrows is given little attention by Josephus, cf. §233 and §240 — "after doing what had been prearranged"). If appropriate, in this version a storyteller could ignore the whole issue of the danger of Jonathan's being followed.

Verses 18-22 introduce a quite different plan, proposed by Jonathan — [*II.B.var*]. The known hiding place is specified and a coded signal is pre-arranged between David and Jonathan. The fall of the arrows will be supplemented by the directions shouted to the attendant. They contain a code for good news (near side, v. 21) or bad news (far side, v. 22). Whether the text refers to arrows (plural) or arrow (singular) in these verses (vv. 20-22, 36-38) does not affect the code or the story and need not be dealt with here (see commentaries). In this version, then, on arrival near David's hiding place Jonathan would execute the agreed code and so would communicate the message to David — [*III.B.1.var*].

A storyteller using this version, or a reader actualizing this version, would need to have allowed for an adequate farewell between Jonathan and David earlier in the story, perhaps after the plan has been agreed on and before David has left to hide. Alternatively, this version could be supplemented by the final farewell scene (vv. 40-42). In such a case, however, the coded message is totally unnecessary. A storyteller would need to go beyond the present text to insist on the spontaneity of Jonathan's action, driven by the natural pressure of emotion and the sudden realization of the impossibility of definitive separation from David without a proper farewell. The text does not hint at this spontaneity. The story outline can leave some spontaneity to the storyteller or the reader.

A further minor variant has been noted above: the words of v. 38 are meant for David: "Hurry, be quick, do not linger." It is possible that they are meant simply to impress on David the urgency of the situation communicated in the code (cf. Smith, *Samuel*, 195). It is possible that in the story they are to be understood as meant for the attendant; Jonathan is overwhelmed by emotion and in a hurry to do what has to be done, whether leaving the scene or farewelling David. For this to be clearly the case, it would make more sense for v. 38 to follow v. 39 rather than precede it. In its present position, v. 38 offers the possibility of an additional version in which no code is used but a message is shouted, apparently at the attendant, but in fact for David's benefit. Were this version to be used for the telling, vv. 20-22 would need to be replaced by a different arrangement; vv. 36-37 would be ignored altogether.

It is essential to the understanding of a story outline or reported story to realize that while an outline might offer more than one version of a story, in the telling (or reading) of a story only one version ought be actualized at any given time.

Two areas remain for reflection. One concerns the assurances sought by Jonathan in vv. 14-17, 23, and 42 — [II.C and III.B.2.b.2)]. The other concerns the attribution of vv. 11-17 in whole or in part to dtr circles — [cf. II.B and C].

On the issue of the assurance sought by Jonathan, it is worth noting that such assurance occurs in three places in the narrative: in vv. 14-17 (or at least vv. 16-17), in v. 23, and in v. 42. The correlation between them is minor. The last five words of v. 23 are found in v. 42; "forever" occurs in vv. 15, 23, and 42 (although not necessarily with identical meaning) and "to swear" occurs in

v. 17 and v. 42. The concern addressed here is clearly alive later (e.g., 2 Sam 9, 11-20, 21). The attribution of the texts is far from clear.

Within the traditions of David's rise to power, the language of 20:17 echoes that of 18:1, 3-4, "he loved him as his own soul/life," and the concern for Jonathan in 1 Sam 23:16-18 is restricted to his role as second to David — not explicit in ch. 20. The concern for Jonathan's house and his descendants after him is certainly alive in David's later years (cf. 2 Sam 9:1-13; 16:1-4; 19:24-30; 21:7). Against McCarter, the text of 2 Sam 9:1-13 cannot originally have followed 2 Sam 21:1-14; David's question in 9:1 or 3 would be bitterly cynical following 21:7 (or for that matter, 21:1-6, 8-14; see McCarter, *I Samuel,* 344; *II Samuel,* 13, 262-63). On the other hand, the situation of 2 Sam 9:1-13 is not that presupposed by Mephibosheth in 2 Sam 19:28. So it seems that there are probably three versions about the sparing of Mephibosheth that have collected around the story of David's middle years. Settings and chronologies are not easy to establish. What is clear in 1 Sam 20 is that the concern is expressed variously at all levels in the story; a story cannot be faithfully actualized from the outline without including this theme. When and how these concerns came into the text of the story outline can scarcely be more than a matter for conjecture.

On the dtr issue, we need a clear understanding of the difference between what is demonstrably dtr language and what might be dtr language. If dtr circles wanted to speak of the ordinary business of life, they had to use the same Hebrew as any other group. If dtr circles wanted to address issues relevant to their own particular ideology (above all, exclusive fidelity to YHWH, God of Israel, and the centralization of worship in Jerusalem), they had at their disposal a range of language and set phrases that had been hammered out, formalized, and handed down within the dtr circles. It is this characteristic language in the service of dtr ideology that can be called "demonstrably dtr language"; reference to the ordinary business of life might be due to dtr circles, but this normally lies outside the possibility of demonstration.

Where 1 Sam 20:11-17 is concerned, the academic spadework has been done by Veijola (*Ewige Dynastie,* 81-87). A primary error lies in the claim that David's question in v. 10 is not concretely answered until vv. 18-23 (ibid., 82-83); in fact, the answer in vv. 12-13 is fully adequate — unless it is assumed that the answer must be in code. Veijola (ibid., 84) uses three phrases to argue for dtr origin: the use of the title "YHWH God of Israel" (20:12), the proper name (Jonathan) in place of the personal pronoun in the oath formula (20:13), and the comparative (or double) prayer for YHWH's support (20:13, with you . . . as with my father). The first of these, the title, is certainly used by dtr circles; it is equally certainly not exclusive to dtr circles (as Veijola himself notes). The change in the oath formula is too minor and too far removed from any dtr concern to carry weight. In fact, the first of Veijola's two claimed dtr occurrences (1 Sam 25:22) is too uncertain to be helpful; a euphemism, "the enemies of David," is used so that the original could have been "to me" or "to David" (with the Greek). Furthermore, Veijola's attribution of both passages (1 Sam 25:22 and 2 Sam 3:9) to dtr circles is highly dubious. In the third case, there is no way that the occurrences can be described as dtr language in the service of dtr ideology. They are not demonstrably dtr language. They can be understood simply as different responses to different contexts. After inspection of the alleged dtr occurrences, the claim of dtr provenance seems unsustainable. No one can say that 1 Sam 20:11-17 is definitely not dtr. No one can demonstrate that 1 Sam 20:11-17 is dtr. Dtr responsibility for 20:11-17, 23, 40-42 has been asserted by McCarter, but without convincing linguistic evidence (see pp. 16-17, 296-97, 344). The understanding of ch. 20 presented here nullifies the need for dtr intervention in these verses. The colloquialisms of 20:11-17 are unlikely candidates for dtr authorship.

Genre

The text as we have it, if it has been correctly interpreted with its variant version, is a (→) story outline. What it outlines is a (→) story. There is a dual problem running in it: how Jonathan is to be convinced and David is to know if there is a threat to his life; and what David is to do about it. What David is to do about it is largely taken for granted: get out of town. As Jonathan puts it: I will "send you away, so that you may go in safety" (20:13). The more worrisome problem to be solved is how to get the news to David if it is bad. In the basic version, if the news is bad, Jonathan will manage to bring it to David himself. In the variant version, a code is carefully arranged to communicate the news, whether good or bad.

As was pointed out in the discussion, a storyteller or a reader must adjust the structure of the narrative to accommodate the variant chosen. If there is to be no meeting at the end, then the appropriate farewell must be fitted in somewhere. If there is to be a meeting at the end, then the talk of codes must be left out — unless, as part of the story, Jonathan is to be overcome with emotion and radically change the plan.

Setting

The earliest probable setting for the story would be among the circles of David's followers. This sort of cleverness on the part of both David and Jonathan was what enabled David to survive and become king. David did not usurp Jonathan's place as future king; David had Jonathan's full backing.

The temptation is strong to assign the assurances for the future of Jonathan and his descendants to later hands. There is nothing linguistically to identify their origin. The issue would have been a live one from the moment Jonathan died with Saul on Mt. Gilboa and David was seen to have ambitions for the crown of Judah and then Israel. Saul's descendants had good reason to fear for their lives (cf. 2 Sam 21:1-14), and Jonathan's descendants were among them. There is motivation for the assurances from very early on. The recognition of a story outline increases the difficulty of attributing such concerns. First, with only one variant actualized in a performance of the story, the aspect of repeti-

217

tion is less significant. Second, in an outline it may be expected that transitions will be terse or abrupt.

The creation of a story outline or reported story, shorter by far than the version told in full, was probably made necessary by the composition of a story of David's rise. As we noted, the story does not fit perfectly within its present context. But it is clearly too good a story and, as its variants show, too popular a story to be left out. Storytellers and readers need to adjust a little if they want to focus on the broader context.

Meaning

The meaning of the story as an independent entity is slightly different from its meaning as part of the larger composition. As an independent story, it celebrates the cleverness of David and Jonathan in spiriting David away from the certainly angry Saul. Beyond that, it drives home the point that Saul's hostility drove David away from the court of Saul; it was not David's ambition that made him leave. Finally, it brings out in story form what 1 Sam 23:16-18 reports briefly: Jonathan was aiding and abetting David and was well aware that in a future situation he, Jonathan, would be playing second fiddle to David's king; "I shall be second to you" (23:17). The need for this to be bruited abroad in David's favor would have been as early as the need on the part of Jonathan's descendants to lay claim to the favor of David on Jonathan's behalf.

With the integration of the story outline into a story of David's rise, its meaning takes on another dimension. Michal, Saul's daughter, saved David from her father. Now Jonathan, Saul's son and heir, saves David from his father. Clearly God and the support of Saul's own family are on the side of David. To this, the present text adds the figure of Samuel, Saul's anointer, and also the prophet who dismissed him from office.

Bibliography of Works Cited Above

Brettler, Marc Zvi. *The Creation of History in Ancient Israel.* London: Routledge, 1995.

Esler, Philip F. "The Madness of Saul: A Cultural Reading of 1 Samuel 8–31." Pp. 220-62 in *Biblical Studies/Cultural Studies: The Third Sheffield Colloquium.* Edited by J. C. Exum and S. D. Moore. JSOTSup 266. Sheffield: Sheffield Academic Press, 1998.

Grønbaek, Jakob H. *Die Geschichte vom Aufstieg Davids (1. Sam. 15–2. Sam. 5): Tradition und Komposition.* Copenhagen: Munksgaard, 1971.

Güttgemanns, Erhardt. "Introductory Remarks Concerning the Structural Study of Narrative." *Semeia* 6 (1976) 23-125.

Holman, C. Hugh. *A Handbook to Literature.* 3rd ed. Indianapolis: Bobbs-Merrill, 1972.

Josephus, Flavius. *Jewish Antiquities.* Books V-VIII. The Loeb Classical Library. London: Heinemann, 1934.

LaPointe, Roger. "Tradition and Language: The Import of Oral Expression." Pp. 125-42 in *Tradition and Theology in the Old Testament.* Edited by D. A. Knight. Philadelphia: Fortress, 1977.

Noth, Martin. "Das alttestamentliche Bundschliessen im Lichte eines Mari-Textes." Pp. 142-54 in *Gesammelte Studien zum Alten Testament.* ThB 6. Munich: Kaiser, 1957.

Propp, V. *Morphology of the Folktale.* 2nd ed. Austin: University of Texas Press, 1968.

Rendtorff, Rolf. "Beobachtungen zur altisraelitischen Geschichtsschreibung anhand der Geschichte vom Aufstieg Davids." Pp. 428-39 in *Probleme biblischer Theologie.* Edited by H. W. Wolff. Munich: Chr. Kaiser, 1971.

Smith, Henry Preserved. *The Books of Samuel.* ICC. Edinburgh: Clark, 1912.

Stoebe, Hans Joachim. "David und Michal: Überlegungen zur Jugendgeschichte Davids." Pp. 224-43 in *Von Ugarit nach Qumran.* Edited by J. Hempel and L. Rost. *BZAW* 77. Berlin: Töpelmann, 1958.

Talmon, Shemaryahu. "The Textual Study of the Bible — A New Outlook." Pp. 321-400 in *Qumran and the History of the Biblical Text.* Edited by F. M. Cross and S. Talmon. Cambridge: Harvard University Press, 1975.

Veijola, Timo. *Die Ewige Dynastie: David und die Entstehung seiner Dynastie nach der deuteronomistischen Darstellung.* AASF B 193. Helsinki: Suomalainen Tiedeakatemia, 1975.

Chapter 8

Open Rupture between David and Saul (1 Samuel 21:2–27:12)

This major section of the 1 Samuel text, from ch. 21 to ch. 27, is arranged as the narrative of open rupture between Saul and David. What was first restricted to conflict within the court of Saul has broken out into open rupture within the countryside of Judah. The narrative has David forced to flee the court; it will continue the pursuit until David is forced to flee the country — after which the final stages of the political conflict will be played out, involving Saul, David, and the Philistines, and ending in Saul's ultimate failure and death. Within Israel, David is driven to become a fugitive in his own country, because of Saul's hostility. Because of Saul's hostility, David is driven into exile from his own country, beyond Israel. Strange as it may seem, in the structure of the narrative and the content of the stories, Saul's hostility culminates in his final commendation of David (in chs. 24 and 26). The overall movement and organization of the narrative in this section can be seen as follows.

Before looking into these scenes in detail, it is important to pause and direct our attention to what we are not told. The great narrative traditions of David and Saul tell us expansively about both figures; so much so that we need to step back and reflect before we are aware of just how much we are not told and do not know. It is important to recognize all that is not told of David in these ten chapters (chs. 18–27).

We are told David spent a year and four months in Philistine territory (27:7), and we are given a brief description of his activity and his victims — Geshurites, Girzites, and Amalekites (27:8). We are not told how long David was a fugitive and guerrilla leader in the wilderness of Judah, and we are not told about his victims there — or much about his beneficiaries beyond Keilah and Abigail. The threat to Nabal (25:21-22) hints in the direction of the victims as well as the beneficiaries, but it is little more than a hint. The readiness of the people of Keilah to hand David and his followers over to Saul (23:12) and the readiness of some of the Ziphites from Hachilah to betray David's whereabouts and surrender him to Saul (23:19-20; 26:1) both reveal ill will toward David, perhaps the result of the depredations of his guerrilla band. Unless a strong sense of the need for liberation is present, those who live off the land (like guerrillas) are seldom loved by those who live on the land (like farmers). They can be valued, but in David's case it appears likely they were not. The point is plain: we are not given the full story. Earlier, David is reported to have had great success against the Philistines; we know none of the details. Nor are we told the circumstances that motivated David's move of his parents to security with the king of Moab. We may surmise, but we are not told. We learn something of the organization of his forces in 2 Sam 23:8-39, but not here. We know so much about David — and yet so little.

It is one thing to know what we do not know. It is another to surmise what we may not know. But this too we must do. It is a fair surmise that we do not know the ways in which the stories were told of David's early days. There is a careful structure in chs. 28–31 that suggests we have them in the form and sequence in which they were meant to be (see below). Similarly, there is a structure in 23:14–26:25 that holds the stories together; the introduction (23:14-24a — [I.C.1]) followed by the stories (23:24b–26:25 — [I.C.2]).

There is also a structure in the narrative of 21:2 (NRSV, 21:1)–22:23 that can be easily overlooked. Open rupture means flight from court — [I.A.1]. There are two stories, two variant options for this flight (21:2-10 [NRSV, 21:1-9] and 21:11-16 [NRSV, 21:10-15]). The collection of traditions in 22:1-5 sets the scene for the narrative of open rupture, after the flight — [I.A.2]. Finally, 22:6-23 rehearses the first two traditions of the rupture and its effects within Israel. Saul is burdened with slaughtered priests and the guilt of sacrilege; David is blessed with the remaining priest and the gift of guidance from God through the ephod. The position of the two pairs of traditions either side of the little collection in 22:1-5 accounts for the brokenness of the Ahimelech story. It is not so much that the two passages are two separate stories (against Stoebe, 390-91, 411-12). Rather, the meeting at Nob is told within the horizon of David's departure from Saul's court; the slaughter of the priests from Nob is told within the horizon of the start of David's days as fugitive within his own country. The intervening material (21:11-16 [NRSV, 21:10-15] and 22:1-5) is just that — intervening material. It is not intervening time or a record of intervening events. The first part is an alternative story of departure (21:11-16). The second is a collection of background material for use by storytellers as needed (22:1-5). It is appropriately situated between David's departure from the court and the episodes of David's life as a guerrilla leader.

The concern is not one of how the events panned out, but of how the narrative might best be told — or, more accurately, how the stories might best be presented for selective telling. An enduring contribution of form criticism, in the narrative area, is to require focus on the narrative actually being told rather than on the events that might be recovered. Even the "setting in life" is not the event. It is the setting in which the narrative of the event is told. The narrative is primary and the event is largely at its service.

Two traditions are offered us about David's flight from Saul. In the second, David's move to Achish is introduced as "David rose and fled that day from Saul; he went to King Achish of Gath" (21:11; NRSV, 21:10). Within the initial context, they are superficially compatible. One may understand David's flight as being via Nob. As a way of handling the present text, this makes some sense but it may emerge from the juxtaposition of traditions rather than their combination. The introduction, "David rose and fled that day from Saul" (21:11; NRSV, 21:10), poses problems. "Flight" is inappropriate language after David's peaceful dealings with Ahimelech; "from Saul" would need to be interpreted broadly. The understanding that David continued his flight from Saul is possible but is pushing the Hebrew beyond its literal sense. It is an appropriate introduction to David's flight on the occasion of his open rupture with Saul. Where it appropriately belongs in the text is less clear. With the reference to "that day," it can hardly follow on 19:10 (which uses a different verb for flight). It would be possible for it to follow on the episode of the dummy in the bed (19:11-17), although it would be duplicating the flight and escape of v. 12b; v. 18a does so anyway. Graver is the reference to "this day" when David has escaped by night, but the intervening exchange between Michal and Saul might be seen as mitigating this. It would equally be possible for it to follow on 21:1 (NRSV. 20:42). It is remarkable for what it does not say; there is no mention of locality or circumstance. There is a close parallel with the action in 21:1a (NRSV, in 20:42, "He got up and left") where the unexpressed subject must be David (complying with 20:42a ["Go in peace"]; cf. LXX, etc.), so that 21:11 (NRSV, 21:10) could easily take its place. The sequence then would be: And Jonathan went into the city; and David rose and fled that day from Saul. The verses could well function as a replacement for the episode with Ahimelech. The possbilities of a quite different narrative sequence cannot be ignored; speculation is unhelpful.

The greater difficulty for this second introduction is in the more distant context: it is in sharp tension with the tradition of David's coming to the court of Achish in 27:1-7. It has often been noted that David would be unwise and unwelcome to show up at the court of Achish armed with the sword of the Philistine, Goliath. More significantly, in 21:11-16 (NRSV, 21:10-15), David arrives at the court of Achish accompanied by no more than his reputation and, once recognized, fears being perceived as a threat; so he feigns madness. On the other hand, in 27:1-7, David arrives accompanied by a fighting force of six hundred guerrillas and he is welcomed. There is a vast distance between the two contexts. Above all, while the anecdote in 21:11-16 may demonstrate David's resourcefulness, it could not have served as an introduction to chs. 28–30. These require Achish to have complete trust in David's loyalty as a vassal. Without explanation, the tradition enshrined in the anecdote should have dissipated any such trust.

At the same time, it is important to realize how easily a skilled storyteller could accommodate both traditions. The gist of the accommodation can be hinted at in a single sentence: And the servants of Achish said that David was dangerous, because in the past he had successfully led them to believe that he was a madman. Such a sentence is not in the biblical text, but it could easily be developed in any storyteller's presentation where it was felt to be needed. For all that, no pointer to the reconciliation of the two sojourns with Achish is present in the text.

It is also important to recognize the context required for 22:1, "David left there and escaped to the cave of Adullam." "David left there" could easily be an editor's link (so Stoebe, 405), but the "escaped" needs a suitable context. The escape from Achish could provide one; there is no note of David's departure in the final verse (21:16; NRSV, 21:15). In this case, the whole of 22:1-5 could have been introduced here along with the episode at Achish's court. Such a procedure would explain the separation of 21:2-10 (NRSV, 21:1-9) from its sequel in 22:6-23. The apparent and unresolved incompatibility of 21:11-16 (NRSV, 21:10-15) with 27:1-7 militates against this as an original configuration of the text (but see below).

Without 21:11-16 (NRSV, 21:10-15), "David left there and escaped"

(22:1) follows well enough on 21:10 (NRSV, 21:9). There are other possibilities as a context for 22:1 (i.e., after 19:17, 19:24, or 21:1 [NRSV, 20:42 — see above]); but there is little point in speculation about ways of telling the Saul-David story that we do not have. It will be important to note (below) how the first and failed sojourn with Achish introduces significant differences into the Saul-David narrative.

These traditions, which are available to us, have been shaped into a sequential narrative, often with remarkable logic and structure. Even what may be additional has been placed where it can be seen to be most appropriate. At this point we have the traditions of open rupture, but before the final act of chs. 28–31. The section begins with (superficially compatible) options for the narrative of David's flight, after the definitive break with Saul and the recognition and acceptance by Jonathan of this break. Narratively, the section does not end with David's departure from the country; that is told as part of the account of his move to Philistine territory (27:1). David's stay with the Philistines is envisaged as a completed sojourn; its end is known (27:7).

With this in mind, we may turn to the details of the open rupture, first within Israel, with David as fugitive in his own country, his flight and its consequences. As we have noted, the present text offers us two introductions to the stories of open rupture. They are better considered separately, serving as a reminder that there were probably many ways of telling the story of David, beyond the present text that has come down to us.

As the present text stands, therefore, the episode with Achish (21:11-16; NRSV, 21:10-15) can be passed over in favor of David's service with Achish (27:1-12). 27:1-12 is essential for 28:1-2 and 29:1-5. To tell any of the stories of David in the wilderness, 22:1-3 is essential — David must have troops. To tell the story of the deliverance of Keilah, as it is given in the text, Abiathar and the ephod must be with David to speak out God's will. For this, at least the background of the slaughter at Nob is essential. The first visit to the court of Achish is not needed for either sequence. Its inclusion in the present text suggests that it had its role to play in the telling of David's stories; the ease with which, if necessary, it could be accommodated to the episode of 27:1-12 has been noted.

Flight (two options)	**21:2-16 (NRSV, 21:1-15)**
Option 1: David's flight to Ahimelech at Nob	2-10 (NRSV, 1-9)
I. Introductory	2-3
A. David's coming to Nob	2a
B. Ahimelech's anxiety	2b-3
1. Anxiety: narrated and expressed by Ahimelech	2b
2. Response to this anxiety by David: untruth	3
II. David's requests	4-10
A. David's 1st request	4-7
1. The request: five loaves	4
2. The concern	5-6
a. Expressed by the priest: cleanness	5
b. Relieved by David: untruth	6
3. The gift of holy bread	7

Textual Issues

21:6 (NRSV, 21:5) "Vessels" is possible (so: NRSV; Hertzberg, 177; Barthélemy, 203); so too is "gear" or "weapons" (so: Driver, 174; Stoebe, 393; McCarter, 347 [for 2nd use]; Klein, 211 [for 2nd use]).

Discussion

In the next chapter, the association of David's visit to Ahimelech at Nob (21:2-10; NRSV, 21:1-9) with Saul's slaughter of the priests of Nob (22:6-19) is clear. Yet in the present text, the short notices about David's family and followers provide an alternative lead into the story of Saul's slaughter of the priests. David and all his father's house heard (v. 1b); Saul heard (v. 6a).

In the present text, the first introduction is the story of David's flight to Ahimelech at Nob. It is not an easy story. The text has David say he is on a mission from the king. We know he is not; he is on the run from the king. David says he has set up a rendezvous with his soldiers. We know that is a lie; there are no soldiers and no rendezvous. David is not the only one of dubious veracity in the story. Ahimelech and the narrator say there is no bread in the sanctuary, except for the holy bread (vv. 4-7; NRSV, 3-6). In 22:18, we learn there were 85 priests in the community. Is it likely that there was no food available? David asks for a spear or a sword. Ahimelech admits to having nothing beyond the sword of Goliath, the Philistine. Perhaps a combination of 1 Sam 13:19-22 with Doeg's single-handed slaughter (22:18) can render this a plausible response. The fact remains that we are not told why Goliath's sword should be held as a trophy at Nob and surprisingly we never hear of it again. Allegedly, Saul will wipe out a priestly city in Israel over this apparently minor incident. It seems likely that there is more happening in this story than meets the eye. As the ancient wisdom of the adage has it: in all questions of politics and spies, the clearest answers are those least sure and the surest answers are those least clear.

This aspect of uncertainty is visible in the beginning itself (v. 2; NRSV, 1). David's coming results in Ahimelech's anxiety — [I]. Such anxiety is no trifling matter (cf. in 1-2 Samuel, 1 Sam 4:13; 13:7; 14:15; 16:4; 28:5; 2 Sam 17:2). It is not simply a matter of astonishment (Hertzberg, 179) or of attitude towards authority (Smith, *Samuel*, 197); rather, it is a signal in the narrative from the outset that the action to follow will be fraught with consequences. It is part of the stylized nature of the story. Why, for example, should David come to

Nob for food and arms, when home was a mere two hours away (Stoebe, 395)? Why should the priest tremble at the approach of a single visitor? Is something of the wider story and its background in view from the outset?

David is on the run — [cf. II]. Ahimelech is afraid; whether for David or for himself we are not told. What are the options at this point? The tradition knows of Ahimelech's death, so it is not possible for him here either to refuse David or to join David. Either he dies a martyr or he dies innocent. Equally, David either tells the truth and makes Ahimelech a martyr, or David tells a lie and makes Ahimelech his innocent unwitting accomplice. The narrative opts for Ahimelech as the innocent accomplice. What are the possibilities for the portrayal of David, within this option? There could be the cunning of David, who gains support rather than is given it (cf. the Jacob motif; Hertzberg, 180 and Stoebe, 396). There could be the cleverness of David, who gives Ahimelech an excuse for his defense; but it is not used explicitly or effectively, and the question of cleanness suggests Ahimelech is portrayed as believing David (apart from the issue of different traditions; see below). There could be the concern of David not to put Ahimelech in danger. 22:22 suggests this as an interest. The concern appears to be less with the moral issue of truth than with the issue of responsibility for the shedding of innocent blood. No interpretative comment is offered in the text.

Assured, Ahimelech provides the sacred bread. Verse 7a (NRSV, 6a) concludes the gift of the bread; v. 7b appears to be an explanatory note about the precise nature of the bread, repeating a little of v. 6. It is misleading to say that the story has reached a clear conclusion with v. 7a and that the mention of Doeg has no relation to the context (against Stoebe, 397). Even at the level of the prehistory of the story, we cannot dogmatically exclude Doeg. If vv. 9-10 (NRSV, 8-9) are omitted as a later popular addition (so Stoebe, 397-98), there is no problem with a mention of Doeg at the end. From the point of view of the storyteller's art in the present text, it is difficult to see valid objection to Doeg's presence coming between the gift of the food and that of the sword. After the bread has been handed over, the narrator indicates the presence of Saul's henchman. Before the shiver of anticipation has passed, the narrative proceeds to the gift of the sword, the tension now increased by the known presence of the spy. This sword recurs in 22:10 and 13. It is possible that the name of Goliath is an intrusion (see on 17:4, 23). The specification of the Philistine as the one "whom you killed in the valley of Elah" is unnecessary if Goliath had been mentioned by name. It has been widely noted that possession of the Philistine's sword would hardly make David welcome at the Philistine court of Achish. Once we are aware of the independence of the two introductions, it is not important.

Genre

The passage 21:2-10 (NRSV, 21:1-9), in the present text, set apart from 22:6-23, outlines a story that is complete. There is tension from the beginning; a fugitive meets a sanctuary priest and the priest trembles. Words predominate, with prevarication, half-truths and untruths. The presence of Doeg is noted; the note of it renders the presence ominous. Equilibrium is reached: David has food and a sword. The equilibrium can only be temporary; prevarication calls for disclosure and Doeg's presence will not be without weight. As a (→) story outline, the text could well be integrated with 22:6-23 in the telling of the story of Saul's sacrilege. As an outline text, it could be used in other contexts as well.

Setting

As will be noted under Meaning, the story behind 21:2-10 (NRSV, 21:1-9) might possibly have been told in many circles — positive or negative to Ahimelech/Abiathar, positive or negative toward David. In the present context, it comes to us from Davidic circles, incorporated early into a story of David's rise, and later incorporated into the DH.

Meaning

These verses (21:2-10; NRSV, 21:1-9) perform a double function: they are introduction to the flight of David and his open rupture with Saul; they are introduction to the awful story of the slaughter of the priests of Nob.

In either case, the verses could reflect a story illustrating the priestly support for David exemplified by Ahimelech, the gift of the holy bread and the sword. But then Ahimelech's support would need to be freely given, instead of his being the unwitting victim of duplicity (cf. Grønbaek, *Aufstieg Davids*, 138). Alternatively, the story could reflect David's cunning and trickery in winning priestly support, a parallel to the Jacob motif. But then it would reflect negatively on Ahimelech and be likely to have circulated in anti-Abiathar circles under Solomon (cf. ibid., 139-40).

In the present context, the passage does none of these things. It begins David's flight from Saul, underscoring his isolation and aloneness. He needs the barest essentials of food and weapons. He needs to dissemble to stay alive. His situation will change dramatically as he comes to head a powerful fighting force; that development is enhanced by the story of so solitary a beginning. At the same time, the passage sets the scene for the story of Saul's sacrilegious slaughter (22:6-19).

Flight (two options)	**21:2-16 (NRSV, 21:1-15)**
Option 2: David's flight to Achish at Gath	11-16 (NRSV, 10-15)
I. Introductory	11
A. David's flight from Saul	11a
B. David's coming to Achish	11b
II. David in danger at Gath	12-16
A. Recognition by servants of Achish: "the king of the land"	12

Discussion

The first flight to Achish, although a potential introduction to David's time in the wilderness, is not suitable for the present text of the slaughter at Nob story or the deliverance of Keilah story. It could only be used with difficulty for the present form of other stories that have been deftly woven into the narrative. In the present text, it is a reminder of another tradition and other possibilities rather than a variant tradition that can be put to easy use. In the present text, as noted earlier: for the stories of David in the wilderness, troops are needed (22:1-3); for the story of the deliverance of Keilah, Abiathar and the ephod are needed (22:20-23, requiring vv. 6-19); later in the text, for 28:1-2 and 29:1-5, David as a trusted vassal of Achish is essential (27:1-12).

It is not appropriate to look for a place where this episode (21:11-16; NRSV, 21:10-15) might be more properly situated in the present text. What is appropriate is to recognize that it may have functioned as an independent introduction to a different presentation of the stories of David. As an independent episode, narrating David's flight from Saul to the wilderness, via the court of Achish at Gath, it could serve as introduction to any of the major stories of David's days in the wilderness. As an independent introduction, for the relief of Keilah it would need to account for the presence of both Abiathar and the ephod with David, but this would hardly be difficult.

The verses themselves offer a hint to the storyteller that they are not to be used in sequence with the Ahimelech episode. They open with the comment that David fled that day "from Saul" (v. 11; NRSV, 10) — [I]. The subsequent text makes clear that the storyteller (or the reader) is to take this hint. The text preserves an alternative introduction to a different sequence of stories of David's open rupture with Saul.

Used as an introduction, the passage could set up a portrayal of David's separation from Saul that is quite different to the present portrayal. Here, David is not just one of Saul's military commanders who is a threat to Saul's authority and a trigger for his jealousy. Instead, David is "the king of the land" (v. 12; NRSV, 11). Here, David has not been driven into alliance with the enemy at the end of a long struggle with Saul (as at 27:1). Instead, David has gone to the enemy from the very beginning of his breach with Saul. How these possibilities might have been exploited we can only speculate. In the present text, once recognized, David's response is one of fear. A storyteller would need to spell out reasons why David should be so afraid; the same reasons are evidently not in play later in 27:1-7. David's resourcefulness when in danger may be the highlight of the episode. He played the madman and was a good enough actor to get away with it.

The servants of Achish are right in their identification of the person of

David, but wrong in their statement of his role: "Is this not David the king of the land?" There is an opening to irony here — [cf. II]. David is not "king of the land" but he will be. It is because he is not yet and because he will be that he is forced to flee Saul and seek refuge with Achish. It is because of this recognition that he will be forced to flee Achish and seek refuge elsewhere.

Genre

The passage 21:11-16 (NRSV, 21:10-15) as it stands is an (→) anecdote. It focuses on a single experience: how recognition led to fear and fear to resourceful dissimulation. It blends the two motives of David's fame and his astuteness.

Setting

The passage presumably derives from Davidic circles. Other possibilities can be conjured up, but without plausibility. It is now part of the present text; it is unlikely that it was selected for the Story of David's Rise — but not impossible. Whether it was part of the DH or not, we can hardly know. The desire to preserve such a tradition might have been operative at any time.

Meaning

The anecdote could have served as an introduction to stories from the time of open rupture between David and Saul, though not quite as we have those stories now. Even apart from its present context, it may have been attractive as an example of David's resourcefulness.

Consequences of Open Rupture (I): For David	**22:1-5**
I. David's base established: cave of Adullam	1a
II. Gathering of David's support	1b-2
A. Family	1b
B. Others	2
1. Quality of the supporters: in distress, in debt,	
discontented	2aα
2. Quality of David: their leader	2aβ
3. Quantity: about four hundred	2b
III. Safekeeping for David's father and mother	3-4
A. Mission to Moab by David	3a
B. Diplomatic negotiations with Moab	3b-4a
C. Safekeeping in Moab for parents	4b
IV. David's base relocated: forest of Hereth	5

Discussion

As will be noted under the "genre" rubric, this is a collection of (→) short notices. The concept has been thoroughly analyzed by Rendtorff (see "Beobachtungen"). Two aspects are of particular importance. First, the matters recorded would be of little interest without the larger context of a project telling of David's rise to power in Israel, composed from assembled traditions. Second, these notices may be independent of each other and of the context in which they are found.

This latter aspect is of interest on several counts. First, David's base in association with the cave of Adullam plays no part in the subsequent narrative — [I]. It is mentioned in another unconnected fragment of tradition (2 Sam 23:13). It might fit well into a presentation of the narrative that gave David a closer association with the Philistines earlier in the piece than ch. 27 (cf. option two above, 21:11-16; NRSV, 21:10-15). Second, David's negotiations in Moab are conducted with the king of Moab — [III]. David's request is put to the king (v. 3b); the favorable response comes from the king (v. 4a). The kings east of Jordan were not insignificant figures in Israel's tradition. What does it mean that David deals with the king? Was there once a context available to storytellers where David's reputation was as "the king of the land" (cf. at the court of Achish, 21:12; NRSV, 21:11)? Could David be portrayed dealing with Moab on a king-to-king basis? Third, the tradition in v. 4b has David's mother and father stay with the king of Moab "all the time that David was in the stronghold." In the very next verse, the text has a tradition that Gad advised David to quit "the stronghold" and he moved to the forest of Hereth (cf. 2 Sam 23:13-14). Where were his parents? How long did David and his forces operate from "the stronghold"? The compiled traditions are a valuable base for the present narrative. They are also a valuable indication that there may have been other ways of putting together the narrative of David's early days.

The concern of Saul throughout 22:6-19 is with the conspiracy against him (vv. 8, 13); the conspiracy is linked to David's rising against Saul. This is the function of 22:1-5 within the narrative: to describe David's emergence as a potential military threat to Saul. A sizable band of irregulars has gathered under his command (vv. 1-2) — [II]; his parents are out of harm's way for the duration (vv. 3-4); instead of being on the periphery, he has returned to the heartland of Judah (v. 5) — [IV]. If David's flight had culminated in hiding among his family, or in helpless exile at the court of Achish, Saul would have cause for satisfaction, not anger. His anger is motivated by the threat he believes David now constitutes, a threat that is visible on the public scene. The narrative makes this clear in the introduction to vv. 6-23: "Saul heard that David and those who were with him had been located" (v. 6a). Whatever of historical reality, in the present text 22:1-5 forms the link that elevates Ahimelech's support to the level of conspiracy and treason.

Adullam is located west of Bethlehem, in the Shephelah where the Judean hills begin to merge with the Philistine plain. Note that his father's house "went down" to him there; the terminology reflects the geographical reality. Equally, it would be geographically accurate for other locations besides

Adullam. The reaction of his family remains unexplained. It is far from any picture of the shepherd lad and Eliab's angry outburst (17:28). There is potential development of the background here that we do not have.

Those who gathered to David, apart from his own family, are categorized as oppressed, indebted, and embittered. There is always a certain surprise at the honesty of this comment. In Judges, the followers of Abimelech (9:4) and Jephthah (11:3) are described in quite different terms — NRSV, "worthless" or "outlaws" (= 'ănāšîm rêqîm, cf. Stoebe, 404). It may be that the narrator does not intend this as a pejorative judgment on David's followers; rather, there may be a hint of the portrayal of David as a deliverer. There is no question here of formulaic language for the oppressed and underprivileged, like the classic triad of the widow, the orphan, and the stranger. But there is a tendency for the language to occur in what might be called redemptive contexts, situations that call for redemption and deliverance. For the distressed (here: māṣôq), cf. Isa 8:23 (NRSV 9:1); Job 36:16; Pss 25:17; 107:6, 13, 19, 28 (refrain for redemption); 119:143; also Jer 19:9; Zeph 1:15; Deut 28:53, 55, 57. For the indebted (here: 'ăšer lô nōše'), cf. Exod 22:24 (NRSV, 22:25); 2 Kgs 4:1; Isa 50:1; Neh 5:7, 10, 11. For the discontented (here: mar nepeš), cf. 1 Sam 1:10; 30:6; 2 Sam 17:8; Isa 38:15; also Job 3:20; 7:11; 10:1; 21:25; and Prov 31:1-9, cf. v. 6. This evidence does not prove that David is being depicted as a deliverer. But it is enough to invite to reflection on the portrayal and to reticence about his description as the leader of "discontented and reckless elements . . . a dangerous band" (Hertzberg, 184).

Stoebe argues that the figure of 400 for David's irregulars is conventional, and that the 600 of 1 Sam 23:13; 27:2; 30:9 should not be viewed as an increase (Stoebe, 404). While the 400 retainers with Esau (Gen 32:7; 33:1), the 400 virgins of Jabesh-gilead (Judg 21:12), the camel squad of 400 Amalekite fugitives (1 Sam 30:17), and the 400 prophets (1 Kgs 22:6) point in the direction of a conventional figure (cf. Stoebe), we may ask about the origin of the convention. Apart from the numbers for David's force, the 600 figure occurs at Exod 14:7; Judg 18:16, 17; 1 Sam 13:15; 14:2; 2 Sam 15:18. The figures may represent the size of a group it was thought that one commander could effectively control and provide for. The later use of 600 in the present Davidic text, even if originally simply stemming from different traditions, may in the compilation be understood to indicate David's growing strength. The LXX traditions fluctuate regarding these numbers.

The return to the center of Judah is commanded by the prophet Gad; no reason is given. Perhaps a location on the Philistine frontier was strategically dangerous, with the possibility of attack from either side. Perhaps, historically, David sought confrontation with Saul; if so, the Davidic tradition flatly denies it. There is no indication in the text that Gad's advice comes from YHWH, which leaves the question of its origin open. A precise location of Hereth is unknown; an identification with Horesh (23:15, 18) is likely (Hertzberg, 185; Stoebe, 405).

Genre

22:1-5 consists of (→) short notices (vv. 1-2, 3-4, 5), as identified by Rendtorff ("Beobachtungen," 432-36). This is material known to the compiler, and used at key points in the compilation. As Rendtorff describes it, the short notice (or: short communication) is an almost notice-like communication about the past that is significant for the events to come (ibid., 433). The short notice deals with the sort of information that is unlikely to be found in official annals; such information became significant only when David had become king (ibid., 434).

Setting

The origins of the individual traditions are probably lost to us. Rendtorff characterizes the short notice as the result of research ("das Ergebnis von 'Recherchen,'") on the part of the compiler of the Story of David's Rise (ibid., 434).

Meaning

The material serves the formulation of the narrative as part of a story of David's rise. Placing these traditions at this point gives a determined shape to the narrative. It has been claimed that a core of what follows in 22:6-19 might have served as a story of conspiracy while David was still in Saul's service (cf. Grønbaek, *Aufstieg Davids,* 136-38). In the present narrative, that is not how it is presented. The introduction of 22:1-5 is a significant part of the presentation of these Davidic traditions.

Consequences of Open Rupture (II): For Saul — Sacrilege	**22:6-19**
I. Introduction: Saul's situation	6
A. Saul's consciousness of David	6a
B. Saul's court associated with him	6b
II. Sacrilegious slaughter of the priests of Nob	7-18
A. Accusation of conspiracy	7-10
1. General accusation by Saul against his court	7-8
2. Specific accusation by Doeg against Ahimelech	9-10
B. Trial of Ahimelech and the priests for conspiracy	11-16
1. Summons to appear before the king	11
2. Trial of Ahimelech by the king	12-15
a. Formal charge by the king of conspiracy	12-13
b. Defense against the charge by Ahimelech	14-15
3. Sentence passed on Ahimelech and all the priests by the king	16

Textual Issues

22:14 With varying degrees of emendation, the MT can be understood as "captain of your guard" (so: Driver, 181; Stoebe, 410; McCarter, 362; Klein, 220; Barthélemy, 207).

    22:18 Stoebe points to the particular spelling of Doeg's name (in vv. 18, 22: *dôyēg*), and the reference to the linen ephod with *nôśē'* rather than *ḥāgûr* (but only 1 Sam 2:18 and 2 Sam 6:14), and finally the move from Gibeah to Nob without an explicit change of subject to suggest an association with the slaughter attributed to Saul of Gibeonites in 2 Sam 21:1-2 (pp. 414-15; note also Hertzberg, pp. 382-83).

Discussion

The groundwork for this story has been laid earlier, in the first of the presentations of David's flight from the court of Saul. At that time, David sought and received aid from Ahimelech. As we noted there, either David tells the truth and makes Ahimelech a martyr, or David tells a lie and makes Ahimelech his innocent unwitting accomplice. The narrative opted for Ahimelech as the innocent accomplice. Innocence will be the defense Ahimelech advances in this version of the story.

    The opening of the text invites storyteller and audience to focus on the context which is basic to this story — [I]: David is out there and Saul knows it (v. 6a). Attention is given to "all his servants" standing around Saul (v. 6b). The weight of office is with Saul; the balance of success has been with David. Saul's spear in his hand may be a symbol of royal authority; it is certainly Saul's constant companion in the narrative (cf. 18:10; 19:9; 20:33; 22:6; ch. 26, passim).

    The general accusation of conspiracy is leveled against Saul's own court and the people of his own tribe — [II.A.1]. The issue of patronage is spelled out with regard to two areas: lands and offices. It is the other side of 1 Sam 8:11-17. Stripped of the pork-barreling element (v. 7), the accusation is about a conspiracy of silence. In this, it prepares the way for Doeg's intervention. Doeg will soon breach the Benjaminite reluctance to speak against David, just as Doeg will soon breach the Benjaminite reluctance to turn against the priests of God — [II.A.2 and C.2]. From the outset, this is a slanted story; it would be in line with the interests of a Davidic narrator to depict Saul's own tribe as dissatisfied with him and favoring David. Doeg is positioned as an outsider, standing by Saul's servants (cf. v. 6b; the NRSV "in charge of" goes beyond the context here, cf. Stoebe, 409).

Doeg provides the specific accusation against Ahimelech of giving support to David: ascertaining God's will, giving provisions and Goliath's sword (22:10). The correlation with 21:2-10 (NRSV, 21:1-9) is problematic. 22:9 gives no specification of time for what happened. Despite vv. 10 and 13, the story in 22:6-19 is clearly focused on Ahimelech's consulting God for David; it is against this charge alone that Ahimelech makes his defense (v. 15) — [II.B]. In the hypothesis of a story outline, these issues do not cause a problem. The text contains a breadth of options, and the storyteller actualizes what is needed for the occasion. Outside this view, other possibilities can be envisaged. However, it does not seem necessary to assume parallel traditions (against Stoebe, 413-14).

The summons to appear before the king may reflect the technical terminology of legal proceedings (cf. Job 9:16; 13:22; Isa 59:4 — cf. Boecker, *Redeformen,* 58, n. 1 and pp. 87-89; what Boecker appears to overlook is that while storytelling and poetry need to be plausible, they may not need to be factually accurate; the situations they portray need to evoke authenticity, but they may not need to be authentic). What is surprising, however, is that it is not only Ahimelech, the accused, who is summoned, but also "all his father's house, the priests who were at Nob" (v. 11). The *bêt 'āb*, the father's house, is normally understood to extend for three or four generations; but the usage is flexible, which may explain the added precision about the priests at Nob. This summoning of all the priests is a sign that we may not have a completely normal proceeding here. The narrative is presented as a story of sacrilege — we would say of unmotivated and paranoid slaughter. It would be imprudent to use the story as a model for royal legal procedure. However, the formality of the proceedings is made clear by the narrator, who initiates the trial itself with a formal call to order (v. 12). Note the form of address, "son of Ahitub," parallel to "son of Jesse" (20:27 and 22:13). Note, too, that the call is addressed to Ahimelech alone. One accused stands for many defendants.

Saul confronts Ahimelech with the charge against him, expressed in the form of an accusing question (cf. Gen 31:30; 44:4; Exod 2:13; 17:3; 1 Sam 2:23; 26:15; Job 13:24 — Boecker, *Redeformen,* 42). The question conveys the accusation: "Why have you conspired against me, you and the son of Jesse?" Facts are arrayed to support the accusation — bread, sword, and oracle. The outcome of the conspiracy is alleged: "so that he has risen against me, to lie in wait, as he is doing today" (22:13).

Ahimelech's defense is directed against the charge of conspiracy, portraying David as a character of known loyalty (coherent with 18:20-28; 20:5, 25, less so with 18:13). At the same time, Ahimelech overlooks the instances of Saul's hostility to David. Ahimelech after all is at Nob, not at the court of Saul. The instances of hostility are private, within the confines of Saul's court. Only after the conclusion of ch. 20 does the rupture become open and public (22:1-5). Ahimelech's silence regarding David's assurances might indicate a separate tradition from 21:2-10 (NRSV, 21:1-9); other options are open, including a Davidic compiler's reluctance to foreground David's lies. Conspiracy has the advantage, for a storyteller, of more easily involving the other priests, even if it is only alleged between Ahimelech and David (22:13). So Ahimelech concludes with a plea for acquittal for himself and his father's house, alleging complete ignorance of anything that would have rendered his actions culpable (v. 15).

Saul passes sentence of death upon Ahimelech and upon his father's house (v. 16) — [II.B.3]. Saul's guard refuse the command to execute the sentence (v. 17) — [II.C.1]. The narrator does not explain the motivation behind the refusal; the narrator explains very little in this story. The involvement of the foreigner and the reference to "priests of YHWH" (v. 17, twice) and "priests" (v. 18, twice) point to a strong concern with the inviolability of the priestly person. Saul is involved in a shockingly sacrilegious act — [II.C.2]. According to v. 11, the priests were summoned with Ahimelech and "all of them came to the king." So they are at hand for Saul's sacrilege. In v. 19, Doeg's appalling action is extended to Nob. We have no other reference to this act of Saul's; similarly, we have no story of his putting Gibeonites to death (cf. 2 Sam 21:1; see Stoebe, 414-16, Hertzberg, 382-83). We are reminded of how fragmentary our knowledge is.

If the extension of the accusation from Ahimelech to his father's house is unmotivated and unjustified in the narrative, the extension of the slaughter to the whole town of Nob ("the city of the priests," v. 19) is doubly so — [III]. The terms in which the slaughter is described are those of the ban, the *herem;* every living being dies. The sacrilege is here at its most outrageous: The annihilation destined for YHWH's foes in YHWH's wars is here turned on YHWH's priests and their city by the one who was YHWH's anointed. The narrative portrays Saul in an utterly godless light. For the compiler, this is the beginning of the presentation of the open rupture in Judah between David and Saul.

Genre

There is every likelihood that this should be seen as a (→) story outline. It is a major story and is despatched in fourteen verses. Much is left undeveloped or unexplained: the accusation against the Benjaminites, the trial of Ahimelech and all the priests, the role of Doeg and the single-handed slaughter of the priests themselves and the destruction of Nob, "the city of the priests." The complicated interplay of traditions with 21:2-10 (NRSV, 21:1-9) also points to a story outline.

In 21:2-10, the trembling of Ahimelech and the prevarication of David set up a tension that overshadowed the exchanges between the two and was intensified by the mention of Doeg. In 22:6-19, the mention at the beginning of David and the forces with him sets a tension that is taken up in Saul's accusations of conspiracy. The narrative tension in both passages is not fully brought to rest until sentence is executed on Ahimelech, the priests, and the town. This is unquestionably (→) story. For Rendtorff, it is (→) historical story, noting in particular that there is no central heroic figure (Rendtorff, "Beobachtungen," 431-32). The evident bias against Saul cautions against treating the story as history.

Setting

The pro-David and anti-Saul bias of the story suggests a setting in Davidic circles. The references to the Philistine's sword, David as Saul's son-in-law, the friendship between Jonathan and David, and the background of Saul's hostility all bring the setting close to that of the compilation of the stories of David's rise to power. If the genesis of many of the stories of David and his heroes was evenings at court, or the campfire on campaigns, then the presence of the hero at the campfire or the court would be a stimulus to the story.

Meaning

Within the Davidic narratives, the function of this story can be best summarized as reflecting the situation of David's public break with Saul and Saul's public break with YHWH. David has been driven to flee Saul's court. Saul, in his suspicion of conspiracy, is led into precipitate action, a highhanded trial, and the sacrilegious killing of the priests of YHWH and their dependents. What was said in a sentence in 16:14 — "Now the spirit of the LORD departed from Saul" — is here unfolded in the telling of a story. What might have been seen, within the court of Saul, as personal antagonism and paranoia radically changes in character as it becomes here alienation from his own supporters and alienation from the priesthood of the God whose anointed he has been.

In the following narrative, Saul is to be portrayed in pursuit of David's life. That narrative is prefaced with this picture of Saul as a ruthless killer who will put to the ban even the priests of his own people.

Consequences of Open Rupture (III):
For David — Abiathar's Presence   **22:20-23**
   I. Abiathar's escape and flight to David   20-21
      A. His identity and flight   20
      B. His information for David   21
  II. Abiathar's acceptance by David   22-23
      A. David's acceptance of responsibility for the slaughter   22
      B. David's acceptance of responsibility for the safety of
         Abiathar   23

Textual Issues

22:22   Doeg: see above, v. 18.

236

Discussion

This minuscule snippet of tradition packs a single punch: the priest with the ephod is on the side of David. God and the future are with David — [I]. What is passed over in silence is remarkable: when, where, how, who, etc.? It is the reverse of what will be dwelt on in story form when Saul consults Samuel to know God's will. David has the wherewithal to inquire of God; Saul does not.

The text is attached to the story of 22:6-19; it does not have to be. The story ends with Doeg's slaughter of the priests and his destruction of the city of Nob; as it stands, this tradition is attached to it. The same tradition could equally be attached to other tellings. There is no mention of when or where this happened. It is not said who did the killing for which Saul was responsible. It is not said how Abiathar managed to escape.

The tradition is at pains to identify Abiathar as son of Ahimelech, son of Ahitub. The information he gives David is all that is needed to burden Saul with sacrilege: "that Saul had killed the priests of the LORD" (v. 21). The death of his father Ahimelech is not singled out. David's comment carries an implied reflection on Saul. David admits he knew that Doeg would tell Saul what he had seen; the implication is that Saul could be counted on to act murderously. There is an irony in the certainty with which the tradition concludes. Saul, the king, is murderously disposed toward David; Abiathar, the priest, will be safe with David. And he was — [cf. II].

Genre

The piece is a (→) short notice, a snippet of tradition, necessary to the larger narrative and unlikely to have existed on its own. As noted, it may have been associated in the tradition with the larger story of vv. 6-19, but it could have survived in association with other traditions (cf. 23:6).

Setting

The setting is difficult to pin down. The Davidic circles are one obvious possibility; circles associated with Abiathar are another.

Meaning

Following on the preceding story, the imagery is clear. Saul kills the priests of God; David protects them. It is a fearful introduction to what follows, with its mirror image in ch. 28. Saul, the killer of the priests, is bereft of communication with God; David, the protector of the priest, is assured of God's guidance.

David is about to be portrayed as a guerrilla leader, chief of a band of irregulars, living off the land — people not overly endowed with respect for life.
The Nob story gives a picture of David who tried to avoid compromising
Ahimelech (21:2-6; NRSV, 21:1-5) and had a keen sense of responsibility for
the lives of others (22:22).

The Contrast of David and Saul, of Fugitive and King

The narrative has brought out the open rupture between Saul and David, David's flight from the court of Saul, and the consequences that have ensued. David heads a military force, a threat to Saul, apparently with long-term strategies.
Saul has brought on himself the odium of priest-killing. David has benefited as
protector of the sole survivor.

As the story moves out from the court of Saul, the focus of the narrative
widens to include more of the country — the story of Keilah. Before David is to
be driven into exile from his own country, his actions within his country are delineated. The Philistines are the foe; at great risk, David delivers an Israelite
town from starvation. The story of Saul's response has multiple impacts. For
Saul, David is the foe. To destroy David, Saul will destroy an Israelite town. To
save their skins, the townsfolk will betray David.

We are not given any formal account of David's days in the wilderness;
we have a few stories. We are given this picture in which David is the deliverer,
Saul the destroyer, and the people fickle.

Contrast of David and Saul: The Keilah Story   **23:1-13**
- I. David: as deliverer of Keilah   23:1-5
  - A. Introduction: David told of the Philistine threat to Keilah   1
  - B. Consultation of YHWH   2-4
    - 1. 1st consultation   2
    - 2. Objection by David's men   3
    - 3. 2nd consultation   4
  - C. Deliverance of Keilah   5
    - 1. David and his men: successful operation   5a
    - 2. David: saved the inhabitants of Keilah   5b
- II. The ephod: now with David   6
- III. Saul: as would-be destroyer of David   7-13
  - A. Introduction: Saul told of David's presence in Keilah   7a
  - B. Reactions to this information   7b-12
    - 1. Saul's reactions   7b-8
      - a. His thought: God has given him into my hand   7b
      - b. His action: mobilization against David   8
    - 2. David's reactions   9-12
      - a. His action: call for ephod   9
      - b. His consultation of YHWH   10-12
        - 1) 1st consultation   10-11

Textual Issues

23:6 According to 22:20, Abiathar fled to David before David moved on Keilah. The LXX has Abiathar flee to David and with David go down to Keilah, ephod in hand. Unless the independence and difference of the traditions is allowed, some such emendation is needed (so: McCarter, 369; Klein, 228). Alternatively, Nowack reads: in his flight to David, he went down to Keilah, an ephod in his hand (*Bücher Samuelis,* 117). For discussion of both, see Driver, 184; see also Pisano, 207-8.

    23:7 Adjustments in Ugaritic research open up the possibility of understanding the MT *nikkar* as: God has handed him over (Stoebe, 419; Barthélemy, 208-9).

    23:11 The MT asks two questions but answers only one. The NRSV omits the first question (with 4QSam[b], cf. McCarter, 370), assuming it is a duplication from v. 12. Not without reason, Stoebe retains the MT (pp. 419-20). For the story — this is narrative not event — the question of betrayal is uppermost; God's answer that Saul will come down may be read as leading to and requiring an explicit answer to the primary question. The content of the betrayal question is the same in v. 11 and v. 12; the detail of the formulation, however, is not identical. See Pisano, 260-67.

Discussion

Verses 1-13 could easily be conceived as two relatively independent vignettes, connected perhaps by the explanatory note that the ephod, needed in both, had been brought to David with Abiathar — [II]. In vv. 1-5, David is portrayed as deliverer in Israel — [I]; in vv. 7-13, Saul is portrayed as would-be destroyer of the deliverer — [III]. There are close parallels: David is told of the threat to Keilah, and Saul is told of David's presence in Keilah. David's reaction is to consult his God. Saul's reaction is to assume God has given him David. The parallels in structure should not be taken too far. Thematically, the two passages may be independent: David as deliverer (vv. 1-5); Saul as destroyer (vv. 7-13); narratively, they are associated by Saul's being told that David had come to Keilah (v. 7). If the two traditions are treated independently, their narrative juxtaposition contrasts the deliverer (David) with the deliverer's would-be destroyer (Saul). It is appropriate to treat both together. In the narrative, together is where they are and there is nothing to suggest that they should not be.

    The narrative opens with the news brought to David of Philistine oppression. The action is more than just a passing raid. If the harvest is plundered from the threshing floors, it might be a matter of life or death for the people of Keilah.

The core of vv. 1-5, as the structure reveals, is the consultation with God (vv. 2-4). The point of the story is made in the divine response where "and save Keilah" (v. 2) goes beyond David's original questions. As we understand texts about the ephod, the procedure with it offers three responses: affirmative (yes), negative (no), and no answer (silence). The "and save Keilah" is, therefore, an interpretation from the narrator — its emphasis is all the more important coming from the storyteller. The objection raised by David's men makes clear that the odds are stacked against success: we are on the run before Saul; what chance do we have against the Philistines? So the story takes David back to God in a second consultation. God's response is again affirmative. The added interpretation, "for I will give the Philistines into your hand" (v. 4), must again be assumed to be from the narrator.

The opening of the story serves to spell out in detail what is latent in most of the Davidic stories: David succeeds because God is with him. Far from a power-hungry ambitious upstart, David is portrayed as directed by God to act as deliverer in Israel and to save the inhabitants of this town in Israel. Verse 5 underlines David's role: the military operation is carried through by David and his men (v. 5a); but it is David who *saves* Keilah (v. 5b) — [I].

The ephod is necessary to both parts of the story — [II]. David must have it to consult the LORD in vv. 2-4 and again in vv. 10-12. There is no mention of it when Abiathar's coming is reported in 20:22-23; there is no mention of Abiathar in 23:1-5. There is no suggestion in 20:22-23 that David is at Keilah. The tradition in 23:6 that Abiathar "fled to David at Keilah" may delicately indicate a complexity of the traditions that escapes us. What matters for the immediate context is given in v. 6b: an ephod came down with him. David has access to God's guidance.

The first part of the story portrayed David as the successful deliverer of an Israelite town. Now vv. 7-13 place Saul in brutal contrast: he seeks to destroy the deliverer — [III]. The contrast is emphasized ironically: Saul interprets the event as God's having given David into his power. On the other hand, v. 9a indicates that David had informants or sympathizers presumably close enough to Saul to give advance notice of Saul's plans. Not everyone, however, is sympathetic to David; despite their deliverance, the inhabitants of Keilah will surrender David to Saul (v. 12).

There is a marked contrast in the passage between Saul's assumption about God's action (v. 7b) and the divine guidance given David (vv. 9-12; see the textual note above). David seeks and is given a guidance that, in the narrative, Saul does not even seek. In the narrative's portrayal, God is clearly on the side of David. The fact that David explicitly calls for Abiathar and the ephod, which passed unmentioned in vv. 2-4, indicates the possibility of an independent existence for these two stories; an indication of shift of emphasis is equally possible.

Thanks to the information gained from God, David and his men, now 600, are safely on the move again. Saul gives up the expedition against them.

This is the first report of a public attempt on Saul's part to attack David, after his establishment as leader of a band of irregulars. As such, it sets a pattern for what is to come.

Genre

The passage is best understood as a (→) story or (→) story outline. The possibilities are there for considerable expansion by a storyteller: the nature of the Philistine threat, the details of the objection by David's men, the military tactics of the operation, Saul's assumptions about God's plan, David's reflections on betrayal by the people of Keilah, etc. What the text offers are the barest details of an outline. What the initial verses make clear is that David saved Keilah under God's guidance.

As story or story outline, there is adequate scope for narrative tension — although its focus is narrowed to each of the two main parts rather than extending to the passage as a whole. In the first, there is the tension of pitting David's faith against the Philistines' military might. In the second, there is the tension of Saul's assumption ("God has given him into my hand") and the narrative's confidence that God is on David's side. The whole is brought to equilibrium with God's information to David, David's departure, and Saul's abandoning the expedition.

Setting

The setting is most likely to have been in Davidic circles. The emphasis on the divine guidance sought through the ephod allows for interest from the priestly circles associated with Abiathar. The interest in Abiathar and the ephod, however, is subsidiary rather than dominant.

Meaning

The immediate meaning of vv. 1-5 is clear: David saved Keilah under God's guidance. It is the only case given of David's action within Israel to the benefit of an Israelite town. We may be expected to conclude from it that, after being forced to flee Saul's court, David and his guerrillas acted as delivering saviors within Israel. The voices to the contrary are few. A lawyer for David might argue from this text; lawyers for the opposition might make a different case.

In conjunction with vv. 1-5, vv. 7-13 contrast David the deliverer with Saul the destroyer of deliverance. These latter verses highlight Saul's desire to destroy David and the protection given David, both by sympathizers (v. 9) and by God (vv. 10-12).

241

Whether the passages are taken separately or together, divine guidance through the ephod is central to both vv. 1-5 and vv. 7-13. What is happening in these texts of oracular divination (cf. 1 Sam 30:7-8; 2 Sam 2:1; 5:19, 23) is the interpretation of David's actions as the obedient and courageous following of God's guidance and, at the same time, the insistence on God's support of David in his actions. The need for such explicit statement is clear; David's actions were susceptible to a quite different interpretation, involving ambition and bloodshed. They were interpreted in this way by some of his contemporaries — the examples preserved for us are Shimei ben Gera (2 Sam 16:7-8) and proba bly Sheba ben Bichri (2 Sam 20:1).

God's will has been in the background during the private conflicts that drove David from Saul's court. In this first presentation of public conflict between the armed camps of David and Saul, it is all the more necessary to place David's position in a clear light: he is Israel's deliverer; he is YHWH's instrument; YHWH is with him. This sets the tone for the episodes to follow. David is on the increase; Saul is on the decrease.

David: Innocence of Bloodshed and
Unexpected Commendation

Once we have recognized the level of sophistication running in the structuring of these traditions, it will come as no surprise to realize that long stretches of the text are carefully structured in what follows. This will be evidently the case in chs. 28–31; it is also the case here in 23:14–26:25. At issue: David's innocence of bloodshed and the commendation offered David by Saul, by Abigail, and by Saul again. These two are "final commendations" for Saul, who will die in battle on Mt. Gilboa; as such they are all the more remarkable. The two final commendations from Saul form an inclusion around the forward-looking commendation from Abigail.

The clue to the structure of the present text is offered by the presence of the Ziphite pledge to betray David as early in the text as 23:19-24a. The offer is not taken up until ch. 26. Details will be discussed below. It is enough to note here that this is the case and that the story of Saul's being spared in the cave (ch. 24) and the story of David's being spared bloodshed in the case of Nabal (ch. 25) are both sandwiched in the envelope between the Ziphite pledge (23:19-24a) and Saul's action on it (ch. 26).

Once this has been seen, the meaning of the text in its structural layout is clear: it demonstrates beyond all doubt the implacable hostility of Saul for David. Between the first foreshadowing of the Ziphite betrayal of David (23:19-24a) and Saul's move to implement it (ch. 26), it is made abundantly clear to Saul (ch. 24) and to the audience (ch. 25) that David will not take the life of Saul, the anointed, and that David is deeply grateful not to be forced to shed blood. According to this composition, Shimei ben Gera is wrong; according to this, the "man of blood" is Saul.

With this structure recognized in 23:19–26:25, its beginnings can be traced back to 23:14. Verses 14-15 portray the state of the two adversarial parties. David and his men are in the wilderness. Saul is in daily pursuit of David. David was in the Wilderness of Ziph, at Horesh. It was there that Jonathan came to pledge his support. It was there that the Ziphites claimed David could be found and would be surrendered by them to Saul.

In stark contrast to this implacable hostility of Saul's, the aspect of commendation makes this section the grand finale of the Saul-David conflict. In what follows, Saul will die (chs. 28–31) and David will fight a long civil war with his heirs to take over his kingdom (2 Sam 2–5; cf. esp. 3:1). After the two encounters here (chs. 24 and 26), Saul and David will not meet again. The structure of the section (23:19–26:25) is determined by issues of both composition and content. Content can lead us too easily to put emphasis on David's innocence of murderous intent, with attention sidetracked onto the parallels between chs. 24 and 26. Content, however, has both chapters conclude with Saul's commendation of David. Saul says that David will be king of Israel (24:21; NRSV, 24:20). Saul blesses David, with assurance of success (26:25). The conflict has ended; Saul has capitulated. As these texts portray the conflict, Saul has not succumbed to superior force or military skill; Saul has succumbed to superior goodness.

This aspect of content has been reinforced by the compositional structure. The report of Samuel's death is hardly haphazard or simply a necessity in view of ch. 28. Samuel anointed David to replace Saul. With Saul proclaiming David as future king of Israel (24:21; NRSV, 24:20), Samuel's work is done; he is no longer needed (25:1). Two further pointers can be seen in the structure of the narrative. First, the report of Samuel's death and burial is the prelude to the story of Abigail and Nabal, at Carmel. So too, as postlude, the report of David's marriages is appended to the story. David is established independently, no longer dependent on Saul. Second, the commendations from Saul, which bring an era to an end, surround a different commendation that opens up an era to come. Abigail commends David for refraining from vengeance and points to a future when God will have made David "prince over Israel" (25:30). The story points to a watershed, not too far into the future.

This overarching structure does not greatly affect the individual components of the text. What it reveals is the narrative artistry that can be seen in the composition of the present text. Note the claim: "can be seen." It is a claim that can be made by the modern interpreter. The signals are there in the present text. The nature of the original materials does not take away the artistry of the composition of the present text into which they have been shaped.

Readers will recognize that this discussion reflects a shift from exclusiveness to inclusiveness in the paradigms dominant in biblical studies. Until recently, the dominant paradigm saw the exclusive business of scholarship as concern with the origins and historical value of traditions. More recently, a shift in paradigms has been occurring, making room in scholarship for concern with the meaning of the biblical text that has been forged from these traditions. The reasons for this shift are complex; their discussion is not appropriate here. It is appropriate to insist on the inclusive aspect: concern for the present text cannot dismiss concern for its origins and historical value; neither can the latter dismiss the former.

Confronted with two traditions focused on one theme — chs. 24 and 26 focused on Saul's life in David's hands — the older paradigm demanded to know which version was original and which the imitation. In this case, for example, Klaus Koch sees ch. 26 as "a later stage of the tale" (*Growth*, 143) while for McCarter "we must regard 23:14–24:23 as a tendentiously fashioned equivalent to 26:1-25" (p. 387). Others seek to explain the presence of both traditions on grounds that are extraneous to the meaning of the larger narrative itself. For example, Hertzberg points to "remarkable differences in places and events" (p. 207); similarly, for Stoebe two independent formulations of the same tradition were associated by piety with different localities, allowing for a triad of meetings in chs. 24–25–26 (pp. 430-31). Note that Alfons Schulz appeals to the "folkloric triad" for chs. 23–24 (Saul's attempts to apprehend David: at Keilah, at Maon, and at En-gedi; "Narrative Art," 143. Schulz does not integrate ch. 26 with these).

In these treatments, the concern with original traditions (whether in the foreground or the background) excludes attention to and concern with the composition of the text. The narrative composition sandwiches chs. 24 and 25 between the Ziphite promise of betrayal and Saul's action on it. Scholarship has trained us to be alert to original traditions and their impact. The narrative here challenges us to find meaning in the composition that has been forged from these traditions.

The structure of this section may be represented as follows.

Commendation of the Innocent David   **23:14–26:25**
- I. Introductory indications   23:14-24a
  - A. State of the adversaries   14-15
  - B. State of their support   16-24a
    - 1. Jonathan: pledge to support David after Saul   16-18
    - 2. Ziphites: pledge to surrender David to Saul   19-24a
- II. Commendation of (innocent) David   23:24b–26:25
  - A. By Saul — David as future king:
    cave story   23:24b–24:23 (NRSV, 24:22)
  - B. By Abigail — David as future leader:
    Carmel story   25:1-44
  - C. By Saul — David as blessed and successful:
    camp story   26:1-25

It is appropriate to look at these sections in detail.

Introductory Indications   **23:14-24a**
- I. State of the adversaries   14-15
  - A. Location: David — various places of flight   14a
  - B. State: contrast of activities   14b-15a
    - 1. Saul: daily pursuit of David unsuccessful   14b
    - 2. David: aware of this pursuit   15a
  - C. Location: David — at Horesh, in the wilderness
    of Ziph   15b

II. State of their support   16-24a
  A. Jonathan: pledge to support David after Saul   16-18
    1. Location: Jonathan comes to David at Horesh   16a
    2. Jonathan's support for David   16b-18a
      a. Expressed generally   16b
      b. Unfolded specifically   17
      c. Pledged in covenant   18a
    3. Location: David remains and Jonathan returns   18b
  B. Ziphites: pledge to surrender David to Saul   19-24a
    1. Location: Ziphites come to Saul at Gibeah   19a
    2. Pledge to surrender David to Saul   19b-23
      a. Offer by Ziphites to Saul   19b-20
        1) Concerning location of David   19b
        2) Concerning offer of surrender to Saul 20
      b. Response of Saul to Ziphites   21-23
        1) Grateful blessing   21
        2) David's location: more precision requested 22-23a
        3) Promise of rigorous pursuit   23b
    3. Location: Ziphites went to Ziph ahead of Saul   24a

Discussion

It is clear that the issue of David's willingness to shed blood is central to the stories of chs. 24, 25, and 26. Less clear is the question whether this concern extends further back in the text and, if so, how far.

Against the paragraphing of the NRSV, it is widely recognized that 23:14 belongs with what follows. While the statement that "God did not give him into his hand" (v. 14) may be seen as echoing Saul's false assumption in v. 7, the primary signal is given in v. 13: Saul "gave up the expedition." What was begun in vv. 7-8 is at an end. The signal of a new beginning is given in v. 14: "Saul sought him every day." The two verbs are different, but the core difference is between giving up pursuit (v. 13) and pursuing constantly (v. 14). While these two can be reconciled, they do not belong together in the concluding pair of verses of the same passage.

Bridging the two passages, on the other hand, is the language of David being "surrendered" to Saul; it occurs twice in v. 12 and again in v. 20. What this points to as a signal is the commonality of theme across these traditions. Saul has hounded David out of his court. With the rupture in the open, Saul has slaughtered priests accused of supporting David while David has protected the survivor. David has delivered Keilah; Saul has sought to destroy the deliverer. God is helping David with information; God is not giving David into Saul's hand. Saul is in pursuit of David constantly (v. 14); David is remaining out of reach in the remoteness of the wilderness. The "man of blood" is Saul. On the defensive is David. At least, that is the picture these traditions present — [I].

The material in 23:1-13, 14-15, 16-24a prepares the way for the major stories that follow.

In 23:14, the narrative summarizes succinctly what is to come, in much the same way as 1 Sam 18:14-16 summarized what was to come in the narrative composition of David's rise to power in Israel (David had success; Saul was in awe; all Israel and Judah loved David). David had success because "the LORD was with him" (18:14). So here. David will be in the fastnesses of the wilderness (23:14a). Saul will pursue him constantly (v. 14b). God will not give David into Saul's hand (v. 14b; cf. Hertzberg, 193). David is at Horesh in the Wilderness of Ziph (v. 15). It is a stative sentence (with Stoebe, 424). It gives David's situation, his whereabouts for the future text. Jonathan will come to him there. The Ziphites will report that he is there. He will move to Maon, En-gedi, and Paran. But it will be in the Wilderness of Ziph that, at the end, he has the final confrontation with Saul, a confrontation that ends in his compulsion to quit the country.

The narrative moves from Saul and David to their supporters; David's support from Jonathan — [II.A] — and Saul's support from some of the inhabitants of Ziph — [II.B]. This is the last reported meeting between Jonathan and David. Even with 20:14-17 in view, it is also the first time that there is any fully explicit reference by Jonathan to David's future kingship and Jonathan's own role in that future. His statement is a remarkable one. After the classic formula of encouragement, "Do not be afraid," Jonathan adds a reason: "for the hand of my father Saul shall not find you." What is the source of his confidence? Verses 24b-28 prove him right at one level; yet more than a military judgment is surely meant. The statements about the future, especially with the note that Saul knows this, could quite naturally derive from Saul's own outburst (cf. 20:31). The "I shall be second to you" need not designate a specific post, but a secondary role; nor need it be the expression of a prior agreement (cf. Stoebe, 427-28). Since it did not eventuate and is not necessary in the context, it casts doubt on any attempt to see this tradition as a later construction (against Veijola, *Ewige Dynastie*, 88-90).

With the explicit support of Saul's eldest son and heir (cf. 20:31), the text has David free of the charge of ambitiously supplanting the rightful royal house in Israel. The source of Jonathan's confidence is not given us. A covenant is made between the two and they part. David remains; Jonathan returns.

The focus shifts to Saul's supporters. Some of the Ziphites are eager to surrender David to Saul. The place of the tradition here has caused its difficulties. As we have seen above, it demands close scrutiny. What must be taken into account in the MT is Saul's command to the Ziphites: "Come back to me with sure information" (23:23). In the present text, the Ziphites do not return to Saul until 26:1 — except for Hertzberg who inserts "when they returned" into his text at the start of 23:24 (p. 192 and cf. p. 194). In my judgment, it is more credible to view 26:1 as a faint echo of these verses than to see 23:19-24a as "an expanded version of 26:1" (McCarter, 379). It is clear that ch. 24 is derived from the tradition narrated in ch. 26 (see below); the reduplication may not extend beyond the core of both stories. As the Hebrew stands, Ziphites leave in 23:24a and Ziphites are not mentioned again until 26:1.

Saul asks the Ziphites to double-check their information, be sure of where

David is and who has seen him there; they are to check out all the possible hiding places (vv. 22-23). Saul has been told how cunning David is; so the Ziphites are to do their homework thoroughly before reporting back to Saul. The problem of the text, however, is that when they come to Saul in 26:1 they have no more information to offer than they had already in 23:19. Storytellers should have little problem handling such material. Modern interpreters make adjustments. Whatever may have happened to the original traditions in organizing the present composition, the Ziphite offer is now made in ch. 23 and acted on in ch. 26.

As noted, the present text *(lectio difficilior)* sets the events of the cave story and the Carmel story (Abigail and Nabal) within the envelope of the camp (or: Ziphite) story. Our task is to ascertain whether we can find meaning in this. Given the evidence of David's innocence in both stories, but above all Saul's avowal in the cave story, Saul's continued pursuit in the Ziphite story is a measure of his implacable desire to destroy David. It offers the context for yet another proof of David's innocence.

It is not simply a matter of Saul's command for the Ziphites to return to him. The exchange in vv. 19-24a is full of fussy details (see vv. 22-23). The Ziphites are to do some serious detective work, and only then can they call in Saul and his troops. This makes no narrative sense if they are simply Saul's advance guard, going into Ziph (v. 24). Hertzberg is right to see the gap and wrong to fill it with "a brief section, at least one word" that has fallen out (p. 194). Hertzberg is also right to ask the question "Why should it stand here?" (p. 208); and his answer points in the right direction: "to show that David remains constantly exposed to Saul's pursuit, and therefore in the utmost danger" (p. 208). What the unfolding of this story in ch. 26 shows, coming after the story of the cave, is that Saul is implacably determined to destroy David. For David, exile is inevitable. What the Carmel story does, in this narrative context, is bring to the fore Abigail's insistence on David's freedom from bloodguilt — the subject of this entire section — "my lord shall have no cause of grief, or pangs of conscience, for having shed blood without cause or for having saved himself" (25:31).

At this point in the text, the Ziphites as supporters of Saul stand sharply contrasted with Jonathan as supporter of David. The son pledges his support to the future king; the father commits himself to his rival's pursuit.

Genre

The opening verses on the state of the adversaries (vv. 14-15) are (→) comment. The two following traditions on the state of their support may be described as (→) notices, as they stand in the present text, and may also be recognized as (→) story outlines.

23:14 sketches the three players involved: David in flight mode, Saul in pursuit, and God who is not on Saul's side. After the complexity of David's location in v. 14 (in strongholds, in the wilderness, in the hill country, in the Wilderness of Ziph), 23:15 focuses on Horesh, setting up what is to come. Jonathan

247

will come to David at Horesh. The Ziphites will report that he is at Horesh, on the hill of Hachilah, south of Jeshimon (23:19). When they next appear in the text, Hachilah and Jeshimon form the link to the unmentioned Horesh (26:1). The comment delineates the situation after 23:1-13. The situation depicted is unfolded in the stories that follow.

It is tempting to consign vv. 16-18 and 19-24a to the (→) notice category and leave it at that. This would be to sell them short and overlook the possibilities for their development from (→) story outlines. In the larger narrative composition, they have the specific role that has been discussed. In themselves, though, each has the potential for considerable expansion by storytellers. The tension is there to be built up: Jonathan, the heir to the throne, in the presence of David, the future king; Saul, portrayed as the would-be destroyer of Israel's hope, in the presence of those who want to betray David to him.

These are possibilities either behind the present text (as abbreviated from past storytelling) or in front of the present text (as a base for future storytelling). Within the text as it stands, vv. 16-18 are indeed a (→) notice and vv. 19-24a are a (→) notice that is also the introduction to a story that will not be told until ch. 26. To that extent, a narrative composition is quite different from the individual stories that may go to make it up.

Setting

The setting for vv. 14-15 is evidently the narrative composition. They are unlikely to have had an independent existence, but emerge as comment on the surrounding traditions.

Of the conversation between David and Michal in 2 Sam 6:20-23, the great Hugo Greßmann once remarked that "only a poet could know what the royal couple may have said to one another in their chamber" (*Schriften,* 135). Greßmann forgot two things. First, it did not happen in "their chamber"; Michal "came out to meet David" (v. 20). Second, neither Michal nor David was obliged to secrecy; either of them could have talked. Here, for vv. 16-18, there is not much time for Jonathan's telling of the story to take root before his death, nor any indication that Ziba or Mephibosheth — much less Ishbosheth — would have cultivated the tradition. The source has to be Davidic. The same circle of people who recalled the meeting of the two men (18:1, 3-4) might be also those who recalled the tradition of their parting.

The original setting for vv. 19-24a has to be sought in conjunction with the story of ch. 26. In its present form, of course, the setting is this narrative composition in which we now have it.

Meaning

Verses 14-15 not only offer a summary setting for the traditions to come; they also contribute to creating the context within which these traditions are heard.

The pursuer and the pursued are clearly identified. The later imagery is more vivid: "Against whom has the king of Israel come out? Whom do you pursue? A dead dog? A single flea?" (24:14). The message here is the same: it is Saul who is the relentless pursuer of David. In what precedes, David has just been identified as the one achieving deliverance in Israel. Verse 14 ends with the comment that God did not hand over David to Saul. Verse 15 confirms Saul's aggression and situates David in view of what is to come.

The meaning of vv. 16-18 is clear: the passage supports the legitimacy of David's succession to Saul. Much of the narrative is concerned with the theological legitimation of David's rise; these few verses climax the political legitimation. After legitimation by God in 23:1-13 comes legitimation by Jonathan, Saul's legitimate heir, in 23:16-18.

The importance of vv. 19-24a at this point in the composition is not so much in the story they introduce as in the emphasis they bring to bear on Saul's unending pursuit of David. In the narrative to come, Saul will chase David on the mountainside in Maon (23:24b-28). Saul will experience David's respect for Saul's life. The confession given him will be generous: "He said to David, 'You are more righteous than I; for you have repaid me good, whereas I have repaid you evil'" (24:17). David's eloquence to Abigail will portray himself as anything but a ruthless killer. "Blessed be your good sense, and blessed be you, who have kept me today from bloodguilt and from avenging myself by my own hand!" (25:33). Then the Ziphites return to Saul, and the betrayal promised in 23:19-24a is begun. Saul can be experienced only as ruthless and implacable.

As noted, these stories portray Saul's unrelenting pursuit of David and David's innocence of any bloodshed. However, also as noted above, an element of their content as well as the compositional structure in which they have been arranged go beyond this: these stories become the commendation of David. The stories of ch. 24 and ch. 26 relate the last encounters between Saul and David before Saul's death in battle on Mt. Gilboa. Chapter 24 has Saul acknowledge David as Israel's future king (24:21; NRSV, 24:20). Chapter 26 has Saul's last words bless David with success (26:25). In between, Abigail speaks of David as destined by God to be "prince" over Israel (*nāgîd,* 25:30).

With Saul's acknowledgment that David "shall surely be king, and that the kingdom of Israel shall be established in your hand" (24:21; NRSV, 24:20), the narrative can introduce the death and burial of Samuel. "It is as though Samuel has lingered over the narrative, waiting until even Saul has finally acknowledged the turn of destiny" (Brueggemann, 175). At the end of the Carmel story, David has taken not only Abigail as his wife but also Ahinoam of Jezreel. David has his own wives; he is not dependent on Saul, who has given Michal to Palti ben Laish. Samuel's role as protector is over. A beautiful and intelligent woman has recognized David's destiny. Wives have joined David realizing the possibility of a dynasty.

After the introductory indications, from Saul's son, Jonathan, and Saul's supporters, the Ziphites, three stories spell out these commendations of David.

Commendation by Saul — as Future King:
The Cave Story 23:24b–24:23 (NRSV, 24:22)
I. Saul in pursuit of David 23:24b-28
  A. Introduction: location of David 24b
  B. Story of the pursuit 25-28a
    1. Pursuit prepared 25
    2. Pursuit unfolded 26
    3. Pursuit abandoned 27-28a
  C. Conclusion: etiology of place name 28b
II. Saul in the power of David 24:1-23 (NRSV, 23:29–24:22)
  A. Introduction: location of David 1-2 (NRSV, 23:29–24:1)
  B. Story of Saul in the power of David 3-23a (NRSV, 2-22a)
    1. Inside the cave 3-8 (NRSV, 2-7)
     a. Introduction 3-4 (NRSV, 2-3)
      1) Saul and his men 3-4a (NRSV, 2-3a)
      2) David and his men 4b (NRSV, 3b)
     b. Episode in the cave 5-8a (NRSV, 4-7a)
      1) Incitement to David 5a (NRSV, 4a)
      2) Action by David 5b (NRSV, 4b)
      3) Remorse of David 6-8a (NRSV, 5-7a)
     c. Conclusion 8b (NRSV, 7b)
    2. Outside the cave 9-23a (NRSV, 8-22a)
     a. Speech of David 9-16 (NRSV, 8-15)
      1) Introduction 9 (NRSV, 8)
      2) Speech itself 10-16 (NRSV, 9-15)
       a) Protestation of innocence 10-12 (NRSV, 9-11)
       b) Appeal to God as judge 13-16 (NRSV, 12-15)
     b. Speech of Saul 17-22 (NRSV, 16-21)
      1) Introduction 17 (NRSV, 16)
      2) Speech itself 18-22 (NRSV, 17-21)
       a) Concerning the past 18-20 (NRSV, 17-19)
       b) Concerning the future 21-22 (NRSV, 20-21)
     c. Outcome: David's oath to Saul 23a (NRSV, 22a)
  C. Conclusion 23b (NRSV, 22b)

Discussion

An issue that has to come up early in any discussion is whether the mountain-side pursuit (23:24b-28) belongs with the cave story (ch. 24) in a single narrative. The answer is remarkably simple; it is both Yes and No. Just as the text in 23:1-13 could be treated as two separate traditions following one another in the narrative or as two traditions presented as a single story, so here the pursuit story and the cave story could be treated as two separate traditions or as parts of a single story.

Quite clearly the two episodes are not unconnected in the narrative. Just as Saul was told that "David had come to Keilah" (23:7), so in this narrative the episodes are linked by the note, "When Saul returned from following the Philistines" (24:2; NRSV, 24:1). A hint of a stronger connection is given. Saul is not said to have "stopped pursuing David" in 23:28 (despite the NRSV translation); instead, the literal Hebrew is: Saul returned from pursuing David. In 23:13, Saul gave up the expedition; the literal Hebrew is "he ceased to go out." It is a clear end. The use of "return" in both 23:28 and 24:2 (NRSV, 24:1) suggests a certain continuity, even if only as part of a redactional linkage. The two passages are now linked.

The juxtaposition of both traditions, mountainside and cave, as parts of the one story allows the contrast between Saul and David to be present, almost unmentioned, yet in the foreground of the narrative. According to the narrative, Saul is in hot pursuit of David, closing in on him, to be frustrated at the crucial moment by the Philistines. Equally according to the narrative, David is in flight from Saul, has him at his mercy, and at the crucial moment is frustrated by his own commitment not to take the life of the LORD's anointed. The story is going to end with a touching scene of reconciliation and with words from Saul that are almost unbelievable. It helps to have Saul's fierce pursuit in the recent context.

Fierce pursuit is exactly what 23:24b-28 provides — [I]. With v. 26, the two groups are on opposite sides of the mountain. The interest is on the closeness of the pursuit, with David and his troops hurrying to escape from Saul, and Saul and his troops closing in for the capture. In the interests of breathless, cliffhanging urgency, one would like to imagine the two groups just below the skyline, either side of one of those razor-like ridges dividing two wadis in the Judean desert. It need not be quite so close. The text would be adequately reflected if David and his troops were making their escape along one wadi, while his lookouts on the ridge observed the progress of Saul and his troops in the adjoining wadi. These choices have to be left to the storytellers.

Saul's return to fight the Philistines is one of the few points in these stories, apart from his death, where we see him fulfilling his royal function. It also gives a momentary pause in the narrative, before the episode at the cave, in the wilderness of En-gedi (ch. 24).

Early in any discussion reflection on the relationships between ch. 24 (the "cave in the daytime" story) and ch. 26 (the "camp in the nighttime" story) is unavoidable. There is widespread agreement that one tradition is coming to expression in both stories. That one tradition is present seems clear. Saul, in pursuit of David, is found in David's power and is spared by the man whose life he seeks; full-bodied reconciliation ensues. More and more, commentators are agreeing that the interpreter's task is to find a meaning for these stories in their context, rather than to debate their mutual dependence and age.

The version in ch. 26 is ready-made for performance. It is night. David and Abishai penetrate Saul's camp and stand over Saul's sleeping body. One spear thrust will kill him. David takes the spear, disappears into the night, and cries out from across the intervening valley. The version in ch. 24 requires a lot more work on the part of the storyteller; there is not a close fit between the deed and the drama — [cf. II]. Saul has three thousand chosen men with him as he

251

pops into the cave — surely in daytime. Why use a cave if it was night? David emerges from the cave, a bit behind Saul, and cries out to him. The storyteller has to make two aspects plausible. Saul, in broad daylight, asks the nighttime question: "Is this your voice, my son David?" (24:17 [NRSV, 24:16]; cf. 26:17). David, in broad daylight, is not seized by the three thousand who are out hunting for him. A storyteller would have to have David slip out of the cave unseen and gain a vantage point where he could not be trapped and would not be visible. Alter has Saul "blinded with tears"; but in the text the weeping comes afterwards, at the end of the verse, and the three thousand are still there to be dealt with (p. 151). Alter wrestles with the three thousand earlier (p. 148); the text does not attend to them. The biblical text reveals faithfully where it has come from; Alter reveals brilliantly where it might be taken.

Inside the cave, there is a pointer to the complexity in the telling that again leaves options open for the storyteller. David's men in the rear of the cave, seeing Saul in the light at the mouth of the cave, urge David to seize this God-given opportunity to do to his enemy Saul as it seems good to David — in a word, kill him! According to the text, David crept up sneakily and "cut off a corner of Saul's cloak" (24:5; NRSV, 24:4). The next verse is odd: "Afterward David was stricken to the heart because he had cut off a corner of Saul's cloak" (24:6; NRSV, 24:5). This is stretching credulity a bit far. The guerrilla chief has remorse over a bit of royal garment snipping. Appeal to royal mystique and the sacredness of all that is associated with the king is a distraction; the central issue is life or death, to kill or to spare. Later, David will wave the same corner of the cloak at Saul as proof of his goodness (24:12; NRSV, 24:11). The remorse is badly out of place in this context. But worse is to come. Having spared Saul's life and cut the corner off his cloak instead, David is portrayed berating his men for their wickedness in wanting to attack Saul (24:7-8; NRSV, 24:6-7). If Joab were present with a speaking role in the story (cf. 2 Sam 19:2-9; NRSV, 19:1-8), he might well have pointed out to David that the heroics were in place before the garment snipping; they were completely out of place after it. So there is more to this scene than meets the eye. Storytellers, start your imaginations! Was there a version with no incitement to kill expressed in the cave? Was the incitement to kill Saul an extra option offered by the text?

There is little point in looking for a relationship of dependence between the two tellings. It is enough that there are two tellings of one tradition, each quite capable of standing on its own. As will be emphasized under "Meaning," the involvement of both traditions in this narrative heightens the intensity of Saul's enmity toward David and makes David's move into exile utterly inevitable. Exile among the Philistines is dangerous for David's reputation as a loyal Israelite. We will look closely at this in treating chs. 28–31. For Davidic supporters, it is important that David had absolutely no choice and was forced into this exile. Reconciliation with Saul could not be trusted.

As to the episode in the cave, it is storytelling and popular storytelling at that (cf. Stoebe, 437-38). Such storytelling requires plausibility; it is unlikely that a performance had all David's band lurking in the cave or conducting a noisy debate followed by a voice vote on the issue of killing Saul or snipping his cloak. As noted above, the implausibility inside the cave lies with David's reproach to his men after he himself has done the deed for which he later takes moral credit — [II.B.1]; outside the cave, the storyteller has to deal with the major difficulty that David peaceably discourses with Saul as though the three thousand chosen troops had never been mobilized — [II.B.2].

A YHWH saying is quoted by David's men that is not preserved for us; in this respect, it is parallel to the unattested sayings quoted in 20:8; 25:30; 2 Sam 3:9-10, 18; 5:2. It has aroused a variety of views; it does not appear possible to reach a verdict. The use of a word of God, understood by soldiers in their own particular way, is quite possible — cf. Abner's military theology: "For just what the LORD has sworn to David, that will I accomplish for him" (2 Sam 3:9-10). The emphasis, in any case, is on David's thinking rather than that of his troops.

 As noted above, David's restraint is exercised after David has done the deed — not before it. The relocation of vv. 5b-6 after v. 8a (NRSV, 4b-5 after 7a) smoothes the logic, but does not make a very good link with vv. 9-16 (NRSV, 8-15) where David's remorse is not reflected at all. In the present text, David's remorse at least motivates the subsequent restraint. If vv. 5b-6 (NRSV, 4b-5) are removed, then the remainder tells a short and simple story. Saul entered a cave where David and his men were. David's men incited him to action, since Saul was now in his power. David restrained them out of respect for YHWH's anointed. So Saul went his way, unharmed and unaware of his danger, until David emerged to point it out for him. The addition of vv. 5b-6 (NRSV, 4b-5) allows for the introduction of Saul's cloak into David's speech outside the cave (v. 12; NRSV, 11) and the closer modeling of the story on ch. 26. The insertion is not perfectly smooth. As it stands, the text does not create a new and unified version of the tradition; instead, it points to a couple of ways in which the tradition might be actualized.

David's speech to Saul is remarkably aggressive. He begins his protestation of innocence by reproaching Saul for listening to slander (v. 10; NRSV, 9). This is a different picture again from the one so far provided in the stories, where Saul's jealousy has been spontaneously ignited by the evidence of David's success. The reproach permits the transition to the issue of judgment. Since David has not taken Saul's life, he relies instead upon God for judgment and vengeance. David's insistence that his hand will not be against Saul frames the proverb (v. 14; NRSV, 13). The proverb itself is susceptible to two very different applications (cf. Alter, 150). Applied to Saul, the wickedness emanating from Saul will ultimately envelop him in its own mesh. Applied to David, the implication is that Saul has nothing to fear from David's hand. Since wickedness proceeds from the wicked, from David who is innocent nothing wicked will be forthcoming (so Stoebe, 441). In either case, the emphasis at this point is on David's renunciation of personal action toward vengeance or vindication. This is confirmed both in his appeal to Saul, with its claim that David is no threat to Saul, and in his final prayer that God vindicate him against Saul (vv. 15-16; NRSV, 14-15).

The difficulty raised by Saul's introductory question — "Is that your voice?" — has already been discussed. Structurally, Saul's speech falls into two parts: concerning guilt and innocence arising from the past; concerning the future of David and of Saul's house. The former is an incredible confession. Saul's acceptance of David's innocence, "You are more righteous than I; for you have repaid me good, whereas I have repaid you evil," puts in a nutshell the Davidic verdict on the events of 1 Sam 18–31. As to the future, Saul asserts what Jonathan has already claimed Saul knew (cf. 23:17). "In a desperate instant of truth, Saul says, 'You shall be king'" (Brueggemann, 173). Saul's concern for the preservation of his descendants and his name is a natural consequence of his belief that David is to be king. Storytelling might choose not to advert to 2 Sam 21:1-14. David swore the oath; it is not referred to again! Saul goes home. David stays in the wilderness. It is a story — and it is at an end. But what an end: it signifies Saul's total capitulation before the rightness of David's cause.

Genre

Saul's pursuit of David is best classed as an (→) anecdote. Its brevity, the pungent irony, and the tension of the situation mark the treatment as anecdotal. Saul in David's power is a (→) story, but it is strongly charged by the legal tones of the speeches of both David and Saul. Once out of the cave, the story turns into two legal speeches: David's protestation of innocence and his call for judgment by God; Saul's delivery of his own judgment in David's favor and his call for David's care for his house.

Setting

The origins of the mountainside pursuit tradition we would expect to trace to the campfires of David's army. Both the military flavor and the good fortune of David exhibited in it point in this direction. Its origins need not coincide with the use to which it is now being put, a use that points to its literary setting.

A setting for the story of Saul in David's power is not easily pinpointed. The cave episode, as an independent story, could easily have circulated among David's troops, at his court, or elsewhere. The speeches that develop the episode point to more than military concerns. Concern for the innocence of David and his respect for the anointed, as well as his justification and legitimation by Saul, could all stem from the Davidic court. On the other hand, Saul's appeal for his descendants can be associated with Jonathan's appeal in 20:14-17. Both are susceptible of association with 2 Sam 9 (favorable to David) or 2 Sam 21:1-14 (not so favorable to David).

Meaning

The anecdote bears out the observation of the storyteller following the Keilah episode (23:14), and also exemplifies Jonathan's prediction, "the hand of my father Saul shall not find you" (23:17). This is an excellent example of the compositional use of traditional material (cf. Rendtorff, "Beobachtungen," 431, n. 17). The earlier picture is maintained: Saul is the aggressor; David is forced to resort to flight. But the earlier conclusion that God did not give David into Saul's hand (23:14), motivated there by the role of the divine guidance in the preceding story, cannot help but influence the interpretation of this passage too. Along with the background of Jonathan's confident assertion, this makes clear that David's escape is indeed providential — it is God's doing. Of this, the anecdote itself says not a word.

Two aspects to the story of Saul in David's power contribute to determining its meaning. One is the emphasis on the harried and pursued David who will not raise his hand against the LORD's anointed; the other is of the weeping and repentant Saul whose descendants and name David swears to protect. The two combine to demonstrate David's innocence of bloodguilt: David claims it and Saul accepts it. Beyond both is the amazing commendation of David attributed to Saul: David is righteous and will surely be king over Israel.

The text portrays David as pursued first on the mountainside and then in the wilderness of En-gedi, as refusing in the cave to act against his pursuer ("for he is the LORD's anointed"), and as having this picture of the situation openly accepted and admitted by Saul. Consequent on this, Saul's recognition of David's future kingship is a clear legitimation of his later accession to kingship over all Israel (v. 21; NRSV, 20). From a self-serving Davidic standpoint, the importance of respect for the anointed of YHWH is evident; later, David was the anointed of YHWH. From a Davidic point of view here, the less said about 2 Sam 21:1-14 the better. From a Davidic point of view, Saul's acknowledgment of David as innocent and as future king is all important.

Commendation by Abigail — as Future Leader:

Textual Issues

25:1 The MT and the LXX^L, with Targum and Vulgate, read Paran; the LXX^B reads Maon. If Paran reflects an original tradition, then we know nothing of a sojourn of David's in the Sinai peninsula and we would have no link to 25:2; this makes Maon the more acceptable reading. It is possible, of course, that the LXX^B is assimilating a different location to the better known tradition (so Stoebe, 446). Barthélemy inclines to Dhorme's suggestion of a location for Paran between southern Palestine and the Egyptian border (p. 211).

25:6 Probably to be understood as "thus [i.e., in peace and prosperity] may it be for next year," a wish for continual prosperity along with the salutation of peace to himself, his house, and all he has (see Barthélemy, 212).

25:22 The MT's text, "enemies of David," is probably a scribal correction, avoiding direct reference to David (cf. Tov, *Textual Criticism,* 272); the correction is secondary (Barthélemy, 213).

Discussion

As the earlier discussion has noted, the structure of the composition and content of the traditions coincide here to emphasize two otherwise contradictory aspects of the narrative: Saul's implacable hostility to David and Saul's unexpected commendation of David. Sandwiched between the stories of ch. 24 and ch. 26 is the Carmel story of David's encounter with Nabal and Abigail. It is a story with a strong message for the future. Nabal spurns David and dies; Abigail commends David as future "prince over Israel" and herself becomes queen.

Two traditions have been associated with this story, as prelude and postlude. The latter tradition (the wives of David) is inherently tied to the Abigail story — [Postlude]. The former tradition's connection with it is more tenuous (death and burial of Samuel) — [Prelude]. Given the tight compositional structure visible in the arrangement of these Davidic traditions, it is likely that composition has more influence on the placement of this information than does chronology or history. At the end of ch. 24, Saul confesses that David will be future king of Israel (v. 21; NRSV, 20). In ch. 25, Abigail, wife of one of Israel's landed gentry, confesses that David is future prince *(nāgîd)* over Israel. Samuel anointed David as replacement for Saul. The replacement has been recognized by Saul and will be soon by Abigail. Samuel's era is over; his job is done. David's descent into the wilderness (25:1b) appears to be a transitional link to the story to come.

Equally, as has been said, the two wives give David his independence and his house its potential foundation. Saul's withdrawal of Michal is significant only in closing off Saulide access to David's kingdom. Both prelude and postlude belong around this story, themselves enclosed by Saul's commendations in ch. 24 and ch. 26.

The story of David, Nabal, and Abigail (in order of appearance) is brilliantly told (cf. Levenson, "1 Samuel 25"). Its beginning has all the marks of classical storytelling (cf. esp. Job 1:1-3) — [I]. The note of residence at Maon while farming at Carmel suggests realism; there is also the reality that Abigail was one of David's wives. On the other hand, no attention is given to family identity beyond the personal names. The two are named and characterized; that is all. They have no need of insertion into historical families; they are individuals who encounter David. In the beginning, named and characterized, they are almost type figures; in the story of their encounter and its consequences, they become de facto type figures. So it is important that Abigail be intelligent and beautiful and that Nabal be surly and mean. It is also important to recognize the insights that honor, shame, and mediation can bring to this story (cf. Stansell, "Honor and Shame," 101-5).

The hermeneutics of suspicion have led us to wonder how stories would look had women told them. This is a story where the woman has the smart and dominant role, where her husband is the archetypal loser. We are not informed enough to know whether male or female storytellers predominated in ancient Israel (cf. 2 Sam 14's wise woman from Tekoa, apparently a professional and certainly a skillful storyteller, unknown to the king; cf. also 2 Sam 19:36 [NRSV, 19:35]; Qoh 2:8; 2 Chron 35:25). Despite Abigail's role, this does not appear as a woman's story. The dominant figure is David, the guerrilla chief, the protector, the avenger, the gracious outlaw, the king-to-be, the husband. For all that we might like it to be different, this is primarily a story about David, not about Abigail. Perhaps for those oppressed by the patriarchy of these texts this is a plus. In a story exalting the male, it is not seen as surprising or particularly out of the ordinary that a wealthy woman in the country was intelligent, proactive, able to override her husband's decisions, and diplomat enough to provide not merely wise counsel but significant political service to the future king of Israel.

Abigail defended David's future against his own vengeful instincts — a major contribution. She was not alone as a contributor among the women of early Israelite tradition. Sarah and Rebekah are portrayed as deciding the course of election in Israel (Isaac over Ishmael, Gen 21; Jacob over Esau, Gen 27). Tamar is celebrated defending her own rights against the patriarch Judah (Gen 38). Deborah and Jael delivered Israel from twenty years' cruel oppression (Judg 4–5). Tamar, daughter of David, is portrayed with an integrity and moral strength totally lacking in the crown prince Amnon (2 Sam 13). A wise woman's action saved a city in Israel (2 Sam 20). Bathsheba is portrayed as instrumental in winning the throne of Israel for her son (1 Kgs 1). Jezebel, a king's daughter as well as a king's wife, wielded power and died with pride (1 Kgs 18:4; 19:1-3; 21:5-15; 2 Kgs 9:30-34). A wealthy woman in the country, at Shunem, befriended Elisha and proved more insightful than he (2 Kgs 4). Queen Athaliah reigned in Jerusalem for more than six years and was no better but also no worse than most of her male counterparts (2 Kgs 11). Deborah was a prophetess (Judg 4:4); Isaiah's child was born to a prophetess (Isa 8:3); Huldah was a prophetess (2 Kgs 22:14). For all of its patriarchy — and ours — Israel was not lacking in women of wisdom and action, some of whom were remembered in its texts. Abigail was one of such women and is remembered in this text. Yet this is not her story; it is David's — he begins it, its encounters are with him, he ends it.

The introduction begins with time and place. The place: a property in Carmel. The time: shearing of the sheep. The two main characters are presented chiastically: Nabal and Abigail; she is intelligent and beautiful and he is surly and mean. The story will concern their behavior toward David and its consequences for their lives. It is also a story that will illustrate not so much the character as rather the destiny of David. In this regard, the overall structure of the story is important. After the introduction, the story of the encounter falls into three sections: Nabal's encounter with David (although they never meet directly) — [II.A]; Abigail's encounter with David — [II.B]; the consequences for Nabal and Abigail respectively — [II.C]. The consequences for David and the revelation of his destiny transpire during his encounter with Abigail. Within the complexity of the chapter, this structure is clear.

David's request triggers the encounter with Nabal. Ten of David's young men are commissioned to take a message to Nabal in David's name. The message consists of a formal greeting, a motivation for the request, and then the request itself, couched in general terms. The greeting is almost fulsome; "peace" (šālôm) occurs four times in the context — the "greeting" in David's name

(v. 5), and the wishes of peace for Nabal himself, his house, and all that he has (v. 6). It may reflect the rhetoric expected of a protection racketeer; it may anticipate and adumbrate the movement of the story; it may do both. In the light of what is to come, it may be prudent for the narrator to associate David from the outset with the blessings of peace and prosperity.

The request, with which the message is to conclude, is given a twofold motivation: the implication of services rendered, and the festive nature of the shearing season. There is an almost irresistible temptation to probe the stories concerning this period in David's career for indications of the historical reality. Did he and his band constitute some sort of loose tribal unit, effectively protecting the southern flanks of Judah from the incursions of hostile marauders? Or were they more of an outlaw band, living off the land, extorting provisions in return for so-called protection (discussed by Stoebe, 455-56)? It is a highly dubious procedure to use this story as a source for historical inquiry. Clearly, in the terms of the story, David is freedom fighter and protector, not freebooter and extortioner (cf. vv. 15-16). But this is a story, not a historical report. It is told from a standpoint favorable to David, and probably from the period when David was already established as king. It has its own point to make and is hardly a suitable quarry for historical information.

The request is for whatever Nabal is able to give; the context suggests that Nabal is well enough placed to be able to respond generously. It is important to note that the request ends on a note of personal reference to David (v. 8b). Minor detail as it is, it points to the structuring of the story around the responses to the figure of David.

Nabal's response remains on the same plane with the figure of David: Who is David? Who is the son of Jesse? (v. 10). It is a distancing move: not my son but Jesse's (note: the narrative has not mentioned Jesse). Who is David? The question is not directly addressed by the story, but it is present at all times. Abigail's answer: David is the future prince over Israel. The structure's answer: David is the touchstone of future destiny. Nabal's description of the background, while part of the storytelling, suggests troubled times, a time in which David might not have found it difficult to recruit his 400-600 men.

Nabal asked no questions. Neither does David — just a simple command, "Every man strap on his sword!" The division of forces may reflect David's standard tactics (cf. 30:23-25) or, with round numbers involved, it may be a matter of narrative convention (with 30:9-10 as a possible origin).

Abigail's encounter with David begins with the report to Abigail of David's request and its rejection by Nabal. The economy of style is deft. The request and its rejection receive a verb each; they are already known to the audience — they have been told. Instead, the occasion is taken to confirm the positive picture of David and his men, and to extend it explicitly in terms of the protection they afforded (vv. 15-16). This serves to balance the increasingly explicit statement of the danger that now threatens, and that motivates the young man's exhortation to Abigail to act. At the same time as the threat is spoken of, Nabal, the cause of it all, is characterized as a "son of Belial," a worthless fellow (the NRSV's "ill-natured" here and in v. 25 is a trifle polite; cf. 1 Sam 2:12; 10:27; 2 Sam 16:7; 20:1; 23:6). It is important for the narrative that, at this

259

stage when "evil is determined," when bloodshed threatens, the cause of it should be characterized as a worthless fellow, one of those in the camp opposed to God.

Abigail's response is the opposite of Nabal's. She puts together the necessary provisions, on a somewhat more generous scale than Ziba later (2 Sam 16:1; cf. also 1 Sam 17:17-18; 2 Sam 17:28-29). The gifts precede; she follows. The same strategy was used by Jacob in his encounter with Esau (Gen 32:13-21); it is common sense. The storyteller retards the narrative a moment, in sketching the approach of the two parties (the NRSV's "as she rode" correctly reflects the Hebrew syntax; no progression in the narrative is intended; cf. 1 Sam 1:12; 10:9; 17:48; 2 Sam 6:16). As the two parties approach the critical moment of this encounter, the text spells out in full detail, for the first time, the nature of the impending threat. Verse 21 is an example in Hebrew of the context demanding a pluperfect translation; cf. NAB, "David had just been saying," which catches the sense well (NRSV less vividly, "Now David had said"). The attitude and intention attributed to David make clear that the punitive raid on Nabal's house is to be one of total destruction (v. 22). It is brilliantly situated here, directly before Abigail's speech of appeasement that successfully averts the disaster. The magnitude of the potential bloodshed motivates David's gratitude in being prevented from it (vv. 32-34); it provides the background of urgency for Abigail's speech.

With this speech, the story reaches its high point. Far from being a piece of typical garrulousness (so, with unusual insensitivity, Budde, *Bücher Samuel*, 166), it is carefully and logically constructed. Close attention has to be paid to the syntactical structure, especially the relationship of main clauses to subordinate clauses. To reduce this exchange to vv. 27 and 35 (so Veijola, *Ewige Dynastie*, 47-54) would be to eviscerate the story unmercifully and unnecessarily (see discussion below). For Abigail's prostration, as a gesture of respect, cf. 2 Kgs 4:37 and also Gen 33:3.

Abigail's speech falls into two clear parts: first, concerning the offense that has been given to David; second, concerning the future that awaits David. She begins with a plea to be heard. In seeking to take upon herself the responsibility, she ensures that she has a right to be heard. The Hebrew ʿāwôn, translated "guilt" by the NRSV, involves the whole semantic field of crime-guilt-punishment. The key request is expressed by a prohibitive: "do not take seriously" (v. 25). Nabal is again characterized as a "man of Belial"; he is excused responsibility on the grounds that gross folly (nĕbālâ) is so inherent in his nature that it is reflected in his name (nābāl; cf. Barr, "Symbolism of Names," 21-28). After having claimed the responsibility, Abigail excuses herself on the ground that she was unaware of the request.

Having successfully insinuated excuses for what has happened, the storyteller has Abigail utter a prayer on David's behalf. The motivation precedes the prayer itself. Skillfully, it presumes what Abigail is in fact pleading for: restraint from the shedding of blood. God is credited with restraining David from bloodshed and vengeance. The prayer itself strikes at the roots of David's motivation for the punitive action, i.e., to make an example of Nabal. In praying that David's enemies, those who wish him evil, may be as Nabal, the implication is that Nabal has already been made an example of. At one level, this may refer to the folly recognized in him, characterized by his name. At another, the text subtly reflects the end of the story (Hertzberg, a little clumsily: Abigail "represents the prophetic voice," 203). Further, at a third level, those who wish David evil include Saul, so he too is drawn into the circle of, or under the condemnation of, folly *(nĕbālâ)*.

Finally, the gift of provisions is presented, and a plea for forgiveness uttered. The mention of forgiveness has been held back until now. It is requested for herself and motivated by the assurance that God will provide a sure house for David. This prophetic assurance is in turn motivated by the assertion that David is fighting YHWH's wars and so cannot fall into evil. This again strikes at the root of David's punitive motivation: God will establish David; there is no reason for him to bring evil upon himself. The reference to the sure house *(bayit ne'ĕmān)* that God will make for David (cf. 2 Sam 7:16; also 1 Kgs 11:38; 1 Sam 2:35) provides the transition to the concern with David's future. But as motivating Abigail's request for forgiveness, it logically belongs with what precedes. It does not have to depend on any other occurrence; it is what every king wants for his kingdom (cf. Saul to Jonathan, 1 Sam 20:31).

The concern for the future is introduced by the condition, "if anyone should rise up to pursue you and to seek your life" (v. 29). The assurance of YHWH's protection is exquisitely expressed. The narrator, while having Abigail speak of the future, is surely looking also into the past. It is Saul who has pursued David and sought his life — particularly eloquent in the singular of the Hebrew idiom, "if a man should arise" *(wayyāqom 'ādām)*. The image of the hollow of a sling *(kap haqqālaʿ)* directly evokes the association with YHWH's protection of David against the Philistine Goliath.

Looking further to the future, for the first time reference is made to a word of YHWH related to David's ultimate destiny as prince *(nāgîd)* over Israel (cf. 2 Sam 3:9-10, 18; 5:2), and this serves to introduce the final plea to avoid bloodshed. The future ruler *(nāgîd)* should not be burdened by needless bloodshed or by the taking of vengeance. This is the exact accusation that David's supporters needed to refute: that he was a man burdened by bloodguilt. Shimei ben Gera of the house of Saul later gives voice to this accusation: "Murderer! Scoundrel! On you the LORD has avenged all the blood [Heb.; NRSV, on all of you the blood] of the house of Saul, in whose place you have reigned. . . . You are a man of blood" (2 Sam 16:7-8). Here, the speech has Abigail undermine this accusation before it is even voiced. Her speech ends with a plea on her own behalf.

The speech is superbly constructed in its movement from the overlooking of Nabal's offense to the protecting of David from the burden of bloodshed. It is to this last aspect that David's reply is initially addressed, giving thanks both to YHWH and to Abigail, and not hesitating to stress the seriousness of the danger that has just been avoided. Then, in accepting the provisions, David grants the forgiveness that Abigail had requested.

The final section of the story moves swiftly to its end. It must not be overlooked, for it completes the story's structure. Nabal and Abigail have each encountered David. Each has responded to that encounter according to their nature, he churlishly and she intelligently. Now the consequences of these encounters are told. Nabal dies, struck by YHWH. Abigail becomes David's wife.

Where David's courting of Abigail is concerned, the Hebrew does not reveal any of the eloquence we might hope for, but it does suggest more than mere royal command. The NRSV's "Then David sent and wooed Abigail, to make her his wife" is a smooth rendering of some jerky Hebrew. Represented more literally, it says: "And David sent and spoke concerning Abigail, to take her to him to wife" (JPS; v. 39b). Coming to Abigail at Carmel, David's messengers say to her: David has sent us to you to take you to him to wife (v. 40b). Two verses describe her reaction — an elegant response and a rapid organization of the party that returns with David's messengers — and her becoming his wife (vv. 41-42). Is this greatly different from David's treatment of Bathsheba, then still a married woman: So David sent messengers, and they took her, and she came to him, and he lay with her (2 Sam 11:4aα)? In terms of the courteous language we would wish to see here winning a woman's consent, no, certainly not. The added attention given to the proposal — the "speaking" for or concerning Abigail — does point to something more than a royal summons (cf. Song 8:8). It would be the storyteller's task to give this appropriate expression.

Genre

There is theology here, politics here, perhaps even history here, but above all this is a (→) story. It is a story told with every possible invitation offered to a first-rate storyteller. With the wide horizons of its vision, it is in a class of its own over against the other stories of David's flight; its only competition is, perhaps, 1 Sam 26. Yet it has in common with these Davidic stories a theological understanding and probably a political aim in the portrayal of David's rise.

Setting

The presence of Abigail at David's court would be cause enough for the story of her wooing to be sung. But this is no simple hearthside story. Its concern with the far wider issue of bloodshed and the story's obvious looking forward to David's establishment as king point to a setting not only at David's court but in a time when his kingship was contested. It may be that stories like 1 Sam 25, 1 Sam 26, and 2 Sam 3:6–4:12 were the first creative stirrings from which a story of David's rise began. A setting among, or influenced by, the wise counselors of the royal court is not to be overlooked. Such figures are central to the Stories of David's Middle Years (2 Sam 11–20) and are likely to have played a role in the shaping of 1 Sam 26. Their influence is likely here as well.

Whatever the original context of this story, its literary setting now within the narrative of David's rise to power is apt. It provides a chiaroscuro counterpart to Saul, steeped in the blood of the priests (ch. 22) and stubborn in vengeful pursuit of David (ch. 23). Before his encounter with Saul in ch. 26 and before the extensive narrative leading up to Saul's death, this story depicts David as acutely aware of the danger of being guilty of bloodshed and as emerging from the Nabal experience profoundly opposed to the shedding of blood or the taking of vengeance.

Meaning

It is difficult to see how a story so profoundly thought through could be concerned simply with how David found a wife, who and what sort of a wife she was (against Stoebe, 454). Nor is the compiler simply concerned with preventing David taking matters into his own hand and becoming master of his own fate instead of letting it be guided by the LORD (against Hertzberg, 204).

The meaning is conveyed in two ways: the structure of the story carries it and the speeches give it expression. The structure of the story portrays the different responses of Nabal and Abigail to their encounters with David and the very different consequences that result. The emphasis on the avoidance of bloodshed in Abigail's speech bears this out in its own way. The conclusion forces itself on the reader that these two, Nabal and Abigail, are type figures. Those who resist and reject David involve themselves in folly (so Nabal); God will return their evildoing upon their own heads (cf. v. 39). As was Nabal's fate, so will the fate of all David's enemies be (cf. v. 26). We might think of Saul and Abner and Ishbosheth; or of Absalom and Sheba ben Bichri later. Those, however, who respond graciously to David, receive him, and bless him will in their turn be richly rewarded (so Abigail).

This structural theme of fate as determined by one's behavior toward David is closely related to the theme of the avoidance of bloodshed. YHWH brings about a person's fate; there is no need for David to do so. Behind the insistence in Abigail's speech, we can hear the shrill accusing cry of Shimei to David, "You are a man of blood!" (2 Sam 16:8). If David was concerned to spare Nabal — if he could at least be prevailed on to spare him — how much less likely was he to shed the blood of important figures like Saul and his house. There was no need for David to have shed blood, for his protection was from God.

Commendation by Saul — as Blessed and Successful: The Camp Story 26:1-25

I. Introduction: Saul in pursuit of David	1-4
A. Arrival of the Ziphites with information	1
B. Saul's expedition and encampment	2-3a
C. David's whereabouts and awareness	3b-4
II. The story proper: David spares Saul	4-25
A. Preparation	4-5
1. Remote: sending out spies	4
2. Proximate: approach to camp of the sleeping Saul	5

Discussion

In all likelihood, this story had an existence of its own before it was incorporated into the larger narrative where we have it now. The preparation for it in 23:19-24a is not properly integrated with the story as we have it here. Saul sends the Ziphites back to "find out exactly where he is and who has seen him there . . . and come back to me with sure information" (23:22-23). There is no suggestion in ch. 26 of the Ziphites returning to Saul with more exact information; no more is said than was said in ch. 23.

This observation throws light on three significant areas. First, the careful compositional structure. The move from 23:19-24a to ch. 26 is not controlled by the flow of remembered events: Saul wanted more precise information, so the Ziphites were sent back home to gather it. The information available in 23:19-24a is basically the same as the information available in ch. 26. Instead, 23:19-24a sets up the image of Saul the pursuer and, at the same time, acts as the introduction to a narrative sequence that will end with ch. 26.

Second, the social climate of the times. This tradition about the Ziphites — almost buried within the larger tradition of how David had Saul at his mercy and spared his life — brings home the reality of opposition to David within Judah. There were those out there who wanted David dead. We risk seeing Saul as king by prophetic anointing. Whatever Samuel's role, Saul was made king by popular acclamation and popular support (cf. 10:24b and 11:15). Support for Saul was still out there, to be reckoned with. The earlier text's programmatic statement, "all Israel and Judah loved David" (18:16), is a claim made by David's supporters. The Ziphites and figures like Nabal and Shimei remind us that dissenting voices existed. The text does not tell us whether the Ziphites felt uneasy and mistrustful about the presence of an armed force in their area — the Nabal story gives them indirect justification — or whether it was a matter of their loyalty to Saul, the king. Whatever the cause, it is an initial pointer to the troubles later in David's reign.

Third, the situation of the compilers who shaped this narrative. It is extremely difficult to date biblical text or situate it adequately in society. This difficulty gives added interest to the dissonance between the request in the introduction (23:19-24a) — "find out exactly where he is and who has seen him there . . . and come back to me with sure information" — and the failure to fulfill this request in ch. 26. The compilers report the request and do not report an answer. Apparently, they are not close enough to the time of events to be able to find out what the answer should have been. At the same time, these compilers who have asked the question do not invent the answer; there appears to be a respect for the narrative tradition that does not allow for fictive invention. It would seem that the compilers were not close enough to the events to ascertain what the Ziphites would have learned; they are not distanced enough from the tradition to invent as fiction the information they did not have. The introduction and the story both have their respective role to play within the structure of the larger narrative: the introduction portrays Saul as pursuer and the Ziphites as hostile; the story portrays David as unwilling to kill and Saul as commending David before they part permanently.

This is not simply a story of pursuer and pursued, as for example 23:24b-28. Nor is it a story of chance confrontation, as for example ch. 24. As told, this story moves a stage beyond its predecessors. The introduction sets up the preliminaries. Brought information, Saul's force camps in the area where David is reported to be ("on the hill of Hachilah," vv. 1, 3). We do not know exactly where David was ("in the wilderness"); apparently David did not know exactly where Saul was, but he was aware of Saul's arrival — [I].

The story proper starts with David sending out spies, moving in on Saul's camp, and even observing precisely where Saul was sleeping — [II.A]. This information is repeated in vv. 5 and 7; v. 7 specifies that it was night and that Saul was asleep. A storyteller might stress that, before night fell, what David saw in v. 5 was the layout of the camp, the "place" where Saul slept, with the army camped around him.

The story then moves in two stages: inside Saul's camp — [II.B.1] — and outside it — [II.B.2]. The first allows for the demonstration of David's refusal to kill the LORD's anointed. The second allows for both an insistence on David's innocence and for Saul's final commendation and blessing of David.

This story holds a challenge, both for its hearers or readers and for its storytellers. The parallel story in ch. 24 is quite different. There Saul walked in on David's territory (24:4; NRSV, 24:3). There, following the present text, David's men urged him against Saul, David approached Saul stealthily, and then David was stricken to the heart (24:5-6; NRSV, 24:4-5). The problems at issue were discussed in ch. 24 and need not be repeated here. That Saul walked in on David's territory is unproblematic. That David was urged against Saul is clear, although its context may be problematic. That David was "stricken to the heart" is equally clear, but its context is quite uncertain. The present text says because he had cut off a corner of Saul's cloak. The context suggests because he had entertained the thought of killing Saul.

The story of ch. 26 is quite different. David intrudes on Saul's territory, his camp. No mention whatsoever is made of David's being repentant or "stricken to the heart." The challenge of the story: Why did David risk his life penetrating Saul's camp by night and putting himself at risk in the middle of Saul's army? Certainly not with a view to killing Saul. That may have been Abishai's intention; in the story, it certainly cannot be David's, for two reasons. First, the narrative so far has been insistent that Saul is the aggressor and David the innocent victim (cf. esp. ch. 24). Second, and paramount for the telling of the story, we know and all Israel knew that Saul died in battle on Mount Gilboa. Why then did the story have David risk his life entering Saul's camp at night? Certainly not to kill Saul. Instead, it has David risk his life to demonstrate his innocence and, within the story, to receive Saul's blessing and commendation. The challenge of the story is to make this plausible.

In the context of chs. 24 and 26, we need to recognize how inauspicious a start to a royal reign it would have been to have killed a king who crept quietly into a cave, urged by a need of nature. How much more inauspicious to pin the sleeping monarch to the ground with his own spear in his own camp — not in battle but in bed. Neither matter, since Saul was to die on Mount Gilboa. Neither is likely to have been told at the royal court of Saul's heir, King Ishbosheth (2 Sam 2:8-10a), or at the hearth of the last known claimant to Saul's throne, the crippled Mephibosheth (cf. 2 Sam 9; 16:3).

Abishai as David's companion is valuable as a foil in the story and as a witness to its truth; two figures make a better story than one (cf. Gideon and Purah, Judg 7:10-11; Jonathan and his armor-bearer, 1 Sam 14:1). The text gives no hint of either man's intention; along with the evident danger, it is left to the imagination. Twice, however, it is mentioned that Saul is sleeping in the middle of his armed force (vv. 5 and 7). The danger is evident.

The proposal to enter the camp came from David. The proposal to kill Saul comes from Abishai. His reaction is the same as Saul's in 23:7. It is told as an interpretation of the event. It is also explicitly a proposal to kill, by contrast with 24:5 (NRSV, 24:4); but the killer is to be Abishai, not David (cf. 24:8 [NRSV, 24:7] where a version involving the others is possible). To pin Saul to the ground with his own spear would be a fitting retribution for Saul's own efforts with the spear against David (18:10-11; 19:8-10; 20:33).

David's response, prohibiting Abishai's proposal to kill Saul, moves toward the nub of the story. Respect for the person of the king is featured here in David's response to Abishai; it is latent in David's accusation against Abner; and it is approached in a different vein in David's appeal to Saul. Finally, the

266

rightness of David's position is acknowledged by Saul. The commendation is the climax.

David is reported justifying his prohibition to Abishai by respect for YHWH's anointed. David's concern to remain guiltless follows satisfactorily on the preceding story with Abigail. David's readiness to let fate run its course, whether by YHWH's intervention or the ordinary course of events, reflects a view that appears frequently in sentiments attributed to him (cf. 1 Sam 22:3; 2 Sam 12:22-23; 15:25-26; 16:10-12). A repeated refusal to touch the life of the anointed leads to the command to take the spear and the water jar. There is good reason for a Davidic narrator to insist on the inviolability of the life of God's anointed (see below under Meaning); it is unnecessary, therefore, to view v. 11a as an addition (against Stoebe, 468). The absence of the jar from v. 22 is not surprising and hardly grounds enough to reconstruct a prehistory of the story. The king's spear has value, symbolic and otherwise, that is not attached to a water jar. It is possible to imagine a version without Abishai, omitting vv. 6-11 (cf. Hertzberg, 210); it is not necessary to do so and would impoverish the narrative. Without Abishai's involvement, v. 15b would be open to the implication of David's own intention to kill Saul.

The final note in v. 12b, "they were all asleep, because a deep sleep from the LORD had fallen upon them," has the potential to strip David's deed of its heroism. A skilled storyteller could easily avoid the trap. Despite his constant trust in the LORD, David knew nothing of the "deep sleep"; his heroism was undiminished. The LORD, on the other hand, was constantly on the lookout to protect David; David had the LORD's favor as no other.

The exchange between David and Saul begins with Saul's recognition of David's voice; at night and at a distance, this is perfectly in place. David begins with an appeal, couched in formal and courtly terms, to know why Saul pursues him; it is motivated by a protestation of innocence. Two options are entertained: (i) that this comes from YHWH (cf. 2 Sam 16:10-11), in which case a propitiatory sacrifice would be in order; (ii) that this comes from a human source (cf. 24:10), in which case David invokes a curse. The possibility that it comes from Saul himself is not explicitly raised, but the dichotomy is between divine and human. Saul is certainly included in the second category and the phrasing may intend to implicate him (differently, Hertzberg, 210; Stoebe, 469-70). The stakes are high: "Go, serve other gods" (v. 19). David's final appeal is made to the king, where ultimately responsibility lies.

Saul responds to David's appeal with a confession of his sin. His call to return, addressing David as "my son," is motivated by David's having spared his life. His confession is threefold: I have done wrong. . . . I have been a fool. . . . I have made a mistake. The concept of foolishness is not taken lightly (cf. 1 Sam 13:13; 2 Sam 15:31; 24:10); making a mistake, apart from its cultic use, occurs primarily in wisdom contexts.

The story does not develop this admission at all, but has David proceed to the return of the spear. David then returns to the theme of the LORD's anointed; his sparing of Saul will bring him his reward from YHWH. His address is to Saul; within it lies his prayer that his life be precious in YHWH's eyes, as Saul's life was in his eyes (26:23-24). Behind the prayer is a distrust of Saul that motivates ch. 27, and a trust in YHWH that characterizes David in all this extensive narrative.

Saul's blessing sums up another facet of the narrative's presentation of David: a man of action, who is successful. The blessing is the last word that Saul will have for David. It allows the story to have the parting occur on a remarkably peaceful note, with David fully vindicated by the man who had sought so long to take his life. But David does not return; he goes his way — [III].

Heroes perform deeds of individual bravery and daring; that is the stuff of national legend. So too in ancient Israel. But it is a heroism not attributed to other kings: no king of Israel before David and no king after David is portrayed doing such deeds. Among the heroes of the past are the deliverer-judges: Ehud who gained entry to Eglon's presence; Jael who entered her own tent to kill Sisera; and Gideon who penetrated the Midianite camp for pre-battle intelligence. Of the stories associated with Saul's court, there is Jonathan's exploit against the Philistines at Michmash (1 Sam 14:1-46; cf. Stoebe, 467); nothing, however, for Saul. Among David's warrior heroes were giant-killers (2 Sam 21:15-22), Philistine killers (2 Sam 23:8-12, 18), and a master exponent of single combat (23:20-21); most stirring may have been the three warriors who broke through the Philistine camp at Bethlehem to get water for David — which he poured out rather than drink (23:13-17).

1 Samuel 26 may not end with Saul's most spectacular endorsement of David; that surely belongs to 1 Sam 24. To the contrary, Brueggemann: "Saul asserts a sweeping blessing upon David; again, a rhetorical, theological escalation beyond chapter 24" (p. 188). Certainly, 1 Sam 26 provides David's most spectacular act of individual bravery and daring — apart from facing Goliath. David sought out Saul's camp (26:4-5). David penetrated the camp by night and stood over the sleeping Saul (26:6-12). Since, as we have noted, no Davidic storyteller would have suggested for a moment that David was after Saul's skin, what did David seek and what did he gain? Even in story, why play the hero, why run the risk? Because, in legend-making story, his gain is as spectacular as his deed: his own innocence is vindicated; he gains Saul's confession (23:21) and he gains Saul's blessing (23:25). On this high note, the drama of David's confrontation with Saul can end.

Genre

Once again, the literary genre is that of (→) story. As with ch. 24, so here a possible popular story of the night raid on Saul's camp has been considerably expanded. It has become the story of the end of a relationship. The relationship began when Saul summoned David to his service (16:14-23). Here it is David who has taken the initiative to provoke a confrontation with Saul. The result is the bringing to resolution of a long-standing tension: not the tension of the daredevil night raid on an armed camp, but the tension of rivalry and pursuit that has dominated chs. 18–26.

Setting

The first setting for the raid-on-the-camp story may well have been the circles of soldiers around the campfires or, when the campaigns were over, around the hearths. Not so the story in its present form. The concerns that intersect in this story witness to a remarkable breadth: the Davidic theology of destiny (v. 10), the language of law (v. 16), of cult (v. 20), of wisdom (v. 21), and of tension and competition between Saul and David (vv. 18-25). Such a combination suggests a setting among the wise counselors of the royal court. The charge against Abner might indicate some military input by those seeking to demean his memory; equally, it serves to heighten the sense of David's bravery. From such a setting, the story would easily find its way into the composition of the story of David's rise to power, into the PR, and finally into the DH.

Meaning

Within the narrative of how David rose to power, ch. 26 brings to an end the face-to-face relationship of David and Saul. David has been driven from the court and driven from the country. A shadow of suspicion can hang over David's intentions and behavior in this period coming from Saul's charges of conspiracy, from the opposition of figures such as Nabal and the Ziphites, and even from the makeup of David's band of irregulars. Is David a brigand, a lawless leader of revolution, wanting Saul dead? At least within the narrative, the import of this story is to set these potential suspicions to rest.

The story functions well between chs. 25 and 27. Abigail's admonition to David to remain free from the guilt of bloodshed prepares for this scene with Saul. There is no blood on David's hands — and it is not for want of an opportunity. We have noted that the insistence on the sacrosanct status of the anointed of YHWH may not be without ulterior motives at the Davidic court. It is not simply a matter of clearing David's name of any whisper of complicity in Saul's death. It may also be a matter of creating a precedent by which the life of the anointed is in the hands of YHWH alone. There is sufficient evidence of threat to David's life (cf. 2 Sam 15–20, esp. 17:2) to give David and his court every reason to seek to perpetuate the idea that it is an utterly heinous crime to put forth one's hand against the LORD's anointed. This thought lies in the background of David's prayer (26:24). In the light of the episode in the cave (ch. 24), it is important to recognize that the concern is for the life of God's anointed, not with any mystique associated with garments, etc.

David's sojourn among the Philistines would have been open to misunderstanding and suspicion. What was David doing fraternizing with the enemy at a time of greatest danger for Israel? This story, especially with David's appeal against his pursuer (vv. 18-20, contrast with ch. 24), serves to transfer the blame for David's exile on to Saul himself, portraying David's unwillingness to be driven out from his share in the heritage of the LORD. This may account for the scant treatment accorded Saul's offer of reconciliation; it is almost lost sight of between the admissions of guilt. Enough is said within the chapter to create a background in which David's reasons for escape to Philistine country are plausible (27:1).

Finally, the story betrays again the concern that has been present throughout this narrative: David succeeds because the LORD is with him. While this may be claimed implicitly by David for himself (cf. v. 23), it is expressed as the storyteller's own conviction in v. 12 — the exploit was possible because of YHWH's aid.

Saul, the anointed of YHWH and king of Israel, is to be succeeded by David. The progress of the narrative has shown David receiving the favor of Michal, Jonathan, the priests, and the people (if one may have recourse to 18:16). Now, in their last meeting, David receives Saul's blessing also. The narrative clears David of any shadow of complicity in conspiracy or treason and has Saul confess his error. The compiled narrative, which began the relationship with such promise in 16:14-23, has the LORD's rejection of Saul (16:14) work its way through the web of human affairs little by little, and here reach resolution. The relationship between the rejected king and the anointed king-to-be is at an end. "So David went his way, and Saul returned to his place."

Textual Matters

27:7 The MT has literally "days and four months." In such a context, "days" is to be understood as a full year; see Lev 25:29; Judg 17:10; 1 Sam 1:3 (cf. Driver, 210).

27:8 A place name is almost certainly required before "on the way to Shur." Telam should be read (see Josh 15:24; 1 Sam 15:4; cf. Driver, 211-12; Barthélemy, 215).

27:10 It is possible to understand the MT as "where" have you raided today? (cf. Stoebe, 474; Barthélemy, 216). The LXX "against whom?" renders this more clearly.

Discussion

While the literary unity of this chapter has been defended by most commentators, others have seen grounds for source-critical analysis or the transposition of verses. The indications are that the narrator has drawn on disparate traditions to put together this picture of David's operations in Philistine territory. The structure analysis brings this out, without prejudice to the overall unity.

In the first section in the analysis, this compositional activity can be seen in the reference to David's motivation for departing: the thought that Saul would despair of seeking him any longer within the borders of Israel (27:1). Alongside it is the comment that this is precisely what occurred (27:4). The implication of this note is that David's judgment of Saul's intentions was correct — [I]. The second section does not have an independent beginning of its own; it is clearly a function of what precedes. But it concludes with a notice which, in giving the precise length of David's stay in Philistine territory, is looking at the sojourn from the standpoint of its conclusion. Verse 6b, of course, has all the appearances of a later historical note (Stoebe, 478-79) — [II]. The third section has a unified concern — David's plundering operations and the cover-up he used to conceal them. It is vague, however, as to the geographical locality of these operations — [III].

Verse 1 serves to motivate David's departure despite the relatively harmonious conclusion of ch. 26. It does not permit David to debate the other options that might have been open to him (e.g., Moab); it takes for granted that his only shelter was with the Philistines. David is portrayed as driven into exile for fear of his life.

The notice of the move gives some insight into the kind of force that has now gathered around David. His troops are not simply a band of scattered outlaws, but they are sufficiently organized to have their wives and families with them as a small army with its camp followers (cf. 30:1-3). It is pedantic to exclude the reference to David's wives by name; the overwhelming interest is on the person of David. Camp followers are not named; those accompanying David are.

The description of David's practice in plundering foes to the south is succinctly expressed (for the problem of Geshurites and Girzites, cf. Driver, 211).

It is unlikely that the practice of permitting no survivors was a cause for moral scruple among his supporters. If known among his enemies, it might have caused criticism. Amos pilloried excessive violence in war (Amos 1:3–2:3); Hosea condemned the bloodshed of Jehu's rebellion (Hos 1:4); we have already noted Shimei ben Gera's condemnation of David as "a man of blood" (2 Sam 16:8). There is no hint of unease; we presume that the story comes from David's supporters. Given the vagueness of our knowledge about the geography and political alliances, the specifics of what David was doing escape us. The comment by Achish in v. 12, however, makes the basic strategy clear. David managed to convince Achish that his victims belonged to "his people Israel" so that his raids made him "utterly abhorrent" to them; in fact, being to the south and on the coast, his victims were presumably friendly to the Philistines.

Within the broader narrative, David has occasionally been depicted as already acting as deliverer in Israel (e.g., 23:1-5); here this role is extended to include aggression against those probably dangerous to Israel. At the same time, it is hardly appropriate to appeal to the motif of the YHWH war to justify the extermination (against Stoebe, 480-81). There is no reference to YHWH's wars or to the ban. The YHWH war ban is not practiced; to the contrary, booty is specifically taken. The strategy might have been judged a matter of tactical necessity, akin to taking no prisoners in modern commando raids. To our modern sensitivities, it was and is morally obscene, then and now. Whether as a matter of fact it was actually achieved may remain open to doubt (cf. 30:17). But it is necessary for the storyteller, in order to create a plausible narrative — the narrative needs Achish to trust David!

The difficulty of geographical precision for David's base comes from the placing of vv. 8-12 after the notice concerning the acquisition of Ziklag. Without this, the natural tendency would be to assume from vv. 9b-11a that David is in proximity to Achish at Gath (cf. esp. v. 9b and v. 11a). The probability of a compilation of traditions in the chapter leaves the historical and/or geographical question beyond solution; the compiler was presumably thinking of Ziklag as the base of operations. A report could be brought to Achish at Gath (v. 11a); David's coming back to Achish (v. 9b) is not so easily blended in, but a regular report by the vassal to his lord is not beyond a storyteller's competence. Any reconstruction is made harder by the recognition that the narrative here is celebrating the resourcefulness of David and the cleverness of his ruse. A historical basis is likely, but it cannot be recovered with enough exactitude to draw conclusions about the length of time David would have needed for such operations, nor how long he could have maintained such a cover, nor precisely how many such raids were carried out or where from. The two triads (v. 8 and v. 10) may point to a schematic rather than a historically accurate presentation.

Genre

The brilliance of the chapter lies in bringing together traditions that make the transition from David's time in Israel to the situation of his embarrassment as a

Philistine vassal in the army that was about to destroy Saul. Probably we should identify three (→) short notices (vv. 2-4, 5-6a, 7). Rather than Rendtorff's identification of vv. 8-12 as a historical story ("Beobachtungen"), it is more accurate to class this as a (→) story outline. It is likely to have a historical basis. David needed to have won the trust of Achish to show up among the Philistines as his vassal; David's near-participation in the Philistine battle force is not a candidate for fictional creation. His enemies would not have let him off so lightly; his friends are unlikely to have felt it as other than an embarrassment. The brief account of how David comported himself with Achish (vv. 8-12) cries out for full telling as a story. 27:1, providing David's motivation for the move, is likely to have come from the compiler of the narrative.

Setting

As Rendtorff has shown ("Beobachtungen"), the setting for the short notice is the literary activity of creating the longer narrative itself. Certainly, the information would have been readily available among the old-timers of David's entourage. We can presume that the exploits so briefly referred to in vv. 8-12 were the subject of many a well-told story. Of these, only ch. 30 has come down to us, in a rather different context.

Meaning

Confronted with the potentially embarrassing fact of David's having served as a Philistine mercenary, the text portrays David as driven into mercenary service rather than having freely sought it; and the text claims that, as a Philistine mercenary, David did nothing prejudicial to his own people.

"Potentially embarrassing" reflects our encounter with literature rather than history. It may have been well known in Judah that David had restricted his raids to enemies in the south; his activities may have enhanced his reputation. It is possible that gifts, like those noted in 30:26-31, had created favorable memories. It may have been well known among David's soldiers that, had they been with the Philistines at the battle of Gilboa, they would have fought for Israel and Saul (cf. 29:4-5). The strategy might have been mooted in advance, if for no other reason than to avoid desertions. These historical possibilities affect the impact of the story. In such cases, telling the story would be recounting one more in the series of David's valorous deeds that formed part of his reputation. We simply do not know (cf. Soggin, "Davidic-Solomonic Kingdom," 345). We should not be too quick to prejudge the issue in one way or the other.

The narrative has shown David harried from court and country in chs. 18-23, and has skillfully resumed this in 26:17-20. So 27:1 is sufficient to bring this issue into focus at the moment of the narrative of departure. The reference

273

to Saul's no longer seeking David after learning that he had fled the country is aptly placed (v. 4); indirectly, it confirms the correctness of David's fears.

The notice concerning Ziklag introduces the story of David's stay with a verifiable fact that was to David's credit and to Judah's benefit — possession of a city. The story outline (vv. 8-12) not only claims that David did nothing prejudicial to Judah, but shows him actively at war against some of Israel's enemies. In this sense, the misfortune of exile is turned to positive gain (cf. Hertzberg, 213). The culmination of the story is in v. 12: David's success in convincing Achish that he is a loyal vassal, to be trusted — which he is not. It is this very success that constitutes the trap from which David must be freed in the stories to come.

David's success again shows that YHWH is with him, even without any explicit comment. It is notable that not a word is said of YHWH's intervention or YHWH's role in these crucial decisions. The chapter is entirely secular in its presentation. Stoebe (pp. 476-77) compares it with 2 Sam 17:1-14; one might also compare it with 1 Sam 23. The distinction between the old sacral world of the earlier Davidic traditions and the brave new secular world of the later Davidic traditions should not be overstated.

Bibliography of Works Cited Above

Barr, James. "The Symbolism of Names in the Old Testament." *BJRL* 52 (1969-70) 11-29.

Boecker, Hans Jochen. *Redeformen des Rechtslebens im Alten Testament.* 2nd ed. WMANT 14. Neukirchen: Neukirchener Verlag, 1964/1970.

Budde, Karl. *Die Bücher Samuel.* KHC 8. Tübingen: Mohr, 1902.

Greßmann, Hugo. *Die Schriften des Alten Testaments.* Part 2, vol. 1: *Die älteste Geschichtsschreibung und Prophetie Israels (von Samuel bis Amos und Hosea).* Göttingen: Vandenhoeck & Ruprecht, 1921.

Grønbaek, Jakob H. *Die Geschichte vom Aufstieg Davids (1. Sam. 15–2. Sam. 5): Tradition und Komposition.* Copenhagen: Munksgaard, 1971.

Koch, Klaus. *The Growth of the Biblical Tradition: The Form-Critical Method.* New York: Scribner's, 1969.

Levenson, Jon D. "1 Samuel 25 as Literature and as History." *CBQ* 40 (1978) 11-28.

Nowack, Wilhelm. *Die Bücher Samuelis.* HAT. Göttingen: Vandenhoeck & Ruprecht, 1902.

Rendtorff, Rolf. "Beobachtungen zur altisraelitischen Geschichtsschreibung anhand der Geschichte vom Aufstieg Davids." Pp. 428-39 in *Probleme biblischer Theologie.* Edited by H. W. Wolff. Munich: Chr. Kaiser, 1971.

Schulz, Alfons. "Narrative Art in the Books of Samuel." Pp. 119-70 in *Narrative and Novella in Samuel: Studies by Hugo Gressmann and Other Scholars, 1906-1923.* Edited by D. M. Gunn. Sheffield: Almond, 1991.

Smith, Henry Preserved. *The Books of Samuel.* ICC. Edinburgh: Clark, 1912.

Soggin, J. Alberto. "The Davidic-Solomonic Kingdom." Pp. 332-80 in *Israelite and Judaean History.* Edited by J. H. Hayes and J. M. Miller. Philadelphia: Westminster, 1977.

Stansell, Gary. "Honor and Shame in the David Narratives." Pp. 94-114 in *Was ist der Mensch? Beiträge zur Anthropologie des Alten Testaments. Hans Walter Wolff zum 80. Geburtstag.* Edited by F. Crüsemann, C. Hardmeier, and R. Kessler. Munich: Kaiser, 1992.

Tov, Emanuel. *Textual Criticism of the Hebrew Bible.* Minneapolis: Fortress, 1992.

Veijola, Timo. *Die Ewige Dynastie: David und die Entstehung seiner Dynastie nach der deuteronomistischen Darstellung.* AASF B 193. Helsinki: Suomalainen Tiedeakatemia, 1975.

Chapter 9

THE ULTIMATE FAILURE OF SAUL (1 Samuel 28–31)

The disposition of the material in chs. 28–31 shows a compositional skill that clothes the whole in a certain unity. Earlier suggestions for reorganizing the text frequently failed to recognize these compositional issues. More recent respect for the biblical compiler has still fallen short of the total picture. 28:1a reports the Philistine preparation for war against Israel. Against this background, 28:1b-2 reports David's engagement to serve under Achish in this war. This report is continued in 29:1-2, where the purpose of the war (28:1a) and the engagement of David (28:1b-2) are both presumed. The story in 28:3-25 also is told against the background of the preparations for war (28:4-5). On the other hand, 28:3-25 presupposes a later stage in these preparations than 29:1-11. The reasons for this will be discussed below; what was once seen as textual accident or editorial error can on further reflection demand serious consideration as editorial skill and compositional structure (cf. Edelman, *King Saul,* 238).

In the present text, 30:1 depends on ch. 29. It has no self-contained report or reference to explain David's absence from Ziklag or his return on the third day. By way of contrast, note how 2 Sam 1:1 refers to the earlier events involved. Finally, 31:1 does not contain the normal preliminaries to a report of battle — the gathering of forces, the place of camp or battle. These have already been given in 28:1-2; 29:1, and 11b.

These observations say nothing of the origin of the various traditions. What the observations point to is a structural unity in the composition of the traditions in chs. 28–31. An interpretation will be faithful to the text and recognize the skill of the compiler if it regards these chapters as forming a carefully structured narrative unity.

To emphasize this unity, the structure analysis below will cover all four chapters. Many details will have to be left to the discussion. The structure analysis given follows the biblical text in presenting a narrative without transforming it into the drama that is implicit. The drama is left latent in the narrative. Before looking closely at the structure of the narrative, it will help to look closely at what is implicit.

The drama is set in train with the Philistine mobilization (28:1-2). The moment of conflict has finally come that has been lurking in the background throughout Saul's reign. One tradition has it as the reason for Saul's becoming king: "He shall save my people from the hand of the Philistines" (1 Sam 9:16). It came to the fore with the challenge of the Philistine champion, Goliath; on that occasion, it was resolved by David. It has been in the background since the stories of Samson; it will not be concluded until the reign of David. At stake is the fate of Israel.

The Philistines mobilize to fight Israel. The drama is not only Saul's; it is also David's. By force of Saul's hostility, David is now a Philistine vassal. He will be there; he will be part of the Philistine force (28:1-2). The dilemma for David is inescapable. If he fights for the Philistines, he will unquestionably be "utterly abhorrent to his people Israel" (cf. 27:12). If he turns against the Philistines from within their own ranks, he could possibly save Israel (cf. 29:4b). In two verses, the narrative sets up the drama for Saul and all Israel and the dilemma for David. Brueggemann catches it well: "David cannot afford to fight against Israel, for that would vindicate Saul and leave David utterly discredited at home. But David also cannot side with Israel, for that would place in jeopardy David's relationship with Achish and the power base that relationship makes possible" (p. 191).

The resolution moves in two stages: it is indicated and it is achieved. The indication comes first for Saul; it is needed early in the piece because it is part of the resolution of David's dilemma. Saul is rejected by God; Saul will die in battle against the Philistines — and Israel will be defeated. In Samuel's words, nothing is more certain: "The LORD has done to you just as he spoke by me. . . . Tomorrow you and your sons shall be with me" (28:17-19). At this high level of divine determination, David's dilemma is irrelevant. Saul will die; it does not matter what David does. God has determined Saul's death and Israel's defeat. For David's people, this faith-claim is critically important.

The indication for David comes from the Philistine commanders, chronologically at an earlier stage in the proceedings. Narratively, this is less important than God's decision to destroy Saul. Its impact is on the politically troublesome question: Where was David when Saul was destroyed? Despite Achish's trust, David is rejected by the Philistine commanders. He is dismissed from the Philistine force. The reason given is both good strategy for the Philistines and excellent public relations for David: "he may become an adversary to us in the battle" (29:4). The possibility that David might have acted in the battle on behalf of Israel is raised as real by the Philistines themselves. They act to prevent it. The possibility that David and his force might have come to Saul's aid in whatever fashion is also eliminated. David's rejection occurred at Aphek on the coastal plain (29:1) and David was sent back to Ziklag (29:4). The narrative text highlights the opposed directions (29:11): David returned to the land of the Philistines; the Philistines went up to the land of Israel — to Jezreel, the plain of Esdraelon.

All that is left for the narrative is to tell how the resolution of the drama was achieved. David found Ziklag ravaged and, in pursuit of the Amalekite raiders, was taken to the far south of Israel, far from the events unfolding in the plain of Esdraelon. David's dilemma had been resolved for him. Saul, having had the condemned man's last meal, met defeat and death against the Philistines. What God had determined was done.

A structural outline of this movement reveals the drama.

Saul's Ultimate Failure **1 Samuel 28–31**
I. The drama set in motion 28:1-2
II. The resolution in Israel's story 28:3–31:13
   A. Resolution indicated 28:3–29:11
      1. For Saul: rejection by God 28:3-25
      2. For David: rejection by Philistines 29:1-11
   B. Resolution achieved 30:1–31:13
      1. For David: success 30:1-31
      2. For Saul: failure 31:1-13

The textual observations noted here are well known (cf. in 1913, Driver, 213-14). Most recent commentators treat 28:1-2 with ch. 27 and discuss the location of 28:3-25 separately. Error and clumsiness are no longer accepted as explanations; a variety of aspects flowing from the location are emphasized. The overall drama discussed here is not highlighted. For example: for Hertzberg, the contrast is between the David of ch. 27 and Saul of ch. 28 (p. 217; cf. p. 222); for Stoebe, the forsakenness of Saul in ch. 16 is brought to conclusion in ch. 28 (pp. 487-88); for McCarter, the reminder of Saul's failure with the Amalekites is a preparation for their punishment by David (p. 422); similarly for Klein, David's victory over the Amalekites contrasts with Saul's failure against them (p. 269); for Brueggemann, the location of 28:3-25 is "a deliberate move by the narrator to hold us in suspense," while contrasting Saul and David (p. 191). These insights are valuable; their value is heightened when placed within the structural composition of the whole.

The structure of the composition is remarkable. After the initial move to war (28:1-2), both the Philistines and Saul with all Israel are at the plain of Esdraelon (see 28:4). David's actions are handled in a flashback: with the Philistines, he is on the coastal plain (29:1); against the Amalekites, he is far to the south (30:9-10). The final battle takes us back to the Philistines and Saul, to the plain of Esdraelon and Mount Gilboa. The message is plain. Saul's death was not David's doing, but destined by God. David's absence was not David's doing, but demanded by the Philistines. Saul was rejected by God; David was rejected by the Philistines. David was victorious, in the deep south near the Egyptian border, while Saul died in defeat on Mount Gilboa. Thanks to God and the Philistines, David could not be blamed. Thanks to the people of Jabesh-gilead, Saul and his sons were buried. The result is a skillful narrative composition in which the battle of Gilboa, foreshadowed in 28:1, is dominated by the inclusion formed by the despair and death of Saul (chs. 28 and 31), while within this frame, David is extricated from a dangerous dilemma. That is the story a carefully structured text presents.

Textual Issues in Chs. 28–29

28:1 Neither the MT or the LXX have a place name here for the gathering of the Philistines. 4QSam[a] adds "toward Jezreel" at the end of v. 1b, while, within a paraphrastic rendering of v. 1a, Josephus refers to an unknown location (cf. *Antiquities,* VI. §325). This would be a prime suspect as a case of assimilation to the details of the later story (with McCarter, 412, 414; Klein, 262).

28:16   "Your enemy" can be read with the MT (cf. Barthélemy, 217-18).

28:17   At the start of the verse, the MT has "to him" (= David) and the LXX has "to you" (= Saul); in view of what follows, either is possible and both make sense (cf. Barthélemy, 218-19, opting for the MT as *lectio difficilior*).

29:10   Pisano offers a thorough discussion of the issues and concludes: either read the longer text with the LXX or accept a double reading in the MT (with Talmon), since "no accident of haplography can account for MT's shorter text" (cf. pp. 298-317).

Textual Issues in Ch. 30

30:20   The NRSV is not helpful; there are no "other cattle" mentioned (unless we assume a distinction between booty that was won and property that was recovered or even between Amalekite booty and Amalekite property; cf. Stoebe, 508). Jerome's Vulgate text is the most minimal and, whether it results from good judgment or good rabbinic advice on the Hebrew tradition, is also the most likely: "And he took all the sheep and cattle and drove them before him; and they said, 'This is David's spoil'" (cf. McCarter, 432; Klein, 280; also Driver, 224).

Textual Issues in Ch. 31

31:3   The NRSV's "the archers" is more complicated in the MT. Stoebe offers two possibilities: either a choice of readings, with two offered; or a gloss ("men of the bow") to explain *hammôrîm* (p. 521). 1 Chron 10:3 offers a third but doubtful option; cf. Driver, 228.

31:9   The LXX has the simpler "their idols" (as 1 Chron 10:9; cf. Driver, 230); Barthélemy affirms the relative autonomy of the texts of Samuel and Chronicles, against assimilation (pp. 224-25).

Discussion

It is probably unwise to associate 28:1-2 with the preceding chapter, beyond its background role as the source of Achish's trust in David (against most commentators; for example: Hertzberg, Stoebe, McCarter, Klein, Brueggemann [p. 189], Alter [p. 171]). The redactional link, "in those days," makes an association, but the reality of the Philistine forces gathering for war against Israel points to something far larger than raids and skirmishes. It is clear that 28:1-2 is followed up by 29:1 and then by 31:1. Scarcely anyone today would argue for a Pentateuch-style source running through Samuel. If stories and traditions are being gathered together, then ch. 26 was one such story and ch. 27 is a tradition bringing a period to a close. David had left Saul's territory; David was with the Philistines for a year and four months (27:7). While with the Philistines, David deceived Achish and gained his trust.

With 28:1-2, something new is begun — [I]. David's engagement to participate with Achish in the campaign needs to be close to ch. 27; its distance from the continuation in ch. 29 creates narrative tension. As noted above, in 29:1-2 the purpose of the war (28:1a) and the engagement of David (28:1b-2) are both presumed; equally, 30:1 depends on ch. 29, having no self-contained report to explain David's absence from Ziklag or his return on the third day; finally, 31:1 does not contain the normal preliminaries to a report of battle — i.e., the gathering of forces and the place of camp or battle (provided in 28:1-2; 29:1, 11b). The formal statement that the Philistines mobilized their armed forces for war against Israel (28:1a) is a pointer to the definitive conflict that lies ahead in ch. 31.

28:1b-2 brings to the fore the dilemma created for David. If he and his troops do not join with the forces of Achish, he blows his cover and his security outside the territory of Saul. If he does join the forces of Achish and the Philistines in the victory ahead, he will incur the contempt of all Israel, as destroyer rather than deliverer. He will be unfit to be Israel's king. David's response in v. 2a is brilliantly ambivalent: he could fulfill Achish's hopes; he could fulfill the Philistine commanders' fears. The narrative leaves the answers for the following text to provide. Drama and dilemma have been set.

The answers, as the structure analysis emphasizes, are revealed in two stages: first for Saul, rejected by God — [II.A]; then for David, rejected by the Philistines — [II.B]. For Saul, it means death; for David, it means deliverance from the dangers of his dilemma. These are the answers of the text; whether they correspond with the realities of history we do not and cannot know. Nowhere are David's intentions disclosed.

God's intentions for Saul provide the first stage of the answer. Saul's fear is at the center of the story's opening verses (v. 5 of vv. 3-7). The attentive hearer or reader may recall Saul's fear at the Philistine challenge (17:11); the wheel has turned full circle. In between time, Saul has feared David (18:12, 29); now the focus of his fear has returned to the Philistines. The details leading up to this fear are briefly sketched (vv. 3-4). Two are not new occurrences, but a description of the existing situation (note the Hebrew tenses): Samuel has died; Saul has banished the mediums and wizards. Both elements are needed in the story ahead with its clandestine summoning of Samuel. The narrative moves again with the comment that the Philistines have come up to Shunem in Gilboa. The text gives no reason why Saul undertook this religious purge, or why the Philistines have come so far north for battle. This is the region where God brought about the defeat of Sisera's chariots on the plain (Judg 4:12-16); it is near where Elijah will kill the 450 prophets of Baal (1 Kgs 18:40). For Saul, it will be the place of defeat.

Following the statement of Saul's fear, two verses set the scene for the story to come. First, Saul's attempts at finding divine guidance are in vain; YHWH is not answering Saul's inquiries made by any of the usual means (v. 6). So Saul, who had purged the land of mediums and wizards, is reduced to ordering his staff to find him a medium (v. 7). The omens are not good. The statement of 16:14 is working itself out in the history from which, presumably, it was derived. One aspect of the meaning of rejection is spelled out in v. 6; there can be no guidance from YHWH (contrast 30:7-8).

The consultation with the medium is set on the eve of the battle (28:19). The Philistines are camped at Shunem (28:4a), on slightly elevated ground in the middle of the valley of Esdraelon, a few miles from Endor. Saul's army is positioned "at Gilboa" (28:4b). The geographical details are not precise. 29:1 has the Philistines at Aphek (probably in the coastal plain, see below) and Israel "by the fountain that is in Jezreel" — more likely in the plain rather than on the mountain. Obviously, against chariots, Israel would have a better chance strategically in the hills. The mountain is specifically mentioned in 31:1, where fleeing Israelites die "on Mount Gilboa"; but they are in flight. A progression from the plain (29:1b) to the hill (28:4) to the battle or flight (31:1) would make tactical sense but may not reflect the reality of events and traditions. With its "at Gilboa" in 28:4, the MT is discreetly vague and general.

The consultation does focus on Samuel's message for Saul, but it begins with the exchange between Saul and the medium and it concludes with the medium's care for Saul. The exchange between Saul and the medium is remarkably unclear and learned suggestions have not been particularly helpful in shedding light on it. First and foremost, it fits into the category of a reported story. The basics are there for a storyteller to work with; the actual telling of the story is not given. The puzzlement concerns four issues of identity and recognition. In v. 8, Saul conceals the identity of the spirit to be consulted: "bring up for me the one whom I name to you." In vv. 9-10, the disguised Saul promises that no punishment will befall the woman for what she sees as a capital crime. How can such a promise be made by one who is not the king? Alternatively, the oath can be understood as: I will not betray you. The decision lies with the storyteller; it is not in the text. In v. 12, when the woman sees Samuel she recognizes the identity of Saul: "Why have you deceived me? You are Saul!" In v. 14, we are not told how Saul "knew that it was Samuel."

We may puzzle over how these issues are resolved. More fundamental is why they are there in the first place. We do not know. With the first, in v. 8, we may perhaps speak of retarding the moment of disclosure. In the telling of a story, the effect could be extended beyond the few verses involved here. From the woman's reaction in v. 12, it is clear that the reassurance given her in v. 10 does not reveal the inquirer's identity. What remains unclear is why seeing Samuel she should recognize Saul (v. 12). Saul's question about appearance suggests there is more at stake than the arrival of the spirit Saul had asked for. What, though, we do not know.

Emendation of the text does not help. The claim of prophetic reworking, replacing an anonymous ghost with the figure of Samuel (cf. McCarter, 421; as in vv. 17-19aα), does not originate in the text (as in 9:1–10:16) but in its difficulties and is not effective in fully resolving these difficulties. The classical understanding that Samuel identified Saul relates to only one of the four issues and does not indicate how the identification happened. It is possible that Samuel's gestures betrayed the identity of Saul (Budde, *Bücher Samuel,* 180). Rather than speculate, it is more honest to recognize the issues in the text and leave their resolution to the storyteller of the moment. Nothing I have read so far has been able to shine light for me on these aspects of darkness. Storytellers must have their day. The text indicates issues that are significant for the telling of the story — a significance that escapes us. The handling of these issues in the telling of the story is left to the storytellers.

McCarter's suggestion opens the way to two areas of reflection. With prophetic redaction assumed later (vv. 17-19aα), does it help to assume it here? Was Samuel involved in this story before any prophetic redaction? As to the first, if vv. 11-12a are regarded as later prophetic redaction (with McCarter), then two issues remain unresolved. First, the identity of the one Saul would name — v. 8: was it an earlier figure? Second, the reason Saul "knew that it was Samuel" — v. 14: or was it the earlier figure? Any prophetic redaction has to be more extensive than simply vv. 11-12a. As to the second area, that of Samuel's involvement, is any prophetic redaction necessary to introduce Samuel at this point? At the earliest level of the Samuel texts, an anonymous prophet commissioned Saul (original of 9:1–10:16), in some pre-dtr texts Samuel was involved in Saul's selection for kingship (cf. 10:20-25), and — in a possible early version of 1 Sam 15 — Saul was rebuked by Samuel for disobedience rather than rejected (cf. 15:22, 24-25, 31). The tradition knew of the awareness of some that "an evil spirit from God" was tormenting Saul (cf. 16:15). Against this background, it is not surprising that Samuel should in due course say to Saul "the LORD has turned from you and become your enemy" (28:16). No prophetic redaction is needed before vv. 17-19aα. To summon an unnamed prophet is not impossible but the suppression of vv. 11-12a does not achieve this. Substituting the unnamed figure for Samuel is possible but unnecessary; it does nothing to resolve the puzzles. We are left with a puzzling text, some parts more puzzling than others — the storyteller's challenge.

The exchange between Saul and Samuel opens badly. It is ominous and threatening, especially given that in the tradition Saul was present to witness one of Samuel's wilder performances: "Samuel hewed Agag in pieces before the LORD in Gilgal" (15:33). When a prophet who has chopped up a king in a sanctuary such as Gilgal asks why he has been disturbed (28:15), it is not a heart-warming opening to an exchange. Saul's answer is chilling: he is facing threat from the Philistines and silence from God. The freeze deepens with Samuel's words: "the LORD has turned from you and become your enemy" (28:16). As is widely recognized, vv. 16 and 19aβb would convey the message. Verses 17-18 recall Samuel's part in ch. 15. Verse 19aα rejoins and repeats the statement of v. 19b: "the LORD will give . . . Israel into the hands of the Philistines." The scene ends with Saul in terror, stretched full length on the ground. The spiritual and physical take their toll. Samuel's words and an empty stomach have unmanned him.

Verse 21 opens a new scene. The woman comes to Saul and sees his terror. In a remarkable exchange, she says to the king: I have risked my life to listen to you; now you listen to me (vv. 21-22). There is little that the woman or Saul's two companions can do to remove the spiritual fear. But the repast they organize and persuade Saul to share can at least alleviate the physical weakness. The text offers a remarkable image of caring by the medium and the men. Strengthened, they rise and depart into the night; the day to come will bring death. In this last image of the rejected king, Saul is not an ignoble figure.

With Saul's fate decided — "tomorrow you and your sons shall be with me" — the narrative can turn to David. What God wills is one thing. What David does is another. Political and military events have to be brought into line with divine decisions. How this happens will be the decision of the Philistine commanders.

When Saul and his sons died, "tomorrow," and the army of Israel was defeated, it would be helpful to David's reputation if David and his group were as far from the scene as possible. So the narrative takes us back to the coastal plain, with the gathering of the Philistine forces at Aphek (29:1; cf. 4:1). Which of several Apheks was most suitable for the Philistine rendezvous is disputed, but the Aphek of the coastal plain is the most likely — where previously Israel fought on the plain and lost. The Philistines are on their way to war; they will probably march up the coastal plain and through the Carmel range by way of the narrow valley, guarded by Megiddo, that gives access to the plain of Esdraelon (cf. Stoebe, 500). The Israelites were already in Jezreel (29:1; in this context = the plain of Esdraelon).

To military historians and strategists the problem is obvious: What on earth are the Israelites doing waiting for the Philistines on the broad plain of Esdraelon? Given the military inequality described in 13:19-22, in any set-piece battle on relatively equal terms Israel will lose — which, of course, they do. On the other hand, David has fought with Philistines and won; they are not invincible. The detailed location of the actual battle is never clearly specified. According to 28:4, the Philistines were at Shunem in the middle of the valley of Esdraelon and Saul and all Israel were at Gilboa, on the fringe of the valley, whether on the mountain or at its foot is not said (see above). "By the fountain" (29:1) suggests in the plain. After the battle, not described in 31:1, many Israelites fell "on Mount Gilboa"; but this does not say that they fought there, only that they fell there in their flight.

So what was Saul doing fighting a strategic battle in a most unstrategic place — if indeed the battle is to be located on the plain? The reality is that we do not know. The Philistine occupation of towns (31:7) may indicate an expansionary thrust on their part that Saul had to try to repel. The military inequality described in 13:19-22 may not have been general; a territorial struggle of balanced forces seems more likely, given David's later successes. At least this is clear: the narrative is not concerned with the historical and strategic details.

As the structure analysis indicates, the narrative falls easily into three parts. The inquiry of the Philistine commanders is followed by their rejection of David and Achish's communication of this rejection to David. A storyteller would have little problem with the relative roles of "lords" and "commanders." As noted, the scene is critical for David's apologists. With a force that feared Saul, David was no match for the Philistines in open battle. A surprise attack from within the Philistine ranks could be devastating for the Philistines and highly advantageous to David and Saul (cf. 29:4). The unfolding of events closed off any access to David's intentions. However, there is an ironic hint in the narrative that a storyteller might exploit. Achish describes David as honest and deserving to be included in the campaign (cf. 29:3, 6, 9). From ch. 27, the reader or hearer knows that Achish was wrong about the past. Would he also have been wrong about the future? Given how the future unfolds, we have no answer. David's statement of commitment, claiming the right to "fight against the enemies of my lord the king" (29:8), is ambiguous. Is "my lord the king" Achish or Saul? The ambiguity is never put to the test.

The irony of Achish's commendation, "I know that you are as blameless in my sight as an angel of God" (v. 9a), is left hanging. David and his men move south toward the land of the Philistines. The Philistines move north to battle with Israel.

Both Saul and David have suffered rejection: Saul by God; David by the Philistines. Now, in reverse order, the narrative unfolds the implications of those rejections; first for David, then for Saul. For David, victory — [III.A]; for Saul, defeat and death — [III.B].

David's victory begins with the horror of defeat. The scene of discovery is brilliantly sketched (30:1-3): the notice of arrival on the third day; the report of what had happened in the meantime; the notice of discovery. The translation, "they found it burned down," is flat (v. 3). The Hebrew has the drama of discovery: and there it was, burned by fire — their wives and their sons and daughters captured. Impact and feeling follow observation. The focus is first on David and those with him; tears flow to the point of exhaustion (v. 4). Then the focus narrows to David himself: his wives, his life, and his faith. David's two wives are gone. His life is in danger because the band he has led is ready to stone him. The leader of such a band lives by his successes and can die for his failures. David's hold on power is fragile — now and later! And David gets his strength from God. Just four words in the Hebrew; nothing more (NRSV: But David strengthened himself in the LORD his God). For others it was an exhortation (cf. Josh 1:6; 1 Kgs 2:2); in the narrative here, for David it was a fact. The comparison with Saul is inevitable.

It is worth noting that for all David's campaigns and battles, outside 2 Sam 15–20, this is the only sustained narrative of one of David's expeditions. It begins with David's consultation of YHWH. A storyteller can decide whether to put the questions in due form; the text provides the answers. Clearly, YHWH is favorable to David and a successful rescue is promised. Earlier, Saul could get no answer from his God; killing the priests of Nob had deprived him of the ephod. The comparison is stark.

The pursuit of the raiding Amalekites has YHWH's blessing; the text has its difficulties in vv. 9-10 and 11-12. Suggestions for excision or rearrangement need to explain how the confusion arose. The recognition that the text is a reported story rather than a reported performance of the story is important. What helps most is attention to the narrative technique in which a general statement precedes the specific details. So v. 10 unfolds the details not given in v. 9; v. 12 unfolds the details not given in v. 11. The storyteller will know how to use the details to best advantage. The division of forces at the wadi will be important later in the story.

The episode of the Egyptian straggler is unusual in such stories. To some degree, it is paralleled by the episode of the Amalekite in 2 Sam 1. The Egyptian's story creates a minor problem with regard to historical verisimilitude. He had been left behind three days ago, but he had taken part in the raids, including the raid on Ziklag itself. Therefore, an audience might calculate that the Amalekite raiders have about a three-day start on David. Is David's rapid overtaking of the group compatible with narrative verisimilitude? An affirmative response is possible, in several scenarios: hot pursuit would not be feared, since David is presumed by the raiders to be away with the Philistines; the Amalekites have regained their home territory or at least an intermediate base, since the Egyptian can lead David straight to them; and so on. Within the narrative context, the meeting with the Egyptian facilitates the plausibility of the rapid overtaking of the raiders. This, in its turn, renders plausible the complete recovery of the booty and the captives, unharmed. At issue is not historical reality but narrative satisfaction and verisimilitude.

In contrast to the details associated with the Egyptian, the report of the raiders' defeat is practically devoid of tactical details. We are told that the Amalekites had spread out in a loose and open formation, not in a closed camp circle, and that revelry was the order of the day. The state of the Amalekite camp on David's arrival confirms the first possibility suggested above: pursuit was not expected and the raiders were taken by surprise. The length of the battle is uncertain. The Hebrew *nešep* (NRSV, twilight) can refer to either dusk or dawn; compounding matters, the NRSV's "of the next day" translates an abnormal and uncertain Hebrew form. Most moderns favor a dawn attack (so: Hertzberg, Klein, McCarter, Stoebe); whether it was one or two days for the battle remains unclear.

The real challenge for a storyteller is less the length of the battle — a lightning strike or a prolonged skirmish — than how David with four hundred troops totally defeats an apparently much larger force, to the extent that *only* four hundred escape — the elite camel corps. No details are given; no tactics are indicated. Nothing was missing; not one Israelite captive was killed. Such is the stuff of legend.

The recovery of the captive wives and children, all the booty taken by the Amalekites, and perhaps more is important to the story. Even more important is the distribution of the spoil back at the wadi, but also at Ziklag.

Verses 18-19 are emphatic that David recovered everything the Amalekites had taken; they open and close with the general statement (cf. vv. 18a and 19b). David's two wives are given separate mention, then v. 19a goes into detail on all that was recovered. The reconstruction and interpretation of v. 20 are tenuous. No mention of flocks driven off from Ziklag by the raiders was made in vv. 1-2; no distinction is attempted between the possessions of the Amalekites and the plunder taken in their raid. Minimally, a special class of booty is attributed to David. Jerome's Vulgate makes plain sense: "And he [David] took all the sheep and cattle and drove them before him; and they said, 'This is David's spoil'" (cf. McCarter, 432). Driver disagrees, opting for plural verbs throughout: they took . . . they drove . . . and they said (p. 224). Probably more important than the exact nature of the spoil involved is the statement, "This is David's spoil" (v. 20). David is back in high esteem.

High esteem for David is continued in the treatment of the division of the spoil among David's troops at Wadi Besor. David's ruling was accepted as a permanent statute and ordinance for Israel (v. 25). Narrative favor for David's ruling is expressed early in the piece; disagreement comes from those characterized as "all the corrupt and worthless fellows" (v. 22). David's position is alleged as common sense: "Who would listen to you in this matter?" (v. 24). If spoil were not equally divided, there would never be a worthwhile warrior to guard the baggage. It is typical of the style attributed to David that common sense is backed by spirituality. The spoil is described as "what the LORD has given us" (v. 23). Because the spoil is YHWH's gift, it is divided among the whole community of YHWH's people.

It is this principle that may underlie the next stage of the narrative — as well as sound politics. Some of the spoil is distributed among the elders of Judah, spoil described as coming from "the enemies of the LORD." The list contains thirteen localities, with a final generalizing conclusion. The generalizing conclusion may have been added because a number of the places we might expect to find here are not listed, e.g., Bethlehem, Maon, Jezreel, Carmel. It could be that the list reflects gifts sent by David in connection with his being chosen king of Judah (cf. Stoebe, 519). This might explain the absence from the list of those places with which David's connections were already well established.

Finally the narrative comes to the moment of Saul's ultimate failure. What Samuel predicted in ch. 28 becomes reality on the battlefield. David is far away in Ziklag, making decrees for Israel and distributing spoil to his friends (30:25-26); Saul and his sons are up against the Philistines and an ignominious death. As the structure analysis shows, the narrative moves in two stages: first, the defeat of Israel and the death of Saul's sons and of Saul himself; second, the aftermath of defeat, with the treatment of the bodies of Saul and his sons, first by the Philistines and second by the people of Jabesh-gilead.

The tone of the reports is factual and neutral; there is no comment. The loyalty of the armor-bearer (v. 5) and of the people of Jabesh-gilead (vv. 11-13) is hardly enough to qualify the tone of the whole as "described with great solemnity, even reverence" (Hertzberg, 231) nor as tragic or heroic (Stoebe, 523). The events may have been; the text is not. The narrative does not exclude this understanding; it does not express it.

The passage begins with the report of Israel's defeat. The preliminary information on the gathering of the forces and the places of encampment has already been given (28:1, 4; 29:1, 11). Verse 1's use of a present participle, "as the Philistines were fighting" (Heb., *nilḥāmîm;* NRSV, "fought"), throws the emphasis onto Israel's flight; contrast the use of a past verb form in Chronicles (1 Chron 10:1; Stoebe, 520; McCarter follows Chronicles, p. 440).

As in ch. 30, the precise details of the military situation are not reported; they are not the center of interest. We do not know whether the Philistine archers were operating from chariots (cf. 2 Sam 1:6; Stoebe, 525). The exact terrain involved and its effect on the fighting are not described. The reference to overtaking may indicate that Saul and his attendants were involved in Israel's withdrawal, if not flight. But the sequence of deaths in vv. 2-5 is far more a matter of narrative stylization than any reflection of a pursuit such as 2 Sam 2:18-23. Saul's sons die; Ishbosheth alone is absent.

The weight of narrative interest as well as the weight of the war (cf. v. 3aα) falls upon Saul. He is pressed hard by the archers and wounded (textual issues abound, but the NRSV rendering is acceptable; cf. Driver, 228). The report is made from Saul's viewpoint; there is no need to assume that the archers were aware of the identity of their victim (cf. v. 8). Saul's anxiety is understandable and the motivation for his request is in the text. The armor-bearer's fear is left unqualified; and no ethical consideration is permitted to obtrude upon the report of Saul's death. As Stoebe comments: "Saul's deed is only the recognition of a fate that has already been decided" (p. 527). It is the nearest approach to the heroic in the passage; his example is followed by his armor-bearer. "There is no self-pity here, but courage. . . . Saul is a man with a last heroic gesture" (Brueggemann, 207).

The resumptive summary (v. 6) brings this section to a conclusion, listing the dead, not in the order they fell but in the order of their rank and importance. It is possible that v. 7 is not from the same tradition as vv. 1-6 (Stoebe, 528); it is certainly witness to a wider perspective. In the narrative composition, it deals with the consequences of the defeat and so belongs with the account of the defeat itself. The extent of the Philistine domination is unclear and should not be exaggerated. It would appear to include the northern borders of the valley of Esdraelon and the western approaches to the Jordan crossings (cf. Hertzberg, 232; Stoebe, 528-29).

On the day after the battle, the Philistines come to strip the dead and take their trophies. There is no indication of the battle's duration; it would appear that Saul was not recognized in the course of the fighting. The gruesome practices of victory are known elsewhere (cf. 17:51, 54). The good news was spread through the Philistine territories and trophies were probably lodged in the temples. Saul's armor was placed in the temple of Astarte; her temple in Ashkelon (mentioned by Herodotus) is a possible but not a certain candidate (cf. Driver, 230, and Stoebe, 530; McCarter, 443, opts for Beth-shan).

The passage concludes with the noble deed of the inhabitants of Jabesh-gilead, who recover the bodies and give them respectful burial. One may assume a connection with Saul's act of deliverance on their behalf (ch. 11). The inclusion of the bodies of Saul's sons in the report may be assimilation to the preceding or may indicate that the material was not originally homogeneous (v. 12a; LXX mentions only Jonathan). The reason for the unusual burning of the bodies is not explained, although disfigurement, corruption, and distance from the family burial ground are all possible contributing causes (cf. Klein, 290).

The bones were buried under a sacred tree (cf. 22:6) and a secondary rite of mourning observed. According to 2 Sam 21:12-14, they remained in Jabesh-gilead until their transfer, in David's reign, to the family burial ground in Geba, in the land of Benjamin.

Genre

Fundamentally, what chs. 28–31 give us is a (→) narrative composition, built up substantially from two (→) stories (more accurately: two → reported stories) and two (→) reports. A narrative composition is an arrangement of various narrative traditions to form a narrative text without necessarily forming a flowing literary unity. Here we have the issue recognized by all commentators that ch. 28 is chronologically and geographically later than chs. 29–30; there is not a flowing literary unity. A narrative composition can accommodate variant versions of tradition or contradictory views that need to be juxtaposed and that cannot be held together within a single story; such is the case for 1 Sam 8-12. A narrative composition can also hold in a single narrative line traditions or stories that do not belong in a single chronological line; such is the case here for 1 Sam 28–31.

One of the general difficulties in the interpretation of chs. 28–31 has been the recognition of the commonality that holds together 27:1–28:2 and chs. 29–31. There is a tendency to speak of these as if it were a source, while almost all scholars know that extensive sources on the pentateuchal model do not exist in the books of Samuel. What has been missing is the recognition that chs. 28–31 constitute a narrative composition that extends for four chapters. The model of the source has been a distraction.

As has been discussed at the start of this section, the composition creates a plot of its own. Aristotle, in *The Poetics,* called plot "the imitation of an action" and also "the arrangement of the incidents." For E. M. Forster, story concerns the narrative of events "in their time-sequence," while plot concerns a narrative of events with "the emphasis falling on causality" (see Holman, *Handbook to Literature,* 396-99, esp. p. 396). It is fair here to speak of a plot that is triggered by the Philistine mobilization against Israel and Achish's order for David to join his contingent (28:1-2). The relevant incidents are then organized, not in their time-sequence, but with a view to displaying causality. God's rejection of Saul is the cause of his death: "tomorrow you and your sons shall be with me" (28:19). The Philistines' rejection of David's participation is the cause of his absence. With this causality established, the composition can go on to narrate the contrasting outcomes for David and Saul.

So much for the whole; it is time to turn to the parts. First among these is the (→) battle report. Battle reports have a particular structure, dictated by their subject matter. Battles must have armies opposed to each other, a location where they are fought, and an outcome, usually detailed with reference to casualty figures. Such a report is spread over at least 28:1a; 29:1; and 31:1.

Of the (→) stories, the first is 28:3-25 (more accurately: a → reported story). The consultation of the medium at Endor has potential for entertainment: the anxious need for an answer, the reluctance of the medium, the ghost-like apparition, the identification of the spirit, and the fateful message it brings — and all this spiced by the mystery of a communication from beyond the grave. It is significant that, in the story as reported here, there is very little of such elaboration. There is as much emphasis on the woman's reluctance as there is on the appearance of the spirit. The gravity of the occasion pervades the telling of the story and is crowned by the fearful utterance of Samuel.

Such an incident is not without parallel in ancient literature. There is the consultation of the dead Enkidu by Gilgamesh (cf. *ANET,* 98) and of Teiresias by Odysseus (*Odyssey* XI, 13ff. — for further literature, see Stoebe, 491-92).

The second (→) story is in ch. 30 (more accurately: → reported story); it moves close to (→) legend. The plot moves in a relatively straight line, from the severe loss discovered at Ziklag to the recovery of all that was lost and of abundant spoil to boot. From a narrative point of view, the issues raised by the exhausted who have to drop out of the pursuit and the chance finding of the Egyptian who can guide the pursuit all add to the interest and liveliness of the story.

It is also worth noting that the two items incorporated into the story — the decree (v. 24b) and the list of David's beneficiaries (vv. 27-30) — expand the narrative beyond what might have been its original bounds. Both look to the larger narrative horizon of David's rise to power in Israel.

The first of the (→) reports concerns David's rejection by the Philistine leaders (ch. 29). It is not cast in story form: there is no tension aroused, no plot, no resolution — although tension lurks in the context and could easily be emphasized. It is a report within a narrative context. The predominance of speeches is remarkable: 49 words of plain narrative; 33 words introducing speeches; and 176 words of speeches, constituting 68 percent of the whole. Speeches may serve to create mood or convey intention and meaning. So this account of David's dismissal is heavily overlaid with a message that goes beyond the basic information.

The second (→) report is closer to the simple variety (ch. 31). It has been seen as composed of several (→) short communications, consisting of vv. 1, 2, 3-5, 6, 7, 8-10, and 11-13 (Rendtorff, "Beobachtungen," 437). However, they have not simply been juxtaposed; they have been assimilated into their present context and bonded into a coherent unity. Awareness of the potential of a reported story cautions against excessive literary fragmentation.

Setting

The story of the episode of Endor may have been preserved in popular circles and been stripped of its more popular elements in its present telling. Or it may have circulated and/or originated among specialists in divination (for example, Abiathar and followers) almost as a cautionary tale. It cannot be facilely assumed to be merely a piece of local tradition (cf. Hertzberg, 217; Stoebe, 488). Which of the four participants told the story? Before David's establishment on the throne, it might have cost the medium her life to do so. It is possible that here too we could have the results of contemporary inquiries. The editorial stitching around vv. 17-19aα suggesting a prophetic insertion cautions against too late a date for the original.

The report of David's dismissal is most likely to have originated in and been preserved by the military circles of his followers. Perhaps even the distinction between the lords (*seren*, 29:2, 6-7) and the commanders (*śar*, 29:3-4, 9) of the Philistines is from those who served with David under Achish and knew these things. The need to tell their story would surely have been felt, and we may presume that both their exploits and their explanations were often enough retailed. Fiction is obviously not impossible but without a core it would have wide ramifications; evidence is difficult to find.

The prophetic insertion (vv. 17-19aα) is most economically attributed to the redaction of the Prophetic Record. Such additions, forging links between stories, can occur early in the independent history of stories or later, after they have been incorporated into more extensive documents. Without denying such possibilities, economy of hypothesis suggests the time and setting of the compilation of a more extensive narrative such as the PR.

The emphasis on David, his wives, his deeds, his spoil, and his decree makes it clear that the story of ch. 30 originates from Davidic circles. The lack of details of military tactics, coupled with details such as the provisions given the starving Egyptian, make it doubtful whether we should look to military circles for the preservation of the story. It is the absence of details of interest that place it on the fringes of (→) legend. The specific concern with Judah might suggest a connection with David's court at Hebron. The vividness of some of the details might favor an early date. Little as it is, more than this can hardly be said.

The setting that obviously comes to mind for the traditions of ch. 31 is among the people of Jabesh-gilead, whom we would expect to tell of the death of the king to whom they were loyal and to celebrate their demonstration of respectful loyalty to him in death. From there, the information might well have passed into Davidic circles (cf. 2 Sam 2:4a-7; 21:11-14). At the same time, 2 Sam 1 shows the interest in Saul's death among David's people too, so that it is impossible to narrow down a setting with any certainty.

Meaning

The first two chapters (chs. 28–29) deal with the destinies of Saul and David, setting both Saul's death and David's absence from the battle scene in an appropriate light. The announcement of the Philistine preparations for war (28:1a) opens a section that will conclude with Saul's death. David is inevitably involved (28:1b-2). The alternatives for David, unsaid of course, are fighting on the Philistine side or acting as Saul's fifth column and becoming an adversary to the Philistines. The episode at Endor shows Saul as doomed — and it is YHWH's doing. Then David is saved by the emergence of a third option: he is compelled to be absent from the scene of battle in which YHWH's will is to be achieved.

In this sense, the primary meaning of the passage reveals Israel's defeat and Saul's death as the result neither of David's doing nor of David's failure but as the result of Saul's rejection by YHWH. Not only is it YHWH's doing, but according to 28:17-19a it is the outcome of Saul's own failure to obey.

291

The narrator allows Saul to see the meaning of events (28:15b) that in the narrative have long been clear (16:14). Later, much the same will occur for David (cf. 2 Sam 5:12). Ch. 28 spells out in clear terms what has been implicit in earlier stories in the tradition: YHWH has turned away from Saul. From the point of view of narrative technique, we must say that the compiler has the threads of the story under close control. From the point of view of theology, it would seem that the perception of the meaning and significance of events is gained only from the end, when one looks back upon the complicated shape of reality. Those who compiled these texts knew it: "Now the spirit of the LORD departed from Saul, and an evil spirit from the LORD tormented him" (16:14). The prophetic circle took it on themselves to read history and to determine that the departure of the LORD's spirit spelled the rejection of Saul (1 Sam 15:1–16:13 etc.). This prophetic vision is now granted us in the present text; it need not have been present when the text began.

As we have noted, respect for Saul is present in the text. Josephus's eulogy of Saul is worth noting at this point, even if his rhetoric is in tension with 28:20-21. It is a fitting encomium for Saul.

> For he, although he knew of what was to come and his impending death, which the prophet had foretold, yet determined not to flee from it or, by clinging to life, to betray his people to the enemy and dishonour the dignity of kingship; instead, he thought it noble to expose himself, his house and his children to these perils and, along with them, to fall fighting for his subjects. . . . Such a man alone, in my opinion, is just, valiant and wise, and he, if any has been or shall be such, deserves to have all men acknowledge his virtue. . . . To harbour in one's heart no hope of success, but to know beforehand that one must die and die fighting, and then not to fear nor be appalled at this terrible fate, but to meet it with full knowledge of what is coming — that, in my judgement, is proof of true valour. (*Antiquities,* VI. §§344-50)

Where ch. 30 is concerned, pointers to its meaning can be seen in the episode's beginning and end. At its beginning: in the threat to the life and leadership of David, followed by his being strengthened in YHWH and his use of the ephod. At its end: in the total recovery of what was lost and the role given David in the distribution of the spoils.

Clearly, there is a contrast with Saul. Saul in distress turns to YHWH and is unanswered. David, in distress, is strengthened in YHWH and guided by YHWH. The emphasis on David's charisma and leadership is evident in the insistence that "David recovered all that the Amalekites had taken. . . . David brought back everything" (vv. 18-19). Precisely this insistence on what must have seemed unlikely brings out the fundamental act: YHWH is with David. The exchange over the distribution of the spoils provides an apt opportunity to emphasize this; it is YHWH who has given the victory (v. 23). Part of the emphasis and part of the irony lie in the realization that at about the same time YHWH's anointed was dying in defeat on Mt. Gilboa.

The distribution of the spoil, which forms a major part of the story, portrays David functioning in a kingly role. As Saul's kingship was evident in his decree concerning the "worthless fellows" who protested his crowning (cf. 10:27; 11:12-13), so David exercises kingly power in issuing a decree that becomes customary law in Israel, also triggered by the grumbling of "worthless fellows" (30:22). As David acted as deliverer in Judah before his time as king (23:1-5), so here he now acts as distributor of favors in Judah (vv. 26-31, contrast 22:7-8).

All of this is depicted in a situation that is not of David's doing or David's seeking. The beginning is painted in colors of catastrophe; the fragility of David's situation is made evident. But out of this disaster, David is able — with YHWH's guidance and help in the background — to achieve an operation that is successful beyond expectations. This success is won against the Amalekites, an archenemy. It was a flawed expedition against the Amalekites that won for Saul his rejection as king (ch. 15). Now Saul is going down to defeat and failure against Israel's other archenemy, the Philistines. The irony is overwhelming.

The expansion of the narrative beyond the story of a highly successful punitive foray is completely in line with its place in the broader narrative. Here David is presented as the consummate leader, favored by YHWH, with success and reputation on a broad scale, at the precise moment when Saul is passing from the scene, under the cloud of YHWH's rejection.

The final act in ch. 31 is simply reported, noting Saul's death and its accompanying circumstances. A note of condemnation and judgment is added in 1 Chron 10:13-14; it is absent here. The events are portrayed in a remarkably neutral fashion. In the preceding narrative, the judgment has already been passed and the interpretation of the events made clear (e.g., 16:14; 28:3-25; etc.). There is no need, therefore, for it to be repeated at this point.

The events have led inexorably, perhaps inevitably, to this the nadir of Saul's reign. In the narrative, the theological judgment passed on these events is that they express YHWH's rejection of Saul: YHWH has turned from you and become your enemy; tomorrow you and your sons shall be with me (28:16, 19). The event itself, and its aftermath, is presented neutrally. The king who rose by the sword (ch. 11) dies as a warrior, among his troops on the battlefield, and receives in the end a warrior's grave.

With his death, the story of Saul is brought to a close. David's is not. 2 Sam 1 is already concerned more with the attitude of David in his rise to power. But already, earlier in the broad narrative, the concern has been shown for the events that lie beyond the death of Saul. Saul's rejection was in view of another (cf. 13:14; 15:28; 16:1). This awareness is present in the comparison of Saul and David in 16:14–18:13 (text common to MT and LXX), in 18:14-16, in the assurances of David's success (26:25) or succession (23:17; 25:28, 30), as well as in the immediately preceding passage (30:26-31). The destiny of Saul has been realized; the destiny of David and Israel lies ahead. The narrative must go on.

Bibliography of Works Cited Above

ANET. Ancient Near Eastern Texts Relating to the Old Testament. 3rd ed. with Supplement. Edited by James B. Pritchard. Princeton: Princeton University Press, 1969.

Budde, Karl. *Die Bücher Samuel.* KHC 8. Tübingen: Mohr, 1902.

Edelman, Diana Vikander. *King Saul in the Historiography of Judah.* JSOTSup 121. Sheffield: Sheffield Academic Press, 1991.

Holman, C. Hugh. *A Handbook to Literature.* 3rd ed. Indianapolis: Bobbs-Merrill, 1972.

Josephus, Flavius. *Jewish Antiquities.* Books V-VIII. The Loeb Classical Library. London: Heinemann, 1934.

Rendtorff, Rolf. "Beobachtungen zur altisraelitischen Geschichtsschreibung anhand der Geschichte vom Aufstieg Davids." Pp. 428-39 in *Probleme biblischer Theologie.* Edited by H. W. Wolff. Munich: Chr. Kaiser, 1971.

Chapter 10

DIACHRONIC DIMENSION: FROM PAST TEXTS TO PRESENT TEXT

The Production of Literature in Ancient Israel

Before we look at the growth of the text of Samuel, it will be helpful to look more generally at the production of texts in ancient Israel. Everything that we take for granted now could not be taken for granted then. With the relatively recent decipherment of key languages — Assyrian (1857), Egyptian (1822), Hittite (1947), Ugaritic (1932), for example — and with the discoveries made by archaeology, our knowledge of ancient Israel and the ancient Near East is an immense improvement over what it was until all too recently. At the same time, we need to allow ourselves to be surprised by just how little we know about the production of literature in ancient Israel or even in the ancient Near East. A valuable recent resource in this area is Susan Niditch, *Oral World and Written Word.*

The Bible's most cynical sage, Qohelet, had his complaint even in biblical times: "of making many books there is no end" (Qoh 12:12). Probably Qohelet meant something like "documents." His Hebrew word is *sēper,* used a little under two hundred times in the Hebrew Bible. The term *sēper* ("book") has many uses. We are familiar with the book of the law and the books of the prophets and various books referred to as sources. But those are far from all. The victory over the Amalekites was to be written "as a reminder in a book" and recited in Joshua's hearing (Exod 17:14). There was "the book of the covenant" (Exod 24:7). Curses are put "in writing," literally: in the book (Num 5:23). "Book" *(sēper)* is the word for a "certificate" of divorce (Deut 24:1; Isa 50:1; Jer 3:8). The same word is used for the letter that Uriah carried from David to Joab (2 Sam 11:14-15), for the letter that Naaman carried to the king of Israel (2 Kgs 5:5-7), for the letter that Jeremiah sent to the exiles (29:1). It is the term used for the letters Jezebel sent in Ahab's name to Naboth's neighbors (1 Kgs 21:8-11). The same word serves for Jehu's correspondence ordering the killing of Ahab's royal family (2 Kgs 10:1-2, 6-7). It serves for the documents delivered by messengers and envoys (2 Kgs 19:14; 20:12). The same word *(sēper)* is used in Isaiah for a sealed document (29:11-12), a scroll (29:18; 34:4), and the equivalent of a tablet (30:8). In Jeremiah, it is used for a property deed (32:10-16) and for the famous scroll of Baruch (ch. 36; cf. 45:1; 51:60, 63). The phrase is used for Ezekiel's scroll too (2:9). Job wanted his words inscribed "in a book" *(sēper,* 19:23).

So what concerns us is the writing of documents, the writing industry. Three central questions will do: Who wrote the documents? Who read the documents? Who kept the documents? Royal courts and temples probably had writers, readers, and keepers. It is likely that wealthy families had them too (cf. the private library at Ugarit; the Shaphan family in Jerusalem). Annals and records were among the documents kept at royal courts. Rituals and psalms were among the documents kept at the temple. Laws were needed in towns and villages where judgment was passed "in the gate," but documents need not have replaced memory. Where were the documents kept and updated? Were collections such as 2 Sam 21–24 kept at court? If priestly writings and a possible Priestly Document were kept in the temple, where would we look for the Yahwist text and the Deuteronomistic History? At the royal court? The books of the prophets began in the hands of the prophet's disciples; where did they end up? There is so much where we can only guess.

Before printing (Gutenberg, 15th century), documents were copied. In the Middle Ages, monks did it in monasteries. In ancient Israel, some copyists did it in scriptoria; we have an example at Qumran. How available such copies were in earlier times we have no idea, but a limited distribution is almost certain. Stories must have been written, because we have them. We assume stories were told; we have minimal information about those who told them. "Singers, both men and women," are mentioned three times in the Older Testament, in association with the royal court (2 Sam 19:35 [NRSV; Heb., 19:36]; Qoh 2:8; 2 Chron 35:25). Perhaps these court performers were the elite of the storytellers' guild. Probably, but we do not know.

When we come down to it, in all honesty we do not know with certainty who wrote, read, or kept the books of Samuel. As part of a DH associated with King Josiah's reform, did they belong in the royal court? As part of the record of God's dealings with Israel, capable of criticism of kings and people, did they belong in the temple? Permeated with prophetic influence, did they belong elsewhere?

If we are uncertain about the production and preservation of the final form of these books, can we be more definite about some earlier stages? Probably not. It would seem obvious, for example, that stories about David's early days and his rise to power were told among his supporters. To others it seems equally obvious that Davidic traditions could be largely fictional compositions from a later time. It is also possible that the texts we have are only shadows of the stories that were told. The texts report what the stories were that were told; the texts may have served as a base from which to begin telling the stories. The texts reflect a storytelling culture; they do not record it. So who wrote these texts? Who read them? Who kept them?

Documents and letters were written when they were needed. Annals were written when events were over or years and reigns completed. Prophetic books (documents) seem to have been written when periods of prophecy ceased (Isa 8:16-17) or when a prophet was silenced (cf. Jer 36:5-6). A first version of the DH is likely to have been composed in anticipatory support of Josiah's reform and modified afterwards. A Prophetic Record may have been composed in support of Jehu's revolt; whether before or after is uncertain. So documents could be written before events or after them. What of the stories of David?

That stories of David were told or sung at court, in the private houses of powerful supporters, and at hearths and campfires across the country is likely — in particular, in places where people struggled to name the meaning of what had happened for them and their tribes. Our texts, the documents, are different: the stories brilliantly condensed, the narrative skillfully composed. What triggered the composition? Who was responsible? Where were they kept? We do not know.

It would be apparently easy to appeal to a DH and lodge them at court or temple or with some significant family or group. The ease is only apparent. The reality, like most reality, is more complex. There were prior stages; the text is loaded with their signals. Apart from the Ark Narrative (in whatever manifestations), a narrative composition about David's rise to power — as a written text — and another reflecting David's middle years seem likely to have been part of the process. At least one later intermediate stage is likely, when other traditions were blended into the Davidic stories — for example, what I call the PR. A PR can be produced by the prophetic groups around Elisha; its preservation is another question. But before that, there is the question of the Davidic stories. Who wrote them as documents? Who read them? Who kept them? Why?

We do not know. We can only guess. My suspicions lie with vested interests, factions at court, and powerful families in Jerusalem, as well as those who needed to articulate and bolster their belief in God's action in their midst. The narrative of David's rise to power is flattering enough that it could have been composed at court. Perhaps it was — but when power is established, how strongly felt is the need to legitimate it? Perhaps it is felt most urgently by those who want to establish their share of it more securely or by those who need to articulate its meaning. The narrative about David's middle years — insightful enough to be called the story of David's fragility — is remarkably ambivalent toward the king. On the one hand, David is presented as a great military tactician and inspirer of huge loyalty; on the other hand, he is womanizer, murderer, incompetent administrator, and victim of rebellion. Was a document such as this more likely to have originated in the houses of the influential than in the courts of the kings? We do not know. We can only guess. We are entitled to our suspicions. (It is principally this ambivalence that makes the Stories of David's Middle Years a poor candidate for a post-exilic challenge to Davidic messianism and a good candidate for the formation of royal counselors.)

Early origins for Israel's texts are not "flavor of the month" in the recent climate of scholarship. However, two aspects of the Samuel text must be accounted for. One is the close resemblance in some of the texts of David's rise to power to what we call "oral history." The primary study here is Rendtorff's "Beobachtungen" in the von Rad Festschrift. What Rendtorff calls "short communications" *(kurze Mitteilungen)* are described as the results of research undertaken by the compiler of the narrative (cf. "Beobachtungen," 434). This is a matter of literary genre for specific verses, the record of fragments of information gathered while still remembered — and unlikely to be remembered without the link to the wider context. Such material need not reflect fictive invention or imaginative power. The other aspect to be considered is the reworking or overwriting of older texts, particularly in ways that require written operations. The best example of this is 1 Sam 9:1–10:16; there are others. The processes within these texts have to be accounted for. If the overwriting is to be attributed to prophetic activities associated with Jehu's revolt (cf. the PR), the older texts are necessarily quite early. Close attention to the text is needed before any generalizations can be made — much less sweeping ones.

The Stories of David's Middle Years (e.g., 2 Sam 11–20) reflect the world of the royal court, with an emphasis on the role of royal counselors and an ambivalence highly suited to stressing the importance of wise counsel for the proper governance of court and people. Abiathar and Zadok as priests tend to appear together; there is no hint of rivalry or favoritism. Such a document might well come from a private family, powerful supporters of Davidic royalty, with a vested interest in the smooth functioning of the court. Or it might have originated at the court of Jeroboam, after the division of the kingdom into north and south. The need for wise counselors at Jeroboam's newly established royal court would have been acute. Only one thing is certain: that we do not know.

Comparative study has not helped much. Assyria and Egypt do not throw great light on these particular issues. As classicists well know, the literary industries of Greece and Rome were different from that of Israel. Their products are different. Their cultural institutions also differed. The law may have been read at major festivals in Israel. Some ancestral stories may have been rehearsed. The law apart, such possibilities account for a small sprinkling of Israel's texts; for festival use, many of the ancestral stories would have badly needed bowdlerizing. The ancient world does not help us greatly.

Before we even ask about early traditions that are identifiable, it is appropriate these days to ask why we bother trying to identify early traditions. Have we any right to? Is there any reason to? Once upon a time, asking these questions would have seemed absurd. It is no longer absurd; it has become necessary.

In the time of ancient Israel, texts and traditions were brought together to form a Bible that Israel claimed as its sacred scripture. Centuries of scholarly work have made it undeniably clear that this ancient Israel brought together texts and traditions (plural, diachronic) to form a collection — its book, its sacred scripture (singular, synchronic). In that plurality and singularity lies the justification for two strands in modern biblical scholarship. Singularity claims the Hebrew Bible as ancient Israel's sacred scripture, does not fuss over its origins, and — at its best — does struggle to engage with this book in search of its meaning and value. Plurality too claims the Hebrew Bible as Israel's sacred book, but struggles with its origins, believing that in the multiplicity of these origins there is something of value for understanding where meaning is to be found.

Both strands are needed; either extreme alone is dangerous. Singularity at its extreme, denying the relevance of plurality (origins), can verge on a precritical denial of the human contribution within these texts. Plurality at its extreme, ignoring the relevance of singularity (book), can virtually deny the art and meaning of the final text. Both strands are needed if the text is to be engaged in a dialogue with the life and context of any generation. The challenge for the diachronic (plurality) is to find in the growth of the text light for the final text and meaning for the contemporary reader. The challenge for the synchronic (singularity) is — while respecting the reality of the text's origin within diverse human experiences — to find meaning in the final product of this growth. The challenge for the future is to find an integration of these two approaches that does them both justice — more felicitously than has happened so far.

Almost invariably when we come to look at the origins of a project, a family, or an idea, we run into complications and uncertainty. Everybody is in for his or her own two bits somewhere. It is no different with the origins of the books of Samuel. At this level, we will treat the two books together. The earliest overall structure for much of the whole, as maintained in this volume, goes back to prophetic activity, probably best envisaged as the PR.

With certainty out of reach, we look to probability. There probably were traditions about the Elides and about the circumstances of Samuel's birth and beginnings. The Ark Narrative was there before the PR; probably 1 Sam 4–6 and 2 Sam 6, possibly not so complete. Traditions probably existed about the reasons that pushed Israel into setting up a monarchy. One set of traditions seems to have based this move on the need for defense, especially against the Philistines. Another set of traditions seems to have based the move on the need for justice within Israel. Further traditions expressed a theological negativity toward the idea of kingship over YHWH's people.

There are extensive traditions in the text about David's rise to power in Israel and some brilliant literary narrative about the middle years of David's reign. These are often referred to respectively as the Story of David's Rise and the Succession Narrative. There are also the account of Nathan's prophetic word to David assuring him of a secure dynasty (2 Sam 7) and the list of David's successes (2 Sam 8). Finally, there is the remarkable collection in 2 Sam 21–24. It is structured chiastically, framed at beginning and end with stories of cultic impact, with otherwise unknown traditions of Davidic military exploits and organization placed either side of a core of Davidic poetry. The collection reveals to us just how much of David's history and activity are unknown to us.

Sketched broadly, these are the building blocks with which the books of Samuel began or, in some cases, were completed. The trajectory of diachronic development enables us to see how from these traditions the books of Samuel emerged and became the present text that has been the subject of this volume thus far.

It will be helpful in some cases to ask the following questions.

- Did these traditions ever exist as an independent narrative before our text?
- If so, what was the extent of the narrative?

- If so, what do we know about the composition and significance of the narrative?
- What do we know about the antecedents of such a narrative?

It makes sense to ask something like this about texts called the Ark Narrative, the Story of David's Rise, and the Stories of David's Middle Years; equally, it makes sense to give some attention to the PR, the Josianic DH, and the fully revised DH, for these works have been or are the literary context for the books of Samuel. The other building blocks do not need to be treated here, separately from the commentary.

The Ark Narrative

The question whether there is or ever was such a document as an Ark Narrative does need to be asked. The fundamental response is that there are four chapters in the books of Samuel — 1 Sam 4–6 and 2 Sam 6 — that focus exclusively on the ark and its function as a symbol of God's presence and God's power and purpose for Israel. Even the anecdotes about the deaths of Eli and his daughter-in-law are told to illustrate the significance of the ark. As such, the texts of these chapters are unique in the Older Testament. While there are other traditions about the ark — for example, its role in the wilderness or at the Jordan crossing or in military campaigns — nowhere else is text of this nature to be found. In these chapters, wonders are associated with the ark that are quite different in kind from military victory or the like. The statue of Dagon falls twice before the ark; the Philistines are struck with diseases and panic because of the ark; two cows walk away from their calves in an unnaturally straight line when pulling a cart with the ark; a crowd of people drop dead at Beth-shemesh because of the ark; a guardian of the ark drops dead on the way to Jerusalem because of the ark; a Gittite prospers because of the ark. Transparent in these texts is a mentality where certain aspects of Israel's history and God's activity are interpreted exclusively in reference to the ark. Vocabulary statistics can be assembled and style analyzed (so Rost, *Succession*), but ultimately these merely confirm what is evidently present: an unusual and exclusive focus on the ark as the symbol of God's presence and the focus of God's power and purpose in Israel. In some shape, there was an Ark Narrative.

The implications of this conclusion have been extensively debated in scholarship over the years. The literature up to 1974 has been discussed in my dissertation (Campbell, *Ark Narrative*, 1-54); it need not be rehashed here. Beyond these, two monographs have advocated different views of the extent and meaning of the Ark Narrative. For Franz Schicklberger, *Ladeerzählungen*, the text is substantially 1 Sam 4:1–6:16, its time of composition was ca. 700 B.C.E., and its assertion is that YHWH is bound to the ark and that the ark and its God can demonstrate their power and have done so (see Campbell, "Yahweh and the Ark," esp. p. 32). For P. D. Miller and J. J. M. Roberts, *Hand of the Lord,* the text includes much of 1 Sam 2:12-36, followed by 4:1–7:1, its time of composition was prior to David's victories over the Philistines, and YHWH's power and purpose are the point of the story — YHWH is in control of history (see ibid.). Both these studies refrain from extending the narrative into 2 Sam 6.

Schicklberger's work depends on his analysis of layers in 1 Sam 4:1–6:16 and the interpretation given to these. In his judgment, an association with 2 Sam 6 is not sustained. For Miller and Roberts, the composition of their ark narrative preceded David's move on Jerusalem (*Hand of the Lord*, 73-75); 2 Sam 6 would have been written later but with the earlier chapters in mind (ibid., 24). What any interpretation must do is account for the total text of the traditions; the claim of a post-Solomonic date must either create a distance from 2 Sam 6 or account for a text that leaves the ark at the Davidic tent-sanctuary in Jerusalem (6:17; 7:2) without somehow including its installation in Solomon's temple — surely the jewel in the crown of the ark's coming to Jerusalem.

What was the extent of the ark narrative? The specific focus on the ark of God is restricted to 1 Sam 4–6 and 2 Sam 6. Whether the move to Jerusalem was part of the narrative from the outset is open to discussion. Two issues are important. First, the plausibility of ending a narrative with the ark shipped off to out-of-the-way Kiriath-jearim (1 Sam 6:19–7:1). Second, the judgment by some that there is continuous text from 1 Sam 7:2aα to 2 Sam 6:2. In this understanding, "from there" in 2 Sam 6:2 refers to Kiriath-jearim; the "Baale-judah," correctly understood, can refer naturally to the citizens of Judah and need not be emended to provide a place name (Campbell, "Yahweh and the Ark," 39-40). The continuous text would then read:

> From the day that the ark was lodged at Kiriath-jearim, a long time passed (1 Sam 7:2aα). And David arose and went with all the people who were with him from the citizens of Judah to bring up from there the ark of God (2 Sam 6:2).

This is disputed and it is not of major importance. If the shaping of the text involved a later inclusion of the ark's move to Jerusalem, it is likely that 2 Sam 6 was composed with 1 Sam 4–6 in view (so Miller and Roberts, *Hand of the Lord*). In this scenario, the two blocks constitute virtually a single text.

What matters is our understanding of the significance of these chapters. At the level of the present text, the issue of date of composition is unimportant. In terms of the text that is focused exclusively on the ark of God, it is almost unthinkable that Israel should be without the ark for a sustained period. At the level of the present text, the ark is not the exclusive symbol of God's presence and activity; there are also prophets who speak God's word. In texts where the ark is the exclusive focus of God's presence in Israel, the ark cannot be left in obscurity for long. If 1 Sam 4–6 and 2 Sam 6 were written together, they could be written at almost any time prior to the consecration of Solomon's temple; they end with the return of the ark of God to Jerusalem, where God is present again to Israel. If 1 Sam 4–6 were written as a totality, without a concluding passage that brought the ark back to the mainstream of Israel, the text leaves Israel deprived of a major traditional symbol of God's presence. As a temporary staging place, Kiriath-jearim is acceptable; as a final resting place, Kiriath-jearim can be no more than a repository for outworn sacral objects.

As noted earlier in the commentary, no theology could leave the ark of God in obscurity without adequately accounting for the absence of God from Israel. Departure is a correlative either of abandonment or return. Once the presence of the ark in Jerusalem is acknowledged, its departure from Shiloh is a correlative of its return to Jerusalem. Until the presence of the ark in Jerusalem is acknowledged, for those for whom the ark is the exclusive symbol of God's presence in Israel, its departure from Shiloh is shrouded in uncertainty. It is a departure that may ultimately signify either abandonment or return. There is no weightier theological issue for Israel.

An outline of this understanding of the ark narrative in its present form can be presented structurally:

The Ark Narrative   **1 Samuel 4–6; 2 Samuel 6**
  I. The ark and Shiloh: Israel's glory departs   1 Sam 4:1-22
    A. Events
      1. First battle: loss of battle
      2. **Pause**: why and what?
      3. Second battle: loss of battle and loss of ark
    B. Interpretations
      1. Eli anecdote: death
      2. Ichabod anecdote: departure
 II. The ark after departure   1 Sam 5:1–6:21 + 7:1-2aα
    A. Remaining with the Philistines: no lasting joy
    B. Returning to the Israelites: no lasting joy
    C. **Pause**: why and what?
III. The ark and Jerusalem: Israel's glory returns   2 Sam 6:2-23
    A. The move to Jerusalem begun under David's auspices
    B. **Pause**: why and what?
    C. The move to Jerusalem completed under YHWH's auspices

The significance of the three cases that I have termed "Pause: why and what?" is clearly visible only when the overall text is surveyed. These are moments in which the narrative pauses in its forward movement; they are moments in which the hearers or readers are invited to pause and reflect: Why has this happened? What does it mean for Israel and for us?

In the first two cases, these questions are only partly answered. It is only in the third case that the answers for all three can become clear. Like the best writing of any age, however, the answers are implied within the text for the thoughtful to find; they are not spelled out with brutal bluntness. Here, we can review them briefly.

The first "pause" is at 1 Sam 4:3-9. Earlier, I referred to this as an intermezzo. The "why?" question is both answered and not answered. After v. 3, the question has to be: Why were we defeated? Verse 3's explicit question is: "Why has the LORD put us to rout today?" It is assumed, in the narrative, that YHWH defeated Israel. The absence of the ark is shown not to account for the defeat.

That initial question — Why were we defeated? — is not answered implicitly until the third "pause." The "what?" question relates to meaning. The ultimate reality is that the Philistines did not defeat us; our own God defeated us, "put us to rout today before the Philistines." What does it mean that our God has defeated us? Will our God abandon us or will our God remain with us?

The second "pause" really comes with 1 Sam 7:1. Because it is invited by a gap in the text — a gap that is not to be filled — it is difficult to locate appropriately within a structure. As with the first "pause," its "why?" question is both answered and not answered. After 7:1, the question has to be: Why has the ark retired to the cultic backwater of Kiriath-jearim? The answer in 6:19-20 is: because the people of Beth-shemesh wanted to be rid of it. Left unanswered is the question: Why did the God of Israel behave so obnoxiously to the Israelites — treating them as the Philistines were treated? This question too is not answered until the third "pause," and then only implicitly. The meaning question is clear: What does it mean that God has withdrawn to Kiriath-jearim? Will our God abandon us? Will our God remain with us? The answer lies in 2 Sam 6.

The third "pause" is at 2 Sam 6:6-11. The statement is that David's procession with the ark stopped dead when Uzzah dropped dead. According to the text, Uzzah was struck by God. If Uzzah did what he should not have done, it is oddly out of place for the narrative to report David's anger and fear; God has merely punished a cultic infraction. If Uzzah did what he was expected to do as a guardian of the ark, the question has to be faced: Why should the text report David as angered and afraid? Why turn the ark aside to a Gittite's house? It is a "why?" question, Why is this anger and fear of David's told? The answer: because the calamity is understood as an expression of YHWH's disfavor, an understanding heightened by YHWH's subsequent blessing of Obed-edom's house, where the ark has been parked for three months. YHWH brings the ark to Jerusalem, not David. David's procession has been stopped; the movement to Jerusalem will resume when YHWH, by dispensing favor to Obed-edom, gives the green light to proceed. The "what?" question — what does it mean for Israel? — then elicits a retrospective answer to the whole narrative and to the question that was asked in 1 Sam 4:3, back at the beginning. What does it mean that God did this? It means that YHWH is moving from the Israel of Shiloh to the Israel of Jerusalem. It is the faith claim that what is primary in all that has happened between Saul's failure and David's success is not primarily the result of David's politics but of God's will to be associated with a different Israel. Fundamentally, David has not changed the reality of Israel; YHWH has. In the past, YHWH was with Israel at Shiloh (or its equivalent); now YHWH is with Israel in Jerusalem. In the past, there were no kings in Israel; now and in the future there will be kings in Israel. This is not David's doing; it is YHWH's. What is signified in Samuel's anointing of David is equally signified in the narrative of the ark's move to Jerusalem.

Given the importance attributed to the Ark Narrative here, there is worth in exploring what we know about its antecedents. Georg Fohrer has attempted a reconstruction of the early history of the Ark Narrative, based on an examination of the distribution of the titles for the ark (cf. "Ladeerzählung"). Within the narrative, a number of terms are used for the ark: ark of YHWH, ark of God, ark of the covenant of YHWH, ark of the covenant of God, ark of the God of Israel, and the ark. The distribution of the titles is as follows:

	1 Sam 4	1 Sam 5	1 Sam 6	1 Sam 7	2 Sam 6
Ark of YHWH	v. 6	vv. 3, 4	vv. 1, 2, 8, 11, 15, 18, 19, 21	v. 1 [x2]	vv. 9, 10, 11, 13, 15, 16, 17
Ark of God	vv. 11*, 13, 17, 18, 19, 21, 22	1, 2, 10 [x2]			vv. 2, 3, 4, 6, 7, 12 [x2]
Ark of the covenant of YHWH	vv. 3, 4, 5				
Ark of the covenant of God	v. 4				
Ark of the God of Israel		vv. 7, 8 [x3], 10, 11	v. 3		
The ark			v. 13	v. 2	v. 4

*1 Sam 4:11 alone has no definite article before God (i.e., *ărôn 'ĕlōhîm* for *ărôn ha'ĕlōhîm*). For Fohrer, the titles referring to the covenant (in 4:3-5) need not be taken into account; they are regarded as later insertions, under dtr influence.

Fohrer has drawn attention to the implications of the distinction between the use of the "ark of God" and the "ark of YHWH" for the growth of the Ark Narrative. Within the "ark of God" material, I am not convinced by further divisions, where Fohrer omits 1 Sam 4:4b, 11b-22 and 5:6-9, 10*, 11-12 and 2 Sam 6:3-8; there are other explanations. What is possible is not, by that fact, necessary — especially when other possibilities exist. The fluctuation among the occurrences of the two main titles is as follows:

Ark of God: 1 Sam 4:11*, 13, 17, 18, 19, 21, 22; 5:1, 2, 7, 8 (3x), 10 (3x), 11; 2 Sam 6:2, 3, 4, 6, 7, 12 (2x).
Ark of YHWH: 1 Sam 4:6; 5:3, 4; 6:1, 2, 8, 11, 15, 18, 19, 21; 7:1 (2x); 2 Sam 6:9, 10, 11, 13, 15, 16, 17.

If the "ark of God" material is taken as a whole, it forms a plausible narrative: 1 Sam 4:1-4, 10-22; 5:1-2, 6-12; . . . 2 Sam 6:2-8, 12 (omitting 2 Sam 6:1). Included are: the two defeats of Israel; the loss of the ark; the deaths of Eli's sons and of Eli and his daughter-in-law; then the discomfiture of the three Philistine cities; the bringing up of the ark is begun; finally the ark is brought to the city of

David with rejoicing (v. 12). Two assumptions are required for the reconstruction to be considered adequate. First, that 1 Sam 6:1–7:1 has replaced an earlier account of the transfer of the ark from Philistine territory (1 Sam 5:11) to the house of Abinadab (2 Sam 6:3). Second, that 2 Sam 6:10-11 has replaced an earlier mention of a sojourn in the house of Obed-edom.

A simpler narrative than the present text, this is still interpretatively rich. The two anecdotes, if they belonged in this earliest form of the text, emphasize the fatal seriousness of the loss of the ark. YHWH's clear mastery over the Philistines still raises the question as to who was in control of the battlefield at Ebenezer-Aphek. The incident of Uzzah's death may still have manifested God's control of the movement of the ark, though less obviously than in the present text. It is also significant that, in this early kernel, the Ark Narrative does not end before the coming of the ark to Jerusalem.

The redaction of this story, using the title "ark of YHWH" (1 Sam 4:5-9; 5:3-5; 6:1–7:1; 2 Sam 6:9-11, 13-15, 17-19), carries further and makes more explicit what was already present or implicit in the earlier narrative. The redactor has presumably perceived the potential of the story as a vehicle for expressing God's will. This potential has been discussed in the commentary (or will be for 2nd Samuel).

The reconstruction cannot be regarded as certain. A major drawback is the need to assume that 1 Sam 6:1–7:1 and 2 Sam 6:10-11 have completely replaced passages of the original text. Nevertheless, the reconstruction accounts for variations in the title used for the ark and is in harmony with some other literary-critical observations and form-critical structures of the text. While uncertain, it opens avenues for insight into the theological processes at work in 10th-century Israel; it requires consideration. The consideration becomes more acute when the contours of David's rise to power are explored.

As was noted in *Unfolding the Deuteronomistic History,* a Story of David's Rise "may have begun with the earliest traditions of Saul's rise to kingship, a prerequisite for David's; it would have ended with David's accession to the throne of Judah and Israel (perhaps including early texts of the ark's coming to Jerusalem and YHWH's commitment to David's dynastic security, concluding with 8:15; . . .)" (Campbell and O'Brien, *Unfolding,* 219).

"Early texts of the ark's coming to Jerusalem" therefore involves an understanding of the Story of David's Rise. It may be reasonable to assume that any composition of the traditions associated with David's rise to power in Israel would have included early texts of the ark's coming to Jerusalem and of YHWH's commitment to David's dynastic security. We need to be clear that we have no knowledge — and should claim none — of any text known as the Story of David's Rise (see below). What we have are traditions about the early years of David from his anointing by Samuel to his establishment as king of Israel. What we do not have is evidence for the precise nature of any composition involving these traditions in the early storytelling tradition of ancient Israel.

Comparison with other texts may help clarify what is meant. For the Stories of David's Middle Years (2 Sam 11–20), we have a coherence of sequence and a level of literary artistry that is not found elsewhere. For the PR, there are arcs of theme, concept, or language that hold together a wide range of traditions. The narrative of David's early years by definition escapes these pointers to the continuity and content of documentary status. It is a collection of traditions. Common to them is the theme that David's success was due to YHWH's support. There is a possible beginning; there is a possible end. There is the possibility that, at some point, these rich traditions were woven into a narrative composition. It is possible; it is not certain. We do not know. We can argue about the possibility. We may indeed believe. We would be unwise to do more.

In the context of our totally legitimate ignorance, we are obliged to ask whether such a composition would have included something on the coming of the ark to Jerusalem and God's promise of a Davidic dynasty. Is it reasonable to think of the narrative of David's rise to power stopping with the capture of Jerusalem, with or without the building of David's palace there? In my judgment, taking such a composition through to 2 Sam 8:15 is more reasonable than ending with 2 Sam 5:10 or 12.

If we take seriously the possibility of the story of David's rise to power being conceptualized with the inclusion of his religious and dynastic establishment (i.e., to 2 Sam 8:15), major questions arise for the earlier ark tradition. Can the coming of the ark to Jerusalem be narrated without the traditions of its going from Shiloh? How is the editing of this material about the ark, and its comings and goings, to be understood? Was there an independent Ark Narrative? What was its relationship to this material assumed to have been available for a Story of David's Rise?

In addressing these questions, it will help to have before us a text of an assumed early account of the ark of God's coming to Jerusalem, using the title, "ark of God." (Note: what is deemed significant here is not the term used for God but the title used for the ark, "ark of God.") Omitting 2 Sam 6:1, a possible text would read as follows.

> David and all the people with him . . . (omitting: from the citizens of Judah) set out and went to bring up . . . (omitting: from there) the ark of God . . . (omitting the further title of the ark). They carried the ark of God on a new cart, and brought it out of the house of Abinadab, which was on the hill. Uzzah and Ahio, the sons of Abinadab, were driving the new cart with the ark of God; and Ahio went in front of the ark . . . (omitting v. 5 as potentially late). When they came to the threshing floor of Nacon, Uzzah reached out his hand to the ark of God and took hold of it, for the oxen shook it. The anger of the LORD was kindled against Uzzah; and God struck him there because he reached out his hand to the ark; and he died there beside the ark of God. . . . It was told King David, "The LORD has blessed the household of Obed-edom and all that belongs to him, because of the ark of God." So David went and brought up the ark of God from the house of Obed-edom to the city of David with rejoicing. (cf. 2 Sam 6:2-7, 12)

In this context, it is important to have in mind the early text that, immediately following in 2 Sam 7, may have been at the core of Nathan's communication to David of God's dynastic promise — it is associated with the title "ark of God."

And [Heb.; NRSV, Now] when the king was settled in his house, the king said to the prophet Nathan, "See now, I am living in a house of cedar, but the ark of God stays in a tent." The word of the LORD came to Nathan: Go and tell my servant David: Thus says the LORD: Are you the one to build me a house to live in? . . . Did I ever speak a word with any of the tribal leaders of Israel, whom I commanded to shepherd my people Israel, saying, "Why have you not built me a house of cedar?" . . . And [Heb.; NRSV, Moreover] the LORD says to you that the LORD will make you a house. . . . Your house and your kingdom shall be made sure forever before you [Heb.; NRSV, me]; your throne shall be established forever. (2 Sam 7:1a, 2, 4-7*, 11b, 16; cf. *Unfolding*, 290-91)

If a final line were needed after this, the conclusion in 2 Sam 8:15 would provide it. It is attributed to the PR (*Unfolding*, 293), but something similar could have been formulated in any appropriate circumstance. It reads:

And [Heb.; NRSV, So] David ruled over all Israel; and David administered justice and equity to all his people.

Two factors carry particular weight in assessing these texts. One is the alternation of the titles for the ark, "ark of God" and "ark of YHWH" — their occurrence, despite difficulties, is a little too significant to be accidental. The other is the eminent reasonableness of wrapping up the story of David's rise to power with more than the defeat of the Philistines, moving further to include the coming of the ark to Jerusalem, and the promise of God to give David dynastic security. Either factor on its own would arouse interest but could be ignored. Together, they arouse interest and really cannot be ignored.

It is possible to take a strictly present-text approach. 2 Sam 6 is there. What does it mean in its context? Any feel for interpretation has to correlate this chapter with 1 Samuel 4–6. Faith's message about the power and purpose of God of the ark is there for those who wish to read it. It can be read without probing behind the present text. Those who are content with that can rest there. Those whose intellectual curiosity will not let them rest there are likely to be drawn by the two factors just mentioned: the titles of the ark and the need of the narrative.

A variety of options might be offered, each based on different assumptions about Israel's literary past. The following is economic and plausible. An early version of how the ark came to Jerusalem was probably told among the traditions of David's rise to power. All things considered, it might well have been along the lines of the passage above, from 2 Sam 6:2-7, 12. It takes for granted that people knew where the ark had been for the previous couple of decades — Kiriath-jearim, of course.

Once the ark was established in Jerusalem, a story would have been needed to celebrate its importance and explain what it was doing in Jerusalem. The "ark of God" text of 1 Sam 4–6 would have served well enough (so, 1 Sam 4:1-4, 10-22; 5:1-2, 6-12), prefixed to the story of the ark's coming to Jerusalem. The only gap to be filled is the transfer from Philistine territory to Kiriath-jearim.

After some experience, when it had been realized that some of the less intelligent listeners thought it was wonderful without getting the point of God's part in it all, the "ark of YHWH" verses may have been added to heighten the emphasis on God's power and purpose. This would have been basically the Ark Narrative as we know it now (1 Sam 4–6; 2 Sam 6). We may assume it was associated with the ark sanctuary in Jerusalem. Owing nothing to prophets, it may not have been a part of the PR; certainly, there are no signals to suggest such attribution.

When the DH drew together the traditions of the story of Israel under prophets and kings, the Ark Narrative came into its own. The emergence of Samuel as prophet in Israel gave hope of something new. The retreat of the ark from Shiloh and its absence from mainstream Israel (1 Sam 4–6) made room for a change of institutions. The move of the ark to Jerusalem endorsed the new unity of Israel under prophets and kings (2 Sam 6). The emphasis of the "ark of YHWH" editing served to highlight that all of this was, of course, God's doing, revelatory of the power and purpose of YHWH. The revision of the DH that produced our present biblical text did nothing to change this.

Genre

The genre is clearly → theological narrative. It is a very good example of narrative traditions being used to communicate theological conviction. It is storytelling. Interest is artfully aroused in the opening verses by the movement from simple defeat to the loss of the ark, through expectations of victory that have been raised and shattered. The relationship of the defeat to God's will and the issue of God's presence to Israel are raised. They are not resolved and brought into equilibrium until the ark has come to rest in its new and permanent location. The plot is apparently simple: the movement from loss to recovery, from Shiloh to Jerusalem. Principally, it involves first the Philistines and Israel and possession of the ark, then the Philistines and the ark, then Israel and the ark, and finally David and the ark and Jerusalem. But at a deeper level, God is present throughout and is the principal actor in the story (cf. 1 Sam 4:3; 5:6; 6:9; 6:20; 2 Sam 6:11-12). It is this constant question of God which forces us to realize that this is more than a mere story: it is concerned with the presence and absence of God to Israel — not merely with the modalities of Israel's relationship to its God, but with the very existence of that relationship. As theological narrative, it seeks to present events in Israel's history in such a way as to communicate an interpretation of them in terms of God's dealings with Israel, in terms of God's rejection of an old order and election of a new.

Setting

An understanding of the narrative which extends its horizons also throws light on its setting. In Jerusalem it must be; the whole import of the story assures us of that. Favorable to the Davidic monarchy it surely is; it is in David's Jerusalem that the ark has finally found "its place." But from what circles might the text have come, and on what occasion might the story have been told? The priests of the ark sanctuary remain the most obvious candidates for authorship — provided they were not afraid to leave their sanctuary and engage in the broader arena as men of theological vision and no little political courage (cf. Campbell, *Ark Narrative*, 251-52). If there were a royal Zion festival, the Ark Narrative might well have had its place in that festival and at its core. By insisting that God's choice of Zion involved far more than the election of a king, the capture of a city, and the installation of a sacred object, by insisting that what is involved is the establishment of a new order in Israel, the return of God's favor to Israel, and the beginning of a new era of salvation, the Ark Narrative would have given massive significance to such a festival.

Meaning

The concern of the Ark Narrative is one that I believe is fundamentally foreign to Christian theology. I trust that on the part of Christian theologians this is due to a proper evaluation of the incarnation rather than a lack of theological courage. The concern is whether God will abandon God's own people. It is not unknown in the ancient Near East; we find it in the laments over Sumer and Ur (see Campbell, *Ark Narrative*, 179-91). It is evident in the Older Testament in the dtr passages of Exod 32:7-14 and Num 14:11-25. It has echoes in Ps 78:59-65. It is the central theme of 1 Sam 4–6. It is the correlative of God's unconditional commitment in the face of human failure. It must be explored before faith in unconditional commitment can be held.

   If the hypothesis of an Ark Narrative is correct, including the coming of the ark to Jerusalem, it is not concerned with the events of secular history that brought David to power in Jerusalem; they are presumed or they are passed over (as is also the case in Ps 78:59-72). In the present text of 1-2 Samuel, they are reported at considerable length. Their omission within the four chapters of this narrative is a reminder of the singular nature of the theological outlook apparently represented in the Ark Narrative. It is best understood as reflecting the narrative's intense concentration on the ark. To say that the ark took no part in the story of David's rise is not to say that God took no part in it. But a special significance is given to the action of God in the coming of the ark to Jerusalem. It crowns and confirms the achievement of David. In this medium of expression, it brings God into relationship with David's history, not in the fluidity of the vicissitudes of his rise to power, but in the stability of the place where his dynasty will hold power for some four centuries.

309

The Story of David's Rise

It is possible to talk about a Story of David's Rise, but it is important to be clear what is meant. We have texts from the traditions of David's early years that could be arranged to form a narrative composition detailing the story of David's rise to power in Israel. We have such texts. We have no evidence for the actual existence of such a narrative composition. We have the possibility; we do not have the fact. In the present biblical text, we have a splendid composition arranged from these Davidic traditions. We have no evidence for the existence of such a composition prior to the present text. We may assume such an arrangement existed — or indeed several of them. We cannot know their shape and the precise details of the traditions they comprised.

As noted in the Introduction, the Story of David's Rise is different from the other narratives claimed for the literary heritage of ancient Israel. If we leave aside pentateuchal narratives, at least two comparisons may be made: (i) with the Stories of David's Middle Years (2 Sam 11–20) and (ii) with the PR (1 Sam 1:1 — 2 Kgs 10:28). 2 Sam 11–20 is held together by a coherence of narrative theme and by a level of literary excellence that is not found elsewhere in Israel's narrative literature. The thematic coherence is clear in that no major episode may be omitted without diminishing the whole. Act and consequence unfold throughout the narrative; God's intervention is rarely noted. The PR is held together by ties of theme, concept, and language. Evidence of written composition is given, for example, by the presence of prophetic editing (over-writing 1 Sam 9:1–10:16 and 15:1-35) and later dtr overwriting of the prophetic speeches (1 Kgs 14:4-13; 21:17-26; 2 Kgs 10:4-10).

The Story of David's Rise is different from both of these. What we have are stories about the period from the emergence of David at the court of Saul until the establishment of David in Jerusalem as king over Israel and Judah. While a skeleton chronology is followed, not all but certainly one or another of several stories could be omitted without detriment to the whole picture. There is a consistent portrayal of Saul as bereft of the spirit and David as successful because of YHWH's spirit. While this does not argue against a narrative composition, it is not evidence for one; it is evidence for the political climate that such stories reflect. As document, what we may legitimately call a Story of David's Rise is a hypothesis; we have no evidence pointing to its existence as a totality, or literary document, before the PR (not to be confused with Friedrich Mildenberger's prophetic editing of the Saul-David traditions). Instead what we have are a number of stories and traditions that could readily be composed into a narrative composition portraying David's rise to power in Israel. We have the stories and traditions; we do not have the composition.

The nearest thing we might have to evidence of such a narrative composition are the "short communications" identified by Rolf Rendtorff, noted earlier. These are snippets of information which, in themselves, are unlikely to have been important enough to find their way into official annals or chronicles and which are hardly substantial enough to have existed as independent traditions or stories. But they are necessary for the telling of a story or they have their part in the telling of a story, and they are collected by the compiler or storyteller in order to provide the proper setting for the story. They are found at a series of points in the Davidic stories and traditions (cf. 1 Sam 18:1-30, esp. vv. 1, 3-4; 22:1-5; 23:14-18; 27:1-7; 2 Sam 2:1-4a, 8-9, 10b; 5:3, 6-7 and 9, 11; to these we might add 2 Sam 4:4). They are evidence that some of the stories and traditions were probably told together in blocks. They are not evidence for the existence of a total narrative composition, such as we might call the Story of David's Rise. Not all the blocks needed to have been told; not all the traditions within a specific block needed to be told. On the other hand, these short snippets are pointers to the likelihood of such a composition. They are reinforced by the narrative organization in areas such as 1 Sam 17–18, 23–26, and 28–31. Pointers and reinforcement do not demonstrate the existence of a composition; they are, however, clear evidence of its possibility. To be wholly honest, we must admit that we do not know. The Story of David's Rise does not admit of even hypothetical certainty. What is certain is that it would have been possible.

To constitute a Story of David's Rise, many short and scattered traditions need to have been brought together to form a large narrative sweep from the beginnings of monarchy to the establishment of David upon the throne of Israel. A case has been made in the commentary that at least with the story of David's single combat with the Philistine Goliath a conceptualization is formulated that points to David's throne in Jerusalem (2 Sam 5; cf. Campbell, "Philistine to Throne"). As the closer study of the text will show, this narrative sweep may well have begun with 1 Sam 9, the inauguration of monarchy and the beginnings of Saul's ill-fated reign, before depicting David's slow and faultless progression to the throne of all Israel. Prior to the formation of the PR, the Saul traditions were scanty enough, and probably unfavorable enough, to form a suitable introduction to the fulsome compilation of David's successes and enjoyment of divine favor.

Precisely what is understood to constitute David's establishment upon the throne of all Israel is open for reflection. It has been usual to close the Story of David's Rise with either 2 Sam 5:10 or 5:12. Clearly, the two verses mark a significant stage in the political life of both David and Israel. However, both contain a reference to what is beyond the merely political and what has been present throughout the stories of David's rise to power: the role of God. In this context — that of the role of God — the account of the ark's coming to Jerusalem (2 Sam 6) and the account of God's commitment to the Davidic dynasty (2 Sam 7) are properly to be associated with the establishment of David upon the throne of Israel. Viewed in this light, the Story of David's Rise might well have included an early level of 2 Sam 6 and 7, perhaps ending with 8:15 (siding on this issue therefore with Wellhausen [*Composition*, 246-55] rather than Rost and von Rad, cf. Rendtorff, "Beobachtungen," 428). With 5:10, David has the city; with 5:12, David has a palace; if we include 5:17-25, David has secured liberty for his people; with 6:17-19, the ark has come to David's city; with 7:16, God has promised David dynastic security; with 8:15, David's rule is affirmed as bringing "justice and equity to all his people."

To argue that "a conceptualization is formulated" or that "short snippets" and "narrative organization" are pointers to the likelihood of such a composition as the Story of David's Rise indicates that such a composition was possible. As noted above, pointers and reinforcement do not demonstrate the existence of a composition, only its possibility. Given the significance of the texts related to David's rise to power, it is helpful to give concrete examples of what is otherwise an abstract assertion.

It was certainly possible to trace the story of David's rise to power as Israel's king back to the beginnings of Saul's kingship (in the early pre-PR texts). We do not know whether it was done in concerted literary form and, if so, what particular traditions may have been used in various versions. Similarly, two versions most probably existed of David's combat with the Philistine, Goliath — involving either Saul's theologically inspired armor-bearer or Jesse's ambitious son from the farm. Either could have suited different approaches; we do not know of their use. Furthermore, five attempts to kill David while at Saul's court are narrated and are largely independent of one another (as are most of these traditions); we cannot know whether any or all of the five would have been used.

Short communications are clustered at 22:1-5 and elsewhere (see above). They point to an overall context for reflection or storytelling; they do not point to a particular text. We do not know whether the Nob or Keilah traditions were employed in any particular version of how David rose to power. The same has to be said of the traditions of chs. 24, 25, and 26. David's sojourn with the Philistines is likely to have been featured, but traditions of his participation in the joint Philistine force may not have been used. Even David's lament over Saul and Jonathan can be passed over, as can the traditions from David's civil war with Ishbosheth and Abner.

An extensive compilation is certainly possible and probably existed in some form or other. Given the independent nature of the various traditions, judgment has to be reserved as to which specific traditions might have been part of any particular version of the story of David's rise. A wide range of these traditions exists in the present biblical text. Most are probably owed to the PR, gathering together what was available, whether as a structured account or as various collections of traditions; particular traditions may have been incorporated at other times.

In these circumstances, it is hardly surprising that scholarly opinions have varied. Concerning the idea of a larger work describing the rise of David, Hertzberg comments: "The difficulties of this hypothesis have been discussed earlier, but for want of a better it must remain as a working hypothesis" (p. 296). McCarter accepts a unified composition, from 1 Sam 16:14 to 2 Sam 5:10, "a document from the time of David himself, written before the development of the theology of dynastic promise under Solomon" (p. 29). Klein speaks of "a hypothetical document whose exact limits cannot be determined" (p. xxxii). Stoebe notes that, while 1 Sam 16–2 Sam 5 correctly reflects the historical sequence of events, this observation does not pay sufficient attention to the form-critically diverse nature of the material. He assesses 1 Sam 16 to 2 Sam 1 as containing very different elements, including what is legendary or primarily theologically formed tradition; from 2 Sam 2 on, the presentation is much more pragmatic. His conclusion: the text is a compositional arrangement of independent traditions (pp. 296-97).

A recent study by J. Vermeylen begins the original text with 1 Sam 11 and concludes it with 2 Sam 7 ("Maison de Saül"). Vermeylen bases his study on an analysis (to be published elsewhere) that identifies an early document from Davidic times, with substantial Solomonic editing, and later editing in the dtr and post-exilic periods. Despite valuable insights, where justification of the analysis is offered the work appears to be too subjective and too speculative to be helpful. In the same volume, the study by J. Briend offers an initially synchronic reading of the text from 1 Sam 16:1-13 to 2 Sam 5:3, moving on to issues of unevenness, tension, and multiple narratives, and finally to questions of history ("Figures de David," 11). Inadequate control of a complex reading and a lack of substantiating reflection lead to a fluctuation from paraphrase to historicization and diminish the value of the approach.

The structure analysis presented below is less concerned with the formal or generic aspects of the material; that is treated within each of the units. Here the concern is rather to bring out the function of each section within the text: either to articulate what is going on in the text, or, alternatively, to express the meaning discernible in the text. It is important to be aware that this is not an analysis of a claimed ancient document, the Story of David's Rise. Rather, it is an analysis of the potentially early traditions preserved in the present biblical text, portraying the time of Saul and David, that might — if all were brought together — form a compilation susceptible of a structure such as is suggested here. In these early texts, there is no pattern, no plot, that can demand the presence of this or that set of traditions in the compilation. While a logical and chronological sequence is discernible in the traditions, there is also an independence within the various traditions that requires us to allow for a variety of compilations at any given time. It is suggested that the (pre-PR) traditions associated with David's rise to power may well have gone back to the beginnings under Saul and that they may well have extended beyond David's capture of Jerusalem to his firm establishment there. What is not suggested is that there was ever a document marked by precisely these parameters. There were traditions. Storytellers and others were free to select from this panoply of traditions those that best suited their needs at any given time.

The Story of David's Rise	**1 Sam 9:1–2 Sam 8:18***
I. Emergence of kingship in Israel	1 Sam 9:1–2 Sam 5:16*
A. Saul: a first king	9:1–15:35*
1. Commissioned by an anonymous prophet	9:1–
2. Crowned after the relief of Jabesh-gilead	11:1–
3. Failed	
a. Concerning the Philistines: rebuked by the people and/or	14:1–
b. Concerning the Amalekites: rebuked by the prophet	15:1–
B. David: a stable king	1 Sam 16:14–2 Sam 5:16*
1. Emergence as a rival to Saul	16:14–18:16*
2. Stories showing that YHWH is with David	18:20–31:13*

313

Saul's commissioning by an anonymous prophet is the earlier text underlying the present 1 Sam 9:1–10:16; his crowning follows the successful deliverance of Jabesh-gilead, threatened by Nahash (11:1-11, 15). In the present text, Saul's rejection is presented as early as 13:7b-15a, followed up in 15:1-35. The potential for Saul's being rebuked rather than rejected is, however, also present. The strange episode of Saul's almost nullifying Jonathan's exploit against the Philistine garrison (14:1-46), with the express resistance of the people to Saul (cf. v. 45), can be read as rebuke by the people; the episode of Saul's failure to annihilate the Amalekites is clearly one of rebuke by the prophet, in the earlier text within 15:1-35 (overwritten to express rejection by Samuel). Either of these could have been used to portray Saul as the king who failed. His instability is then reflected against the stability of David until Saul's death at Gilboa and David's triumph as sole king.

The portrayal of Saul in the various traditions is indeed of a failed and unstable king, just as David is portrayed as unceasingly successful. David exhibits kingly courage in facing the Philistine, Goliath; Saul does not. At court, Saul attempts to kill David and fails five times: (i) through his daughters (18:20-29a); (ii) through his son and servants (19:1-7); (iii) with his spear (19:8-10); (iv) at Michal's house (19:11-17); and finally (v) when David is missed at court while hiding in the field (20:1b–21:1 [Heb]). In flight, David increases and Saul decreases: the sacrilege at Nob reflects badly on Saul (21:2–22:23); the deliverance of Keilah reflects well on David (23:1-14). At the head of his band, David is acknowledged as future leader by Saul (23:24b–24:22), by Abigail (25:2-42), and again by Saul (23:19-24 and 26:1-25). Finally, Saul dies in the battle of Gilboa — according to the text, not because David failed to come to his aid, but because YHWH had decided his fate. In the civil war that followed Saul's death, David prevailed.

The traditions are available to affirm the consolidation of the institution of kingship in ancient Israel. David was militarily successful against the Philistines; his new capital, Jerusalem, was religiously blessed by the coming of the ark; his dynasty received God's promise of stability; he successfully imposed his authority on the surrounding peoples; and he established an administrative structure that could have given institutional permanence to his personal achievements. (2 Sam 8:16-18 makes sense as a conclusion to David's rise to power, but may not have been of interest to prophetic editors; its provenance — and that too of 20:23-26 — has to remain uncertain.)

Genre

The basic characteristic of these traditions is clearly (→) narrative, ranging from notices and accounts to story outlines and stories. A question arises over the qualifier to be applied to this "narrative" material. Information is communicated about a series of events, but not merely information. The events are open to interpretation: either by the structure of the stories narrated, or by the juxtaposition of the material, or by the comments of the narrator. In its narrative context, a single combat reveals who is YHWH's instrument in Israel. A long series of apparently random events shows — despite human malice, almost despite human endeavor — that YHWH is with David. The narrative of David's assumption of kingly power may be highly secular (2 Sam 1–5), but YHWH's presence is brought to the fore at the crucial moments. It is YHWH's initiative, through the lot, that brings David to Hebron; the initiative of the men of Judah that brings him to the throne (2:1-4a). When the tribes of Israel come to David at Hebron, their motivation is portrayed as both historical (5:2a: "it was you that led out and brought in Israel") and theological (5:2b: "and the LORD said . . .").

What we have here is the potential material for a complex narrative compilation which sets out to recount and display the events of David's rise to power in such a way as to interpret them so that YHWH's will and YHWH's work may be seen within the events. These traditions constitute or have the potential for (→) theological narrative.

Setting

The question of setting suggests circles associated with David and favorable to him. An early date seems likely; the concerns are Davidic, not Solomonic. The tendency to place these traditions of the story of David's rise earlier than the Stories of David's Middle Years, arguing that the former are steeped in a sacred world while the latter have emerged into the brave new world of secularism, is to be very carefully scrutinized before being accepted. The three places in which YHWH's will bursts through the veil of events in the Stories of David's Middle Years have been emphasized by von Rad: 2 Sam 11:27b; 12:24b; 17:14 (*Old Testament Theology,* 1.314-15). But in these traditions of David's rise, about twice as long as the Stories of David's Middle Years, there are only four such occurrences: 1 Sam 16:14; 18:14; 23:14; 25:38. Perhaps 28:6 is a fifth occurrence; it remains, however, in the realm of observable cultic procedures. In

2 Sam 5:12, the final statement is not made by the narrator as his own; it is attributed to David. The narrator has allowed Jonathan (1 Sam 23:17a), Abigail (25:30), Saul (23:17b; 26:25), and even Abner (2 Sam 3:9-10, 17-18) to perceive YHWH's hand in the movement of events. Perhaps it is a reflection of David's own almost fatalistic theology (1 Sam 26:10; 2 Sam 15:25-26) that constrains the narrator to permit this perception to David only when history has run its course and the narrative sequence reaches or approaches its term.

It is the events recorded in the Stories of David's Middle Years (esp. 2 Sam 15–20) that make clear how great a need there was to have a proper understanding of the events of David's rise to power. The words of Shimei, "You man of blood, you worthless fellow" (2 Sam 16:7), and of Sheba, "We have no portion in David" (2 Sam 20:1), show clearly that different interpretations of these events and different judgments of David were possible.

Factors of narrative style, immediacy of detail, and an overall concern which does not extend beyond David all combine to suggest a setting for most of these traditions in close association with the period of David's reign. Narrower definition of the setting is difficult. However, not only the assumption of the existence of guilds of minstrel singers but also the evidence of David's own presence at the court of Saul (1 Sam 16:14-23) shows that singers and presumably singer-narrators had their place at court (cf. also 2 Sam 19:36 [Heb.; NRSV, 19:35]; Qoh 2:8; 2 Chron 35:25). The nature of many of these narratives suggests that these "singers of tales" were not mere storytellers, purveyors of entertainment at the hearth. They appear to have taken on the task of interpreting the events of which they sang, of relating the stories they told to the religious traditions of their people. In short, among the hats they wore was a theologian's cap.

Meaning

A historian's judgment of the events of David's rise to power may be adequately expressed by M. Noth: "Unlike Saul, David set out on the road to political power quite deliberately and consistently from the very beginning. . . . He was skilled in the great art of waiting until things came within his grasp, and this was the way he created the great empire which represents the climax in the development of political power in the history of Israel" (*History of Israel*, 179, 181; cf. Lemche, "David's Rise"). Be that as it may, it is clearly not a complete expression of what is portrayed in these traditions of David's rise. It is one of the fascinating qualities of these stories that while, from one point of view, their thought and purpose move at a lofty level of theological abstraction, they do not seek to avoid or cover over the mundane and sometimes sordid realities of life. YHWH's will is not divorced from the realities of human destiny.

Whatever the reality may have been from which these traditions derive, in them David is generally depicted, not as one who initiated action through personal drive or ambition, but as one who reacted to the demands of the situation, which at key moments appear as revelations of YHWH's will. So David comes to the court for the benefit of Saul. There, faced with the demand of the Philistine challenge, he reacts with trust in YHWH (but there is the tradition of the ambitious shepherd from the farm). Set by Saul the goal of a hundred Philistine foreskins, he succeeds, for the LORD was with him (18:28a). When told of Keilah's straits, he responds, against great odds, to the call of the LORD (23:1-5). With Saul at his mercy, he leaves Saul's fate in the hands of YHWH (26:9-11). And so on.

If there is a constant theme through these traditions, it would appear to be: David did not reach for greatness and the crown; he had it thrust upon him. Expressed in the terms of Israel's traditions, David is no Abimelech; his rise results not from a desire for power, but as a result of Israel's needs and YHWH's will. It can be summed up in the perception that YHWH established him king over Israel, and that YHWH had exalted David's kingdom for the sake of God's people Israel (2 Sam 5:12).

Is this theology? Is it propaganda? Is it history? As I claimed in the Introduction, the articulation of an experience can be a theological task. The experience here is that, at the end of a prolonged process, David has emerged as the stable and established king of Israel. An institution is in place. The past that Israel knew is no longer its present. The theologians among ancient Israel's thinkers were obliged to ask themselves: Is this change of God or have we abandoned what constitutes us as a people of God?

Coupled with profound theology, is this also propaganda as well as insightful history (cf. Whitelam, "Defence of David," esp. 71-76)? It is one thing to articulate experience and give it meaning for oneself. It is another to place this articulation before others; above all, to seek to convince others of the truth of one's understanding. In the strict sense of propaganda — spreading ideas beneficial to a cause — these traditions can indeed be deemed propaganda. But in the broader, more pejorative sense of propaganda, distortion of the truth is involved. Such propaganda did not begin with the abuses of modern media. Nor is it only works like Stefan Heym's *King David Report* that raise the issue. Shimei raised it; Sheba raised it. In a sense, the traditions themselves raise it in their characterization of David's followers (1 Sam 22:2) and in the rather strange story of David's initial participation in the preparation for the Philistine offensive against Saul (1 Sam 29).

The texts are clear: David is brought to power by a sequence of events which can ultimately be understood (according to the texts) only as being YHWH's will. To impute a measure of dishonesty, or more mildly, of prejudicial bias, some form of independent access to the events would be needed — another account for example. And that we do not have. We have Shimei ben Gera, but this is hardly "some form of independent access." The question is therefore largely otiose: there is no answer, so there can be no question. However, it may at least be remarked that whatever grounds there are for a charge of prejudice against the Davidic narrators should begin with their own texts.

317

The Stories of David's Middle Years

What has often been called the Succession Narrative has classically been delineated as at least 2 Sam 9–20 and 1 Kgs 1–2. It has been seen responding to David's penultimate recorded utterance: "Blessed be the LORD, the God of Israel, who today has granted one of my offspring to sit on my throne and permitted me to witness it" (1 Kgs 1:48). The royal word here is surely too feeble to justify more than a dozen chapters of the best and most superbly complex narratives in Israelite literature. The central focus of these narratives is hardly on Solomon's accession to David's throne. An alternative focus, without 1 Kgs 1–2, has been termed the Court History. In many ways, the text might be called the stories of David's fragility. The classic literary qualities of this narrative begin with what is now the prophetic story of 2 Sam 11–12. The Mephibosheth story of 2 Sam 9 is in uncomfortable tension with the tradition assumed in the Mephibosheth material in 2 Sam 19; 2 Sam 10 is not of the same elevated literary caliber as 2 Sam 11–12. We may regard 2 Sam 11–20 as one of the major building blocks of the books of Samuel. It is neutrally titled: The Stories of David's Middle Years.

Second Samuel 2–4 is a story of remarkably high literary caliber. For this reason, the claim has been made that it belongs with the later narrative in 2 Sam 11–20 (e.g., Gunn, *Story of King David,* 66-84). While the literary observation is accurate, we have to take account of broader contexts and horizons. 2 Sam 2–4 deals with the elimination of Saulide contenders to David's throne. As such, it has some bearing on the succession to David's throne — if that were in fact central to chs. 11–20 (with or without 1 Kgs 1–2). It has more immediate bearing on David's accession to the throne. The traditions of 1 Samuel can hardly end with the death of Saul (1 Sam 31) and David's eulogy (2 Sam 1). David is anointed to be king. David facing the Philistine Goliath with faith and without fear replaces Saul as deliverer of Israel, abandoned by God's spirit (1 Sam 16:14) and paralyzed by fear (1 Sam 17:11). This story ends with the throne of Israel in view (cf. 1 Sam 18:14-16). The traditions of David's rise to power cannot be broken off before David is on Israel's throne; 2 Sam 2–4 belongs with these accession traditions.

To anticipate the 2 Samuel volume, we may note that these are stories not history. An affair, a death in battle, and two pregnancies are not the stuff of courtly chronicles. A princely rape might precipitate fratricide; it would not make the chronicles in detail. A major rebellion might well be matter for a chronicler, but scarcely the details of David's flight and return. Sheba's revolt might be of interest, but not Joab's recovery of power, without appropriate follow-up.

A policy of unasked and unanswered questions is visible in these stories. A course of action is taken from which the narrative develops. Spaces (gaps) are open throughout the stories; the narrative could have moved differently into one or another of these spaces and the outcome might have been so very different. The narrative did not and so the outcome is not. It will help to note some examples. Bathsheba's attitude toward David is left ambiguous. Was she willing or unwilling? Was she submissive, seductive, scheming, or victim? The text is silent. Various attempts to sketch a convincing plot fail to do so. The ambiguity here is not so much an unasked question as a background that reflects the complexity of human motivation every leader needs to be aware of.

Might these stories have been told for royal courtiers to explore the boundaries of counsel given the king? At what points in the stories would counsel have been desirable? What options might have been proposed and what consequences might have followed from them? Such a function would account for this peculiar capacity of the stories to leave space for questions that could be asked and to close off almost none. Such is the wisdom of a counselor: to open unthought-of options for reflection and to choose wisely.

Details will need to wait for *2 Samuel*. Within the diachronic dimension of the books of Samuel, the great text of the Stories of David's Middle Years has its place. The stories show David sometimes in a good light (usually out of the city) and sometimes in a bad light (usually in the city). A setting too close to David's time or too far from David's time is unlikely. The court of Jeroboam, first king of northern Israel, is a possibility. With the court in late-10th-century Shechem or Penuel, such a setting would be far enough away from David in time and space to be safe. It is early enough and northern enough that the ideal image of David would not have taken root. Many of Jeroboam's courtiers would have been at court in Jerusalem and been well aware of the Davidic traditions. With the establishment of a new kingdom and a new court, a high value would have been set on the availability of courtiers capable of giving counsel to the king.

Certainty will escape us always. It is enough to say here that, in the trajectory of the books of Samuel, this tightly woven and largely independent work had its place.

The Prophetic Record

Before outlining the hypothesis of a Prophetic Record, it is useful to note that two earlier studies have argued for a prophetic editing of original traditions in this Samuel material. In 1962, in an unpublished dissertation, Friedrich Mildenberger attributed the following texts to this prophetic editing: 1 Sam 9:1–10:16; 11; 13:4b-5, 7b-15a; 15; 16:1-14a; 18:10-16 ptm; 25(?); 28:3-25 (*Saul-Davidüberlieferung*, 29). In 1976, Bruce Birch isolated the following texts as prophetic: 1 Sam 9:15-17, 20-21, (25-26), 27–10:1 (LXX), 5-8, 16b; 10:17-19, 25; 11:12-14; 12:1-5; 13:7b-15a; 15:1-35 (*Israelite Monarchy*, 141). In 1980, McCarter proposed "that it was at some pre-Deuteronomistic stage that the stories were set in their basic order" and that "the older sources were systematically reworked to produce a continuous prophetic history of the origins of monarchy in Israel" (p. 18). His summary concluded "that the First Book of Samuel derives its basic shape from a prophetic history of the origin of the monarchy that was intended to present the advent of kingship in Israel as a concession to the wanton demand of the people" (ibid., 21).

To put things briefly, Mildenberger and Birch do not go far enough, while

McCarter goes too far. McCarter operates with the unjustified assumption that whatever is prophetic belongs within the "prophetic history"; adequate weight is not given to differences of view within "prophetic texts" in relation to the monarchy and its origins in Israel.

The following presentation of the PR is largely shared with *Unfolding the Deuteronomistic History.* The revision of both volumes for publication occurred about the same time. In the view of Martin Noth, the Deuteronomistic Historian was "not merely an editor but the author of a history which brought together material from highly varied traditions and arranged it according to a carefully conceived plan" (*Deuteronomistic History,* 26). However, "of the approximately 156 chapters in Noth's DH, he attributed more than two-thirds to prefabricated sources. No wonder that Noth comments: 'In general, then, Dtr. gave his narrative very markedly the character of a traditional work, the intention was to be a compilation and explanation of the extant traditions concerning the history of his people'" (Campbell, "Martin Noth and the Deuteronomistic History," 38; the comment quoted is from p. 133 of Noth's *Deuteronomistic History*).

In the book of Deuteronomy, Noth assumed such an "extant tradition": the deuteronomic lawbook, with its introduction and conclusion (cf. 2 Kgs 22:8-10). In the book of Joshua, Noth argued for an earlier source in Josh 2-11. Noth did not isolate a source collection in the book of Judges; however, such a collection has been claimed by Wolfgang Richter *(Untersuchungen* and *Bearbeitung).* In the books of Samuel and Kings, Noth's stance was more nuanced. He accepted that the Saul and David traditions formed an adequate base that "absolved Dtr. from the need to organize and construct the narrative himself" (*Deuteronomistic History,* 86). Among the sources for the books of Kings, Noth saw "some narrative cycles, each of which accumulated around one prophetic figure" (ibid., 107). Noth spoke of the Elijah and Elisha cycle, the Isaiah cycle, the story of Ahijah of Shiloh, of Micaiah ben Imlah, and others. As Noth saw these traditions, the prophets "appear chiefly as opponents to the kings" (ibid.). Even with Samuel set apart (for Noth) in the period of the Judges, the fact that Ahijah designates Jeroboam as future king and Elisha's disciple anoints Jehu as king did not receive significant attention from Noth — although it may have contributed to the need for the adverb "chiefly" *(vorzugsweise).* The prophetic texts in Kings cannot be dealt with adequately unless they are associated with those in Samuel. The claim for a PR, as a source for the Deuteronomist, emerges out of a closer study of the signals embedded in these traditions in the books of both Samuel and Kings.

There are certain clusters of signals in Samuel-Kings that need explaining. They are in passages spread widely across the books and bear remarkable similarities to each other. They are not identical; but they are too similar for the similarity to be coincidental. It matters little whether they are the work of one hand, editing the traditions, or result from several generations mulling over the traditions they handed on. What they point to is a striking concern for the understanding of Israel's past, for the role of the prophets in establishing and dismissing kings, and for the remarkable ways in which the prophetic word may be realized in the unfolding of events. They are not dtr, neither in language nor in concern. They need to be accounted for.

The existence of a PR was first proposed as a hypothesis by Antony F. Campbell (the present writer) in *Of Prophets and Kings* (1986).

Discovery of the Hypothesis

The observations that suggested the need for this hypothesis can be briefly summarized. A first set of observations concerns Saul, David, and Jehu; a second set concerns Jeroboam, Ahab, and Jehu. Jehu is the figure common to both sets.

Saul, David, and Jehu

Both Saul and David were designated by a prophet in remarkably similar circumstances. Of all Israel's kings, only Jehu received a similar designation from a prophet.

The similar circumstances are:

a. anointing by a prophet
b. done in relative privacy, variously expressed
c. direct attribution of the anointing to YHWH
d. recipient named king-designate *(nāgîd)*, king-to-be, or simply king
e. empowering consequences that flow from the anointing (for these, see Campbell, *Of Prophets and Kings,* 17-23).

It needs to be noted that Saul was also dismissed by the same prophet who designated or anointed him. The effective impact of the prophetic word, realized in the unfolding of events, is claimed in 1 Sam 28 and 2 Sam 7.

The text is substantially a revision and expansion of the early traditions of David's rise to power in the united kingdom, taking in both the future southern and northern kingdoms.

Jeroboam, Ahab, and Jehu

Speeches of remarkable similarity were spoken by prophets to kings within stories about Jeroboam and Ahab. Along with these two archetypal figures, of all Israel's kings, once again only Jehu was the recipient of a similar speech from a prophet.

Jeroboam was designated and subsequently dismissed — as was Saul. Ahab was dismissed. Jehu was commissioned to destroy the house of Ahab.

The similarities are particularly noteworthy within the three speeches about dismissal. As in the anointing texts, there is a strong element of direct attribution of the action to YHWH.

The common elements are:

a. the bringing of evil (not in these words in 2 Kgs 9)
b. the extirpation of the royal house
c. the cutting off of every male

d. a comparison with the fate of the house of Jeroboam (not in 1 Kgs 14 of course)
e. the specific fate of those who die in the city or the country (not in 2 Kgs 9:1-13, but cf. 9:26, 36) — for these speeches, see Campbell, *Of Prophets and Kings,* 23-41; note that 1 Kgs 16:1-4 is not within a story.

The elements listed here have often been classified as dtr, because of a bevy of dtr characteristics to be found in the present text of these prophetic speeches. These elements, however, form a core within the speeches that can be read as independent and free-standing. The combined elements themselves are exclusive to these speeches. The possibility has to be envisaged that the core within the speeches is pre-dtr, subject understandably to later dtr expansion. The imagery owes nothing to dtr characteristics.

The ideology, common language, and common reference to the fate of the house of Jeroboam hold this series together. The designation of Jeroboam is bound to the dismissal of Saul by the prophetic action of tearing a cloak and the prophetic speech interpreting that action (see Campbell, *Of Prophets and Kings,* 41-63).

The text is substantially a revision and expansion of the early traditions of Elijah's conflict with Ahab over the worship of Baal and the murder of Naboth, but extended back to the prophetic legitimation of Jeroboam and his rejection for apostasy (associated with illegitimate clergy) and concluded with the prophetic legitimation of Jehu, the brutal destruction of Ahab's house, and Jehu's elimination of Baalism from Israel.

Conclusion

These signals in the text constitute a set of similarities that needs to be accounted for. One explanation is the hypothesis of a PR, from the prophetic circles around Elisha, extending from 1 Sam 1 to 2 Kgs 10, building on earlier traditions such as the stories of David's rise and the Elijah stories, concluding by bringing Jehu's coup under the legitimation of major prophetic authority (i.e., Samuel in association with Saul and David, Ahijah for Jeroboam, and Elijah for Ahab).

The northern provenance should not surprise. The PR's claim has Samuel (a northerner if anyone was — although he set up his sons in Beer-sheba!) anoint Saul, a Benjaminite, and David, a Bethlehemite. It has Ahijah (like Samuel associated with Shiloh) transfer the Davidic heritage to Jeroboam for the north. Divisive forces are evident in 2 Sam 15–20; for all that, David's was a united kingdom of north and south.

The Recovery of the Text

The observations that lead to the shaping of the hypothesis and the identification of its text can be discussed from the standpoint of Jehu's coup (2 Kgs 9–10), the anointing, and the dismissal of the dynasty.

Jehu's Coup

The story of Jehu's coup is told in 2 Kgs 9–10, a coup that according to the text wiped out the house of Ahab in Israel and with it the worship of the god Baal. It is a story that puts itself under the patronage of the prophet Elijah. What Jehu does, in all its awfulness, is portrayed as fulfilling the prophecy of Elijah. Three times Elijah's prophecy is explicitly invoked (2 Kgs 9:36; 10:10, 17). An anonymous oracle is also invoked (2 Kgs 9:25-26). We have no other trace of it, but the reference to the "plot of ground" and the blood of Naboth's children, as well as the circumstances of the divine oracle, suggest the circulation of more versions of the story than the one we have from 1 Kgs 21 (cf. 2 Kgs 9:21).

After 2 Kgs 9:1-13, there is no mention in the coup narrative of Jehu's having been anointed or commissioned by Elisha's disciple. It is likely that 9:1-13 was placed before the story of Jehu's coup in order to bring Jehu's action explicitly under the authority and legitimation of the prophetic circles associated with Elisha. The Elisha circles are likely to have been the bearers of the Elijah traditions and probably of many of the earlier prophetic traditions.

The Anointing Texts

Elisha's disciple anointed Jehu, in private, away from the other army commanders. Samuel's anointing of Saul, also in private (cf. 1 Sam 9:27), shows clear signs of being an overwriting of an older story of a chance meeting with an anonymous prophet, provoked by Saul's search for his father's asses. Samuel's anointing of David, apparently in the relative privacy of his family circle (cf. 1 Sam 16:5), is an account of an event unmentioned in the early traditions about David's rise to power.

If the prophetic circle around Elisha were to claim the legitimate authority to designate kings by anointing in YHWH's name, they could do no better than go back to the figure of Samuel and the establishment of Saul and David. The image of Saul, dismissed from kingly office and replaced by David (1 Sam 15:1–16:13), provides the foundational understanding of the kingship as being in the gift of the prophets, to bestow or withdraw as God wills.

For this portrayal, an account of the emergence of Samuel as a prophet to all Israel would be needed, along with the stories of Samuel's dealings with Saul and David, through to the successful establishment of David as Israel's king, in fulfillment of the word of the LORD through Samuel. Such a narrative can be easily traced within the texts from 1 Sam 1:1 to 2 Sam 8:15.

Samuel dismisses Saul and anoints David. The realization in history of Saul's dismissal is found in the same events that are the realization in history of David's designation by the prophetic anointing. For Saul, the dismissal's realization extends to 1 Sam 31. For David, the anointing's realization extends at least to 2 Sam 5:3. Elijah condemns Ahab; Elisha's disciple anoints Jehu. The realization in history of Elijah's prophetic words is brought to completion by Jehu's coup, itself presented as the realization in history of his anointing by a prophet.

The Dismissal of Dynasties

Elisha's disciple commissioned Jehu to wipe out the house of Ahab, making it like the house of Jeroboam, son of Nebat. There is strong traditional preparation for this. First, in YHWH's name, the prophet Ahijah of Shiloh transfers to Jeroboam what the prophets gave to David: "I will be with you, and will build you an enduring house, as I built for David, and I will give Israel to you" (1 Kgs 11:38b; cf. vv. 29-31, 37). Subsequently, Ahijah predicts that the house of Jeroboam will be wiped out because of Jeroboam's apostasy: "[you] have thrust me behind your back" (1 Kgs 14:9b).

The stereotyped phrases used of the house of Jeroboam are applied to the house of Ahab, patron of the worship in Israel of the god Baal (cf. 1 Kgs 21:17-24). They are spoken to Ahab by the prophet Elijah; as we have noted, the main narrative of Jehu's coup is placed under the patronage of Elijah. They are spoken to Jehu by Elisha's disciple; those responsible for the organization of these traditions can lay claim to the prophetic heritage from Samuel on down for the action of Jehu by which he "wiped out Baal from Israel" (2 Kgs 10:28). Given Elijah's departure before the arrival of Jehu on the scene and the likelihood that the Elijah traditions were preserved in the circles associated with Elisha, it is appropriate that a disciple of Elisha's anoint Jehu — with the figure of Elijah an unmentioned power and presence.

It may help to see these stereotyped phrases without the dtr additions that are part of their present context. They are:

Jeroboam (1 Kgs 14)

Crime:
- [You] have thrust me behind your back

Consequences:
- I will bring evil *(rā'â)* upon the house of Jeroboam
- I will cut off from Jeroboam every male *(maštîn bĕqîr),* both bond and free in Israel
- [I] will consume *(bi'artî 'aḥăr'ê)* the house of Jeroboam, just as one burns up dung . . .
- Anyone belonging to Jeroboam who dies in the city, the dogs shall eat; and anyone who dies in the open country, the birds of the air shall eat. . . .

Ahab (1 Kgs 21)

Crime:
- Have you killed, and also taken possession?

Consequences:
- I will bring disaster *(rā'a)* on you
- I will consume *(bi'artî 'aḥăr'ê)* you
- [I] will cut off from Ahab every male *(maštîn bĕqîr),* bond or free, in Israel

- I will make your house like the house of Jeroboam son of Nebat
- Anyone belonging to Ahab who dies in the city the dogs shall eat; and anyone of his who dies in the open country the birds of the air shall eat.

Jehu (2 Kgs 9)

Commission:
- I anoint you king over the people of the LORD, over Israel

Consequences:
- You shall strike down the house of your master Ahab, . . . the whole house of Ahab shall perish
- I will cut off from Ahab every male *(maštîn bĕqîr)*, bond or free, in Israel
- I will make the house of Ahab like the house of Jeroboam son of Nebat.

The same language is found in the dtr condemnation of the dynasty of Baasha, attributed to the prophet Jehu ben Hanani (1 Kgs 16:1-4). There is no story as context for this prophetic speech, and there are grounds for seeing it as a dtr construction modeled on the speeches above. 1 Kgs 16:1-4 apart, these phrases are not characteristic of dtr language in any way. Of course it is possible for the dtr editors to employ language in one context that they use nowhere else. The occurrence however raises questions. There is an imagistic and figurative quality to the language that is not usually present in dtr passages. The role of the prophet, the anointing, and the language of *nāgîd* (e.g., 1 Kgs 14:7) tie these speeches into the realm of prophetic redactional activity and the PR (for *nāgîd,* in particular, see the excursus in Campbell, *Of Prophets and Kings,* 47-61).

The Shape of the Text

The similarities have been too obvious to be overlooked. They have been explained as the result of dtr composition; there has been the appeal to cycles of stories told in prophetic circles. This latter may appear the easy approach, but there are certain features of the texts concerned that sit uncomfortably with the idea of story cycles. While material may, of course, have been drawn extensively from such cycles, an overarching concern has been imprinted on them that extends beyond the individual stories and even the individual cycles.

In the case of the anointing stories, it is clear that the theme of anointing has been superimposed on 1 Sam 9:1–10:16 in a way that demands literary reworking not oral retelling. The treatment of 1 Sam 15:1-35 is similar. In the case of the later prophetic speeches, there is consistent comparison with the house of Jeroboam son of Nebat, thus involving both Ahijah and Elijah. The stories do not have the independence expected within cycles. The stories of prophetic anointing or designation require later stories of realization within history; the stories of prophetic rejection need a wider context and also stand in

325

need of realization in history. In this, these stories of the PR are quite different from the stories found in 1 Kgs 13, 20, and 22.

The stories of the PR are clustered at the start of the unified monarchy (Saul and David) and early in the divided monarchy (Jeroboam, Ahab, Jehu). An intervening text is needed between these clusters. It bears marks of concerns common to the stories (e.g., 1 Sam 28:17-19aα; 2 Sam 7:4b, 8-10, 11b-12, 14-17). All of this militates against the idea of a cycle of stories, much less of two or more narrative cycles.

Over and above these issues, there are a movement of narrative logic and a central focus of thematic interest that bind the whole together from Samuel to Jehu. Samuel is needed to set up and put down Saul, establishing David in his place. God's will, mediated by Samuel, is effective and David succeeds splendidly. No such figure as Samuel has been profiled in Israel since Moses and Joshua. Nathan takes up the thread and points back to what God has done and forward to what God will do (2 Sam 7). Mediated by the prophet Ahijah of Shiloh, the legitimacy given David is transferred to Jeroboam with regard to the ten tribes. Jeroboam is then rejected by Ahijah, Ahab emerges and is equally rejected by the prophet Elijah, and finally under Jehu God's will becomes effective. There is a unity here that escapes the simply cyclical.

There is a clear and coherent text from Samuel to the assertion of David's success (2 Sam 8:15); it is an expanded form of the early David traditions. There is an equally clear and coherent text from Ahab to Jehu; it is an expanded form of the early Elijah traditions. A text can be identified from Jeroboam to Ahab. There is, of course, no question of the Omrides, and especially the Baal-worshipping Ahab, receiving legitimation or designation from the prophets of YHWH. The rejection of Jeroboam's house is concluded in 1 Kgs 15:29; the story leading to the condemnation of Ahab's house is begun in 17:1 with the figure of Elijah. The trace of the PR can be followed across 1 Kgs 16, in the wild and turbulent times of Nadab and Baasha, Elah and Zimri, and the triumph of Omri over Tibni. A text is needed and present (within 1 Kgs 16:6-32); prophetic guidance is conspicuously absent.

The text, like that of the rest of the PR, employs the linear system of reporting the royal succession: X died and Y reigned in his stead. The system's exclusive use in the list of the kings of Edom (Gen 36:31-39) is evidence that it could exist independently; a few cases of superfluous repetition provide evidence that this linear system did in fact coexist in Kings alongside the synchronistic system used in the DH (cf. 1 Kgs 16:28-29; 2 Kgs 8:24-25; 13:9-10; 15:22-23; 15:38–16:1) — see Campbell, *Of Prophets and Kings*, 139.

Where Solomon's reign is concerned, the situation concerning prophetic guidance is different. Without naming him, the prophets had already promised David's offspring and successor (2 Sam 7:12) — who turned out to be Solomon. Already they had prepared the ground for his lack of fidelity (2 Sam 7:14-15). Ahead, secure in the narrative to come, they had his partial replacement waiting in the wings — Jeroboam. Was that enough? Alternatively, was there a gap in substantially a two-part story? Was Solomon well enough known among the many rotten apples in the royal barrel? Was it known only too well that by the end of his time he had rotted to the core? As administrator and temple-builder, Solomon receives extensive treatment from the Deuteronomists; by comparison, he attracts no attention from the prophetic editors. Was it possible that Solomon was too bad to hire and too big to fire? Or was there no tradition available for the prophetic editors to build on?

Certainly there is no prophetic designation for Solomon. He was anointed by the priest Zadok although the prophet Nathan was present (1 Kgs 1:38-39; vv. 34 and 45 associate Nathan more closely with the anointing, but v. 39 is explicit about the act: Zadok did it). There is no prophetic condemnation or dismissal either. It would be possible for the PR to be seen in two parts, concluding the first with 2 Sam 8:15 and, in the second, resuming the narrative thread with Jeroboam at 1 Kgs 11:26. There are similar disjunctions in Israel's narratives.

On the other hand, there are the apparently related references to Solomon's building activity in 3:1 and 9:15a, coupled with the oddly placed references to Pharaoh's daughter so early at 3:1 and correlatively at 9:24, as well as the issue of forced labor in 9:15a and Solomon's apostasy in 11:7. These texts need a setting and the PR as a hypothesis is a strong candidate for the provision of that setting. In which case, it is possible that 1 Kgs 2:10 and 12 belonged originally to the PR or have replaced the Record's notice of David's death and Solomon's accession.

The texts of the PR as we have them indicate that it should not be seen as a record of Israel's history. It is a record of the prophetic activity claimed in the guidance of Israel with regard to its kings, from Saul to Jehu.

Given the misunderstanding that has occasionally surfaced, it is worth insisting that all of the above is totally independent of any analysis of the royal judgment formulas. The judgment formulas are significant for any consideration of the history of the text after the PR. They are of no significance in the establishment of the hypothesis of a PR. One other misunderstanding needs to be corrected. My judgment was ("My personal inclination, however, is to think that it was not included") and is that 2 Sam 11–20 did not form part of the PR (see Campbell, *Of Prophets and Kings*, 83; despite Dietrich, "David-Saul Narrative," 311-12).

A rudimentary structure analysis may help identify the shape and concerns of the text.

The Prophetic Record   **1 Sam 1:1–2 Kgs 10:28**

I. Emergence of the prophetic figure in Israel: Samuel   1 Sam 1:1–4:1a

II. Record of prophetic guidance of Israel's destiny   1 Sam 9:1– 2 Kgs 10:28

     A. Concerning SAUL   1 Sam 9:1–

        1. Establishment as king

           a. Designation by prophet: Samuel

           b. Realization in history

        2. Summary of Saul's reign

        3. Rejection as king by prophet: Samuel

     B. Concerning DAVID   1 Sam 16:1–

        1. Establishment as king

a. Designation by prophet: Samuel
b. Realization in history
2. Consummation of David's reign
a. Promise of a secure dynasty: Nathan
b. Summary of David's success
3. Aftermath with Solomon
C. Concerning JEROBOAM   1 Kgs 11:26–
1. Establishment as king
a. Designation by prophet: Ahijah
b. Realization in history
2. Summary of Jeroboam's reign
3. Rejection of house of Jeroboam
a. Prophetic word of rejection: Ahijah
b. Realization in history
D. Concerning AHAB   1 Kgs 16:6–
1. Anarchic prelude to Ahab's reign
2. Elijah's triumph over Baalism
3. Rejection of house of Ahab
a. Prophetic word of rejection: Elijah
b. Initial realization in history
E. Concerning JEHU   2 Kgs 9:1–
1. Establishment as king
a. Designation by prophet: Elisha's disciple
b. Realization in history
2. Extermination of Baal worship from Israel

Genre

"The genre of the Prophetic Record is most accurately described as theologically inspired history. Insofar as it gives an account of the past, it is history. Yet its interpretative base is so strongly theological, in terms of addressing the divine impact on human affairs, that it cannot be neglected. . . . It is a record of the prophets' views, rather than a portrayal of what actually was" (Campbell, *Of Prophets and Kings,* 105-6).

Setting

The setting claimed as most appropriate for the PR is that of the prophetic circles surrounding Elisha. It was Elisha's disciple who is credited with having anointed Jehu. In this connection, some views on the dating of the Elijah and Elisha traditions may be noted. According to O. H. Steck, the Elijah tradition concerning anointing (1 Kgs 19:15-16) does not belong to the earliest kernel of the Horeb passage, but depends on the anointing of Jehu in 2 Kgs 9; both are to

328

be dated in the late 9th century, in the time of Jehoahaz (*Überlieferung und Zeitgeschichte*, 28, 95-97). A late-9th-century date for the original formation of the Elijah traditions, including 1 Kgs 19:15-18, is also affirmed by G. Fohrer (*Elia*, 39, 50-55). On the other hand, H. C. Schmitt argues against a 9th-century and northern collection of Elijah traditions and sees the Elisha traditions as having undergone a lengthy and complex process of growth (*Elisa*, 119-26, 137-38).

The principal link to the 9th-century prophetic tradition is the anointing of kings, and the primary datum for this association is the anointing of Jehu. Two factors affected Israel in this time. Internally, the emergence of Jezebel as queen mother, with her predilection for Canaanite practices, posed a grave threat as far as YHWH believers were concerned. Externally, Hazael of Damascus constituted a serious threat to Israel (cf. Steck, *Überlieferung und Zeitgeschichte*, 83-102). It would have been an appropriate time to formulate the activity of Samuel in terms of the anointing of Saul and David. These stories could, as it were, have underwritten the prophetic legitimation of Jehu. The fact that Saul and David were anointed for the purpose of national deliverance would give these stories all the more force in a period when Damascus threatened Israel's existence. Finally, the image of the prophet playing a prominent role in the life of a nation might well be bolstered by the figure of Samuel, as portrayed in the prophetic redaction.

Meaning

The importance of this move by the PR is enormous. By claiming Samuel, the prophet, as God's agent who anointed and rejected Saul and then anointed David in Saul's place, the prophets have laid a claim to placing Davidic legitimacy in their own gift. It was a prophet, acting as God's agent, who gave David royal power (1 Sam 16:1-13); it was a prophet, acting as God's agent, who transferred Davidic legitimacy to Jeroboam ("I will be with you, and will build you an enduring house, as I built for David, and I will give Israel to you," 1 Kgs 11:38b); it is a prophet, acting as God's agent, who anoints Jehu as king of Israel, to eradicate the house of Ahab and eliminate Baal worship from Israel (2 Kgs 10:28). This transfer of Davidic legitimacy is a major move, unthinkable in southern circles. To achieve it, northerners have made their own the traditions of the united kingdom, Davidic in origin though they were.

To do this, the prophetic circles took over the traditions of David's rise to power and extended the story. They quite radically rebuilt the front end of the narrative. They built up the figure of Samuel as trustworthy prophet of God to all Israel. They had Samuel preside over the emergence of monarchy in Israel. They overwrote an older text to have Samuel anoint Saul as king-designate (1 Sam 9:1–10:16) before the victory at Jabesh-gilead. They overwrote another older text so that, very early in Saul's reign, instead of suffering a prophetic rebuke Saul is rejected by Samuel (15:1-35). They have Samuel anoint David as king-to-be, in Saul's place (16:1-13). They have Nathan reaffirm God's commitment to David and his dynasty. The prophetic influence on these texts has effectively put the stamp of prophetic authority on the traditions of David's rise to power over Israel. According to their claim, kingship in Israel was God's gift, given and taken away by the authority of God's prophets. It is an astounding claim, but the texts back it up with the anointing of Saul and his rejection, before the gift of legitimacy to David through his anointing. These moves at the front end of the story have put the prophets in a position to exercise legitimate authority in transferring royal power to Jeroboam and ultimately to Jehu.

At the other end of the story, the prophetic circles needed to move from David to Jehu. Solomon is skipped around discreetly; the summary of his reign emphasizes his unpopular building program, including the high places east of Jerusalem that foreshadow apostasy (cf. 1 Kgs 3:1; 9:15-24*; 11:7). Ahijah of Shiloh is the prophet entrusted with transferring to Jeroboam almost all that has been given David (1 Kgs 11:26-31, 37, 38b, 40). Later, Ahijah dismisses Jeroboam for apostasy ("you have thrust me behind your back," 14:9b). The follow-up in the north is a period of anarchic rebellion, fundamentally untouched by prophetic authority. Jeroboam was followed by his son Nadab, who was overthrown in a coup by Baasha (eliminating the house of Jeroboam, 15:29a). Baasha was followed by his son Elah, who was overthrown in a coup by Zimri, who reigned seven days (16:15), before being overthrown in his turn by Omri. Omri fought and won a civil war against Tibni (16:22), and Omri became king of northern Israel, established Samaria as its capital, and was succeeded by his son Ahab.

Under Ahab, married to the Sidonian princess Jezebel, the worship of Baal and the power of the prophets of Baal are portrayed as having become deeply entrenched in the kingdom. The circles responsible for the PR use the great figure of Elijah for the dismissal of Ahab and his house, in the classic confrontation over the judicial murder of Naboth and the alienation of his vineyard (1 Kgs 21). Elisha's disciple anoints Jehu as king of Israel, in place of Ahab's son Joram, with the mission of cutting off the house of Ahab (2 Kgs 9:7a, 8-9a). Jehu turns against the worshippers of Baal, and "Jehu wiped out Baal from Israel" (10:28; for the association between the Ahab and Jehu texts, see Marsha White's independent study, "Naboth's Vineyard").

The PR has achieved its goal. What Elijah began in the slaughter of the prophets of Baal (1 Kgs 18:40), Jehu has completed in the slaughter of all the worshippers of Baal (2 Kgs 10:18-27). Elisha's circle claimed to have given Jehu his legitimating authority from God through the act of anointing. The legitimacy of their action goes back to the beginnings of monarchy in Israel: to Samuel who anointed and rejected Saul and who anointed David. Its trajectory extends to Ahijah who designated and dismissed Jeroboam, to Elijah who dismissed Ahab, and finally reaches Jehu who executed what Elijah had commissioned.

How much of this is based on historical memory rather than theological imagination, we do not know (cf. Campbell, *Of Prophets and Kings,* 117-20). "The shaping of the Prophetic Record involved innovation. There is evidence in the tradition to say that this innovation was not simply creative fiction, but that elements existed which could legitimate its plausibility. In their freedom with the tradition, the prophetic redactors gave it new form. In their fidelity to their tradition, that form can be seen emerging out of the interpretation of the past. The figure of the early prophets is not a wholly historical one; nor is it wholly arbitrary" (ibid., 119).

What must be recognized is that the prophetic claims are indisputably present in the biblical text. They need to be accounted for. Some hypothesis is needed to account both for the presence of the prophetic claims in the text and for the particular way that these claims are expressed. The hypothesis of a PR meets this need.

The Josianic Deuteronomistic History

The Deuteronomistic History (within Deuteronomy through Second Kings) extends far more widely than 1 Samuel. For an understanding of this major compilation in the literature of ancient Israel, see Campbell and O'Brien, *Unfolding*. As presented there, the DH first came into existence in support of the reform moves of King Josiah (ca. 622). Josiah's unexpected death in battle (609) was followed by abandonment of the reform and, in due course, the exile of Judah (587-538). The Josianic DH was given an upgrade for the four kings of Judah after Josiah as well as a thorough and extensive revision. Within this revision (presumably exilic), two focuses can be identified, one focusing the blame on Israel's monarchy, the other blaming the people and their failure to observe the law.

The Josianic DH is concerned with the responsibility of Israel's leadership to enforce effectively the central deuteronomic concerns: exclusive fidelity to YHWH, God of Israel, and centralization of all sacrificial worship on Jerusalem. Under Moses, the leadership was impeccable but the people are portrayed as constantly rebellious. Under Joshua, both the leadership and the people, Achan excepted, are portrayed as impeccable. After Joshua, the nation moves into apostasy (Judg 2:10-11); then into a regular cycle of sin, oppression, and deliverance through the judges; and ending up with oppression at the hands of the Philistines for forty years (Judg 13:1), with no effective deliverance in sight until the experience under Samuel. So the Deuteronomists took over much of the theology of the PR. The prophets, mediators of the word of God, installed kings and, if they failed in fidelity, dismissed them. The dismal history of the monarchy is then sketched, down to Josiah who takes us back to where the history began, being directly responsive to the word of God, mediated by Moses in the book of Deuteronomy and authenticated by a prophet, Huldah.

Within 1-2 Samuel, the major contribution of the Josianic DH appears to have been the inclusion of the Ark Narrative (1 Sam 4–6; 2 Sam 6), bringing support to the Davidic epoch from a non-prophetic tradition, and of course the Stories of David's Middle Years (probably along with 2 Sam 9–10). Beyond that, the additions and editing do not have major impact. While 1 Sam 15:1-35 belonged within the PR, the clustering of the three chapters, 1 Sam 13–15, is uncertain and may be attributable to the Josianic Deuteronomist.

The following structure is indicative and does not attempt to specify chapter and verse in detail.

The Josianic Deuteronomistic History	Deuteronomy–2 Kings
I. Story of Israel under Moses and Joshua	Deut 1–Josh 24
A. Instruction: from Moses	Deut 1–34*
B. Occupation: with Joshua	Josh 1–12 and 21:43-45
II. Transition	Josh 24:29–2 Sam 5:25
A. Of generations	Josh 24:29-31; Judg 2:10
B. Of institutions	Judg 2:11–2 Sam 5:25
1. Deliverer-judges: failure	Judg 2:11–13:1
2. Prophets and kings: hope	1 Sam 1:1–16:13
a. Emergence of prophet at Shiloh	1 Sam 1–3
b. Retreat of ark from Shiloh	1 Sam 4–6
c. Coronation of Saul	1 Sam 9–11
d. Rejection of Saul	1 Sam 13–15
e. Designation of David	1 Sam 16:1-13
3. David: success	1 Sam 16:14–2 Sam 5:25
III. Story of Israel under prophets and kings	2 Sam 6–2 Kgs 23
A. Unity: under David and Solomon	2 Sam 6–1 Kgs 8
1. Ark	2 Sam 6
2. Nathan	2 Sam 7
3. Temple	1 Kgs 5–8
B. Disunity	1 Kgs 9–2 Kgs 20
1. Apostasy: Solomon	1 Kgs 9–11
2. Divided kingdom	1 Kgs 12–2 Kgs 17
a. North: to **exile — 722**	1 Kgs 12–2 Kgs 17
b. South: to Ahaz	1 Kgs 12–2 Kgs 16
C. Reform	2 Kgs 18–23
1. Reform I: Hezekiah	2 Kgs 18–20
2. Return to apostasy: Manasseh and Amon	2 Kgs 21
3. **Reform II: Josiah — 622**	2 Kgs 22–23

This Josianic DH accepted the bulk of what is now Deuteronomy as fundamentally God's guidance by which Israel was to live in its land, a law that could be kept: "the word is very near to you; it is in your mouth and in your heart for you to observe" (Deut 30:14). Joshua's generation perpetuated the leadership of Moses; with the death of that generation, leadership deteriorated. With David, a new style of leadership emerged, kingship guided by the prophets. While the Josianic DH gave full approval only to three kings, the third of these was Josiah. The lesson of the history was clear: reform — commitment to YHWH and Jerusalem — would bring to Israel "life and prosperity" (Deut 30:15). Josiah and his generation, guided by Huldah, were committed to reform (2 Kgs 23:1-3).

Genre

Even before the analysis of the origins of the Pentateuch slid into confusion, the literary genre of the so-called sources was itself confused. The use of "epic" in certain quarters is seriously unsatisfactory. The term Deuteronomistic History is well established in biblical usage. History as an intellectual activity is not easily defined; its understanding can probably be stretched enough to fit. Jan Huizinga offers one broad definition: "History is the intellectual form in which a civilization renders account to itself of its past" (cf. Van Seters, *In Search of History,* 1; Halpern, "Davidic State," 44; Brettler, *Creation of History,* 10-12). Another historian's comment is relevant: "Historians are the foot soldiers in the slow business of understanding our species better, and thereby extending the role of reason and humanity in human affairs" (Clendinnen, *Holocaust,* 205). More irreverent but perhaps no less relevant are the remarks by Norman Davies: "People have always had a need to use the past for their own purposes. The writers of scientific monographs are playing a losing game. The past as transmitted to posterity will always be a confused mixture of facts, legends, and downright lies" (Davies, *Europe,* 270). Where the DH is concerned, history of the "how it really was" variety (Ranke's "wie es eigentlich gewesen") it certainly is not. What was said in the Introduction applies here; the usual biblical practice of amalgamation rather than adjudication, of juxtaposition rather than evaluation, renders biblical text extremely unhelpful for the historian. Taking a leaf out of Halpern's essay (ibid., 45), we would do well to attempt to describe what the DH is doing rather than try to define it. For the DH, assessment is complicated by the need to separate the source materials from the editing that has utilized them.

Deuteronomy does not function as historical record but as exhortation to the ideal. The DH's Joshua is an example of amalgamation rather than adjudication, with "We conquered" almost a background to "God conquered for us." Judges witnesses to the absence of permanent leadership resulting in instability; repeated sin leads to repeated oppression before recurring deliverance. The DH's Judges ends with a forty-year Philistine oppression. With Samuel, the Josianic DH prepares for change, has monarchy instituted by divine initiative and Saul fired for disobedience; David is presented as flawed but faithful. In Kings, Solomon — the temple-builder — and his successors on the thrones of north and south are presented as flawed and unfaithful. The examples of Hezekiah and Josiah point to the possibility of renewed leadership. Prophets have been central: Samuel anointed and dismissed Saul, then anointed David; Nathan confirmed David and confronted him; Ahijah designated Jeroboam and later dismissed him; Elijah condemned Ahab; Elisha's disciple anointed Jehu; Jehu ben Hanani spoke against Baasha; Isaiah and Huldah gave support to Hezekiah and Josiah. The leadership of Moses and Joshua has been replaced by the effective leadership of king and prophet.

Deuteronomy's "today" that offered effective hope despite seven centuries of failure (cf. von Rad, *Old Testament Theology,* 1.231) spoke to the adherents of reform under Josiah. The Josianic DH is not a document of historical record. It is a presentation of insight into the past bearing benefit for the present, an evaluation of the past with a view to policy in the present. The evaluation of the past associates it with history; the policy for the present associates it with manifesto, but a remarkably muted manifesto. What it provides is the theological self-understanding, grounded in a reading of Israel's past, that is a secure base for a movement of reform.

In the Josianic DH, the PR has been blended into a wider presentation of Israel's traditions; the introduction of the ark's move from Shiloh to Jerusalem emphasizes an abandonment of the old for the new; and the acceptance of a stable monarchy under David, anointed by Samuel, offers a radically new situation to Israel. In the Stories of David's Middle Years (2 Sam 11–20), significant royal failure does not invalidate the promise of the monarchy — David returns to Jerusalem and the Davidic dynasty continues. The failures of the past need not invalidate the hope of the present, offered by Josiah's reform.

Setting

The setting for the final composition of the Josianic DH would be deuteronomistic circles in Jerusalem, at some time before the date assigned to the reform under King Josiah, i.e., somewhere before the last quarter of the 7th century, B.C.E.

Meaning

The Josianic DH left Deuteronomy fairly much as it found it. Deuteronomy was the datum from which the Josianic DH started. As the opening of a separate document, it needed to be inserted into the story of Israel, so it began with the people's departure from Sinai. At Sinai, Israel as a people had entered into covenant with their God. In Deuteronomy, then, the ten commandments are repeated (Deut 5); the law is rehearsed (Deut 12–26). There, in the plains of Moab, covenant is again celebrated. From covenant, as the Josianic DH has it, blessings or curses flow; its law does not, of course, impose a precondition for becoming God's people, but rather addresses those who are already God's people, specifying behavioral norms with consequences for blessing and life.

The Josianic DH has Joshua promised the land, taking over from Moses (Deut 31:7-8; Josh 1:1-6). The end of the period (now Josh 21:43-45) has the assurance that all of this came to pass, as promised. With the transition of generations and of leadership, instability, infidelity, and deterioration set in (see Judg 2:10-11, 14-16, 18-19). David is established as king, the anointed of God by courtesy of Samuel, beginning a new epoch of leadership — prophet and king. The Josianic DH affirms Solomon as temple-builder and reaffirms the security of David's dynasty (cf. 2 Sam 7:13). Solomon's temple is given permanent status as the place where God's name and God's "eyes and heart" will be (1 Kgs 9:3). The dynastic promise is reaffirmed, but with rule "over Israel" (= united kingdom) subject to an express condition of fidelity (1 Kgs 9:4-5).

Solomon, in old age, becomes a besotted apostate (1 Kgs 11:4, 6). The Josianic DH has God give the northern kingdom to Jeroboam, by courtesy of Ahijah, leaving the Davidic dynasty in Jerusalem; like Saul, Jeroboam is dismissed by the prophet who designated him.

In dtr eyes, the northern kingdom was an aberration of infidelity. After its fall, hope surged in the south with Hezekiah, bolstered by Isaiah, and with Josiah, authorized by Huldah. According to the Josianic DH, Josiah made a covenant before the LORD; all the people joined in the covenant (2 Kgs 23:3). King and people kept the passover, prescribed in the book of the covenant (2 Kgs 23:21-23). Blessing might have been expected to flow from such faithful behavior. Such blessing did not eventuate.

The meaning of the Josianic DH is to be found in this evaluation of Israel's history and in the expected outcome for a reforming and faithful generation.

The Revised Deuteronomistic History

It may have been with the royal focus of the revision (blaming Israel's kings) that traditions were introduced into 1 Samuel tracing the monarchy to a desire by Israel's elders for internal justice, following Samuel's successful intercession against the Philistines, providing a significant alternative to the external defense traditions of 9:1–10:16 and 11:1-11, 15. These alternative traditions are found principally within 7:2–8:22 and 10:17-25. 1 Sam 12, so close to later dtr thinking and yet so often distant from dtr tradition and expression, may have been introduced with this focus of the revision. The national focus (blaming the people) involved a far more extensive revision of the DH, reaching back into Deuteronomy itself and covering the whole history. In 1 Samuel, this revision is restricted to chs. 7–12, interpreting (e.g., 7:3-4), sharpening (e.g., most of 8:7b-9a, 18; 10:18-19), and expanding (e.g., perhaps 12:10). The revision, whether in its royal or national focus, does not appear to have needed to adjust 2 Samuel. The addition of 2 Sam 21–24 does not seem to have depended on the revision. The addition of the last four kings of Judah and the events leading up to exile also bear no marks of the revision.

Preceding 1-2 Samuel, it is important to be aware of the major additions made by the revision, above all in Deuteronomy and Joshua. Among these would be the warning in Deut 4 and the reflections on the consequences of infidelity in Deut 29-31; in the book of Joshua, above all the warning against infidelity in Josh 23. The upshot is a remarkably different DH from its Josianic predecessor. The following structure is indicative rather than detailed.

The Revised Deuteronomistic History	Deuteronomy — 2 Kings
I. Instruction to Israel by Moses	Deut 1–34
A. Retrospect and prospect (exhortation & warning)	Deut 1–3 and 4
B. Instruction (with introduction & conclusion)	Deut 5–28 (+ 30:11-20)
C. Foreboding: consequences of infidelity	Deut 29–34

335

After the death of Josiah, Israel's theologians were confronted by the cold reality of a disordered world with limited predictability. The optimism of the Josianic document had to be blended with a pessimism that prepared for the final outcome. As noted, Deut 4 and 29–31 provided dire warnings early in the piece. Warning was reiterated in Josh 23 and again in 1 Sam 12. Solomon's apostasy was brought to the fore; its reverberations were felt first in the north and finally in the south.

Genre

The revised DH is no longer a base for reform but a revision both preparing for and accounting for the failure of the reform that was implicit in the manifesto aspect of its predecessor. As we have just seen, the genre of history can be stretched enough to accommodate the DH with its strong theological overtones. The evaluation of the past associated it with history; the policy for the present associated it with manifesto, a base for reform. With the experience of failure, the aspect of manifesto lapsed and revision had to reevaluate the history.

The task set the revision by events was relatively simple. The Josianic DH had created the expectation that religious recommitment would lead to political and social well-being. Events replaced kings; kings abandoned recommitment. The revision had to prepare for this eventuality; the revision also had to account for the failure. Various avenues might have been chosen; the one selected was to focus on the kings and their evil (royal focus) and the people's folly in following them (national focus). Ironically, this emphasis and the threat of exile shifted the balance from leadership as such to what should have been its fruits: the land and life in it. Good leadership generated fidelity and the outcome should have been blessing. Bad leadership, on the other hand, generated infidelity and the outcome was loss of the land and the impossibility of autonomous life in the land.

As noted, preparation bulked large in the early stages of the revised DH: for example, Deut 4 and 29–31; Josh 23. Beyond these, references to the possibility of failure and exile recur throughout the revision. The royal focus of the revision blamed Israel's kings; the national focus blamed the people. Neither blamed the dtr theology. The history was reevaluated; the theology was left largely alone. The dtr understanding of covenant was left in place. Deuteronomy and the DH had introduced Israel to the broad use of covenant language for articulating Israel's relationship with God. Perhaps it should have been set in a broader context, with wider emphasis on God's relationship with Israel prior to Sinai.

Setting

At one level, the setting for the revised DH is easily determined: it took place in circles concerned with the DH, after the events of Josiah's unexpected death and the abandonment of his reform. During the time of exile is most likely; just before the exile or after it are of course possible.

Far less easy to determine is the nature of the revision. Was it done in a relatively short time? Was it spread over a longer period? Was it the work of a single individual or group? Was it done in stages and to be attributed to various sources? In speaking of focuses in the revision — the royal focus and the national focus — the language is carefully chosen to avoid prejudicing this issue. The twin focus is evident. We do not know whether it was present from the outset or whether it developed over the course of time. Differing aspects of ideology or vocabulary might suggest differing elements within a group; they do not impose a sequence in time. In a couple of texts (1 Sam 8; 2 Kgs 21), the royal focus has priority over the national focus; again, it would be unwise to universalize this and project it into an enduring process.

Meaning

Since failure happened, the credibility of the DH required that failure be prepared for. Because it had happened, the failure needed to be accounted for. Evil kings were an easy target. National failure in obedience and faith could well be claimed.

What both aspects failed to address was the fidelity of King Josiah and the generation he led. Meaning was sought; meaning may not have been achieved.

Bibliography of Works Cited Above

Birch, Bruce C. *The Rise of the Israelite Monarchy: The Growth and Development of 1 Samuel 7–15.* SBLDS 27. Missoula: Scholars Press, 1976.

Brettler, Marc Zvi. *The Creation of History in Ancient Israel.* London: Routledge, 1995.

Briend, J. "Les Figures de David en 1 S 16,1–2 S 5,3." Pp. 9-34 in *Figures de David à travers la Bible: XVIIᵉ congrès de l'ACFEB* [= l'Association catholique française pour l'étude de la Bible] *(Lille, 1ᵉʳ-5 septembre 1997).* Edited by L. Desrousseaux and J. Vermeylen. Paris: Cerf, 1999.

Campbell, Antony F. *The Ark Narrative (1 Sam 4–6; 2 Sam 6): A Form-Critical and Traditio-Historical Study.* SBLDS 16. Missoula: Scholars Press, 1975.

———. "Yahweh and the Ark: A Case Study in Narrative." *JBL* 98 (1979) 31-43.

———. *Of Prophets and Kings: A Late Ninth-Century Document (1 Samuel 1–2 Kings 10).* CBQMS 17. Washington: Catholic Biblical Association of America, 1986.

———. "From Philistine to Throne (1 Sam 16:14–18:16)." *ABR* 34 (1986) 35-41.

———. "Martin Noth and the Deuteronomistic History." Pp. 31-62 in *The History of Israel's Traditions: The Heritage of Martin Noth.* Edited by S. L. McKenzie and M. P. Graham. JSOTSup 182. Sheffield: Sheffield Academic Press, 1994.

Campbell, Antony F., and Mark A. O'Brien. *Unfolding the Deuteronomistic History: Origins, Upgrades, Present Text.* Minneapolis: Fortress, 2000.

Clendinnen, Inga. *Reading the Holocaust.* Melbourne: Text Publishing, 1998.

Davies, Norman. *Europe: A History.* Oxford: Oxford University Press, 1996.

Dietrich, Walter, and Thomas Naumann. "The David-Saul Narrative." Pp. 276-318 in *Reconsidering Israel and Judah: Recent Studies on the Deuteronomistic History.* Edited by G. N. Knoppers and J. G. McConville. Winona Lake, IN: Eisenbrauns, 2000.

Fohrer, Georg. *Elia.* 2nd ed. ATANT 53. Zurich: Zwingli Verlag, 1968.

———. "Die alttestamentliche Ladeerzählung." *Journal of Northwest Semitic Languages* 1 (1971) 23-31.

Gunn, David M. *The Story of King David: Genre and Interpretation.* JSOTSup 6. Sheffield: JSOT, 1978.

Halpern, Baruch. "The Construction of the Davidic State: An Exercise in Historiography." Pp. 44-75 in *The Origins of the Ancient Israelite States.* Edited by V. Fritz and P. R. Davies. JSOTSup 228. Sheffield: Sheffield Academic Press, 1996.

Lemche, Niels Peter. "David's Rise." *JSOT* 10 (1978) 2-25.

Mildenberger, Friedrich. *Die vordeuteronomistische Saul-Davidüberlieferung.* Unpublished dissertation. Eberhard-Karls-Universität, Tübingen, 1962.

Miller, P. D., Jr., and J. J. M. Roberts. *The Hand of the Lord: A Reassessment of the "Ark Narrative" of 1 Samuel.* The Johns Hopkins Near Eastern Studies. Baltimore: Johns Hopkins, 1977.

Niditch, Susan. *Oral World and Written Word: Ancient Israelite Literature.* Library of Ancient Israel. Louisville: Westminster John Knox, 1996.

Noth, Martin. *The History of Israel.* 2nd ed. London: Adam & Charles Black, 1960.

Rad, Gerhard von. *Old Testament Theology.* 2 vols. Edinburgh: Oliver and Boyd, 1962, 1965.

Rendtorff, Rolf. "Beobachtungen zur altisraelitischen Geschichtsschreibung anhand der Geschichte vom Aufstieg Davids." Pp. 428-39 in *Probleme biblischer Theologie: Gerhard von Rad zum 70. Geburtstag.* Edited by H. W. Wolff. Munich: Chr. Kaiser, 1971.

Richter, Wolfgang. *Die Bearbeitung des "Retterbuches" in der deuteronomischen Epoche.* BBB 21. Bonn: Hanstein, 1964.

—————. *Traditionsgeschichtliche Untersuchungen zum Richterbuch.* 2nd ed. BBB 18. Bonn: Hanstein, 1966.

Rost, Leonhard. *The Succession to the Throne of David.* Historic Texts and Interpreters in Biblical Scholarship 1. Sheffield: Almond, 1982. German original, 1926.

Schicklberger, Franz. *Die Ladeerzählungen des ersten Samuel-Buches: Eine literaturwissenschaftliche und theologiegeschichtliche Untersuchung.* FB 7. Würzburg: Echter, 1973.

Schmitt, Hans-Christoph. *Elisa: Traditionsgeschichtliche Untersuchungen zur vorklassischen nordisraelitischen Prophetie.* Gütersloh: Gerd Mohn, 1972.

Steck, Odil Hannes. *Überlieferung und Zeitgeschichte in den Elia-Erzählungen.* WMANT 26. Neukirchen: Neukirchener Verlag, 1968.

Van Seters, John. *In Search of History: Historiography in the Ancient World and the Origins of Biblical History.* New Haven: Yale University Press, 1983.

Vermeylen, J. "La maison de Saül et la maison de David: Un écrit de propagande théologico-politique, de 1 S 11 à 2 S 7." Pp. 35-74 in *Figures de David à travers la Bible: XVIIe congrès de l'ACFEB* [= l'Association catholique française pour l'étude de la Bible] *(Lille, 1er-5 septembre 1997).* Edited by L. Desrousseaux and J. Vermeylen. Paris: Cerf, 1999.

Wellhausen, Julius. *Die Composition des Hexateuchs und der historischen Bücher des Alten Testaments.* 3rd ed., 1899, reprinted unchanged. Berlin: de Gruyter, 1963.

White, Marsha. "Naboth's Vineyard and Jehu's Coup: The Legitimation of Dynastic Extermination." *VT* 44 (1994) 66-76.

Whitelam, Keith W. "The Defence of David." *JSOT* 29 (1984) 61-87.

GLOSSARY

Genres

Readers of biblical scholarship will be well aware that authors who use the same words as others do not always mean the same things by them. Those who compare the genre listings in this FOTL series, for example, will discover that the same genre term can be used and described differently by different authors. This is not a sign of error or imprecision; it reflects the multi-faceted reality of interpretation as an art. Descriptions will be affected by the insight and articulacy of a scholar, by the different texts on which scholars work, by the concern to describe accurately what a term should mean ideally or by the concern to describe accurately how a term is actually used, and so on. It is an important part of the task of analysis to know what is happening in any given text. It is part of form-critical study to universalize to some degree the outcome of the analysis of various individual texts. Few human activities in the reality of life can be classified and compartmentalized down to the finer details, above all in the interpretative arts. What is offered in a list like this is how one scholar understands specific texts and the terms used to describe them, with attention given to how those terms are used by others. The precision of much scientific work is not a goal; the move toward increasing clarity of understanding, allowing for shades of interpretation, is a hope within the process.

ACCESSION FORMULA (Einführungs Formel) The term may be used for the introductory part of the regnal resumé (see below). The full introductory resumé may contain as many as five elements. For Saul, at 1 Sam 13:1, two are noted: his age at accession and the length of his reign. The numbers involved are contested and difficult: one-year-old and a two-year reign (for discussion, see the commentary). The age at accession is given here, unusual since Saul is a Benjaminite; the note of age is usual only for kings of Judah, but occasionally is missing in the resumé (cf. Long, *1 Kings,* 264).

ACCOUNT (Bericht) Account is one of the literary genres coming under the overarching concept of (→) narrative. It is used where there is concern for the communication of information without any need for plot, raising tension and reaching resolution. It is often found practically as a synonym for (→) report. For some, account is felt to be rather more extensive and explanatory in nature; for others, it is felt to be rather less impersonal; for others again, account is the more general non-plot term, with report being rather more restricted. Precision in definition and use is unlikely to be achieved. Readers will need to be sensitive to context. An allied genre is (→) notice, usually implying greater brevity.

G. Coats (with R. Knierim) characterizes account as relating additional information that brings some particular light to bear on what might otherwise be reported more neutrally; the aspect of accountability is given weight (*Exodus 1–18*, 155-56). The emphasis on accounting for something, rather than neutrally reporting it, is attractive. However, it cannot be taken for granted as a usage among scholars. Readers must exercise judgment.

ACCUSATION (Anklage) The accusation is found as an element of a (→) prophetic judgment speech. As such, the accusation provides a statement of the reasons motivating a judgment. Naturally, its use is not restricted to prophetic contexts. These accusations unfortunately arise naturally from human and social interaction. As such they are part of the trial genres, as well as featuring in prophetic pronouncements of punishment (cf. Sweeney, *Isaiah 1–39*, 512 and 29-34). In a trial situation, the accusation "normally specifies the offense for which the accused is being brought to trial" (ibid., 512). More generally, therefore, an accusation describes the offense that is being alleged.

ANECDOTE (Anekdote) A short narrative of an interesting or amusing or otherwise memorable episode, often told to illustrate a point. See Holman, *Handbook to Literature*, 25.

ANNOUNCEMENT OF JUDGMENT (Gerichtsankündigung) The announcement of judgment is similarly an element of the (→) prophetic judgment speech. It also occurs as an independent literary type. Its essential core is the announcement of forthcoming disaster, whether for an individual or a whole people. Its basic core is the statement that a disaster will be inflicted as God's punishment for crime or sin. It may be associated with the accusation, specifying the reasons for the disaster. An announcement of judgment can be framed and styled as a speech of YHWH through a prophet. Most commonly, then, properly introduced, this would involve a first person speech of YHWH. Passive or impersonal formulations are known as well. In older terminology, the term used for this genre was "threat."

Reading:
Westermann, *Basic Forms.*

341

BATTLE REPORT See REPORT OF BATTLE.

BIRTH STORY See STORY OF BIRTH.

COMMENT (Kommentar, kommentierende Bemerkung) Comment is the general term used to describe a narrator's activity in stepping outside the narrative to express an opinion on what is taking place. Comment is a part of narrative: the activity that occurs when the narrator steps back from the narrative itself and communicates directly with the narrative's audience. It may be purely secular, as in the comment on the lying prophet: "he lied to him" (1 Kgs 13:18). It may express belief, indicating God's action within apparently human affairs: "it was a turn of affairs brought about by the LORD" (1 Kgs 12:15).

COMPOSITE NARRATIVE (Komposition gegensätzlicher Traditionen) Composite narrative is a term that is useful to describe the genre of a text that is a composition of conflicting narrative traditions. Traditions that are not in conflict can be blended into a unity with its own generic characteristics. Traditions that are in conflict are juxtaposed rather than blended. The resulting composition may well be a literary tribute to editorial skill. It would be a mockery of that skill not to recognize the conflict that has been preserved and that calls for reflection or evaluation. Such composite narratives are found, for example, in 1 Sam 8–11 and 28–31.

CURSE STORY See STORY ABOUT CURSE

DECREE (Dekret, Verordnung) An ordinance or decision that has the binding force of law, handed down by the appropriate authority — in 1 Samuel, by the king (1 Sam 11:13; 30:24b).

HERO STORY See STORY ABOUT A HERO

HISTORICAL STORY (Geschichtserzählung) The term was used by Rolf Rendtorff to describe stories where historical rather than heroic elements were to the fore ("Beobachtungen," 431-32). For 1 Samuel, he had in mind 27:8-12; 28:1-25; 29; 30). He considered the designation particularly appropriate where there was no central individual figure involved (e.g., 1 Sam 21:2-10; 22:6-23).

HYMN OF PRAISE (Loblied) According to Erhard Gerstenberger, the hymn is a "joyful song of choir or community extolling the greatness and kindness of Yahweh and his dwelling place. Seasonal and ad hoc festivals for the ancient Israelite give ample occasion to get together at holy places. Sacrifices and celebrations extend over several days. The hymns intoned vary in contents: They praise creation and creator (cf. Psalms 8; 19; 104), and Yahweh's glorious deeds in history (cf. Psalms 68; 105). They admire Mount Zion, his abode (cf. Psalms 46; 48; 76), and jubilate at his just reign (cf. Psalms 24; 47; 93; 96). Hymn-singing always has been a vital part of Jewish-Christian worship services . . ." (*Psalms,* 249).

Hymns tend to celebrate who God is and what God does. The hymn, or more specifically the hymn of praise, is a psalm or song which extols and glorifies YHWH. Typical elements are: a call to praise or worship; praise of YHWH; blessings or petitions. The opening call to praise may be resumed at the conclusion of the hymn. The blessings and petitions play a minor role; the focal point is the descriptive or narrative praise. Modes of expression vary, ranging from solemn measured stanzas to a free narrative style. The Hebrew use of the participle (hymnic participle) is a feature of many hymns of praise; it functions to describe or recall the great deeds of YHWH in creation or salvation (e.g., 1 Sam 2:6-8; Pss 33; 103; 104; 135; 145; 146; Job 5:9-16; Amos 4:13; Isa 40:22-23). Even when hymns seem to glorify intermediate things, YHWH is usually the real subject of praise. Praise is closely associated with thanksgiving.

INSTRUCTION (Unterweisung) Described by Michael Floyd as "a type of discourse that gives guidance on matters of traditional concern to an individual or group. Such discourse is produced by someone in a position of civil, religious, or administrative authority through reflective study of the traditions in question." There are instructions given by scribes regarding the wisdom tradition, as well as priestly and prophetic instructions (cf. Floyd, *Minor Prophets,* 631).

LEGEND (Legende) A (→) narrative primarily concerned with the wonderful and aimed at edification.

The legend has no specific structure of its own. It is concerned not with narrative interest, but with the impressiveness of its contents which are supposed to stimulate its audience to believe or to do something good. Thus legends often serve to inculcate awe for holy places (cf. Judg 6:10-24) and for ritual practices (cf. 2 Macc 1:19-22), and respect for notable figures (cf. the Elijah cycle; 2 Kgs 2:23-24) who may be models of devotion and virtue (cf. Exod 32:27-29; Deut 33:9; Num 25:6-12; Ps 106:30-31).

Legend is distinguished from *märchen,* a genre which shares an interest in the wonderful, by virtue of two characteristics: (i) its specific practical aim; (ii) its claim to belief. Unlike *märchen,* legend is placed in the real world and is often associated with historical characters. This latter characteristic distinguishes legend from myth, which may claim belief but is essentially non-historical, outside time. Legend is distinguished from (→) story by two characteristics: (i) its specific practical aim; (ii) its consequent relative indifference to narrative art. It is the marvelous and not the story line which constitutes the legend's essential claim on attention. Cf. Hals, "Legend."

Adapted from an entry in the FOTL project files by D. J. McCarthy.

LIST (Liste) A simple recounting in writing of names or items assembled under a certain perspective or heading. In an elementary form of list, the names or items may be assembled regardless of any ordering system. In a developed form, elements are logically or explicitly linked together in successive order, providing an artistic form.

Adapted from an entry in the FOTL project files by R. Knierim.

NARRATIVE (Erzählung) Narrative is information about action communicated directly. Narrative is an overarching concept rather than itself constituting a literary genre.

It is characterized as information: it is not primarily concerned with moving an audience to action or creating an attitude. It is characterized as about action: its subject is event or movement; even if the action is emotional or intellectual, it will involve the development of interplay of emotions or ideas in action, not their simple description or logical progression. It is characterized as direct communication: it is addressed to its audience rather than acted out before a group that "overhears" it.

OT narrative takes many different forms. From the point of view of technique: (→) story which moves from created tension to its resolution, (→) report which simply describes events with no overt effort to create tensions and resolution, and (→) legend which seeks to edify. From the point of view of situation: narrative may be historical or non-historical. The first is bound to time and space in ways that are plausible within ordinary or remembered experience (e.g., legend, novella, story). The second moves in a parameter of space or time that transcends, precedes, or follows ordinary experience (e.g., fable, *märchen,* myth). (→) Anecdote and *märchen* are other types of narrative with special techniques and content. For further reading, see Scholes and Kellogg, *Nature of Narrative.*

Adapted from entries in the FOTL project files by D. J. McCarthy.

NOTICE (Notiz) A brief account noting for the record either traditions/information or opinions/views.

PROPHETIC JUDGMENT SPEECH (Prophetische Urteilsrede) A passage in which the prophet speaks on behalf of YHWH to announce judgment against an individual, group, or nation. Examples include: 1 Sam 2:27-36; Isa 22:16-24; Amos 7:14-17; Jer 20:1-6 (individual); Jer 23:9-12; 23:13-15; Mic 3:9-12 (group); Isa 8:5-8; Jer 11:9-12 (nation). The main elements of the genre are: (i) a statement of the reasons for judgment; (ii) a logical transition ("therefore" or equivalent), usually with the messenger formula; (iii) the announcement of punishment. Associated elements may include a call to attention or the oracle formula. The reasons for judgment are presented often but not always in the prophet's own words; the prophet then reports the announcement of punishment by YHWH. Sweeney distinguishes a "Prophetic Announcement of Punishment against an Individual" as employing "a more direct form of the accusation against the individual" (*Isaiah,* 530), probably reflecting judicial proceedings in Israel or Judah.

Adapted from Sweeney, *Isaiah,* 533-34 (cf. 530).

PROPHETIC STORY See STORY ABOUT/OF PROPHET(S)

REGNAL RESUMÉ (Schlußformel) A formulaic summary, above all in the books of Kings, which provides information about the kings of Israel and Judah. The regnal resumé normally appears in two parts, as an introductory and a concluding summary, forming a framework around the account of a particular reign. The introductory part typically includes: (1) name of the king and date of accession; (2) the age of the king at accession (for Judah only); (3) the length of reign and the capital city where he reigned (one or both sometimes given in the concluding summary); (4) the name of the queen mother (for Judah only); (5) a theological evaluation, usually stylized and stereotyped. Occasionally some elements, or even the entire resumé, may be omitted. The concluding part of the regnal resumé, also sometimes omitted, usually includes: (1) a citation formula, referring the reader to other sources for information about the reign; (2) a notice of death and burial of the king; (3) a notice of succession, i.e., who succeeded him. Examples are 2 Kgs 13:10-13 (both parts); 1 Kgs 15:1-5, 33-34 (introductory part); 1 Kgs 14:19-20; 2 Kgs 10:34-35 (concluding part). See also: Accession Formula.

Adapted from Long, *1 Kings*, 259.

REPORT (Bericht) A usually brief (→) narrative, which tells what happened without trying openly to arouse interest by creating tension leading to resolution — by contrast with (→) story. Alternative terms used are (→) account and (→) notice. They may have the same definition; for some authors, account may imply a less impersonal tone than report, with notice tending to imply greater brevity.

REPORT OF BATTLE (Kampfbericht) A short (→) narrative of a battle, providing the basic information about a battle and its outcome. It does not attempt to describe the battle; on the other hand, it is more than a bare notice of the fact of a battle or its result. Quite a number of passages are available for consideration (although not all are to be definitely assessed as battle reports): Josh 7:2-5; 8:3ff.; Judg 3:26-29 (30); 4:12-16; 8:10-12; 20:35; 1 Sam 4:1b-2, 10-11; 13:5; 15:4-8 (9); 17:1-2 (3); 2 Sam 2:12-17; 5:17-21, 22-25; 10:6-14, 15-19; 18:6-7 (8); 1 Kgs 20:19-21, 26-30; 2 Kgs 14:(8-10) 11-14; 2 Chron 14:7-14. For contrast, note: as examples of battle narratives, Josh 8:3-29; Judg 9:34-41; 1 Kgs 22:29-36; 2 Kgs 3:4-27; 2 Chron 13:2b-21; 35:20-25; as examples of campaign notices, 2 Sam 8:1-14; 2 Kgs 12:17-18; 2 Chron 25:5-13; as examples of annalistic notices, 2 Kgs 15:19-20; 17:3-6; 18:9-11.

The structure of a report of battle tends to be dictated by the subject matter: (i) confrontation of forces; (ii) the battle; (iii) consequences of battle. Before the battle, there may be a prophetic consultation, or its equivalent, such as prayer or encouragement. With modifications, this structure is found in Josh 7:2-5; Judg 3:(26) 27-29 (30); 4:12-16; 1 Sam 4:1b-2, 10-11; 15:4-8 (9); 2 Sam 5:17-21, 22-25; 10:15-19; 18:6-7 (8); 1 Kgs 20:26-30; 2 Kgs 14:(8-10) 11-14; 2 Chron 14:7-14. The element of consultation, prayer, or encouragement is absent from 1 Sam 4:1b-2, 10-11; 2 Sam 10:15-19; 18:6-7 (8); 2 Kgs 14:(8-10) 11-14. It may also happen that the gathering of the forces (confrontation) is reported for one side only: e.g., Josh 7:2-5; Judg 3:26-29 (30); 1 Sam 15:4-8 (9); 2 Sam 5:22-25.

The report of battle appears to be used where the text is less concerned with the battle itself than with a particular aspect of it, so that the report reflects the tension between the nature of the event reported and the concern of the text in which it is reported.

For further reading, see Campbell, *Ark Narrative,* 68-70; Gunn, "Battle Report"; Van Seters, "Sihon's Kingdom," esp. pp. 186-89.

REPORTED STORY As a genre, reported story is used of narrative texts that stand in only an indirect relationship to the performance of storytelling. Instead, they look in two directions: rearward, back to the storytelling tradition that they report; forward, to the stories to be told in the future.

The rearward glance is the report of storytelling tradition. We know the texts we have and the high quality of their literary style; it is tribute to the quality of ancient Israel's storytelling. Those who told the stories told them well; those who reported the stories reported them well. The plot structure is there. The gems of dialogue are there. The details that go to make a good story are there. There is enough stuff there to hold a report together. The trimmings that any good story-teller can generate are not there. Variant versions are there, even if only briefly noted. A storyteller may choose to use one; no good storyteller would actualize conflicting ones. Contradictory traditions are sometimes noted. Good storytellers knew how to handle them. Fundamentally, a good report preserved whatever possibilities the tradition contained. The aim of a reported story is to recapitulate the story — not to retell it.

The reported story also looks forward as a base for the storyteller whose task is to retell the story. Choices may be made from that base: which variants to tell, which details to include. A good storyteller knows, on any given occasion, which details to provide and which to withhold, which gaps to fill and which to leave as gaps. A good storyteller knows when to extend a story and when to shorten it. The base may contain several variants; the good storyteller will actualize only one and will know which is the right one to actualize for the particular audience. It is not a matter of being bound to a text but being bound to a story — to the opportunities that a text offered and limited for the telling of a story. To be more nuanced for later generations: canonically, it is a matter of being bound to a text; aesthetically, it may be a matter of being bound to a story, which in its own appropriate fashion is duly bound to the text.

The reported story preserves a past tradition, rehearsed in the telling of the story, and prepares for a future rehearsal of the tradition, in the retelling of the story. There is a structured move from the oral into the written with a view to returning to the oral. We have no certainty that such reported stories functioned as bases for storytelling; it is an assumption, based on respectable grounds. The description given is fully compatible with the processes described in the field studies reported by Culley, *Structure of Hebrew Narrative,* 4-20, and by Long, "Recent Field Studies."

How Israel's traditions, preserved in some instances as reported stories, can be woven into Israel's longer narratives is adequately illustrated in 1 Samuel.

346

Clearly, it is possible for a longer report to be condensed for the sake of an extended narrative. Clearly, it is equally possible for a terse report to be expanded during its incorporation into another narrative. We cannot identify where such possibilities may have been actualized. What we can affirm is this: some texts bear characteristics that point to the reporting of stories rather than the performing of stories. Such characteristics do not affect any canonical aspects of a text, which are unchanged. Instead, they point to the possibility of a text's addressing both readers and also storytellers — which can change matters quite significantly.

For the purposes of this volume, reported story will be suggested as genre when the text appears to require a storyteller's choice, clarification, or expansion; where such development is not required by the text but is merely possible, the genre will be given as the more conventional (→) story. Alternative terms used are (→) story outline and (→) story summary.

Reading:
Campbell, "Reported Story"; "Storyteller's Role."
Campbell and O'Brien, *Sources*, 19; "1-2 Samuel," 580-81; *Unfolding*, 7.
Culley, "Oral Tradition," 1-33, esp. p. 9; *Structure of Hebrew Narrative*,
  1-32, esp. 15-16.
Long, "Recent Field Studies."
Rofé, "Prophetical Stories," 432-33.
Wilcoxen, "Narrative," 65-66.

REPROACH See ACCUSATION

RITUAL (Ritual) In a broad sense, ritual can be used to describe any stylized behavior or its prescription. In a more specialized meaning, it denotes the way in which a community performs or prescribes the ceremonies or observances that symbolize the pivotal events in its life. In the life of Israel, rituals can have a wide range relating to events on the yearly calendar, to the human life-cycle, to acts of worship and celebration, and even to unpredictable events, wars and disasters, joys and successes. However, whether ritual as such constitutes a literary genre is a matter of scholarly debate.

Reading:
Knierim, *Text and Concept*, 93-94.

SHORT COMMUNICATION (Kurze Mitteilung) These are not fully fledged narratives or stories, nor do they appear to stem from annals or chronicles. Rather, they are pieces of information which, in themselves, are unlikely to have been important enough to find their way into official annals or chronicles and which are hardly substantial enough to have existed as independent traditions or stories. But they are necessary for the telling of a story, and they are collected by the compiler or storyteller in order to provide the proper setting for the story. In the case of the story of David's rise to power, for example, we find such short communications interspersed with the stories, which are viable enough to have had a literary independence of their own, and with the data that might be culled from royal chronicles and other records. These short notices contribute background and a certain framework to the whole narrative; they may be traditions that were personally known to the narrator; they may be the result of his inquiries. They are largely details that would be of little interest outside the larger perspective of the narrative.

Reading:
Rendtorff, "Beobachtungen."

SHORT NOTICE (Kurze Mitteilung) An alternative term for Short Communication.

SPEECH (Rede) At a formal level, a speech may be described as a sustained oral presentation. Speeches will then be more narrowly circumscribed by occasion or purpose (e.g., battle speech, farewell speech, disputation, sermon, etc.).

STORY (Geschichte) A (→) narrative that creates interest by arousing tension and resolving it. A story's structure is controlled by plot, moving from exposition and the initial introduction of characters through forms of complication to resolution and conclusion. Plot is understood in the Aristotelian sense of the arrangement of the incidents of an action.

    In the presentation of genres here, narrative is seen as the overarching category, subsuming story, report, and account, etc.

    In some other views, the overarching role is given to story. For C. H. Holman, "*Story* is thus the basis for all literary genres that are narrative or dramatic" (*Handbook to Literature,* 511). According to Holman, "The one merit of *story,* as *story,* is its ability to make us want to know what happened next" (ibid.). Story, in this view, comprises any narrative genre "with any basis in a sequence of events" (ibid.). In the presentation of genres here, reflecting usage in biblical studies, this role is given rather to narrative, and story is understood as a narrative genre involving plot, therefore creating interest by arousing tension and resolving it. A different relationship between story and plot can be seen in a description quoted from E. M. Forster: "A *story* 'is a narrative of events in their time-sequence. A *plot* is also a narrative of events, the emphasis falling on causality.' A story arouses only curiosity; whereas a *plot* demands intelligence and memory" (ibid., 396).

STORY ABOUT CURSE A (→) story specified by content; it is not a separate genre. For example: 1 Sam 14:23b-45.

STORY ABOUT A HERO A (→) story specified by content; it is not a separate genre. For example: 1 Sam 14:1-23a.

STORY ABOUT/OF PROPHET(S) A (→) story specified by content or origin; it is not a separate genre.

STORY OF BIRTH A (→) story specified by content, i.e., birth. Usually involves need or distress, whether before or after the birth, resolution of the need by the promise of a child, and realization of this in the birth of the child, naming, etc. For example: 1 Sam 1:1–2:11a.

STORY OUTLINE/STORY SUMMARY Alternative terms for (→) reported story.

THANKSGIVING SONG (Danklied) A jubilant cultic song to celebrate victory, divine help, and all sorts of joyful occasions. There are personal thanksgiving songs and communal ones. For 1 Sam 2:1-10, see rather Hymn of Praise.

    Adapted from Gerstenberger, *Psalms,* 256-57.

THEOLOGICAL NARRATIVE (Theologische Erzählung) The term is used to describe those cases where the (→) narrative has acquired a new function: the shaping of theological questions and affirmations. Its function is to grapple with theological problems and assertions through the medium of narrative. The same can, of course, be said of a theologically told story. While the terms narrative and story might sometimes seem interchangeable, there are occasions when the mingling of account and comment, report and story, within a single text make it advisable to use the overarching term of narrative.

Reading:
Campbell, *Ark Narrative,* 250-51.
Westermann, "Arten der Erzählung."

Bibliography of Works Cited Above

Campbell, Antony F. *The Ark Narrative (1 Sam 4–6; 2 Sam 6): A Form-Critical and Traditio-Historical Study.* SBLDS 16. Missoula: Scholars Press, 1975.
———. "The Reported Story: Midway between Oral Performance and Literary Art." *Semeia* 46 (1989) 77-85.
———. "The Storyteller's Role: Reported Story and Biblical Text." *CBQ* 64 (220) 427-41.
———. "1-2 Samuel." Pp. 572-607 in *The International Bible Commentary: A Catholic and Ecumenical Commentary for the Twenty-First Century.* Edited by W. R. Farmer. Collegeville: Liturgical Press, 1998.
———. *Unfolding the Deuteronomistic History: Origins, Upgrades, Present Text.* Minneapolis: Fortress, 2000.
Coats, George W. *Exodus 1–18.* FOTL 2A. Grand Rapids: Eerdmans, 1999.
Culley, Robert C. "Oral Tradition and the OT: Some Recent Discussion." *Semeia* 5 (1976) 1-33.
———. *Studies in the Structure of Hebrew Narrative.* Philadelphia: Fortress, 1976.
Floyd, Michael H. *Minor Prophets.* Part 2. FOTL 22. Grand Rapids: Eerdmans, 2000.

Gerstenberger, Erhard S. *Psalms: With an Introduction to Cultic Poetry.* Part 1. FOTL 14. Grand Rapids: Eerdmans, 1988.

Gunn, David M. "The 'Battle Report': Oral or Scribal Convention?" *JBL* 93 (1974) 513-18.

Hals, Ronald M. "Legend: A Case Study in OT Form-Critical Terminology." *CBQ* 34 (1972) 166-76.

Holman, C. Hugh. *A Handbook to Literature.* 3rd ed. Indianapolis: Bobbs-Merrill, 1972.

Knierim, Rolf P. *Text and Concept in Leviticus 1:1-9.* FAT 2. Tübingen: Mohr, 1992.

Long, Burke O. "Recent Field Studies in Oral Literature and Their Bearing on OT Criticism." *VT* 26 (1976) 187-98.

———. *1 Kings: With an Introduction to Historical Literature.* FOTL 9. Grand Rapids: Eerdmans, 1984.

Rendtorff, Rolf. "Beobachtungen zur altisraelitischen Geschichtsschreibung anhand der Geschichte vom Aufstieg Davids." Pp. 428-39 in *Probleme biblischer Theologie.* Edited by H. W. Wolff. Munich: Chr. Kaiser, 1971.

Rofé, Alexander. "The Classification of the Prophetical Stories." *JBL* 89 (1970) 427-40.

Scholes, Robert, and Robert Kellogg. *The Nature of Narrative.* London: Oxford University Press, 1966.

Sweeney, Marvin A. *Isaiah 1–39: With an Introduction to Prophetic Literature.* FOTL 16. Grand Rapids: Eerdmans, 1996.

Van Seters, John. "The Conquest of Sihon's Kingdom: A Literary Examination." *JBL* 91 (1972) 182-97.

Westermann, Claus. "Arten der Erzählung in der Genesis." Pp. 9-91 in *Forschung am Alten Testament. Gesammelte Studien.* TB 24. Munich: Chr. Kaiser, 1964.

———. *Basic Forms of Prophetic Speech.* Philadelphia: Westminster, 1967.

Wilcoxen, Jay A. "Narrative." Pp. 57-98 in *Old Testament Form Criticism.* Edited by J. H. Hayes. San Antonio, TX: Trinity University Press, 1974.